Political Economy of Production and Reproduction

Political Economy of Production and Reproduction

Caste, Custom, and Community in North India

Prem Chowdhry

OXFORD
UNIVERSITY PRESS

OXFORD
UNIVERSITY PRESS

YMCA Library Building, Jai Singh Road, New Delhi 110 001

Oxford University Press is a department of the University of Oxford. It furthers the
University's objective of excellence in research, scholarship, and education
by publishing worldwide in

Oxford New York

Auckland Cape Town Dar es Salaam Hong Kong Karachi Kuala Lumpur
Madrid Melbourne Mexico City Nairobi New Delhi Shanghai Taipei Toronto

With offices in
Argentina Austria Brazil Chile Czech Republic France Greece Guatemala
Hungary Italy Japan Poland Portugal Singapore South Korea Switzerland
Thailand Turkey Ukraine Vietnam

Oxford is a registered trademark of Oxford University Press
in the UK and in certain other countries

Published in India
by Oxford University Press, New Delhi

© Oxford University Press 2011

ISBN-13: 978-019-806770-2
ISBN-10: 0-19-806770-4

Typeset in 10.5/12.4 Dante MT Std
by Excellent Laser Typesetters, Pitampura, Delhi 110 034
Printed in India by Rajshri Photolithographers, Delhi 110 032
Published by Oxford University Press
YMCA Library Building, Jai Singh Road, New Delhi 110 001

To

Uma and Patricia,
friends who care

Contents

Tables

Acknowledgements

I join the publisher to gratefully acknowledge the publishers and copyright holders of the journals and publications cited below for permission to publish the following articles in part or in full:

SAGE PUBLICATIONS INDIA PVT. LTD.

'Contesting Claims and Counter-claims: Questions of the Inheritance and Sexuality of Widows in a Colonial State', *Contributions to Indian Sociology*, 29 (1& 2): 65–82. Copyright © Institute of Economic Growth, Delhi. All rights reserved. Reproduced with the permission of the copyright holders and Sage Publications India Pvt. Ltd., New Delhi (1995).

'Caste Panchayats and the Policing of Marriage in Haryana: Enforcing Kinship and Territorial Exogamy', *Contributions to Indian Sociology*, 38 (1 & 2): 1–42. Copyright © Institute of Economic Growth, Delhi. All rights reserved. Reproduced with the permission of the copyright holders and Sage Publications India Pvt. Ltd., New Delhi (2004).

'Jat Domination in South-east Punjab: Socio-economic Basis of Jat Politics in a Punjab District', *The Indian Economic and Social History Review*, XIX (3–4): 325–46. Copyright © The Indian Economic and Social History Association. All rights reserved. Reproduced with the permission of the copyright holders and Sage Publications India Pvt. Ltd., New Delhi (1982).

'The Advantages of Backwardness: Colonial Policy and Agriculture in Haryana', *The Indian Economic and Social History Review*, 23 (3): 263–88. Copyright © The Indian Economic and Social History Association. All rights reserved. Reproduced with the permission of the copyright holders and Sage Publications India Pvt. Ltd., New Delhi (1986).

'A Matter of Two Shares: A Daughter's Claim to Patrilineal Property in Rural North India', *The Indian Economic and Social History Review*, 34 (3): 289–320. Copyright © The Indian Economic and Social History Association. All rights reserved. Reproduced with the permission of the copyright holders and Sage Publications India Pvt. Ltd., New Delhi (1997).

ECONOMIC AND POLITICAL WEEKLY
'High Participation, Low Evaluation: Women and Work in Rural Haryana', *Economic and Political Weekly*, XXVIII (52): A 135–A 148 (1993).

INDIAN COUNCIL FOR HISTORICAL RESEARCH
'Fluctuating Fortunes of Wives: Creeping Rigidity in Inter-caste Marriages in the Colonial Period', *Indian Historical Review*, XXXIV (I): 210–43 (2007).

INDIAN INSTITUTE OF ADVANCED STUDY
'Ideology, Culture, and Hierarchy: Expenditure–Consumption Patterns in Rural Households', in Uma Chakravarti and Kumkum Sangari (eds), *From Myths to Markets: Essays on Gender*, Shimla: IIAS (1999).

SOCIAL SCIENTIST
'Contours of Communalism: Religion, Caste, and Identity in South-east Punjab', *Social Scientist*, 24 (4–6): 130–63 (1996).

'Persistence of a Custom: Cultural Centrality of *Ghunghat*', *Social Scientist*, 21 (9–11): 91–112 (1993).

CAMBRIDGE UNIVERSITY PRESS
'Private Lives, State Intervention: Cases of Runaway Marriage in Rural North India', *Modern Asian Studies*, 38 (1): 55–84 (2004).

'"First our Jobs then our Girls": The Dominant Caste Perceptions on the "Rising" Dalits', *Modern Asian Studies*, 43 (2): 437–79 (2009).

Introduction

The issues of caste, custom, and community, with gender concerns permeating them all, underlie almost every aspect of our contemporary life from production to reproduction. These are not some unchanging traditional issues and concepts but are very much alive and shifting one. They have remained powerful by re-inventing themselves over different historical periods. What we are witnessing today is a great deal of complexity underlining the contemporary relationship with the colonial past. The multifaceted changes evidenced today in post-colonial India—the process of political democratization and the radically altered legal enactment, especially relating to marriage and inheritance, frontally attacking caste and the existing patrilineal kinship system—have changed the dynamics of power relations and made way for different and complex interactions. These, in combination with the new political economy of the green and post-green revolution, the new economic polices under a greatly liberalized economy, globalization marked by conspicuous consumption, and the kind of quasi-urbanization that rural north India has undergone, have had a fallout on rural society in terms of new class formations, westernization, and notions of social status. These, in return, have impacted familial, inter-generation, and gender relations. The younger members, with radically different aspirations, attitudes, and life styles, are challenging the caste/kinship ideology upheld by the caste leadership of senior male members and/or are breaching sexual codes and taboos, defying cultural norms and customary practices much more openly now than before. These breaches are evoking a sharp and violent reaction from the individuals generally and, more especially, from the community. With caste dynamics taking its own form even in the twenty-first century, the richest regions in north India emerge more regressive than moving towards a modern egalitarian statehood.

The essays included in this volume are selected with a view to achieving an understanding of contemporary north India, with all its contradictions. Spanning a period from mid-nineteenth century to the present 2009, they make a special case study of Haryana, and therefore have an internal coherence. The in-depth analysis is broadly applicable to the whole of northern region of India in sharing socio-cultural concerns.

Haryana has been my fieldwork area for more than two decades. Indeed, in a way, the heart of north India may well be located in the tiny state of Haryana, measuring 27,638 square miles, carved out of Punjab on 1 November 1966. In the colonial period it was part of united Punjab, then measuring altogether 1,35,773 square miles, extending up into the Himalayas to the borders of Tibet and across the river Indus to the borders of Baluchistan. The south-east portion of this Punjab, which is now known as Haryana, had come into the possession of the British much earlier than the rest of Punjab. The British East India Company had established itself in the Delhi territory, including most of the present Haryana, in 1803 itself, after the Maratha failure and their consequent withdrawal to the south. It came to form part of the Delhi division under the Lieutenant Governorship of the North-West Province of Agra and Oudh. However, through repeated territorial rearrangements, especially in the wake of the happenings of 1857, and again in 1911, when the capital was shifted from Calcutta to Delhi, the British created the Ambala division of Punjab which included six districts, that is, Rohtak, Hissar, Gurgaon, Karnal, Ambala, and Simla. The present-day Haryana region in this Punjab roughly approximated to the Ambala division, minus its Simla district. This Ambala division also underwent a few territorial changes after independence. Geographically, the state surrounds the national capital on three sides and is hemmed in between Himachal Pradesh, Uttaranchal, and Uttar Pradesh on the north and north-east, by Punjab in the west, and Rajasthan with its vast deserts in the south.

Divided into two sections, colonial and post-colonial, these essays both separately and in combination map significant social processes which have shaped and reshaped Haryana. The first section, covered by five essays, shows how colonial intervention left a deep imprint on various aspects of Haryanavi society which very largely determined the outcome of the politico-legal and social changes brought about in the immediate aftermath of independence. The seven essays included in the second section study the response and shifts in society taking place due to those dramatic changes introduced by the state. Through these essays, it is argued that the traditions which had been nurtured and customs which had crystallized during the colonial period were to prove detrimental to a very large extent to any changes initiated by the independent state. With patriarchal forms reformulating and refashioning themselves to accommodate these changes, the face of contemporary Haryana has come to be marked with mutually contradictory indices: high economic but low social indices. A running theme in this collection is the overall state domination, both colonial and post-colonial, and the adoption of certain policies which had effects on issues specially relating to women. The other themes cover politics, economy, and society, with particular accent upon caste and gender.

The first essay, 1986, 'The Advantages of Backwardness: Colonial Policy and Agriculture in Haryana', which appeared in *The Indian Economic and Social History Review*, vol. 23, no. 3, October–December, is seminal to the understanding of this region. Haryana, as compared to the other parts of united Punjab, was one of its most backward regions. The needs of imperialism gave low priority to any improvement of agriculture in Haryana which went into sustaining and reinforcing its agricultural stagnation and extreme backwardness. The colonial policy's deliberate slant in keeping this impoverished tract as the supplier of draught animals to Punjab and other parts of India and a major recruiting area for the British Indian army went a long way in determining the character and development of this region's economy, society, and politics—aspects which have been dealt with in subsequent essays. It was only when this carefully maintained pattern of agrarian economy was broken in the post-colonial period and Haryana could emerge from being a perennially deficit region providing, by and large, a subsistence level living, to become a surplus producing state in India that changes in other spheres were to follow.

The socio-economic fabric of this agrarian society is used as a launching pad to understand the emergent casteist politics in the second essay, 'Jat Domination in South-east Punjab: Socio-economic Basis of Jat Politics in a Punjab District', published in *The Indian Economic and Social History Review*, vol. XIX, nos 3 and 4. Based on the study of the ubiquitous domination by a single caste group, that is, the Jats, this essay correlates their triple domination commanded in the social, economic, and numerical spheres to the emerging politics of this region. It highlights the changes occurring roughly over the first four decades of the twentieth century which went into strengthening the upper strata of the landowning classes. Such an analysis helps us to understand the present-day politics and society and why the caste equations continue to be relevant despite the contemporary flux of the caste system. The pulls and pressures, confirmation and challenges co-existing within the caste system are a recurring theme in this volume.

Caste and growing casteism in this region also cut through the sharpening sectarian/religious identities. The picture remains the same even today as, despite attempts by the right-wing forces, the communal divides in Haryana are nowhere being crystallized. The third essay, 1996, 'Contours of Communalism: Religion, Caste, and Identity in South-east Punjab', published in *Social Scientist*, vol. 24, nos 4, 5, and 6, April–June, analyses the Hindu–Muslim confrontations in this region, officially projected as 'communal riots' around construction of places of worship, celebration of religious festivals, and the cow protection movement. Out of these, it is the cow protection movement alone that continues to inflame passions, as seen in the lynching of five Dalits by the landowning caste groups in village Dulina in district Jhajjar in October 2002. Attempts made to communalize the issue by the Vishva Hindu Parishad (VHP) and the Bajrang Dal came to nothing. In the colonial period, despite mobilization around religious symbols, these confrontations emerge as land related, born out of demands of rising social groups to appropriate crucial indices of status formation in their drive towards upward mobility and enforce recognition on other social groups. These attempts posed a challenge to the traditional structure of authority and the dominance of certain castes and classes in rural society, as is visible even today.

The dominant caste groups in general, and the landowning classes among them in particular, coloured the socio-cultural ethos and shaped the customs and attitudes of this region which were seen to be followed by all lower castes as well as classes. The affect of these customs on women, emerging from the growth and demands of a patriarchy and interacting with specific geo-economic needs, is the focus of analysis in the fourth essay, 1995, 'Contesting Claims and Counter-claims: Questions of the Inheritance and Sexuality of Widows in a Colonial State', published in *Contributions to Indian Sociology*, vol. 29, nos 1 and 2, January–December. This essay argues that within a tightly controlled peasant culture, aided and abetted by the colonial government, occurred women's self-assertion and protest as seen in widows' determination to hold on to the landed property and the challenge which women posed to their marriage or remarriage in its levirate form. The analysis underlines that, on the one hand, patriarchal interests were invoking the aid of the law to get certain highly contentious customs and claims accepted, stretching notions of legitimacy and morality and impinging upon rights of widows; and on the other hand, the widows were making use of the new legal and public spaces to counter these moves, activate their inheritance rights, assert their preferences in sexual and marital relationships, and make counter-claims of their own. Despite these attempts, the situation remained ambivalent, with many widows asserting their autonomy and yet others being speedily engulfed in the growing hold of levirate which, as the dominant custom of this region, successfully controlled their inheritance as well as their sexuality.

In the post-colonial period, the state's attempt at a positive intervention in promoting greater equality for women in the sphere of inheritance has had almost paradoxical consequences for widows, leading to the strengthening of the levirate which is in direct contradiction to her inheritance claims. This intervention has meant forcible remarriage, an unmatched and undesirable alliance, polygamy, and the harsh reality of being a co-wife against the legal requirements of monogamy.[1]

More than the widow's right of inheritance, it is the daughter's right sanctioned by the post-colonial state which has created a greater sense of unease in rural society. The ability of the patriarchal forces to control a widow, argued in the fourth essay, was never the same in relation to the daughter. The ninth essay, 1997, 'A Matter of Two Shares: A Daughter's Claim to Patrilineal Property in Rural North India', published in *The Indian Economic and Social History Review*, vol. 34, no. 3, July–September, takes up the question of a daughter's inheritance and how the patriarchal/patrilineal society of Haryana is checkmating this enablement and with what effects. The essay shows the extensive use of

[1] For the contradictory actions of the post-colonial state, which not only subverts the more positive facets of widow remarriage practice but is also privy to the subversion of the revolutionizing effects of the law of inheritance (Act of Succession, 1956) as well as other legislative measures, see my essay, 1998, 'Conjugality, Law and State: Inheritance Rights as Pivot of Control in Northern India', *National Law School Journal*, special issue on Feminism and Law, 1993, pp. 95–116 and *Indo-British Review*, vol. XXI, no. I, pp. 59–72. Reprinted in Srimati Basu (ed.), 2005, *Dowry and Inheritance*, New Delhi: Women Unlimited, pp. 171–93.

selective cultural and ideological controls to make a daughter relinquish her inheritance rights; if that fails, then use of force and violence. Even the newly bestowed marital rights, including divorce and the tradition of remarriage, have come handy in reinforcing the customary norms rather than in breaking them. With women themselves acknowledging the 'ideal pattern' of inheritance of land and property by males from males, the legal enablement has not had any real impact. Yet, breaches have occurred. Such assertions have only made men in northern India more anxious to control women even if it has meant making futile attempts at reversing the legal enablement or in strengthening cultural patterns and festivals which prioritize the claims of the brother at the cost of the sister.

Clearly, as the socio-economic forces changed in the post-colonial period, the cultural ethos and the resultant customs and attitudes which these forces had moulded and determined underwent certain shifts. This is evident in the wide-scale changes brought in the wake of the green revolution, analysed in Section II, which have catapulted this region from a backward subsistence level economy to the second richest state in India. These changes have had deep-rooted socio-cultural effects, especially in relation to women, in either completely or partially diluting many of the customs and social attitudes or sharpening many others, or introducing new ones. These changes have also impacted the role and nature of women's work. The sixth essay, 1993, 'High Participation and Low Evaluation: Women and Work in Rural Haryana', *Economic and Political Weekly*, vol. XXVIII, no. 52, attempts to correlate different aspects and levels of this region's green revolution economy with women's work in agriculture, agricultural processing, and animal husbandry. For this, the work sphere of two categories of women is investigated in great depth, that is, female family workers from landowning households and female agricultural wage earners from landless as well as cultivating households. The analysis highlights the dominant socio-cultural and ideological factors which have made for continuing high participation rate of Haryanavi women along with their cultural devaluation which considers their work to be inferior/secondary/supplementary to that of men.

In fact, the image of women observing *ghunghat* while continuing to work as full working partners of men in the dominant economic activities has come to represent an existing dual reality of Haryana. This dual reality is the theme of seventh essay, 1993, 'Persistence of a Custom: Cultural Centrality of *Ghunghat*', *Social Scientist*, special issue on women, vol. 21, nos 9, 10, and 11, September–November. Clearly, the genuine seclusion of women is uneconomical in this state. The observance of ghunghat even while involved in intensive physical work imposes efficacious constraints upon women, leaving them ineffective in all crucial spheres. Ghunghat imposes the most cogent control on married women which extends from their private and public conduct in purely domestic and familial sphere to the outside social and political structures of the wider village community. This essay analyses the persistence of the custom of ghunghat and the wider factors operating behind its reinforcement and inordinate acceptance, especially in the rapidly changing social milieu of post-colonial Haryana. Ghunghat emerges as an outward symbol of patriarchal control which has retained its hold over women despite dramatic internal politico-legal and socio-economic shifts, and, in fact, as a result of those shifts.

The eighth essay takes this dual reality much further. 'Ideology, Culture and Hierarchy: Expenditure–Consumption Patterns in Rural Households', was published in Uma Chakravarti and Kumkum Sangari (eds), *From Myths to Markets: Essays on Gender*, Shimla: Indian Institute of Advance Studies in 1999. This essay takes the twin factors of ghunghat observance and women's lack of economic worth and social standing to study the expenditure–consumption patterns in rural households of Haryana to argue how gender articulates with other socio-cultural structures not only to reinforce but to further tighten existing gender inequalities. It highlights how women of all classes, with hardly any socio-cultural recognition of a right to a share of resources and control of income which she produces or helps to produce, face gender-based and intra-household inequalities. The new and vastly changed expenditure–consumption patterns, especially in the wake of the green revolution and based upon male priorities, emphasize status symbols and give low priority to women's needs even in crucial domestic sphere. Such patterns can be seen becoming more and more male oriented, creating yet greater nuclei of male control. The old cultural constraints which have been determinedly kept alive have not only ideologically conditioned women's participation in decision-making but have physically inhibited them from decision-making fora with detrimental repercussions.

This almost complete lack of decision-making power in the hands of women is most noticeable in the sphere of marriage. As marriage provides the structural link between kinship and caste, marital alliances have always been under close surveillance. Clearly, challenged to the caste, cultural and customary norms and practices observed for marriage have repeatedly come from within the caste and outside it. The post-colonial processes of democratization and the opening of economic opportunities, drastic social and legal changes have altered the dynamics of power relations, making for complex interaction between members of different caste groups as well as between members of a particular caste. Any breach of the given codes has meant infliction of direct violence by male members of the family, or the community, on the couple generally and on the girl specially. The contemporary newspapers and media reports are full of cases of the so-called 'honour killings', specially located in northern India. The societal pressure to adhere to the prescribed norms is endorsed by the state agencies, which effectively uphold the gender and caste codes espoused by the caste/community leadership.

The colonial period, however, shows that cultural shifts in marriage practices were taking place. Tracing the marriage question in the colonial period, the last essay in Section I deals with the role played by the colonial state in matters concerning inter-caste marriages, specially as they impinged upon wider civil concerns of land, property, and inheritance. This made marriages a target for social and judicial intervention. The fifth essay, 2007, entitled, 'Fluctuating Fortunes of Wives: Creeping Rigidity in Inter-caste Marriages in the Colonial Period', appeared in *Indian Historical Review*, vol. 34, no. I, January. This period emerges as a period of contest when control over a woman was becoming more rigid in every way, aided by the colonial structure and ideology which willingly or unwillingly supported such efforts. Anxious to resolve and settle social matters according to their own interests and assessment of the existing norms and traditions of different caste groups in different regions, the colonial intervention activated conditions which worked towards strengthening the dominant norm of caste endogamy and posed a serious challenge to inter-caste marriages.

The court cases taken up for analysis highlight competing viewpoints and differing social and moral systems vying to gain supremacy and sanctity through colonial procedures. The creeping rigidity in inter-caste marriages and the concomitant emphasis upon caste endogamy underline the enforcement of a more dominating and wilful male-oriented social pattern. It defined the structures of social difference and ranking among high caste/low caste male/male, male/female, and children of different wives, far more sharply and emphatically. The long period of colonial domination set up fresh traditions that determined the social values and interaction in post-colonial India. Further complications were to set in with the legal changes and changes in political economy in independent India.

The role of the independent state and its agencies, specially the state judiciary, in relation to inter-caste couples and their marriage is the focus of attention in the tenth essay, 2004, 'Private Lives, State Intervention: Cases of Runaway Marriage in Rural North India', published in *Modern Asian Studies*, vol. 38, no. 1, February. In tackling the runaway cases, the post-colonial state emerges resembling its predecessor state which operated on norms clearly at odds with modern egalitarian principles enshrined in the constitution. Analysing a series of court cases from Haryana–Punjab involving runaway couples, the essay argues that legal intervention not only delegitimizes such individual attempts at breaking out of the traditional system of marriage alliances, it also criminalizes all such attempts. The state acts and, in fact, is used by patriarchal forces as a primary legitimating institution of popular cultural practices. Standing as an overarching patriarch and acting on behalf of the male guardians of a woman, the state criminalizes female sexuality and constructs it as essentially transgressive, illegitimate, and morally reprehensible. It denies the woman autonomy over her body or to assume agency to gain control of her life. This collusion of the family, community, and the state ends up in tragedy.

The customary rules regulating marriages in Haryana, standing diametrically opposed to the law of the land, are carried much further in the eleventh essay, 2004, 'Caste Panchayats and the Policing of Marriage in Haryana: Enforcing Kinship and Territorial Exogamy', *Contributions to Indian Sociology* (ns), vol. 38, nos 1 and 2, January–August. Based on recent case studies, occurring within a caste group which has breached norms of kinship and territorial exogamy, it examines the social factors operating behind the intervention of the caste panchayat and the success and limitation of this intervention. It reflects upon the working of the caste panchayat, to understand how and why, despite the post-colonial structural changes in law and polity, the caste panchayat continues to wield dictatorial power as an extra-judicial body, and how it is able to use social problems, especially those pertaining to questions of marriage, for legitimization of its authority, which has been severely eroded over the years. It also determines the role of the state agencies in abetting this traditional authority and in legitimizing the illegitimate, even while eroding the moral authority of the panchayat.

The role of the community through its panchayat is again taken up in the twelfth essay, 2009, which deals with inter-caste liaisons, with special reference to the Dalits and upper caste elopements and marriages. Entitled, '"First our Jobs then our Girls": The Dominant Caste Perceptions on the "Rising" Dalits', this essay was published in *Modern Asian Studies*, vol. 43, no. 2. It argues that in the post-colonial shifting of material, legal, and ideological bases, some of the given patterns of relationship between individuals and caste groups have changed and weakened due to the introduction of new, parallel, and alternative structures of relationships. This change has left the dominant caste groups feeling palpably insecure in relation to the Dalits. While delineating this relationship, this essay argues that the cases of Dalit and dominant/upper caste elopement and marriage represent a high point in the ongoing conflictual relationship between them, as these are viewed as forms of Dalit assertion. Although many caste groups and communities are involved in inter-caste marriages and associations that defy customary norms and caste practices and have no social acceptance, it is in relation to a Dalit and non-Dalit association or marriage that certain aspects, which impinge on wider issues, come to the surface more pronouncedly. For the dominant caste groups acting through the caste panchayats, such associations remain the most viable and potent issue to garner a wider collective support, cutting across class/caste/community and age divides. These cases are selectively made a public spectacle by the dominant caste groups to settle wider issues at stake verging on contemporary political and economic interests.

The success of these attempts is curiously supported by the youth that are primarily involved in breaching the norms of caste endogamy. They deny vehemently any desire to marry outside the caste. Anxious not to sound at odds with the dominant opinion, they mouth opinions popularly accepted by the society, occasionally diluting them with what they consider politically correct opinions. The possibilities of a gender divide on this issue exist. In this, the oral tradition of women, who bear the onus of effecting such breaches, emerges with an entirely different ideological position from the one publicly stated that underlines caste endogamy and status considerations in marriage and relationships.[2]

---

[2] For locating voices and opinions of women that have so far remained unheard in the public arena, see my essay: 2001, 'Lustful Women, Elusive Lovers: Identifying Males as Objects of Female Desire', *Indian Journal of Indian Studies*, vol. 8, no. 1, January–June, pp. 23–50. It explores one of the more

This collection of essays, however, remains a limited one. There are many more aspects which have had to be excluded because of constraints of space. Yet other aspects need to be studied further to arrive at a more comprehensive understanding. What this collection does is to initiate and stimulate the interest of the reader and researcher into the study of a region, which shares a large number of characteristics and attributes with the rest of northern India.

popular self-projections of women in oral tradition of rural north India based exclusively upon women's songs produced collectively by women, sung by women for an audience consisting purely of women. Declared 'immoral and indecent', several attempts have been made since the colonial period to abolish the singing of these songs by the reformist and moral police acting through the panchayats. So far, these attempts have not been successful. Women's hidden voices through these songs take a central and even an outright subversive stand towards the dictates of the dominant gender culture and its expectations. Reprinted in Nivedita Menon (ed.), 2007, *Sexualities*, New Delhi: Women Unlimited, pp. 255–88.

State, Law, and Economy: The Colonial Flux

1

The Advantages of Backwardness

*Colonial Policy and Agriculture in Haryana**

What is the present-day Haryana, which constituted the south-eastern part of Punjab in the colonial period,[1] remained one of the most backward and underdeveloped regions of Punjab under the British. This essay seeks to bring out the needs of imperialism which gave low priority to any improvement of agriculture in Haryana. This region was seen primarily as suited for the supply of draught animals to the rest of Punjab, as also to certain other parts of India. The determined efforts of the British to retain it as such are reflected in their irrigational policies, emphasis on low value food-cum-fodder

---

* This chapter was originally published in 1986, *The Indian Economic and Social History Review*, 23(3): 263–88.

[1] The south-east Punjab under the British, called the Ambala division, including the districts of Rohtak, Gurgaon, Karnal, and Ambala minus its Simla division, constituted roughly the present-day Haryana. It was only after independence that this division underwent a few more territorial changes. For example, in 1950, Pataudi state and Bawal pargana of Patiala and East Punjab States Union (PEPSU) were merged with the Gurgaon district; the state of Loharu was merged with Hissar; Kalka, Kurali, and Sahawar were added to the Ambala district; Pinjore Kanungo Circle and Nalagarh *tehsil*, which had been merged with PEPSU on its formation in 1948, were also added to this district in 1959, when PEPSU was merged with Punjab. The state of Haryana, created on 1 November 1966, comprises of 27,638.75 square miles of territory as against 27,254 square miles of the erstwhile Ambala division.

crops, with increasing acreage under fodder cultivation, and in their attempts to curb the limited efforts being made at substitution of fodder crops by other crops, which might adversely affect this region's cattle wealth. Animal husbandry emerged as a necessary supplement to this region's subsistence level economy. However, as encouragement was given only to draught cattle, and not to dairy cattle or to the commercialization of dairy products, animal husbandry never became a high-paying proposition under the British. The perpetuation of this backward economy proved to be very helpful to Imperial interests, as the impoverished tract became a major recruiting area for the British Indian army. The army, in this region, provided the only source of employment and sustenance under conditions of severe economic stagnation, rising population, unemployment, and prices. Whatever capital existed went, in the absence of any other profitable avenue of investment, into moneylending. The ranks of moneylenders, both agriculturist and non-agriculturist, who had come to acquire a pivotal role in the subsistence level economy, swelled noticeably. Usury, land mortgage, and land purchase, mostly for renting out purposes, emerged as more profitable areas of investment than agriculture. The resultant socio-economic changes like growing numbers of land mortgages, land sales, smaller landholdings, the tenants, and agricultural labourers went into sustaining and reinforcing the agricultural stagnation and extreme backwardness of this region. The colonial policy's deliberate slant went a long way in determining the character and development of this region's economy.

The Haryana region had poorer resources than most other parts of Punjab. This region was far away from Punjab's perennial rivers and the river Jamuna's course was along the eastern boundary of the state. The non-perennial River Ghaggar, which passed through the northern parts of this area, caused considerable yearly damage to agriculture. Small rivulets, mostly dry except during the monsoon, caused more damage. Rainfall was low and erratic; and in the peak period, from July to September, there were often early local and widespread floods. The soil was sandy and light in texture. Irrigation through wells was extremely limited. In most parts, there was a paucity of sub-soil water; the level of sub-soil water was considered to be roughly about 25 feet.[2] In extreme cases, as in the western part of Karnal district, the water

[2] *India Office Records (IOR): Proceedings of the Punjab Government*: P/7841/ 1908, see Report of the Deputy Commissioner of Rohtak, 22 September 1906.

table was as deep as 150 feet.[3] In many cases, the water was brackish. Clearly, the labour and cost of sinking an agricultural well and working it was prohibitive, more so as the income was comparatively small, specially when *abiana* (water rates) had to be paid on the *pacca* (masonry) well.[4] In most parts, well sinking was considered something of a 'gamble' as, within 3–4 years, a well produced nothing but liquid mud.[5] In the estimate of the deputy commissioner of Rohtak, in 1906, even the working of a well all day did not result in the irrigation of more than one *kachcha* bigha, that is, one-fifth of an acre.[6] Water was clearly the crucial determinant of agriculture, and this arid region especially needed extensive irrigation. But the massive irrigation facilities provided by the British elsewhere in Punjab were absent in this region. Starved of this basic requirement, this region continued to remain agriculturally backward.

But these unfavourable characteristics proved advantageous to British requirements. An official report, published in 1910, on the question of cattle and dairying in the Punjab, maintained:

The physical features of Haryana constitute an ideal breeding ground [for cattle]. In the dry climate, sandy soil has an amount of lime essential to bone formation in young stock. Few monsoon showers produce plentiful crop of excellent grasses, dry season scarcity of fodder ensures sufficient exercise, as extensive roaming of animals to find it. To supplement grazing, staple fodders are Jowar Chari, Pala, or leaves of the Jhar, wheat and gram Bhusa, Khal or oil cakes in hot seasons and Binaula [cotton seed] in cold.[7]

Agriculturally, therefore, the region seemed eminently suitable for cattle, and very early, the British had realized that 'Haryana produced cattle

---

[3] *Punjab District Census Handbook 1961*, 1962, Karnal, District, Punjab, Chandigarh: Superintendent of Census Operations and Enumeration Commission, p. 18.

[4] *Final Report of the Third Regular Settlement of Rohtak District, 1905–1910*, 1910, Lahore: Government of Punjab, Civil and Military Gazette, p. 42.

[5] India Office Records: Proceedings of the Punjab Government: P/7841/1908, see *Report of the Deputy Commissioner, Ambala, to the Commissioner of Delhi Division*, 12 September 1906.

[6] Ibid.

[7] A.M. Stowe, 1910, *Cattle and Dairying in the Punjab*, Lahore: Civil and Military Gazette, p. 67. A similar opinion had been voiced even earlier, in 1903. See H.T. Pease, 1903, *Breeds of Indian Cattle, Punjab*, Calcutta: Superintendent Government Printing, pp. 35–6.

greatly in excess of its own requirements.'[8] It, therefore, quickly came to be treated as a 'store', from which other parts of Punjab began to be supplied. By World War I, an extensive cattle trade had been built up to ensure supplies all over Punjab, specially Shahpur, Mianwali, Multan, Dera Ghazi Khan, and the Central Colonies, where cattle breeding had been completely pushed out by extensive cultivation.[9] There were also exports to other provinces. The southern portion of the United Provinces absorbed a large number of cattle, as artificial irrigation had made commercial crops such as sugarcane more remunerative than fodder crops there. Bombay, Calcutta, and Benaras also imported Haryana cattle; there was even a growing demand from Rangoon and Java.

As Table 1.1 shows, the Haryana tract had a near monopoly of cattle sales in British Punjab. Haryana contributed 99 per cent of the sale of cattle in British Punjab in 1939, and over half the total number of cattle traded in all India (Table 1.2).

For this all-important economic activity, even the very frequent famines in this region were considered, by the officials, to be 'good for the quality of the breed' as they 'naturally' got rid of the inferior animals.[10] This 'enforced casting' was considered necessary to maintain and improve the quality of the breed. The Punjab officials also bemoaned the fact that such a practice was 'not prevalent in other parts of the province which are more securely placed in regard to cultivation.'[11] Clearly, therefore, irrigational facilities, the one most likely insurance against recurrent famines in this region, were not likely to be made available on a large scale; in fact, net area irrigated increased in only a few districts in the first half of the twentieth century (Table 1.3).

[8] Stowe, *Cattle and Dairying in the Punjab*, p. 67.

[9] The Board of Economic Inquiry, *A Cattle Survey of the Rohtak District in the Punjab*, Lahore: Civil and Military Gazette, 1935, pp. 25, 37–8. For purposes of cattle breeding, half an acre of uncultivated grazing land in the *barani* (dependent on rainfall) land of Haryana region was considered better than three-quarters of an acre of cultivated land in areas like Lahore. See Stowe, *Cattle and Dairying in the Punjab*, p. 20.

[10] The Board of Economic Inquiry, *A Cattle Survey of Rohtak District*, pp. 11, 12. For a similar opinion, see The Board of Economic Inquiry, *Economic Aspects of Animal Husbandry in Hissar: A Famine Area of the Punjab*, Lahore, 1945, p. 11.

[11] Ibid.

TABLE 1.1 Places in the British Punjab, from where Animals were Brought for Sale at the Ten Annual Cattle Fairs held in Punjab in 1939 and 1940

District	Total Nos 1939	Total Nos 1940
Hissar	26,620	19,444
Rohtak	8,171	6,189
Gurgaon	2,645	790
Karnal	1,196	511
Ambala	222	121
Simla	49	–
Ludhiana	71	–
Jullunder	53	26
Ferozepur	182	16
Hoshiyarpur	3	121
Sheikhupura	–	2
Montgomery	24	–
Lahore	11	–
Lyallpur	–	86
Total	39,247	27,394

Source: The Board of Economic Enquiry, 1945, Economic Aspects of Animal Husbandry in Hissar: A Famine Area of the Punjab, Lahore: Civil and Military Gazette, pp. 63–4.

TABLE 1.2 Sources of Cattle Supply in 1939 and 1940 for Trade from All Over India (percentages)

	1939	1940
1. Haryana region	53.3	60.1
2. British Punjab minus the Haryana region	0.6	0.8
3. Punjab states	16.3	16.8
4. Outside Punjab (Delhi)	–	0.2
5. United Provinces	1.3	1.0
6. Native states (Bikaner, Jodhpur, & Jaipur States)	28.2	20.8
7. Other places	0.2	–
8. Vagrant Tribes	0.1	0.3
Grand Total	100	100

Source: The Board of Economic Enquiry, 1945, Economic Aspects of Animal Husbandry in Hissar: A Famine Area of the Punjab, Lahore: Civil and Military Gazette, pp. 63–4.

TABLE 1.3 Percentage of Net Area Irrigated in the
Different Districts of Haryana (derived from the
quinquennial average figures)

	(1898–9 to 1902–3) 1901	(1908–9 to 1912–13) 1911	(1918–19 to 1922–3) 1921	(1928–9 to 1932–3) 1931	(1938–9 to 1942–3) 1941	(1948–9 to 1952–3) 1951
Rohtak	24.66	15.26	28.42	33.11	42.50	37.28
Hissar	20.30	10.93	15.84	13.48	17.08	17.38
Karnal	38.00	26.58	40.38	43.00	54.11	44.66
Gurgaon	24.11	12.95	17.33	17.17	13.06	14.42
Ambala	8.20	3.81	6.79	6.36	8.57	8.21
Total	23.11	13.90	21.75	22.62	27.06	24.39

Source: Calculated from Punjab District Handbooks, 1961, Punjab, Chandigarh: Superintendent of Census Operations and Enumeration Commission, 1962 (Ambala,
Gurgaon, Hissar, Karnal, and Rohtak districts).

However, according to the Urdu weekly, the Jat Gazette, a mouthpiece
of the Hindu Unionists of this region and widely accepted as a 'semi-
government' paper, British administrators did speculate for a while
on the need to provide irrigation in this region, if only as a reward for
its massive contribution to the war effort.[12] Consequently, the Bhakra
dam irrigation scheme was conceived by the Punjab government in the
wake of World War I, to irrigate the arid regions of Hissar, Rohtak,
and Karnal, and a detailed project, on the basis of extensive surveys
carried out in 1915–18, was prepared in 1919.[13] However, no steps
to implement it were taken, although the project itself underwent a
great deal of expert scrutiny from time to time.[14] Doubts regarding the

[12] The Jat Gazette, weekly newspaper in Urdu published from Rohtak, private
collection, now with Nehru Memorial Museum and Library, see issue of
20 April 1927, p. 5. Regarding the origin, nature, and association of this paper
with British officials, see the author's Punjab Politics: The Role of Sir Chhotu Ram,
New Delhi: Vikas, 1984, chapter II.

[13] Punjab Legislative Council Debates (PLCD), XXII, 25 February 1929, pp.
336–7. See answer given on behalf of the Punjab government by Mian Sir
Fazl-i-Husain, member for revenue.

[14] Ibid. Also, see the speeches of Sir Chhotu Ram, a member of the Unionist
Party, and the leaders of the rural Hindu group of this region, who gave the
entire background of the Bhakra dam project since its inception, PLCD, XXIII,
27 March 1933, pp. 758–61.

'detrimental' and 'adverse' effects of irrigation on the existing economy of these parts made the officials hesitant. An official report dated 1935, commenting on the proposed Bhakra dam project, disclosed:

> It is almost certain that if the Bhakra Dam Scheme matures cattle breeding will receive a serious setback and the production of draught bullocks in Hariana tract may be discontinued. This brings us to a very disputed question on which there is a sharp difference of opinion; whether the breeding of good cattle, especially the draught bullock is possible in irrigated areas. Evidence contained shows that canal irrigation ruined the Montgomery breed. In Rohtak district, where the irrigated and the unirrigated areas exist side by side, we find that cattle breeding has shifted to the unirrigated area, except for the breeding of buffaloes.[15]

The debate obviously tipped in favour of those who were against bringing irrigation to this region as the implementation of the Bhakra dam project remained shelved indefinitely. Publicly, the project was declared economically unsound, especially in the light of the existing financial stringency of the province; the objections of the Bombay government and the rulers of the Punjab states were declared unsurmountable.[16] However, in the wake of World War II, two more proposals were tentatively entertained in 1939–42 and in 1946, as a part of the post-war development plans of the province. The backward Ambala division, 'most in need of development', once again formed a part of the proposed schemes because it corresponded 'with the best recruiting

---

[15] The Board of Economic Inquiry, *A Cattle Survey of Rohtak District in the Punjab*, p. 27. The Punjab officials involved in various surveys of the Haryana region had for a long time been declaring that any extension of irrigation to this region would prove to be injurious to cattle breeding. See Pease, *Breeds of Indian Cattle, Punjab*, p. 47; Stowe, *Cattle and Dairying in the Punjab*, pp. 6–7; The Board of Economic Inquiry, *Economic Aspects of Animal Husbandry in Hissar*, p. 32.

[16] In a wide-ranging debate on the Bhakra dam project, Sir Henry Craik, the Finance Member, and R.P. Hadow, the Chief Engineer, Irrigation, highlighted certain reasons which had prompted the Punjab government to shelve the scheme. Among these, the Bombay government featured because it feared that the water supply of its Sukkur Barrage Scheme and other inundation canals would be severely affected if water was allowed to be withdrawn from the river Sutlej for the proposed Bhakra dam project. The rulers of the states of Bikaner, Patiala, Faridkot, Nabha, and Malerkotla were also declared to be unwilling to share the financial burden of this project. The Raja of Bilaspur state, on whose land the project was to come up, was stated to have firmly refused to give permission. For the whole debate, see *PLCD*, XXIII, 27 March 1933, pp. 757–91.

area'.[17] Interestingly, the 1946 project showed a fall in the share of this region in irrigated acreage (Table 1.4).

TABLE 1.4 Projected Irrigation

(thousands of acres)

	1919 Project	1939–42 Project	1946 Project
Haryana	2,362.1	2,392.8	1,863.2
Total Punjab	3,188.9	3,305.8	3,286.3
Share of the Haryana region (percentage)	23.62	23.93	18.63

Source: Haryana Development Committee Final Report, 1966, Chandigarh, Govt of Haryana: Controller, Printing and Stationery, see annexure 23.

These projects, however, did not materialize under the British. This region's continued dependence on its cattle reinforced its existing social ethos; this was reflected in local proverbs, which abound in praise of its cattle. To cite a few only:[18]

Gae dudh ki rakhle, labh uski teen gin
Chha pi kar ghi behle, bachre, bachri bin
[Keep a cow and count its three benefits: drink the buttermilk, sell the *ghee* (clarified butter), and also own the bull and cow calves]

Yet another maintained:

Jin ghar kali roz diwali
[In a house where there is a black she-buffalo every day is a day of Diwali]

The ownership of cattle was valued over the merit of religious observance, according to a Hissar proverb:

Salegram ki sewa main tunbi mala kath ki
Kali bhains ki sewa mein murki rupae ant ki
[In serving 'Salegram' (a black stone worshipped by Hindus), a man possesses a wooden vessel and a rosary, but in serving a black buffalo he possesses a golden earring and a great deal of money]

However, not even animal husbandry could remain unaffected in the chronically drought-prone region, which was exposed to recurring

[17] IOR: P/6045/33, 1945, see *Five Year Plan in Post War Development Schemes*, Lahore: Govt of Punjab, Superintendent, Government Printing, pp. 1–2.
[18] All three proverbs cited are from R. Maconachie (ed.), 1870, *Selected Agricultural Proverbs of the Punjab*, Delhi: Imperial Medical Hall Press, pp. 63, 169.

famines and fodder scarcity.[19] In the fodder scarcity years, the price of fodder rose sharply, for example, in 1931, by nearly 70 per cent.[20] And since fodder in normal times was in any case more expensive elsewhere in Punjab,[21] the cost of importing it in times of famine and drought became prohibitive; speculators, both *zamindars* (landowners) as well as merchants, charged very high prices.[22] Consequently, wide-scale destruction of cattle took place. Perusal of famine reports from 1878 to 1923 show that landowners often let their cattle die rather than exhaust their capital by buying fodder at excessively high prices.[23] At such times, the price of cattle fell dramatically, thereby reducing the owners' wealth. Thus, in 1910, cattle would fetch only one-fourth of their original price.[24] Selective destruction was, as we have seen, good,

---

[19] Famines in this region struck as follows: 1753–4, 1782–3, 1802–3, 1812–13, 1817–18, 1833–4, 1837–8, 1860–1, 1868–9, 1877–8, 1890–1, 1899–1900, 1905–6, 1909–10, 1918–19, 1929–31 (3 years), 1938–40 (3 years). See The Board of Economic Inquiry, *A Cattle Survey of Rohtak District in the Punjab*, pp. 3–4 and *Report on the Famine Relief Operations in the South-East Punjab, 1938–40*, 1946, Lahore, Government of Punjab: Civil and Military Gazette.

[20] The price of fodder rose from 80 seers (a measurement of weight approximately 933 grams, just a little less than a kilogram) per rupee before the famine in 1928 to 11 seers per rupee in February 1931. See M.L. Darling, *Wisdom and Waste in the Punjab Village* (reprint), New Delhi: Vikas, 1977, preface.

[21] Punjab (excluding Haryana region) mainly had surplus of *bhusa* (wheat chaff) which was supplied to the military dairy farms for its cattle, horses, and mules, and to the United Provinces for industrial demands like the manufacturing of strawboard and cardboard. The limited amount, in combination with the heavy demand, pushed up its price. See The Board of Economic Inquiry, *Rise in the Price of Bhusa in the Punjab*, 1949, Lahore: Civil and Military Gazette, pp. 18–19.

[22] *Report of Fodder Famine Operations in the Ambala Division*, 1930, Lahore: Government of Punjab, Civil and Military Gazette, p. 13. Apart from the high prices of fodder, the cost of importing corn was enormous. At concessional rates, the railway freight was 39 pies per mile per wagon for fodder carried over 150 miles. Besides, there were charges for loading and unloading and wastage in the entire operation estimated at 10 per cent. Ibid.

[23] *IOR*: P/1372, 1923, see a note on 'Concession for Export of Cattle during the days of Famine', by W. Roberts, p. 9.

[24] *IOR*: P/8400, 1910, p. 19. Another official report gives the fall in the average price of all cattle as from Rs 71 per head in 1928 to Rs 65 and Rs 62 in the next two years and Rs 45 in 1931. See The Board of Economic Inquiry, *A Cattle Survey of Rohtak District in the Punjab*, p. 10.

but the wholesale destruction of the 'best breed of cattle in the Punjab' led to fear of the danger of 'great injury' being 'done to the province as a whole'.[25] Indeed, the socio-economic effects of this cattle-cum-fodder question, specially in the stagnant agricultural economy, came to be considered so volatile that British officials feared political exploitation of the issue by the Congress.[26] This was another important reason for the official attempts at salvaging at least the best cattle during extensive fodder famines.

Animal husbandry, of course, had its concomitant subsidiary trades, but the periodic official inquiries into animal husbandry hardly paid any notice to them. The subsidiary trades were concentrated in the hands of the landless, mostly menial classes. For example, the trade in hides and bones was handled by *Chuhras* and *Chamars*; and the trade in meat and beef by *Qassais* (butchers), who mainly supplied to the cantonments, civil stations, and larger cities.[27] An exception was the trade in ghee which was in the hands of Banias, but this trade was not widespread.[28] Although animal husbandry and these trades were interdependent, little encouragement was given to the subsidiary trades, except perhaps in a limited way to the export trade in raw hides.[29]

Similarly, there was no official encouragement for dairy farming. No improvement was made in the marketing of milk or its products even by the district boards, which drew the major part of their revenue from the numerous cattle fairs held in this region.[30] Except for a very insignificant flow, milk products continued to be locally consumed in

[25] IOR: P/1372, 1923, p. 9. Even in 1903, such apprehensions had been voiced. See Pease, *Breeds of Indian Cattle, Punjab*.

[26] *Report of the Fodder Famine Operations in the Ambala Division*, pp. 32–3. Because of the importance of cattle in this region, both the Unionist and the Congress parties took up 'the cattle cause' in order to mobilize political support. The frequency with which the Congress championed the 'cow-issue' in this region often imparted to it a communal colour.

[27] Stowe, *Cattle and Dairying in the Punjab*, pp. 38–9.

[28] For limitations on the trade of ghee, see ibid. Also, see The Board of Economic Inquiry, *A Cattle Survey of Rohtak District in the Punjab*, p. 56.

[29] For details, see IOR: P/8121/89, October 1909; also, The Board of Economic Inquiry, 1939, *Tanning Industry in the Punjab*, Lahore: Civil and Military Gazette.

[30] The Board of Economic Inquiry, *Economic Aspects of Animal Husbandry in Hissar*, p. 32.

predominantly vegetarian Haryana.[31] British officials themselves agreed that the cattle breeders did not earn legitimate profits from by-products due to the lack of an efficient marketing organization.[32] On the contrary, improvement of milking performance and encouragement to dairy products were frowned upon as it was considered to be at the expense of the improvement of the draught qualities of cattle. An official report on Hissar reveals:

> The general trend of expert opinion is that nothing should be done which might impair the stamina for which these primarily draught breeds are noted and the limit to which improving milking capacity should be taken is that the cow should be giving sufficient milk to rear her calf properly, with a small surplus for the domestic use of her owners.[33]

The conclusion reached was that the 'development of milk in [Haryana] cattle should not be done at the expense of the draught quality.'

Indeed, the much publicized Hissar Government Farm was primarily concerned with the development of the draught qualities of its bulls and not the increase of milk production.[34] So much so that there were

---

[31] The officials gave the following interesting account of the vegetarian diet of this region: 'The Hindu Jat is a strict vegetarian … the ordinary Jat's diet was said to be half a seer of curds when he gets up; another half-seer in the fields at 10 o'clock; three ounces of ghee at midday, and from three quarters to a seer of milk in the evening; plus of course bread (of millet in winter and wheat in summer) vegetables, sugar and rice' (The Board of Economic Inquiry, *A Cattle Survey of Rohtak District in the Punjab*, pp. 18–19). It may be pointed out that in this region, the word Jat was synonymous with zamindar, that is, landowner.

[32] The Board of Economic Inquiry, *Economic Aspects of Animal Husbandry in Hissar*, p. 44. The report noted that the management and sale of ghee was far from profitable as its methods of production were 'crude and unhygienic'. It also added that 'specially as market facilities did not exist', surplus residue, *lassi* (buttermilk), had to be thrown away which only added to its production costs and consequently hardly left any margin of profit.

[33] Ibid., p. 43.

[34] The Board of Economic Inquiry, *A Cattle Survey of Rohtak District in the Punjab*, p. 56. The management of the Hissar Farm was officially taken over from an English agent in 1813. Cattle breeding, with a view to produce good draught bullocks, for the artillery, were introduced in 1815. In 1899, the Punjab animal husbandry department took over the farm and adopted a policy of breeding 'pedigree bulls' to 'further the draught cattle wealth', which came to be known as the 'Hissar Breed'. See, *Punjab District Census Handbook, 1961, Hissar District*, 1962, Punjab, Chandigarh: Superintendent of Census Operations and Enumeration Commission, p. 19.

repeated complaints from landowners regarding the deterioration in the milking qualities and capacity of the cows which they felt was on account of the emphasis placed on improving the quality of bullocks.[35] In 1935, the Rohtak farmers, much to the chagrin of the official investigators, were markedly recalcitrant regarding the use of Hissar bulls for breeding purposes on the ground that it brought down the milking capacity of cows. In fact, over the years, in all the districts of Ambala division, the buffalo was steadily substituted for the cow because it produced richer milk and milk products, as official reports noted with some urgency.[36]

Since no incentives were given to dairy products, and in uncertain agricultural conditions and frequent famines leading to heavy cattle mortality, animal husbandry did not become a highly paying proposition for the owners. The cattle experts from Hissar observed that 'generally speaking the profits of animal husbandry appear to be small and hazardous.'[37] They went on to conclude that cattle breeding on the existing basis did not pay. They candidly admitted that 'there is

---

[35] The Board of Economic Inquiry, *A Cattle Survey of Rohtak District in the Punjab*, p. 56.

[36] This is clear from all the annual cattle survey reports, 1901–40, including the two special reports on animal husbandry of Rohtak and Hissar cited above.

[37] The Board of Economic Inquiry, *Economic Aspects of Animal Husbandry in Hissar*, p. 12. The difference between the price realized from cattle on attaining maturity and the value of food it consumed was a very narrow one. The given figures show:

	I	II	III	IV (Rs)
Total value of cattle feed in four different				
tracts in the Hissar district:	58	74	58	62
Probable value of calf at three years:	80	100	75	85
Surplus over the cost of feed:	22	26	17	23

The report, while admitting the difficulty in estimating the possible cost and profit of rearing animals, calculated a mere Rs 25 profit per animal in 'normal times'. This estimate, the report admitted, did not take into account the cost of family labour, milk consumed by the calf, and free grazing during the monsoon. Ibid., p. 13. For a similar opinion, see, The Board of Economic Inquiry, *A Cattle Survey of Rohtak District in the Punjab*, p. 48. The severe fall in the price of cattle during the frequent famine and drought conditions also contributed towards bringing down the margin of profit. See fn. 24 given earlier.

little doubt that but for the facility of free grazing during the monsoon months and the practice of taking light plough work from young bullocks in their third year, it would not pay to raise cattle for sale even in normal times, even if the milk yield of the cow is taken into account.' This, consequently, resulted in stagnation in cattle breeding; the total number of cattle showed no upward trend, nor was the quality of cattle significantly improved.[38] As pointed out earlier, the officials had considered that extension of irrigation in this region would discourage the breeding of cattle. Interestingly, the very opposite view was taken in the post-colonial period by the Haryana Development Committee, 1965, which laid down that 'the growth of cattle wealth is, to a large extent, dependent on the availability of fodder. This in turn is dependent on the extension of irrigation facilities. Added emphasis should, accordingly, be given to irrigation in areas with large potential for cattle development.'[39] In the post-colonial period, there was a sharp rise in the numbers of buffaloes, the superior milk producing animal, without affecting the regional wealth of draught cattle. The state led, although belatedly, in providing the infrastructure for an immensely improved animal husbandry which led to the dramatic and widespread commercialization of dairy products called the 'white revolution'.[40] Clearly, the emergence of cattle

[38] To illustrate this point, we take the two most important cattle-rearing districts, Hissar and Rohtak:

Total no. of cattle	1920	1923	1935	1940	1945
Hissar	5,55,132	4,90,000	5,67,509	2,86,825	4,89,893
Rohtak	5,33,737	5,72,295	5,33,833	4,02,162	5,33,948

Source: Punjab District Census Handbook 1961, Hissar District, 1962, Punjab, Chandigarh: Superintendent of Census Operations and Enumeration Commission; Punjab District Census Handbook 1961, Rohtak District, 1962, Punjab, Chandigarh: Superintendent of Census Operations and Enumeration Commission. In fact, 1940 was the last year of a three-year famine (1938–40) in Ambala division. This famine was most severe in Hissar district, which explains the severely depleted figures of its cattle.

[39] Haryana Development Committee, 1965, Interim Report, Chandigarh: Government of Haryana, Controller, Printing and Stationery, p. 62.

[40] For details of the 'white revolution', see Directorate of Public Relations, 1981, Haryana, Prosperity with Social Justice, Chandigarh: Government of Haryana, pp. 28–34; and Facts about Haryana, 1981, 1981, Chandigarh: Government of Haryana, pp. 38–42. Haryana has won distinction as being the home

breeding as an immensely profitable economic activity was itself the best insurance against its much feared non-continuation.

AGRICULTURE: PREDOMINANCE OF LOW VALUE FOOD-CUM-FODDER CROPS

With the region being earmarked as the preserve of cattle supply, attention to its agriculture was hardly considered necessary Agriculturally, therefore, it continued to be backward. The cropping pattern of this region came to be determined by two important factors: first, the cultivator must grow food for himself; and second, for his cattle. This implicit policy decision was adopted right from the beginning; and giving it a candid expression in 1945, the officials firmly laid down:

Cattle breeding tracts may do without commercial crops but they cannot exist without food for the cattle. Animal husbandry is so intimately identified with the economic life of the people of this area that, in judging the utility of the existing agricultural economy, or suggesting improvements, the requirements of the cattle cannot be ignored, and the cultivation of commercial crops, such as sugar cane and cotton, at the expense of fodder cannot be defended.[41]

Therefore, the region, unlike the other parts of Punjab, continued to show predominance of low value food-cum-fodder crops. Without irrigation in most areas, there could only be low value food-cum-fodder crops like bajra, jowar, gram, and maize. Only a few limited irrigated tracts grew wheat and a few others had always shown a distinct preference for high value crops, such as sugarcane and, to a very small extent, cotton.[42]

In studying the major crop trends, we have focussed on one district, Rohtak, since this district represented varied agro-economic conditions which were prevalent more or less all over this region. The trends thrown up are, in fact, confirmed by the available statistics of other districts of Haryana, so the agro-economy of Rohtak district may be

---

of world famous buffaloes and the Haryana cow. The Murrah buffalo leads all other breeds in milk yield; some yield even more than 3,500 kilolitre of milk per lactation.

[41] The Board of Economic Inquiry, *Economic Aspects of Animal Husbandry in Hissar*, p. 20.

[42] *IOR*: P/8400, 1910, pp. 28–9.

used to gain an insight into the nature of agricultural development, its transformation, or lack of transformation, in the entire region during the British period. As Table 1.5 shows, food-cum-fodder crops were important even in 1891–2 and, over the years, showed an increase in share of acreage.[43] Out of these, bajra had the largest area under cultivation; from an average of 14 per cent in 1891–2 to 1895–6, bajra spread to over 30 per cent of the total cultivated area in 1936–7. Indeed, in all the districts of this region, its sown area increased in this period. In Hissar district, for example, the upward trend of bajra cultivation was particularly marked. From 11 per cent of the total sown area in 1895–1900, it increased to 37 per cent in 1935–40.[44] Bajra was considered the staple diet of the people of this region, as a Karnal proverb shows:

Bajra kahe main sughar suhela
Do musalon se men larun akela
Je koi meri khichri kare to
Naumi ghi upar tire
[Bajra says I am a very fine fellow. I can fight alone with two pests. If any one makes Khichri of me, good ghee floats above it][45]

Its continued consumption importance under the British was also due to the fact that wheat, with its limited production, was exported out of this region.[46] And bajra, with its dual advantage of being a food-cum-fodder crop, supplied a huge internal market, so much so that, in famine years, its price rode neck-to-neck with wheat and, during 1937–8 to 1939–40, actually exceeded it.[47] Low productivity during famine years and the heavy demand for it as food and fodder temporarily enhanced its price above that of wheat.

---

[43] Among the drought-resisting crops, jowar alone did not show any increase in acreage. The reason can perhaps be found in its overwhelmingly one-sided value of being a fodder crop. Its acceptability as a food crop has never been very significant in this region. A report from Hissar observed that it was 'usually eaten by the poorer people during famines' (The Board of Economic Inquiry, *Economic Aspects of Animal Husbandry in Hissar*, p. 17).

[44] Ibid.

[45] Maconachie, *Selected Agricultural Proverbs of the Punjab*, p. 260.

[46] Government of India (GoI): Revenue and Agriculture Department (Agriculture and Horticulture Branch), 'Wheat Production and Wheat Trade of India', January 1880, pp. 41–82A.

[47] IOR: *Agricultural Statistics*, V/24/119, 1938–9, pp. 3–4; 1939–40, p. 4.

TABLE 1.5 Rohtak District: Average Percentage of Area Cultivated under Major Crops in Relation to the Total Cultivated Area

	1891-2 to 1895-6	1896-7 to 1900-1	1901-2 to 1905-6	1906-7 to 1910-11	1911-12 to 1915-16	1916-17 to 1920-1	1921-2 to 1925-6	1926-7 to 1930-1	1930-1 to 1935-6	1936-7 to 1940-1	1941-2 to 1945-6	1946-7
1. Rice	–	–	–	–	–	–	–	–	–	–	–	–
2. Wheat	10.00	11.13	10.59	5.80	11.00	11.35	10.95	12.13	10.58	13.73	11.32	12.95
3. Barley	3.90	6.34	4.98	2.47	2.56	2.2	2.08	2.74	1.42	2.17	1.71	1.63
4. Jowar	26.58	15.29	11.49	18.82	17.13	18.47	12.54	14.96	10.59	12.16	8.34	12.98
5. Bajra	14.34	24.54	18.28	27.36	16.13	25.26	23.21	26.31	25.46	30.00	28.80	25.45
6. Gram	22.52	9.02	6.74	21.47	35.00	25.80	30.23	20.07	28.49	13.88	27.13	27.19
7. Sugarcane	1.83	5.07	2.40	1.36	2.59	3.36	2.52	2.49	2.21	2.24	2.02	2.79
8. Cotton	3.50	6.34	10.00	8.24	5.34	4.18	3.29	4.51	4.37	6.05	2.72	1.29
9. Fodder	0.10	4.37	6.20	5.01	7.19	9.85	11.76	12.93	12.86	14.99	13.22	12.55

Source: Agricultural Statistics of British India, New Delhi, 1890–1947, London: India Office Records.

Wheat continued to be sown in the irrigated parts of this region and its cash importance was undoubtedly known, as can be seen from the Karnal proverb:

Gehun kahe main bare gaumbhir
Sab bhaiyon me hue amir
Mere bina puri pukwan
Ae gae rakkhun man
[Wheat says I am a very important personage. I am the richest among all my fellow brother crops. All sweetmeats are made out of me. I bestow honour on the guests][48]

Yet, the acreage barely increased by 1 per cent between 1899–1900 and 1946–7; this was primarily due to lack of irrigation facilities, the continued heavy demand for fodder, necessity of subsistance level farmers with no marketable surplus to grow food for themselves and their cattle, and also, the fact that the colonial government, having already created for export a massive wheat basket elsewhere in Punjab, hardly gave wheat in Haryana any incentive. It was primarily concerned with the cultivation of other crops in this region.

The other high value crops, rice and sugarcane, both needed a great deal of water, which was not available, and also heavy initial investment. Rice, therefore, featured nowhere in this region; but sugarcane, because of the heavy local demand for *gur* (raw sugar) and refined sugar, continued to be produced on a limited scale. The small irrigated parts of Rohtak and Karnal districts came to represent the sugar growing tracts under the British. However, here also great difficulty was experienced in growing sugarcane. A local proverb from Karnal indicates:

Athais bah, giyarah pani, nau khod,
Jab dekhe ganne ka lod.
[If you plough twenty-eight times, water eleven times, and weed nine times, you may look for good sugarcane][49]

The proverb underlines the heavy work and labour involved in sugarcane cultivation, before a good yield could be expected. The heavy local demand for sugarcane and the lack of facilities, even in irrigated parts, had led the Deputy Commissioner of Karnal to recommend 'special allowances for growing of sugarcane' as early as in 1908.[50] There had

[48] Maconachie, *Selected Agricultural Proverbs of the Punjab*, p. 257.
[49] Ibid., p. 93.
[50] IOR: P/7841, 1908, see *Assessment Report of the Gohana Tehsil in the Rohtak District*, 1910, Rohtak, p. 22.

been brief experiments in enlarging the area under sugarcane from 1896–7 to 1900–1 (Table 1.5), but in view of the paucity of facilities like irrigation, they did not prove very successful, and the area once again contracted between 1891–2 and 1946–7; sugarcane accounted for roughly 2 per cent of the total cultivated area. The Sugarcane Machine Press in tehsil Gohana of Rohtak district attracted no customers, as not even the operating costs could be covered by the cash returns to this crop. The officials noted that sugarcane, a very remunerative crop elsewhere in Punjab, was hardly so in this region as it did not make the 'zamindars feel better off'.[51]

Cotton failed miserably (Table 1.5). Its urgent requirement by the British did lead to initial experiments in growing it on larger tracts between 1896–7 and 1910–11. During this time, the area under cultivation fluctuated from 3.5 per cent of the total cultivated area in 1891–2 to 1895–6, to 6.3 per cent in 1896–7 to 1900–1. It increased to a maximum of 10 per cent in 1901–2 to 1905–6, and then declined to 8.2 per cent in 1906–7 to 1910–11. From then onwards, the cultivated area saw successive steep declines and a smaller area was under cotton in the 1940s than in the late nineteenth century. This was primarily because, like rice, cotton also needed an almost perennial canal water supply.[52] During World War I, the export demand for cotton again led the Imperial government to attempt to replace 'Desi inferior cotton' with 'superior American cotton'. This attempt also failed.[53] The factors behind this failure, which were indicated by the landholders themselves, reveal the extent of this region's backwardness and stagnation.[54] For one thing, the longer cropping period of the American cotton could not be maintained by subsistence level cultivators. Further, they could not even afford to lose the dried sticks of the cotton crops used as fuel for gur making, which the American cotton did not supply in time. The crop also demanded more time and labour for which the village *penja*

---

[51] Ibid.

[52] What cotton needed most was irrigation and with that assured in independent India through the Bhakra and the western Jamuna canals, Hissar, and Sirsa districts (the erstwhile Hissar district) have emerged as the major cotton growing areas. They now produce 80 per cent of this region's cotton.

[53] IOR: *Microfilm from Pakistan, Punjab Official Selection (POS)*, 5536, see 'Cotton Survey Report, Rohtak District', undertaken in 1919 by D. Milne.

[54] Ibid.

(labourer) demanded higher wages. Cotton, therefore, continued to be insignificant, meant only for local consumption. And 'barani cotton', considered 'worthless' by the officials, continued to be grown in small areas throughout this region. The most phenomenal increase during this period was, in fact, in fodder cultivation (Table 1.5). From being grown on 0.10 per cent of the total cultivated area between 1891–2 and 1895–6, it rose to occupy 13–15 per cent of the area in the 1940s. In fact, it was mostly against the very large exports of fodder to Delhi and the United Provinces that this region could import foodgrains.[55] In the irrigated tracts of Punjab, the landowners had started to raise high value crops like wheat, cotton, and sugarcane and did not trouble to make sufficient provision for growing of good fodder crops. Regarding a similar attempt in certain irrigated parts of Haryana, an official report, as early as in 1899–1900, laid down: 'It would appear that abiana (water rates) in Hissar (and similar localities) need revision to discourage the cultivation of those commercial crops which yield no fodder on irrigated lands adjacent to barani villages.'[56]

In 1945, another official report, *Economic Aspects of Animal Husbandry in Hissar*, again considered it necessary to recommend: 'It is suggested that in cattle breeding tracts the canal water rates for commercial crops should be raised considerably, and the present rates for fodder crops be lowered still more.'[57] In conclusion, the report maintained: 'The [fodder] crops now extensively grown in the district have been selected after generations of experience and no marked improvement or alterations have so far been suggested.'[58] The consequent retention of this region as a cattle-breeding area was justified by pointing out that this area's food consumption needs were looked after by an assured supply from the rest of Punjab.[59]

---

[55] *IOR*: V/24/117, 1907–8, pp. 6–7.

[56] See 'Report on Punjab Famine in 1899–1900 (Hissar District)', in The Board of Economic Inquiry, *Economic Aspects of Animal Husbandry in Hissar*, p. 20.

[57] Ibid.

[58] Ibid., p. 20.

[59] Ibid., p. iv.

AN ALTERNATIVE PROVISION IN A BACKWARD ECONOMY: THE ARMY

This kind of backward economy needed an alternative but powerful outlet for its growing population[60] since the danger of permanently alienating the agriculturist population was a very real one. This outlet was provided by the recruitment policy of the British. Punjabis, with their fighting experience of regular European style armies gained in the pre-British annexation period had come to form the major bulk of soldier recruits in the British Indian Army. After the 1857 uprising, in which regiments drawn from Oudh participated so conspicuously, the British embarked upon a calculated policy of recruiting soldiers from the Punjab peasantry. At the outbreak of World War I, it was found that Punjab supplied about half the Indian soldiers in the army, and the proportion increased in the next two years.[61] The Haryana region, however, shared only partially in this recruiting system, but the requirements of World War I made the British look at this 'little known area' afresh; so far, it had been looked down upon as being 'comparatively unimportant'.[62] Also, in the background of growing national consciousness elsewhere in the country, it was acknowledged that in this region, 'a crude political consciousness so liable to create hostility towards the

[60] Percentage of growth or decline of population in the Haryana region from 1901–51:

Years	Rohtak	Hissar	Karnal	Gurgaon	Ambala
1910–11	−13.7	+ 3.35	−9.48	−12.80	−16.3
1911–21	+7.8	+ 1.58	+3.52	−6.85	−1.61
1921–31	+4.5	+9.97	+2.79	+9.31	+9.11
1931–41	+13.7	+11.93	+16.71	+14.96	+14.13
1941–51	+13.7	+3.58	+10.06	+8.01	+7.50

Source: *Punjab District Handbook, 1961*, Punjab, Chandigarh: Superintendent of Census Operations and Enumeration Commission, 1962 (Ambala, Gurgaon, Hissar, Karnal, and Rohtak districts).

The decade 1901–11 was characterized by an epidemic of plague and fever of a specially fatal kind which contributed to a death rate which exceeded the birth rate in all the districts except Hissar.

[61] M.S. Leigh, 1922, *The Punjab and the War*, Lahore: Superintendent Government Printing, 1922, p. 7.

[62] Punjab Official Selection: *IOR: POS, 5547, War History of the Rohtak District*, 1920, Lahore: Superintendent Government Printing, London: India Office Records, p. 1.

Government' could be aroused, especially among the 50–60 per cent of 'martial castes' with marked 'martial instincts'.[63] Since, geographically, this area encircled the capital, the political danger was evident.

Special attention was, therefore, given to this region and it came to be flooded with thousands of the so-called 'civil recruiters', who, British officials admitted, used fair and foul means to 'procure' the recruits.[64] The British wooing—at economic, political, and social levels—of the 'martial castes', which overlapped with the 'agricultural castes',[65] proved highly successful, so much so that in certain areas of Haryana, agriculture became a second string to the army. For example, in the village Kalanaur, a Muslim Rajput village in Rohtak district, 90 per cent of the males of military age enlisted by 1939.[66] This district as a whole showed an astounding increase of recruits between the First and Second World Wars, as can be ascertained from the number of pensioners in the district. The number of pensioners in 1910 was 866 and it rose to 6,238 in 1936—an increase of 620 per cent.[67] A large number of families in Rohtak district boasted of having provided more than three recruits each to the army during the two World Wars. It is interesting that in this district, the bulk of recruits came from the unirrigated villages of its Jhajjar tehsil, where living conditions were most insecure.[68] In fact, the official reports acknowledged that the insecure and backward areas

---

[63] Ibid., p. 6.

[64] Rohtak district alone had a thousand civil recruiters. For a most interesting account of how recruits for the army were 'procured' from different villages, see ibid., p. 5.

[65] The Punjab Alienation of Land Act, 1900, created a special category of 'agricultural tribes'. In this region, these were: Jat, Rajput, Pathan, Sayyed, Gujar, Ahir, Biloch, Ror, Moghal, Mali, Taga, Saini, Chauhan, Arain, Gaud-Brahmin, and Qoreshi. Generally, those were also the castes from which recruitment was made. For details, see Prem Chowdhry, 1982, 'Jat Domination in South-East Punjab: Socio-Economic Basis of Jat Politics in a Punjab District', *The Indian Economic and Social History Review*, vol. XIX, no. 4, pp. 326–46.

[66] The Board of Economic Inquiry in Punjab, *Soldiers' Savings and How They Use Them*, Lahore: Civil and Military Gazette, 1940, p. 3. There were a large number of villages in Haryana which contributed 50 per cent of their total male population to the army. See Punjab Official Selection: *IOR: POS, 5540, War Services of the Karnal District August 1914–31 March 1919*, 1920, Lahore: Superintendent Government Printing, India Office Records, p. 17.

[67] The Public Relations Department, 1952, Punjab, *Rohtak District*, Jullunder: Controller, Printing and Stationery, p. 18.

[68] Ibid., pp. 17–18.

of Punjab had provided the best recruiting grounds;[69] and the response of the canal colonies had been most disappointing to the British war effort.[70] Even in the irrigated tracts of the otherwise backward region of Haryana, the Punjab officials had realized quite early that the 'canal irrigation was a distinct obstacle in the way of recruitment and the response of the irrigated villages was extremely disappointing as compared to the unirrigated ones.'[71] In unirrigated areas, fewer human resources and labour were needed to tend the cattle and the rest could be made available for recruitment. Not for nothing was this region allowed to be kept agriculturally backward. In World War I, this region contributed one-fifth of the total recruitment from Punjab (Table 1.6) and came to establish a kind of historical and family tradition of army service which continues to this day.

Interestingly, heavy enrolment in the army did not put an unbearable strain on the number of people available for agriculture, primarily because work in the fields in nearly all agricultural operations was performed by women as well as men.[72] In fact, for the Jatni and Kunbi, it was popularly maintained:

Bhali jati jatni, le khurpi hath
Khet niware apne khawind ke sath
[Good kind Jatni, with hoe in hands, weeds the fields along with her husband][73]

---

[69] IOR: P/6045/33, 1945, *Five Year Plan in Post War Development Schemes*, Lahore: Govt. of Punjab, Superintendent, Government Printing. Also, The Board of Economic Inquiry in Punjab, *Soldiers' Savings and How They Use Them*, p. 4. The most important recruiting grounds, apart from the arid plains of Haryana, were Jhelum, Rawalpindi, and Attock in north-west and Kangra in north-east. All these were arid areas with highly deficient irrigation and prone to recurrent famines. The percentage of males of military age enlisting in these areas was as follows: Rawalpindi, 40.1; Jhelum, 38.7; Attock, 23; Kangra, 13.9. For Haryana, see Table 1.6; Leigh, *The Punjab and the War*, pp. 61–2.

[70] The percentage of males of military age who enlisted during World War I in the canal colonies was as follows: Lyallpur, 5.5; Multan, 3.4; Montgomery, 3.3; Jhang, 1.1. See ibid. An interesting disclosure was made by the Secretary of the District Soldiers' Board, Montgomery, who wrote that during 1934 and 1938, the 60,000 military grantees in Montgomery district returned less than sixty men for recruitment. See The Board of Economic Inquiry in Punjab, *Soldiers' Savings and How They Use Them*, p. 4.

[71] *War Services of Karnal District August 1914–31 March 1919*, p. 7.

[72] *War History of the Rohtak District*, p. 6.

[73] W.E. Purser and H.C. Fanshawe, 1880, *Report on the Land Revenue Settlement of the Rohtak District, 1873–79*, Lahore: W.Ball Printer, p. 53.

TABLE 1.6 Army Recruitment in Haryana during World War I

District	No. of males of military age	Total recruitment till 30 November 1918	Percentage of recruitment
Rohtak	1,18,170	28,245	23.90
Gurgaon	1,24,290	20,181	16.23
Hissar	1,34,000	18,400	13.73
Karnal	1,34,200	6,819	5.08
Ambala	1,20,800	10,254	8.48
Total	6,31,460	83,899	13.28
Provincial total (British territory only)	33,67,060	4,23,006	12.56

Source: M.S. Leigh, The Punjab and the War, Lahore, 1922, pp. 61–2.

Even so, because of the demands of agriculture on manpower which might impinge upon the British recruitment requirements, 'the government took measures to safeguard the interests of agriculturists by stopping the enlistment of agricultural labourers', provided primarily by the menial castes.[74]

A large number of social customs relating to marriage also facilitated heavy recruitment. Not only the Hindu Jats, who constituted the single largest caste in this region and contributed the most to heavy recruitment, but also castes like Ahirs and Gujars practised the ceremony *karewa* (widow remarriage); but, as a rule, it was a levirate marriage in which the widow was accepted as wife by one of the brothers or cousins of the deceased husband.[75] A local proverb, popularly associated with Jats, went:

Aja beti lele phere, yeh mar gaya to aur bahutere
[Come daughter get married, if this husband dies there are many more][76]

The army reinforced this social custom. Since soldiers left behind their wives, children, and share in the ancestral land, the custom of marrying the widows within the family came to have greater economic validity. Yet greater sanctity and respectability was provided by the Arya Samaj movement which worked towards encouraging widow remarriage.

[74] *War Services of Karnal District August 1914–31 March 1919*, p. 6.

[75] *War History of the Rohtak District*, p. 3. Also, see The Public Relations Department, Punjab, *Rohtak District*, p. 22.

[76] *Report of the Land Revenue Settlement of the Rohtak District*, 1873–9, p. 53.

The people of this region were not ritual bound or prone to excessive zeal for religious purity. Brahmins occupied a somewhat lower position in the social hierarchy in this region than the one they occupied in most other parts of India.[77] The influence of the Arya Samaj, with its anti-ritualism and emphasis on religious simplicity certainly worked towards loosening the religious scruples of the inhabitants. Even the recruiting officers confessed that 'freedom from religious scruples adds considerably to their value as soldiers.'[78] The military service limited to the so-called martial castes, who were also the statutory agricultural castes, came to be associated with the higher social strata of this region, as the 'inferior castes' were barred from recruitment. These specially categorized castes got social and economic benefits, especially in the climate of severe unemployment and lack of development and this, in turn, had beneficial political consequences for the colonial masters. Recording this, the official report noted, with satisfaction, 'the deep rooted confidence of the people in the government', which even the political cataclysm of April 1919 could not shake, 'despite the best efforts of agitators and demagogues.'[79]

THE BACKWARD ECONOMY AND EMERGENT ROLE OF MONEYLENDERS: AGRICULTURAL STAGNATION

Economically, the initial prosperity of this region seems to have come with the army. The income from pay, pensions, and gratuities was considerable. For instance, as early as in 1909, the annual income of Rohtak district, accruing from pay and pension of government servants, most of whom had served and were serving in the army, was estimated at Rs 16.5 lakh, whereas land revenue of that year was assessed to Rs 11.86 lakh.[80] Village Jatusana of Karnal district, which had provided 140 recruits, received Rs 76,000 from its Indian officers and men serving in the army during eleven months in 1918, by postal money orders.[81] During the same period, Rs 1,20,000 was received in a similar way at Dharuhera, another village in the same district; other villages like

---

[77] For details, see Prem Chowdhry, 'Jat Domination in South-East Punjab', pp. 326–46.

[78] War History of the *Rohtak District*, p. 3.

[79] *War Services of Karnal District August 1914–31 March 1919*, p. 13.

[80] *Punjab District Gazetteer, Rohtak, 1910*, 1911, III-A, Lahore, Government of Punjab: Civil and Military Gazette, pp. 160, 168.

[81] *War Services of Karnal District August 1914–31 March 1919*, p. 25.

Ghairtpur Bas in Gurgaon district and the entire Rajput circle of the Rohtak district recorded similar remittances.[82] On a rough estimate, 50 per cent of ex-armymen turned into moneylenders, petty or big, after their return from the army.[83] The income from pay and pension sent back home enabled the soldiers to repay old debts, redeem mortgaged property in land, and lend out money on mortgages.[84] In fact, they joined the ranks of richer agriculturists as new moneylenders. Together, they competed directly with and outnumbered the old *sahukars* drawn from the Bania and Mahajan castes.[85]

In this chronically famine-ridden region where large sections of the peasants tended to be subsistent or deficit producers, only a comparatively large holding could be economic. For example, in Rohtak district, a holding of at least 12 acres could be taken as an economic one.[86] This meant that only about 28 per cent of landholdings fell in this category.[87] The same was true, more or less, for the entire Haryana region. This meant that an overwhelming majority needed frequent loans; almost anything—a minor natural calamity, needs for seeds, death of cattle—landed them in debt. Moreover, the barani nature of the region with its concomitant low-yielding inferior crops and chronic crop failures made the pressure of the flat rate per acre land revenue demand in cash of the colonial government harder to bear.[88] The frequent natural calamities, which necessitated the suspension of

[82] Indeed, the total revenue demand from the spring harvest due for the whole of Rewari tehsil in which the above cited two villages were situated amounted to Rs 1,19,000, whereas the remittances of these two villages alone came to Rs. 1,96,000. Ibid.

[83] *The Punjab Provincial Banking Inquiry Committee Report, 1929–30 (PBIR),* 1930, vol. II, Lahore: Superintendent, Government Printing, p. 872.

[84] The Board of Economic Inquiry in Punjab, *Soldiers' Savings and How They Use Them,* pp. 21–4.

[85] Rohtak district, for example, came to have by 1927–8. 562 agriculturist moneylenders as compared to 123 Bania moneylenders. *PBIR,* Vol. I, 1930, Lahore, Superintendent, Government Printing, pp. 138, 332.

[86] *Punjab District Gazetteer, Rohtak,* p. 68.

[87] Calculated from The Board of Economic Inquiry, *The Size and Distribution of Agricultural Holdings in the Punjab,* Lahore, 1925, p. 16.

[88] For the controversy whether the land revenue was declining in Punjab over the years, and how it continued to represent a major part of an average cultivator's income and became responsible for his indebtedness, see Mridula Mukherjee, 'Some Aspects of Agrarian Structure of Punjab, 1925–47', *Economic and Political Weekly,* vol. XV, no. 26, June 1980, pp. A46–58.

land revenue in the region, worsened the economic burden of the cultivators.[89] All this strengthened the position of the moneylender.

Yet, in this region, the cultivator's credit, as compared to other parts
of Punjab, was much poorer. The land had lower sale and mortgage
value and, consequently, a higher rate of interest charged.[90] The creditor, in the general lack of development and employment opportunity,
found moneylending the only outlet for profitable investment. In fact,
an official report candidly confessed: 'All the men who bought or took
land on mortgage were well-off zamindars and had no other immediate use to make of their money.'[91] The agriculturist moneylenders, it
may be repeated, included the 'well-off zamindars' as well as armymen
who were also landholders with varying sizes of landholdings. Quick
to lend, as they coveted land, they undercut the traditional Bania sahukar and took the eventual possession of the debtor's land.[92] The debts
which were not promptly repaid turned into mortgages; and mortgages
became mortgages with possession, which in case of default came under
the creditor's possession. Their hands were strengthened by the fact that
the non-agriculturist moneylenders were severely restricted as regards
possession of land by the Punjab Alienation of Land Act of 1900.[93]

---

[89] *Report of the Land Revenue Committee, 1938*, 1938, Lahore: Civil and Military
Gazette, p. 48; also, see GoI: Home Poll, 77/31, 1931.

[90] An official inquiry into the sale of land in the quinquennium 1922–3
to 1926–7 showed the provincial average of sale price of land per acre as
Rs 206.30. In the backward districts of this region, it was: Hissar, Rs 52.90;
Karnal, Rs 83.30; Gurgaon, Rs 138.30; other backward districts like Attock,
Mianwali, Muzaffargarh, Dera Ghazi Khan, and others, showed similar lower
prices. It was highest in Lyallpur, that is, Rs 626.80. See The Board of Economic
Inquiry, Punjab, 1931, *A Note on Sales of Land between Notified Agricultural Tribes
in the Punjab During the Quinquennium, 1922–3 to 1926–7*, Lahore: Civil and
Military Gazette, p. 36.

[91] The Board of Economic Inquiry in Punjab, *Soldiers' Savings and How They
Use Them*, p. 21.

[92] 'A zamindar will lend more money to bad deals than the sahukar as the
latter cannot get his land in return for a loan.' Evidence of the zaildars and
cooperators of Rohtak district, *PBIR*, II, pp. 872–4.

[93] 'Alienation of Land Bill of 1900', *Gazetteer of India*, 1899, part V, p. 135.
Briefly, the provisions of the act stated that the land of an agriculturist (one
who belonged to the statutory agricultural caste) could not be sold to a non-
agriculturist without the sanction of the deputy commissioner, which was
almost never given. Regarding mortgages, the land of an agriculturist could be
mortgaged to a non-agriculturist for twenty years only.

This region of Punjab, consequently, became very conspicuous in having a predominance of agriculturist moneylenders (Table 1.7). Together, the five districts showed, by 1927–8, a total of 1,959 agriculturist moneylenders, operating Rs 1,514 lakh of capital, being taxed annually on Rs 52.81 lakh.

Apart from those listed for income tax purposes, there were hundreds, indeed thousands of agriculturists, who were small-scale moneylenders, but since their interest collection fell below Rs 2,000 per annum, they did not attract the notice of the income tax authorities.[94] Noticeably, Rohtak and Karnal districts of this region headed the list of Punjab districts with the highest number of agriculturist moneylenders who operated the largest amount of capital in moneylending (Table 1.7).

The single directional thrust of the accumulated capital in usury meant an enormous increase in the number of tenants and the area under tenancy cultivation, as figures of alienation of land in the form of mortgage and sale, mostly by small subsistence landowners, skyrocketed and the region came to be dotted with smaller and smaller holdings. The statistical data of Rohtak district are illustrative enough of the above contention. The available figures of thirty years (Table 1.8) show an 85 per cent rise in sales of land and a 73 per cent rise in mortgages of land.

This prodigious increase in the total number of cases clearly indicates the involvement of so many more agriculturists in land transactions. However, the high prices available for land succeeded in limiting the acreage of land under those transactions. And although the annual acreage of land sold or mortgaged during this period did not radically change, the price of land sold or mortgaged rose five times. Interestingly, even during the period of enormous rise in price of land, the Deputy Commissioner of Rohtak observed, in 1934, that 'the agriculturist moneylender could dictate their terms and get the land of the small zamindar at a price far below what it would have fetched in an open market.'[95]

---

[94] See *The Royal Commission on Agriculture in India*, Punjab, VIII, evidence, Calcutta: Government of India, Central Publication Branch, 1927, Appendix III, p. 594.

[95] *Confidential Files from the Deputy Commissioner's Office, Rohtak*, Q. 27, see Report of E.H. Lincoln, 4 February 1934. The restriction on the purchase of land by the non-agriculturists provided the rich agriculturists and the agriculturist moneylenders in Rohtak district, as elsewhere in Punjab, with a condition of semi-monopoly to buy land.

TABLE 1.7 Return of Capital Employed and Interest Earned
in 1927–8 by the Agriculturist Moneylenders Assessed to
Income Tax in Punjab in 1928–9

District	Number of money-lenders	Total capital employed (lakh Rs)	Income for money-lenders actually taxed (lakh Rs)
Rohtak	562	147	13.25
Karnal	507	120	17.64
Gurgaon	458	73	7.25
Hissar	347	71	11.70
Ambala	85	23	2.97
Gujranwala	125	37	5.23
Sheikhupura	97	28	3.94
Sialkot	297	106	7.04
Lyallpur	285	37	5.60
Multan	81	50	5.70
Muzaffargarh	88	21	2.56
Dera Ghazi Khan	39	11	1.28
Montgomery	330	85	9.80
Gurdaspur	144	33	5.62
Kangra	67	10	1.75
Ferozepur	430	90	13.44
Amritsar	159	39	6.13
Jullunder	324	23	2.98
Hoshiyarpur	114	10	1.55
Ludhiana	155	25	3.69
Simla	2	⅓	0.02
Gujrat	178	34	5.05
Jhelum	88	18	2.65
Sargodha	338	68	10.71
Jhang	197	41	5.03
Rawalpindi	68	13	1.90
Attock	85	14	1.86
Mianwali	185	38	5.41
Lahore	163	41	7.35
Total	3,998	1,306.33	169.70

Source: The Punjab Provincial Banking Inquiry Committee Report, 1929–30, I, Lahore, 1930, statement no. 6, p. 332.

TABLE 1.8 Sale and Mortgages of Land in Rohtak District
from 1901 to 1931

Year	Sale of Land			Mortgage of Land		
	No. of cases	Area in acres	Purchase money (Rs)	No. of cases	Area in acres	Purchase money (Rs)
1901–2 to 1905–6	2,947	15,872	9,77,383	14,770	54,782	21,37,821
1906–7 to 1910–11	2,926	16,402	8,98,550	17,298	50,373	23,69,045
1911–12 to 1915–16	6,457	21,563	20,31,330	21,710	54,553	38,14,535
1916–17 to 1920–1	3,502	15,456	23,42,627	22,680	63,967	91,80,534
1921–2 to 1925–6	3,594	13,370	33,14,682	21,819	56,555	89,19,708
1926–7 to 1930–1	5,436	16,592	48,30,321	25,495	62,024	1,06,48,093

Source: Rohtak District Gazetteer, II, part II, Statistical tables, Lahore, 1936, table no. 21.

Similarly, the number of usufructuary mortgages in less than twenty years showed a sharp increase; between 1921–2 and 1939–40, the figures show a 96 per cent increase (Table 1.9). Moreover, usufructuary mortgages also showed a 76 per cent increase in actual acreage of land in relation to the total cultivated area.

The land made available through the above mentioned transactions was leased out for cash or kind to either the smaller owners whose holdings were uneconomic, or to other tenants who did not own land at all, or to the mortgagees themselves. This added to the number of tenants. Calvert was to pointedly assert, in 1921, that in Punjab, the increase in the number of tenants was due to increase in the number of mortgages, as the mortgagees in a number of cases were entered in the records as tenants cultivating under the landowners who were their mortgagors.[96] Besides, those who lost in these land transactions were mostly petty landowners. The Punjab Banking Inquiry Committee Report pointed out that in 73 per cent of the mortgages in Rohtak district, the mortgagors were owners of not more than 5 acres of

[96] H. Calvert, The Wealth and Welfare of the Punjab (2nd edition), Lahore: Civil and Military Gazette, 1936, p. 87.

TABLE 1.9 Area Owned by Statutory Agricultural Castes with
Details of Portion Held under Usufructuary Mortgage
between 1921–2 and 1939–40 in Rohtak District

Year	Total cultivated area (acres)	Total no. of mortgages	Cultivated area under mortgage (acres)	Percentage of area held under mortgages to the total cultivated area
1921–2	10,42,198	34,752	90,867	7.9
1925–6	10,53,414	39,178	1,00,975	8.7
1930–1	10,44,877	50,793	1,21,652	10.6
1935–6	10,66,455	61,470	1,47,399	12.6
1939–40	10,40,219	68,191	1,58,685	13.9

Source: India Office Records: *Annual Report of the Land Revenue Administration in Punjab, 1921–40*, see statement III of these reports for the relevant years.

land.[97] Land transactions, along with other factors like population growth, irrigation uncertainties, war and the consequent price rise, and the like, were held responsible by the officials for an enormous increase in very small holdings and, consequently, affected the economic status of the agriculturists.[98] The village surveys undertaken by the Punjab Board of Economic Inquiry similarly showed that in seven out of eight villages in different districts, the average area per owner had decreased in the last twenty years.[99] In Rohtak district, the enormous increase in the number of tenants and agricultural labourers, stands confirmed through the census figures of 1911–51.[100] And although the authenticity of these figures is questionable, as they may have been wrongly stated for various reasons, the increase is generally accepted to be real.[101]

[97] *PBIR*, II, pp. 872–4.

[98] See inquiry conducted by M.L. Darling, Financial Commissioner of Punjab, dated 3 June 1936, South Asian Centre, Cambridge, Darling Papers, Box 5, F. No. 1.

[99] Ibid.

[100] See Chapter 5 in this volume.

[101] For severe reservations regarding the authenticity of census figures, see J. Krishnamurty, 'Changing Concepts of Work in the Indian Censuses, 1901–1961', *The Indian Economic and Social History Review*, vol. XIV, no. 3, July–September 1977, pp. 324–40. Also, for the entire controversy regarding reliability of agricultural statistics of Punjab, see Clive Dewey, 'Patwaris and Chaukidars: Subordinate Officials and the Reliability of India's Agricultural

Under colonial domination, the increasing moneylending activities show that the existing capital was going into usury and mortgage and land purchase, mostly for renting out purposes. Cultivation in this backward region, specially with extreme uncertainty and low level of produce, was not advantageous through hired labour.[102] Therefore, cultivation through tenants, who bore all the costs of cultivation as also the whole brunt of any natural or unnatural calamity like a fall in prices, continued to be considered more advantageous. The rents which the tenants paid in this region, as compared to the rest of Punjab were, by and large, paid in cash, which was more attractive to the landowners in the given agricultural insecurity of this region. However, in certain districts of this region, as elsewhere in Punjab, by the beginning of the twentieth century, with the limited extension of irrigation, cash rents were being displaced by the *batai* rents (sharecropping).[103] This shift in the form of rent payment shows the commanding position of the landowners, born, in particular, out of the rising competition for land and its rapid commercialization. As already pointed out, the land was sought not only by tenants but also by the owners of small holdings, with ever decreasing sizes, which necessitated their renting in land in order to achieve an economic holding. This showed a competition for land which meant that renting out of land was more profitable than rich farmer capitalist farming.

Cultivation in the colonial period, therefore, hardly showed any capital investment in the production process. The investment of capital in a few cases, like digging of wells, and even limited utilization of

---

Statistics', in Clive Dewey and A.G. Hopkins (eds), *The Imperial Impact*, London: Athlone Press, 1978; also, Neeladri Bhattacharya, 'The Logic of Tenancy Cultivation: Central and South-east Punjab, 1870–1935', *The Indian Economic and Social History Review*, vol. XX, no. 2, April–June 1983, pp. 121–70.

[102] Even the rising numbers of agricultural labourers in this region do not provide any evidence of the growth of cultivation through hired labourers. In fact, a stagnant economy with no alternative outlets of employment was bound to show a large number among rising agricultural population who eked out their living from periodic hiring out of their labour at the time of required agricultural needs.

[103] Between 1890 and 1922, for example, the proportion of leased area under cash rent decreased by 30 per cent in Hissar, 33 per cent in Rohtak, 5 per cent in Gurgaon, and 26 per cent in Karnal. See Bhattacharya's article, 'The Logic of Tenancy Cultivation', pp. 121–70. Bhattacharya has brought out the reasons behind the formal shift of form of rent charged from and given by the tenants in south-east Punjab over a wide span of time.

improved seeds, and so on, was restricted to the areas that could be cultivated with family labour and some hired labour. But this kind of limited and risky experimentation was hardly possible in the case of small cultivators who were generally deficient in any kind of resources. The tenants, on the other hand, could scarcely be expected to invest in land. Cultivation by the tenants, as all contemporary British officials testified, was certainly not conducive to agricultural improvement and prosperity.[104] Moreover, Punjab had no tenancy legislation worth the name and tenants in this region were primarily tenants-at-will. Tenants-at-will cultivated from year to year without any security of tenure or provision of compensation for improvement in land, if ejected.

The investment in agriculture which meant more profit than usury and rent-out cultivation was to await the increase in productivity which occurred in post-colonial India. Till then, Imperial needs, which demanded that this region retain its basic characteristics, continued to emphasize and underline the extreme agricultural backwardness of this region. It was only when this carefully maintained pattern of agrarian economy was broken in the post-colonial period that Haryana could emerge from being a perennially deficit region providing, by and large, a subsistence level living, to become a surplus producing state in India.

[104] The existence of tenants mitigated against any improvement of land or any experimentation. Calvert testified that tenants generally took less care in preparing the land for crops, ploughed it less often, manured it less, and used fewer implements upon it than owners. They grew less valuable crops, especially avoided those which required sinking of capital in land, and made little or no effort at improving their yields. The system of Batai was considered to accentuate most of those tendencies, including even a proper rotation of crops. See Calvert, *The Wealth and Welfare of the Punjab*, pp. 89–90.

2

Jat Domination in South-east Punjab

Socio-economic Basis of Jat Politics in a Punjab District*

Politics of south-east Punjab has been designated as 'Jat politics'. In fact, the rural Hindu representatives of this region, having formed themselves into a 'Jat Group', provided an indispensable source of support to the very existence and success of the Muslim dominated Unionist Party of Punjab from 1924 to 1946. This essay attempts to offer an explanation to this unique phenomenon—a phenomenon of ubiquitous domination by a single caste. It seeks to correlate the triple domination this caste commanded in the social, economic, and numerical spheres to the emerging politics of this region. In analysing the basis of this casteist politics, it seeks to trace out the actual beneficiaries found among the upper strata of Jat peasantry operating behind the projected 'Jatism'. It also offers a brief comment on the policy of the colonial government in providing an additional boost to this strata in its control of the entire socio-economic fabric of the agrarian society and in gaining an easy access to the seats of political influence and gain. For purposes of illustration of arguments, an in-depth study of the socio-economic composition of a district has been undertaken to highlight the changes occurring roughly over the first four decades of the twentieth century which went into strengthening the

* This essay was originally published in 1982, *The Indian Economic and Social History Review*, XIX (3–4): 325–46.

upper strata of the landowning classes—Jat and non-Jat. The district adopted for this purpose is Rohtak—the acknowledged centre of south-east Punjab and the district responsible for providing the 'Jat' epithet to this region and indeed, to that of the province. This district not only set the tenor for all districts of this region to follow but was also the constituency of Chhotu Ram, the 'Jat leader' behind the mobilization of Jats and responsible for creating the 'Jat Group' in the provincial politics.

Numerically, the Hindu Jats were found in very large numbers in the five districts of this region, namely, Ambala, Gurgaon, Hissar, Karnal, and Rohtak; the last three districts forming the 'homeland of Hindu Jats'.[1] Out of these districts, Rohtak held the largest number of Jats. According to the Census of 1921,[2] the population of Rohtak district was 772,272 and the Jats, as the single largest caste in the district, accounted for 262,195 people or one-third of the total population of the district. The Jats also held the bulk of agricultural land as proprietors.[3] With their twelve major *Gots* (patrineal clans) and 137

---

[1] *Census of India, 1931, Punjab and Delhi*, Punjab Census, 1933, XVII, part 1, Report, Lahore: Civil and Military Gazette, pp. 339–40.

[2] *Punjab Census, 1921*, 1923, XV, part II, Lahore: Civil and Military Gazette p. 2. The other castes in relation to Jats were much smaller in numbers. Jats, therefore, emerge as the single largest caste in Rohtak district. The caste complexion of Rohtak district in 1921 was as follows: Jat, 262,195; Brahmin, 71,917; Chamar, 65,804; Bania, 46,814; Rajput, 46,468; Dhanak, 24,044; Chuhra, 23,514; Ahir, 17,064; Kumhar, 13,954; Tarkhan, 13,390; Nai, 13,070; Mali, 12,106; Faquir, 9,383; Tcli, 9,254; Jhimar, 8,972; Qassab, 8,528; Gujar, 7,789; Pathan, 7,019; Machchi, 6,371; Taga, 6,019; Jogi, 5,872; Chimba,5,406; Dhobi, 4,063; Sunar, 3,295; Saini, 2,922; Mirasi, 2,698; Biloch, 2,386; Lilari, or Rangrez, 2,293; Julaha, 1,945; Changar, 1,217; Kayastha,1,209; Mughal,1,151; Khatri, 1,138; Maniar, 1,132; Bharbhunja, 1,111; Gadaria, 1,128; Kunjra,1,009; Od, 985; Sayyed, 945; Lodha, 663; Rahbari, 511; Bhatiara, 298; Aheri (Heri), 277; Darzi, 245. Ibid., part I, p. 220. Also, *Punjab District Gazetteer, Rohtak*, 1931, 1936, II, part B, statistical tables, Lahore: Civil and Military Gazette.

[3] Classification of 530 villages in Rohtak district according to the caste of the majorty of proprietors:

Caste	No. of villages held in			
	Gohana	Rohtak	Jhajjar	Total
1. Jat	97	99	189	385
2. Rajput (Hindu)	1	6	20	27
3. Brahmin	7	8	12	27

minor ones, they controlled, in 1910, 385 villages in the district out of a total of 530. And significantly, in many of these 'Jat villages', they held a near monopoly of landownership. For example, in village Kanaudha, the Jat landowners were in possession of 99.22 per cent of the total cultivated land.[4] Again, in village Gijhi, the Jats, comprising 83.89 per cent of the landowners, held 92.99 per cent of the total cultivated land.[5] In fact, not only in Rohtak district but in any district of Punjab, the Jats were considered to be foremost among all the landowning castes of Punjab.[6] At a time when agriculture was more or less the solitary prop of the provincial economy, the ownership of agricultural land inevitably established the dominance of Jats in the area. The settlement report of Rohtak district of 1910, which includes the last consolidated list of the caste divisions, throws the social and economic patterns into bold relief.[7] The Hindu Jats emerge as the owners of 60 per cent of cultivated land in the district; there were also five or six villages which were owned by Jats who had converted to Islam. In comparison, Muslim Rajputs owned 7 per cent, Hindu Rajputs about 4½ per cent,

Caste	No. of villages held in			
	Gohana	Rohtak	Jhajjar	Total
4. Ahir	–	–	25	25
5. Rajput (Mohammadan)	12	13	–	25
6. Afghan	3	–	12	15
7. Gujar	–	1	6	7
8. Biloch	–	–	4	4
9. Kayastha	–	2	2	4
10. Mahajan	2	1	–	3
11. Sheikh	–	1	2	3
12. Sayyed	–	2	1	3
13. Fakir	–	–	1	1
14. Ror	1	–	–	1
Total	123	133	274	530

Source: *Punjab District Gazetteer, Rohtak, 1910*, 1911, III-A, Lahore: Civil and Military Gazette, 1911, p. 68.

[4] *Confidential Files from the Superintendent's Office (CFSO)*, Rohtak, 26/51.

[5] The Board of Economic Inquiry, Punjab Village Surveys, 1932, *Gijhi, a Village in Rohtak District*, Lahore: Civil and Military Gazette, p. 132.

[6] *Annual Reports of Administration in the Punjab (PAR)*, 1921–2, 1921, Government of Punjab, Lahore, Superintendent Government Printing, p. 324.

[7] *Final Report of the Third Regular Settlement*, 1905–10, 1910, Rohtak District, Lahore: Civil and Military Gazette, p. 10.

Brahmins 6½ per cent, Ahirs 2½ per cent, Banias and Pathans about 2 per cent each, of the total cultivated land. The remaining 15½ per cent of land was owned by miscellaneous castes and government boards.

Certain administrative changes took place in 1912 when Delhi territory was separated from Punjab, and its Sonepat *tehsil*, with an area of 449 square miles and 241 villages, was merged in Rohtak district. Although there are no official figures relating to the additional cultivated land which this change brought to Rohtak district, the unmistakable similarity between the economic and social patterns of village communities of the newly merged territory on the one hand, and of the village communities of the old Rohtak district on the other, would certainly point to the continued Jat dominance as the single largest caste in the enlarged district both in economic and numerical terms. Certain available figures would support this conclusion. Sonepat area had a Jat population of 49,319, while its total population was 1,73,345.[8] This gives to the Jats the same numerical ratio in the population as that of the old Rohtak district of pre-1912. The Jats in Delhi district comprising of three tehsils, prior to the administrative rearrangement of 1912, owned 48 per cent of land. It is to be noted that the Hindu Jats were numerically strongest in Sonepat tehsil. In terms of percentage, the Jat in Sonepat tehsil were 30 per cent higher than in Delhi tehsil and 70 per cent higher than in Ballabhgarh. Fifty per cent of the villages of Sonepat tehsil were controlled by Jats. As to the rest, 30 per cent of villages were dominated jointly by Jats and Sayyeds or Brahmins. The proprietary body in the Sonepat tehsil consisted exclusively of Jats in 123 villages, of Jats and Brahmins in forty-seven, of Jats and Sayyeds in twenty-one, of Chauhans in twenty-six, and of Tagas (also known as Tyagi Brahmins) in twenty-six villages. Rohtak district, enlarged after the inclusion of Sonepat tehsil, should, therefore, show the continued domination of Jats in both spheres, that is, economic and numerical.

The social status of Jats in Rohtak district is somewhat difficult to define in the ritualistic framework of the caste hierarchies. The census authorities of 1901 confessed that Punjab defied a systematic

[8] *Punjab District Gazetteer, Delhi, 1912*, 1913, V, A, Lahore: Civil and Military Gazette, statistical tables, p. xxxi. Jat population: Delhi, 38,999; Ballabhgarh, 16,380; and Sonepat had a majority of Hindu Jats—out of 49,319, they were 47,365 in numbers with only 29 Sikh Jats and 1,655 Muslim Jats.

classification of castes.[9] For example, the social superiority of the Brahmin did not exist in Punjab, and though Brahmin could be sacredocally superior, yet, socially he was described as 'lowest of the low'.[10] On the other hand, regarding Jats—who were in the ritual hierarchy a peasant caste all over India and were ritually ranked in Punjab after the Brahmin, Rajput, and Khatri—the Punjab census of 1901 laid down: 'there is no caste above the Jat'. The social status of Jat was further complicated by their differing social status in the different regions of Punjab. In central Punjab, for example, a Sikh Jat did not consider anyone his social superior, not even a Rajput. Elsewhere in Punjab, the Jats, by and large, claimed Rajput origin. The Jats of south-east Punjab, who were declared to be of the same stock and type as that of central Punjab, also claimed the Rajput origin.[11] However, following the model of the dominant caste in a given region described by M.N. Srinivas,[12] the

[9] *Punjab Census, 1901*, 1912, XVII, part 1, Report, Lahore: Civil and Military Gazette, p. 337. The report in this connection gives the example of *Janeo* (the sacred thread) which was donned by the twice born, that is, the Brahmins, nearly all over India. In Punjab also, the Brahmins wore the Janeo but apart from them, the Janeo wearers could be found among other castes as well, for example, the Nai who ministered to the castes who wore the Janeo. Among Jats also, Janeo was worn in certain villages but this did not have the effect of raising the Janeo wearing Jat above the level of non-wearing Jat. Ibid., p. 324.

[10] Ibid., p. 338. In this connection, the remark of Prakash Tandon that he discovered the privileged position of the Brahmins only when he went to live outside Punjab is interestingly relevant. See his *Punjabi Century, 1857–1947*, London: Chatto & Windus, 1963, p. 63.

[11] D. Ibbetson, *The Punjab Castes*, Lahore: Government Printing Press, 1916, pp. 100–5. The Hindu Rajputs of Rohtak were in possession of merely four-and-a-half per cent of land as compared to 60 per cent under the Hindu Jats. However, there is no mention of any evidence regarding the socially higher status of the Rajputs. The fact of Jats claiming the Rajput origin may be explained by the ritualistic and traditional norms which held a Rajput to be a *Kshatriya* and as the ideal. In any case, claiming a higher origin did not detract from the fact of a particular caste being the 'dominant caste'. The 'dominant caste', in a given region, was frequently given to claiming a higher origin. In fact, M.N Srinivas specifically mentions Jats as the 'dominant caste' in Punjab. See *Caste and Modern India and Other Essays*, Bombay: Asia Publishing House, 1962, p. 90.

[12] For the concept and features of 'dominant caste', see M.N. Srinivas, 'The Dominant Caste in Rampura', *American Anthropologist*, vol. 61, no. 1, February 1959, pp. 1–16.

status of Jats as a 'dominant' caste can be easily established in Rohtak district. Economically and numerically stronger than any other caste in Rohtak district, the Jats satisfied yet another norm of the 'dominant caste', that is, in the ritual hierarchy also, they did not occupy 'a low ritual status'. In the agrarian society of Punjab, the norms, as seen to be operating and also as encouraged by the British, did not conform to the ritualistic concepts and were necessarily in relation to the amount of land that was held in possession by a particular caste.[13] Seen as such, the Jats in Rohtak district clearly emerge as the 'dominant caste'. In the agraian setup of the district, most of the other castes were in relation of servitude to the landowning Jats who stood as the single largest receivers of services from the other castes. Whatever superiority the Brahmins may have enjoyed declined severely by the early twenties with the propagation and acceptance of Arya Samaj, especially among the landowning Jats of Rohtak.

The Jats were, however, economically and socially not a homogeneous caste or community. In the total population of 1,45,435 landowning or revenue paying families in Rohtak district under the Provincial Autonomy,[14] Jats, who constituted 60 per cent of the landowners, came to about 87,261. In the total Jat population of 2,66,840 in the district in 1931, this left 1,79,579 Jats as belonging to the families of either

---

[13] For details, see *Punjab Census, 1901*, XVIII, part 1, Report, Lahore: Civil and Military Gazette, pp. 324–5.

[14] Figures showing number of land revenue payers in different groups in Rohtak district:

Total number of land revenue payers—1,45,435

		Amount
Land revenue payers who pay Rs 5 or less	63,000	140,898
" " " " " between Rs 5 and 10	33,388	233,585
" " " " " between Rs 10 and 20	28,048	340,372
" " " " " between Rs 20 and 50	17,174	499,641
" " " " " between Rs 50 and 100	1,107	73,294
" " " " " between Rs 100 and 250	274	38.041
" " " " " between Rs 250 and 500	62	7,567
" " " " " between Rs 500 and 1,000	18	12,423
" " " " " between Rs 1,000 and 5,000	4	6,104
" " " " " between Rs 5,000 and 10,000	—	—

Source: *Report of the Land Revenue Committee 1938*, 1938, Lahore, Government of Punjab: Superintendent Government Printing, appendix I.

tenants of all kinds or landless agricultural labourers. It is impossible to further break the figures into actual numbers of tenants and agricultural labourers among Jats of Rohtak. However, Jats were officially proclaimed to be 'dominating' among the tenants as well.[15] That they were found among the agricultural labourers also, is clear from the percentage of agricultural labourers for the Hindu Jats, given in the census of 1931: out of 1,000 males in Punjab, 19 Hindu Jats were agricultural labourers; the corresponding figure for female agricultural labourers was 5 out of 100 males. But again, there are no separate figures for Jats employed as agricultural labourers in Rohtak district. The number of Hindu Jats among the agricultural labourers in Rohtak district was not as large as given for the whole of Punjab, as the agricultural labourers in Rohtak district were deemed to be drawn mainly from among the untouchable castes.

Even the landowning Jats were internally differentiated. The 1924–5 figures of the size and distribution of agricultural land in Rohtak shows varied landholdings:[16] 45.9 per cent of the peasant proprietors were petty owners with holdings of area between 1 acre and 5 acres only; 25.2 per cent with holdings measures between 5 and 10; and 28.9 per cent alone with sizable holdings of 10 acres and over; some holdings were 50 acres and beyond. As the average holding came to 5.7 acres only, nearly half of the total holdings in Rohtak fell well below this average. Apart from this, Rohtak district was notorious for its limited

---

[15] W.E. Purser and H.C. Fanshawe, 1880, *Report on the Revised Land Revenue Settlement of the Rohtak District*, 1873–9, Lahore: W.Ball Printer, p.50.

[16] The size and distribution of 15,379 agricultural holdings in Rohtak district:

Landholdings	Total number	Percentage
Under 1 (one) acre	1,097	7.1
1 and under 3 acres	3,370	21.9
3 and under 5 acres	2,594	16.9
5 and under 10 acres	3,872	25.2
10 and under 15 acres	1,776	11.5
15 and under 20 acres	1,173	7.6
20 and under 25 acres	582	3.8
25 and under 50 acres	721	4.7
50 acres and over	194	1.3

Source: The Board of Economic Inquiry, *The Size and Distribution of Agricultural Holdings in the Punjab*, Lahore: Civil and Military Gazette, 1925, p. 16.

irrigation, precarious rainfall, devastating floods due to the periodic overflow of the river Jamuna, seasonal excesses, and also, frequent *akals* (famines).[17] Irrigation through wells was extremely limited. In most parts of the district, the water level was generally very low and in most places, the sub-soil water was brackish and not useful for agricultural purposes.[18] The district administration was aware of the enormity of water problem that this region faced. Despite incurring enormous cost for constructing masonry well, the income was very meagre especially as water tax had to be paid to the colonial masters. The water made available at the depth of 25 feet irrigated just about 1/5th of an acre, even after having worked the entire day and after three to four years even ceased to produce water.[19]

The irrigated land in Rohtak was, therefore, only 28.4 per cent in 1921 and 33.1 per cent in 1931 of the total cultivated land.[20] This farther reduced the economic viability of the numerous holdings in the district. The average holding of 5.7 acres in Rohtak was too low a figure for a district where nearly 70 per cent of the cultivated area was *barani* (dependent on rainfall). Therefore, if a holding of 12 acres is taken as an economic one, as suggested by the *District Gazetteer* of 1910, then even less than 28 per cent of the population had their 'neck above water'. Thus, a vast multitude of petty and, more or less, impoverished owners greatly outnumbered the comparatively affluent and big landowners, though both continued to be grouped under the title of *zamindars*.[21]

---

[17] In the present century, Rohtak district experienced famines in the following years: 1905–6, 1909–10, 1913–14, 1918–19, 1928–30, and 1938–40. The famines of 1928 and 1938 lasted for three years each. *Haryana District Gazetteer, Rohtak*, 1970, Chandigarh: Haryana District Gazetteers Organization, Revenue Department, pp. 100–1.

[18] *India Office Records, Proceedings of the Punjab Government (IOR: P)*, 7841/1908, 22, see Report, 22 September, 1906.

[19] Ibid.

[20] *Punjab District Census Handbook, Rohtak, 1951*, II, Chandigarh: Superintendent of Census Operations and Enumeration Commission, Punjab, 1965, p. 42.

[21] In Punjab, the word zamindar, unlike in the most other provinces of India where it was generally used for very big owners of land, was applied to anyone who owned land, however little. However, since the enactment of the Punjab Alienation of Land Act of 1900, when certain agricultural castes were created for the first time, the word zamindar also came to stand for a member of any 'statutory agricultural caste'. Zamindar, therefore, became a synonym for an agriculturist.

Right from the beginning, the British officials showed favour to this 28 per cent or so of landowners at the expense of the other petty owners of land in Rohtak district. This was nothing new, for the British had always favoured the upper stratum of landowners from among the rest of the landowners or even at their expense and that of the other categories of agriculturists. In Punjab, the open official favour to this class started with the enactment of the Punjab Alienation of Land Act of 1900.[22] So far as Rohtak district was concerned, this act was especially favourable to the rich Jat landowners. Officially, the object of this measure was to place restrictions on the transfer of agricultural land in Punjab with a view to check its alienation from the agricultural to non-agricultural classes.[23]

For defining 'agriculturists', certain castes, mistakenly referred to as 'tribes' by the British administrators, were set aside and designated as 'agricultural tribes' for the first time in Punjab.[24] A.H. Diack, the

---

[22] The widespread official debate around the Bill of 1900, as covered by N.G. Barrier, *The Punjab Alienation of Land Bill, 1900*, Durham: Duke University, 1966; Clive Dewey, 'The Official Mind and the Problem of Agrarian Indebtedness in India, 1870–1910', Unpublished thesis, Cambridge University, 1972; and P.H.M. van den Dungen, *The Punjab Tradition: Influence and Authority in the 19th Century India*, London: George Allen and Unwin, 1972, certainly gives no indication that the official intention was to 'benefit' or 'help' the richer peasantry of Punjab, as given above. The words most frequently and uniformly used are 'peasantry' or 'agriculturists', without specifying their economic categories. However, it is difficult to accept that the British officials were unaware of the benefits of the act accruing almost entirely to the richer among the notified agriculturists, specially when they themselves acknowledged that the agrarian debt was a necessary evil in Punjab. Moreover, the instructions sent to implement the act clearly indicate the official knowledge about the possible beneficiaries of the act. This fact also surfaced repeatedly when the act came in for discussion. For example, D.C. Johnstone, a British Judge for the Ambala division, commented in October 1900: 'It is not easy to see how all this (the Bill) is going to benefit the poor zamindar himself'. See *Legislative Department Proceedings*, No. II-68, October 1900, appendix A 24, p. 14.

[23] 'Alienation of Land Bill of 1900', *Gazetteer of India*, 1899, part V, p. 135. Under the provisions of the Act, both sale and mortgage of agricultural land came to be highly restricted. It could neither be sold nor alienated or mortgaged to a non-agriculturist for more than twenty years.

[24] The British Indian civil servants had mistakenly used the two kinds of units, that is, tribe and caste, interchangeably. And what are now acknowledged as castes were freely described as tribes and vice-versa. The confusion arose because the nineteenth century British administrators while producing vast

revenue and finance secretary to the Government of Punjab, sent certain instructions regarding castes which should or should not be classed as agricultural castes in any district or group of districts. These instructions[25] clearly favoured the richer castes among the rest. These castes which were represented by 'insignificant numbers' and held a 'trifling amount of land' were not to be 'ordinarily' placed in the deputy commissioner's list, even though they were, in fact, agricultural and were so enumerated in other districts. The British official visualized 'no great harm' if they were left to alienate the 'trifling' area in their possession to the moneylenders. Another 'very important matter to be kept in view', according to the instructions, was the fact that 'agricultural tribes may include professional moneylenders among its members'. The purpose of the act, as revealed through these instructions, therefore, was to enable the persons among favoured agricultural castes 'possessing of sufficient capital' to invest in land. The moneyed classes from among the non-agriculturists, however, were completely excluded. The 'questionable' nature of the policy of giving free access to such persons among agricultural castes to acquire land from their fellow caste men had been recognized but ignored.[26] Consequently, the swallowing up of petty owners by their caste men or members of other agricultural castes was accepted and encouraged by the British administrators.

In keeping with the instructions, ten castes were notified in Rohtak district as 'statutory agricultural tribes' in notification No. 21. S., dated 22 January 1901. This list was enlarged by inclusion of a few more castes

literature on the description and identification of various tribes and castes in the population of India did not follow any clearly formulated system of classification. However, the anthropological definition of tribe makes a clear distinction between the two. A tribe is socially, economically, and politically a self-contained unit—a unit which has within its boundaries all the resources necessary for the continued maintenance of a particular mode of existence. But a caste is not an autonomous entity. Identified with ritual or occupational specialization, it is dependent on others for its survival. For details, see Andre Béteillé, 'On the Concept of Tribe', *International Social Science Journal*, vol. XXXII, no. A, 1980, pp. 825–8.

[25] *CFSO, Rohtak*, I–IV. See instructions contained in a letter dated 12 November 1900 and also, notification, 18 April 1904.

[26] Ibid.

in 1907, 1910, 1925, and 1936.[27] Among these notified agricultural castes, so far as the existence of 'capitalists' and 'moneylenders' was concerned, the Jats were deemed by the British administrators to form a 'class' by themselves. In December 1900, H.J. Maynard, the Deputy Commissioner of Ambala, commenting on the grouping of agricultural castes, had suggested that the Jat should be placed in a 'separate category' on the ground that 'capitalists and moneylenders were specially common in this tribe.'[28]

Restriction on land market imposed by this act, leading to the near elimination of what the British called the 'professional moneylender', that is, Bania, Mahajan, and Khatri, naturally proved very beneficial to the rich agriculturists. Not satisfied with this limitation on the non-agriculturists moneylender, which left the field fairly free for his counterpart among agriculturists, the British officials sought to further restrict the land market for the benefit of the buying rich agriculturists. This necessitated grouping of agricultural castes. Land alienations brought about with the permission of the deputy commissioner were restricted within these groups. This was considered a 'serious evil' by the Deputy Commissioner of Rohtak.[29] Grouping of agricultural castes meant narrowing of the market to such an extent that each caste or group of castes would be restricted to the exploitation of its own caste or group. For the rich Jats of Rohtak district, this further limitation of the land market proved a boon as they could easily exploit their caste fellows by furnishing the necessary capital. This provided the rich Jats of Rohtak with a semi-monopoly condition in buying land cheaply. In fact, despite the rise in prices of land in the mid-1930s the district administration admitted that the richer sections of Jats were able to buy the land of the smaller landowners at much lower a price than available in the marketplace.[30]

---

[27] The castes designated as 'agricultural tribes' in Rohtak district were: Jat, Rajput, Pathan, Sayyed, Gujar, Ahir, Biloch, Ror, Moghal, and Mali. By subsequent notifications, the following were notified: Taga, Saini, Chauhan, Arain, Gaud-Brahmin, and Qoreshi.

[28] *CFSO, Rohtak*, I–IV, H.J. Maynard, the Deputy Commissioner of Ambala, 16 December 1900.

[29] Ibid., P.S.M. Burlton, the Deputy Commissioner of Rohtak district (1897–1900) to the Commissioner of Delhi division, 26 December 1900.

[30] *Confidential Files from the Deputy Commissioner's Office, Rohtak*, Q. 27, see Report of E.H. Lincoln, 4 February 1934.

In the nature of things, the richer Jat landowners emerged as moneylenders. So much so that the word 'Jat' came to be used for all agriculturist moneylenders, whatever their caste.[31] Compared to the rest of Punjab, Rohtak district became very conspicuous in this connection. By 1927–8, the number of agriculturist moneylenders in the district had risen to 562, the highest compared to any other district of Punjab.[32] The total amount invested by them in moneylending was estimated at Rs 147 lakhs as compared to Rs 82 lakhs invested by 123 Bania moneylenders of the district. The agriculturists moneylenders had clearly emerged as strong competitors of the non-agriculturist moneylenders. The income tax assessed on the capital invested by the agriculturist moneylenders in moneylending was Rs 13.25 lakhs. On an average, the outlay or capital per moneylender came to Rs 12,000. A survey of 338 of the 562 assessees made by the income tax officer revealed that 103 assessees had an investment of over Rs 20,000 each.[33] These substantial agriculturist moneylenders had lent out money not only in rural areas, where the rates of interest were very high, but also in *mandis* (grain markets) and towns. The smaller moneylenders among the new class of moneylenders, however, confined themselves to the countryside. A hundred and thirty-one of these moneylenders with individual investment between Rs 10,000–Rs 20,000, and 104 with investments below Rs 10,000 each, had dealings purely with their fellow agriculturists. Besides these, there were hundreds, indeed thousands, of agriculturists who became moneylenders on a small scale and whose

---

[31] *Punjab Legislative Council Debates (PLCD)*, vol. XXV, 1 November 1934, pp. 842–3. See speech of Chhotu Ram.

[32] See Table 1.7, Chapter 1 in this volume.

[33] Sardar Chanda Singh's inquiry (Income Tax Officer, Hissar) of 338 money-lenders in Rohtak district revealed the following:

Range of investment rupees	No. of money-lenders	Total investment	Total interest	Average rate of Interest
20,000 and over	103	33,71,690	424,691	12.6%
Between 10,000 and 20,000	131	19,02,155	284,330	15%
Below 10,000	104	7,19,562	119,379	16%

Source: *Punjab Provincial Banking Inquiry Committee Report, 1929–30 (PBIR)*, I, note K, p. 224.

interest collection being below Rs 2,000 per annum did not attract the notice of income tax authorities.[34]

It was mostly Hindu Jats who were the new moneylenders in Rohtak district. In his evidence before the Punjab Banking Inquiry Committee, Rai Bahadur Lal Chand, a 'Jat leader' and one of the earliest protagonists of the Unionist Party, correctly maintained that the number of increasing agriculturist moneylenders were drawn from among the rich landowners of the villages; regarding their caste he explained that 'in a Rajput village there are Rajput moneylenders and in a Jat village you have Jat money lenders and so on.'[35] There was an interesting enquiry made in 1924–5 in relation to a village Gijhi situated 15 miles south-east of Rohtak. The position revealed by the inquiry was characteristic of the countryside in Rohtak and the neighbouring districts. The inquiry showed:

20 years ago there were only 2 Jat moneylenders while there were 3 Mahajan and 2 Chippi (cloth-printers) who worked on a large scale. The number of moneylenders who do a fair amount of business is now: Jats 13, Mahajans 4, Bairagi 1, and Chippi 1; in addition to about 6 other Jats who also lend small sums for short periods...The number of agriculturist moneylenders is more than double that of all other classes of moneylenders put together. As regards non-agriculturists, almost all the money is lent by Mahajans...It must not be overlooked, however, that the monied zamindar does not care so much for lending money for the sake of interest as for securing a mortgage with the hope of getting possession of the mortgaged land in the future. Each of the 13 Jat moneylenders has several mortgages to his credit...Land hunger on the part of the zamindar is the chief motive in his loan transactions...The Mahajans of the village are fairly well to do without being prosperous, but the agriculturist moneylenders are certainly well off. Some of them have pacca homes built recently; three of these houses cost Rs 20,000/- and Rs 10,000/- and Rs 8,000/- respectively. These people are ever ready to take on mortgages, but their prosperity is not to be wholly ascribed to moneylending as they are also big zamindars on their own account.[36]

[34] *Royal Commission on Agriculture, Punjab*, VIII, evidence, Appendix III, p. 594.

[35] *PBIR*, II, evidence, p. 966.

[36] The Board of Economic Inquiry, Punjab Village Surveys: *Gijhi*, pp. 102–3.

The report also maintained that 'of 170 acres mortgaged, 162 were mort-gaged with Jats'. This position of 'Jats' in the moneylending business confirms the earlier conclusion regarding their growing monopolistic control of money and land transactions.

In fact, the whole of Rohtak district showed similar figures regard-ing land mortgages. The statutory agriculturists of Rohtak district were calculated to be holding 90 per cent or more of the total area under mortgage.[37] In Rohtak district, as in other districts of Punjab, there were rapid alienations of land in the form of mortgages and sales. In thirty years, that is, between 1901 and 1931, the cases of both sales and mortgage of land in the district rose by 84.45 per cent and 72.61 per cent, respectively.[38] The annual average of 2,947 cases of sale of land and 14,770 cases of mortgage of land between 1901–2 and 1905–6 rose to an annual average of 5,436 and 25,495 cases, respectively, between 1926–7 and 1930–1.[39] Similarly, the number of usufructuary mortgages, by far the most popular in Rohtak district, rose by 96.22 per cent in less than twenty years, that is, between 1921–2 and 1939–40. From 34,752 in 1921–2 they reached 68,191 in 1939–40.[40]

The actual acreage of area given by the agricultural castes in usufruc-tuary mortgage to their fellow agriculturists showed 75.94 per cent increase in relation to the total cultivated area owned by them. Mort-gaged area which was 7.9 per cent of the total cultivated area in 1921–2 increased to 13.9 per cent in 1939–40.[41]All these land transactions were between statutory agricultural castes only. The caste-wise figures given for the period 1926–7 to 1939–40 show that among the agricultural

[37] *PBIR*, I, p. 139. The oral evidence of the zaildars and cooperators of Rohtak district shows that unlike the sahukars, the bigger landowners were more than willing to lend money despite knowing the inability of the small landowners to pay back. Such a deal provided them with an opportunity to take over the land of a small landowner—an opportunity which had been closed for the non-agriculturist moneylender. *PBIR*, II, pp. 872–4.

[38] Calculated from the figures of sale and mortgage of land in Rohtak district for the period 1901–31 in *Rohtak District Gazetteer*, II, part II, statistical tables, Lahore, 1936, table no. 21.

[39] See Table 1.8, Chapter 1 in this volume.

[40] Calculated from the figures of usufructuary martgage in Rohtak district given for the period 1921–2 to 1939–40 in *Annual Report of the Land Revenue Administration in the Punjab (PLRA)*, statement III, for the relevant years.

[41] See Table 1.9, Chapter 1 in this volume.

castes also, the major beneficiaries were 'Jats'.[42] The benefits of land transactions as shown accruing to the 'Jats' were, however, a net gain

[42] Detailed caste-wise figures (1926–7 to 1939–40) of the total gain (+) or loss (–) in land transactions (mortgage and sale) of Rohtak district between the members of statutory agricultural castes only:

Caste	1926–7		1927–8		1928–9		1929–30	
	Mort.	Sales	Mort.	Sales	Mort.	Sales	Mort.	Sales
Ahir	+175	–351	+144	+77	+197	+118	+202	+132
Arain	—	+5	—	+4	—	+3	+3	+2
Bairagi	—	—	—	—	—	—	—	—
Biloch	–39	–11	–4	+1	–19	–20	–14	–17
Gaud-Brahmin	+23	+3	+17	–7	–43	–29	+34	–5
Gujar	–22	–12	—	–15	–20	–12	–40	–4
Jat*	+362	+536	+364	+50	+389	+179	+323	–5
Qoreshi	—	—	—	—	—	—	—	—
Mali	+14	–1	—	+20	+2	–2	+244	+1
Moghal	—	–1	+19	–14	–3	+14	+1	–6
Pathan	–58	–81	–72	–178	–17	22	–65	–7
Rajput	–377	–62	–420	+62	–413	–33	–624	–59
Ror	–14	+1	–6	—	–6	—	–9	—
Sayyed	–43	–27	–36	–10	–35	–94	–19	–32
Taga	–21	–2	–16	+2	–32	2	–36	—
Chauhan	—	—	—	—	—	—	—	—

	1930–1		1931–2		1932–3		1933–4		1934–5	
	Mort.	Sales	Mort.	Sales	Mort.	Sales	Mort.	Sales	Mort.	Sales
	+304	+80	+227	+45	+200	+25	+55	+14	+93	+76
	—	–2	—	—	—	—	—	+5	—	—
	—	—	—	—	—	—	—	—	—	—
	–10	–7	–5	–3	+5	–12	+3	—	–7	+6
	+24	–2	+38	+15	–4	–10	+60	–1	+106	+4
	—		–47	–10	–5	–4	–4	+11	–1	+11
	*+76	+145	+481	+25	–14	+99	+74	+43	–40	+76
	—	—	—	—	—	—	—	—	—	—
	–6	+5	+8	+15	+3	–13	+10	–7	–1	+4
	—	–3	–15	–3	+1	–11	—	—	–9	–11
	–11	+1	–36	–12	+89	+42	+8	–10	+85	–61
	–390	–224	–654	–63	–274	–11	–55	–1	–171	–80
	—	—	–1	–9	–2	—	—	—	–7	—
	–3	–3	+10	—	–2	–99	–7	–48	–19	–17
	+12	—	–6	—	–3	+6	–32	–6	–5	–3
	—	—	—	—	–4	–12	—	—	—	—

after subtraction of the losses suffered by the others in the same caste. Those who lost in these land transactions were mostly petty landowners. In fact, figures show that 73 per cent of total mortgages in Rohtak district were mortaged by owners of not more than 5 acres of land.[43] For the other land transactions of the district it can be similarly

1935–6		1936–7		1937–8		1938–9		1939–40	
Mort.	Sales	Mort.	Sales	Mort.	Sales	Mort.	Sales	Mort.	Sales
+87	+55	+218	+7	+104	+105	+116	+54	+172	+33
—	−1	—	—	+1	+1	−5	—	—	+2
—	—	—	—	−5	—	−4	—	−7	–
—	−6	+2	−12	−12	+16	+10	−30	−3	+11
−12	−15	−28	—	−20	+19	−3	+5	−28	+3
−19	+40	−4	+20	−26	+18	−5	−15	−6	+9
*+348	+83	+328	+205	+310	+369	+376	+225	+181	+37
−1	—	−20	−25	−30	−15	−18	−27	−19	−8
−2	+6	−2	+6	+36	+18	—	+21	+4	+10
−2	+10	−2	–	−11	−23	−5	−5	−2	+8
−30	−14	+52	−45	+27	−188	−31	−41	−54	−98
−203	−60	−401	−37	−334	−152	−289	−93	−228	−12
—		+2	—	−6	—	—	—	—	—
−36	−80	−29	−101	−6	−122	−13	−112	−9	−48
−16	−1	−16	—	−28	−46	−26	−8	−14	+42
−5	−1	—	—	—	—	—	—	—	—

Source: Table prepared from statement XXIV appended to the PLRA for the relevant years.

There is some controversy regarding the reliability and authenticity of the figures drawn from the Annual Reports of the Land Revenue Administration in Punjab. However, it may be noted here that Punjab, as compared to other provinces of British India, was in a somewhat better position regarding the reporting of matters relating to land and agriculture. Punjab employed *Patwaris* for all such reporting who, though inefficient, handed in more reliable figures than the *Chowkidars* employed in the southern and eastern provinces. Figures of land and agriculture handed in by the Patwaris were 'under-reported' rather than 'over-reported' and more reliable than the 'whimsical and unchecked' reporting of the Chowkidars. For details, see Clive Dewey, 'Patwaris and Chowkidars—Subordinate Officials and the Reliability of India's Agricultural Statistics', in C. Dewey and A.G. Hopkins (eds), *The Imperial Impact: Studies in the Economic History of Africa and India*, London: Athlone Press, 1978, pp. 280–314.

[43] *PBIR*, II, evidence, pp. 872–4.

maintained, with certainty, that the major beneficiaries were the richer stratum of Jats in the district as a whole, and Jats and Ahirs together in the Jhajjar tehsil who between them dominated the agricultural scene of Rohtak district and acquired, through mortgage or sale, appreciable amounts of land from the small peasant proprietors whatever their caste. M.L. Darling, the Financial Commissioner of Punjab, writing in 1936 attributed the enormous rise in the number of very small holdings and the resultant impact on the economic status of the agriculturist, to not only the population growth, war and consequent price rise, the lack of irrigation facilities in the region, but also to rampant land transactions.[44] Indeed, in Rohtak district, the starting deterioration in the economic status of the petty owner is distinctly noticeable in the swelling of the number of tenants and agricultural labourers. The census figures of 1921 and 1931, relating to different agricultural categories, make this amply clear. Although these two census are regarded as controversial in nature for being recorded in what were termed as unnatural times, the resultant general trend indicated by their figures is fully supported by the earlier census figures of 1911 and of the later ones of the Census of 1951.[45] The figures of different agricultural categories, as

[44] Inquiry conducted by M.L. Darling, Financial Commissioner of Punjab, 1936. See letter of Laithwait, Private Secretary to the Viceroy, 3 June 1936, *Darling Papers,* Box 5, F. no. I

[45] There are severe reservations regarding the authenticity of the census figures of 1921 and 1931 mainly because of the two different definitions adopted for the word 'economic activity' in determining various categories of agricultural classes. Apart from this, the demographic and economic disturbances of influenza epidemic of 1918, and the agricultural depression of 1930, made both the census years somewhat 'unnatural'. This has also been taken to result in 'vagaries in figures' of the two census operations. Therefore, a longer time span indicated by census operations in Punjab from 1911 to 1951 has been taken to interpret the long-term socio-economic trends. The trends as interpreted, leaving a margin for 'vagries in figures' of 1921 and 1931 censuses, may be taken to be authentic trends as they are also supported by other evidence belonging to the same period. For details of this controversy, see J. Krishnamurthy, 1977, 'Changing Concepts of Work in the Indian Censuses: 1901–1961', *The Indian Economic and Social History Review,* vol. XIV, no. 3, pp. 324–40.

available in Rohtak district for 1911 and 1951,[46] show a mere nominal change, less than 1 per cent, in the total number of rent receivers between 1921 and 1951, although there was an increase of 38.5 per cent between 1911 and 1921. This discrepancy merely reinforces the point that bigger landowners were gaining at the expense of smaller land-owners. A phenomenal increase can be seen in the total number of so-called ordinary cultivators, a term which included petty owners and tenants. From 99,355 in 1911, they increased by 30.76 per cent in 1921 and stood at 1,36,723. By 1931 census, an increase of 54.84 per cent had been effected, and by 1951, they had once again risen by 59.23 per cent. It may be safe to infer that big landowners substantially added to their holdings in this period. The agricultural labourers of Rohtak district too showed a 60.77 per cent increase from 1911 to 1921, 56.65 per cent increase from 1921 to 1931, and 43,03 per cent from 1931 to 1951. The rather substantial increase of 66.65 per cent among agricultural labourers during the economically tense period of 1921 and 1931 is therefore fairly well supported by both the 1911 and 1951 census reports.

The richer landowners were not the only ones in Rohtak district who benefited from these land transactions which were mostly the outcome of their moneylending activities. Ex-armymen who returned to their homes on pension, and took to moneylending, also gained significantly. Jats produced half of the total recruits provided by the district to the

[46] Figures of different agricultural categories in Rohtak district:

	1911	% of increase	1922	% of increase	1931	% of increase	1951
Rent Receivers	3,539	+38.5	4,898	+0.8	4,940	+0.9	5,389
Ordinary Cultivators (petty owners and tenants of all kinds)	99,355	+30.76	136,723	+54.84	211.718	+59.23	337,127
Agricultural Labourers	9,916	+60.77	16,610	+66.65	27,681	+43.03	39,593

Source: *Punjab Census 1911*, XIV, part II, table XV, part A, 1921, XV, part II; 1931, XVII, part. I; 1951, table VIII, part. 1-B, Lahore: Civil and Military Gazette.

army during the World War I.[47] The rest of the 50 per cent were spread among five or six other 'martial caste' of Rohtak. The British officials openly acknowledged the contribution of Hindu Jats of Rohtak district to war effort. In fact, Rohtak occupied third place among the districts of Punjab in supplying recruits to the British Indian Army. By 30 November 1918, 23.9 per cent of its total male population of military age had enlisted itself in the army.[48] This greatly added to the total income of the peasantry of the district. Sepoys and officers returned from the army not only with money accumulated over the war years but also, in most cases, with claims to monthly pensions. As early as 1909, the annual income of Rohtak district, made up of the pay and pension of government servants, most of whom had served and were serving in the army, was estimated at 16.5 lakhs.[49] Interestingly, the same amount of money was collected as land revenue in Rohtak district in 1927–8.[50] According to the estimate of the Punjab government, about half of the man-power returning from the army took to moneylending on a small or big scale.[51]

The franchise system granted by the Act of 1919 greatly favoured the classes of above mentioned people. The act granted voting right on the basis of landed property, such as payment of certain amount of land revenue or local rates and of army service. All retired and pensioned personnel of the Indian Army, commissioned or non-commissioned,

[47] Recruitment in Rohtak district during the World War I:

Recruits from:	No. of recruits	Percentage of total recruits (combatants) of the district
Jats	8,361	nearly 50
Brahmins	1,937	11.57
Ahirs	932	5.6
Rajputs (Muslim)	443	2.6
Sikhs	39	Negligible
Other Hindus	2,123	12.68

Source: India Office Records (IOR), Punjab Official Records from the Government of Pakistan (POS), 5547, see War History of the Rohtak District, Lahore, 1920, p. 25.

[48] M.S. Leigh, 1922, The Punjab and the War, Lahore, 1922, pp. 46–7.

[49] Punjab District Gazetteer, Rohtak, p. 168.

[50] Indian Statutory Commission (ISC), II, written evidence, memorandum, Punjab government.

[51] PBIR, II, p. 872.

were enfranchised. This resulted in the military personnel forming 42.96 per cent of the total rural electorate of Rohtak district as against 40 per cent in the whole of Punjab.[52] And, in view of the continued high recruitment figures in between the two World Wars, it is more than likely that this percentage persisted under the Provincial Autonomy despite a somewhat extended franchise. The demand of the representatives of this region to the Indian Statutory Commission in 1927, on behalf of the martial classes, for separate electorate for all those enjoying soldiers' franchise and for special constituencies for the officers,[53] spoke volumes of the support of the army personnel to the Hindu Unionists—majority being that of Jats in this case. This restricted franchise system, based on property qualifications and army service, was highly favourable to the rich Jats, whether landlords, rich peasants, or agriculturist moneylenders. Their dominance in political life was further assured by the creation of thirty-six 'rural seats' in the Punjab Council under the Montagu Chelmsford Reforms Act of 1919 which greatly outnumbered the ten 'urban seats'.

Offices like those of zaildars, *safedposh*, and *lambardars*, which formed the 'non-official' part of the revenue agency in a district, were manned by the chief landowning families and also, the ex-soldiers.[54] These three sets of officials were also voters in the rural constituencies. In fact, they were held responsible for the strength of the '*Jee Huzoor*' (Yes Sir) party, as the Unionist Party in this region was termed by the *Haryana Tilak*, a weekly Congress newspaper of Rohtak, which also accused the administration of favouring Jats for these jobs in the district.[55] The charge of *Haryana Tilak* that the influence of these officers was used

---

[52] Out of a total of 23,860 rural voters in Rohtak district, the military vote, after taking into account 13,608 rural voters belonging to different voting categories, excluding the enfranchised soldiers, amounted to 10,252 or 42.96 per cent of the total electorate. Source: Figures calculated from *Reforms Office*, Franchise B, March 1921, nos 34–9; and *IOR: POS*, 5546, Punjab Electoral Statistics and Maps, 1920.

[53] *ISC*, I, Punjab, see memorandum submitted by the Punjab government.

[54] *Jat Gazette (JG)*, Urdu, Rohtak, Nehru Memorial Museum and Library, New Delhi, 19 September 1923, p. 9. The term 'non-official' was freely used for these officials of the lower revenue agency. See oral evidence of Beazley, Secretary to the Government of Punjab. *ISC*, I, Punjab, 2 October 1928.

[55] *Haryana Tilak (HT)* Urdu, Rohtak, Private Collection, 25 February 1924, pp. 2–3; 30 June 1924, p. 9; 3 May 1926, p. 6; 20 December 1927, p. 9; 21 June 1928, p. 8.

to strengthen the roots of the Unionist Party seems to be correct. The election commission set aside the election of Lal Chand to the Punjab Council on account of a variety of reasons: one being the pressurizing and terrorizing tactics practised by these 'non-officials' on the voters in favour of Lal Chand.[56] Attempts made in 1926, and again in 1937–8, by the Congress members to get these posts of 'non-official' revenue agency filled by election instead of nomination was staunchly opposed by the Unionists.[57] It was clear wherein lay the loyalty and support of these so-called 'natural leaders of society'.

Similarly, the village panchayats, given legal status and some limited power by the Acts of 1912 and 1922, were also, in most castes, controlled by the Jat landowners. In its working, the members of the statutory panchayats showed themselves to be generally under 'local or tribal' influence.[58] Later on, in the reorganized panchayats also, the district panchayat officers for each tehsil of Rohtak district were all Jat by caste.[59] These Jat officers were all declared to be furthering the activities of the party in power. Malcolm Lyall Darling, in the notes on his tours, also noted that the Unionist Party had used the panchayats to get votes.[60] Interestingly, despite the great multiplication in the numbers of official panchayats, Salusbury, the Commissioner of Ambala division, had the following remark to make in 1943: 'Statutory Panchayats are numerous but shallow. The real business in Jat villages at any rate is done by zamindar panchayat, a quasi-political organization.'[61] All in all, in Rohtak district of Chhotu Ram's days, Jat landowners not only dominated the socio-economic field but were also in full control of the emerging political machinery as well.

[56] See *HT*, February–September 1924. Also, see a series of articles published in the *HT* titled, 'Naukar Shahi Ki Alief-Be-Pe', which exposed the pressure exercised by landowners of the district through the offices of zaildar, safedposh, and lambardar. See *HT*, 29 October–31 December 1923.

[57] *HT*, 18 January 1926, p. 9; 25 January 1926, p. 5; All India Congress Committee Papers, 1937–9, p. 10, pp. 102–3.

[58] *Confidential Files of the Deputy Commissioner (CFDC), Rohtak*, 2, part 1, see 'Handing Over Notes' (HO Notes), Malik Zaman Mehdi Khan, 4 November 1931.

[59] Ibid., 'HO Notes', Sultan Lal Hussain, the Deputy Commissioner of Rohtak, 11 January 1944.

[60] *Darling Papers*, (Cambridge), Box No. 5/1, Diary (n.d.).

[61] *Confidential Files from the Office of the Commissioner of Ambala Division (CF Comm. Ambala Div.)*, A/28, 'HO Notes', C.V. Salusbury, 31 October 1943.

In the triennial elections to the Punjab Legislative Council held in 1921, 1924, 1927, and 1931, and the first elections to the Punjab Legislative Assembly in 1937, only Jat landowners were returned from the general rural constituencies of Rohtak district.[62] The explanation is not far to seek. Out of a total population of 772,272 of Rohtak district in 1921, persons with voting right under the 1919 Reforms Act numbered only 23,860.[63] Under the Government of India Act of 1935, with a more 'liberalized' franchise, the total number of voters in the district increased to 127,290 out of a population of 805,621. Clearly, despite the 'liberalized franchise', the number of those enfranchised in Rohtak continued to remain severely limited. It is difficult to know the percentage of Jats among the enfranchised people. That it must have been high is evident not only from the landholding structure available in Rohtak district and the fact that the Jats formed the majority of the retired and serving army personnel and nearly monopolized the 'non-official revenue' agency, and the like, but also from the fact that only Jat candidates were successful from the constituencies of this district. This voting behaviour of the Jat electorate stands confirmed by the observation of Darling on twelve years working of the Reforms Act of 1919 that the votes were cast on personal and caste grounds without reference to political questions.[64] Open and frank appeals for votes were made on the slogan of caste.[65] Among Jats, the emphasis was further laid on their Gots, as recruitment of certain important men belonging to the predominant Got of a village was claimed to result in a complete and successful control of other Jats.[66] And, in fact, for election purposes such men were recruited.[67] The influence and hold of such men operated through the Got panchayats as also through the traditional village panchayats; both were extensively

[62] For details of the successful candidates from 1921 to 1937, see *PLCD*, I, 8 January 1921, p. 1; VII, 2 January 1924, p. 1; X, 3 January 1927, p. 1; XVIII, 25 January 1931, p. 1. Also, *Punjab Legislative Assembly Debates (PLAD)*, I, 5 April 1957, p. 1.

[63] *ISC*, II, Punjab, written evidence, E. 349.

[64] M.L. Darling, 1934, *Wisdom and Waste in a Punjab Village*, London: Oxford University Press, p. 334.

[65] *JG*, 25 April 1923, p. 15; 28 August 1923, p. 14; 19 September 1923, p. 3; 13 May 1925, p. 8; 7 July 1925, p. 7; 15 July 1925, p. 8.

[66] *CFSO Rohtak*, H-18, Chhotu Ram to the Deputy Commissioner, Rohtak, (n.d.), p. 171.

[67] Author's interviews with Hardwari Lal, 9 June 1979.

used for election purposes during the 1920s and 1930s in Punjab.[68] The newly emergent electoral politics came to be effectively controlled by these traditional tools and agencies.

The Hindu Unionists of south-east Punjab were accused, especially by their Congress opponents, of fighting the elections on the basis of Jat and non-Jat.[69] However, the Congress in this region also recognized the importance of the caste factor. This is evident from their choice of candidates from that caste which was 'dominant' in a particular constituency. For example, the choice of Garib Singh, a Jat, as a candidate to contest against Chhotu Ram in 1937 was a recognition of the reality of caste factor in Rohtak district. And although this Jat candidate withdrew and a Brahmin, Mange Ram Vats, of village Mandothi of Rohtak district, who belonged to the Punjab Socialist Party, had to be accepted as the Congress candidate at a very late stage, the pro-Congress *Haryana Tilak* revealed its caste consciousness in the comment it made on the resultant defeat of its candidate. It wrote: 'Chhotu Ram has won due to the overwhelming Jat votes in this constituency. After all we must remember that there are hardly any people in this constituency who belong to the *Biradari* (caste/brotherhood) of comrade Mange Ram.'[70] The Congress leadership of Rohtak repeatedly commented that in south east Punjab, voting was purely on caste basis and while so commenting, it also disclosed its own weakness and the fact that it suffered from the very same defect as the other party in Rohtak. The Congress, despite being the oldest organization and political body, could not offer to the voters of Rohtak district any election programme even during the first elections held under the Provincial Autonomy.[71] It, therefore, projected local caste issues just like others.

Another feature which helped the representatives of rich Jats of Rohtak in occupying the political echelons of the district and the province was the role which money played during elections. In Darling's estimate, a seat in the legislative council, in the 1930s, would often cost Rs 10,000 or even Rs 20,000.[72] Therefore, he observed, the candidate

---

[68] Author's interviews with P.S. Daulta, 17 May 1981; and K.L. Rathi, 19 May 1981.

[69] *HT*, 16 February 1925, pp. 5–6. Also, see *Civil and Military Gazette*, 2 July 1936, p. 2.

[70] *HT*, 9 March 1937, p. 4.

[71] *Proceedings of the Home-Political Department, Fortnightly. Report from Punjab,* 18/11/36, November 1936.

[72] Darling, *Wisdom and Waste in a Punjab Village*, p. 334.

must be rich. Even the *Jat Gazette*, a self-confessed 'mouthpiece of the Jats' and the Unionist Party, remarked that it was common knowledge that heavy amounts were spent on elections. It also mentioned in 1937 a newspaper report where three candidates were said to have spent Rs 5 lakhs and one candidate out of these was credited with an expenditure of Rs 2 lakhs.[73] The restricted franchise, before and after the 1935 Act, and the high cost of fighting elections were major factors in making the rich Jats of Rohtak also politically dominant. This was recognized by the 'Jat leaders'. At the time of the first and second elections to the Punjab Council in 1921 and 1924, it was emphasized by Chhotu Ram that the leadership of 'Jat community' should be reserved for the rich among Jats, with enough income from land, who were intelligent, educated, who knew the English language well, and who had sufficient experience in the running of caste and religious *sabhas*.[74] Emphasis on certain Gots among the Jats, and recruitment of important men from these Gots, also indicates that these 'social superiors' were in a position and, in fact, able to control the rest of their Got men. This phenomenon was also recognized by the British officials who had recorded, as early as in 1901, that certain Jat clans and families could claim the status of 'social superiors' to the rest of the Jats depending on the amount of land they held.[75] In fact, in November 1923, the compilation of a 'Jat directory' for election purposes was proposed which was to include the names and addresses of the important *jagirdar*s (landlords), zamindars (landowners), professionals, and businessmen among Jats, who could be asked to lead the election campaign and render help by making direct financial contributions.[76] The Hindu Unionist leaders of this region, always referred to as the 'Jat leaders', did not attempt to camouflage in the early stage of their career, the attempts of the richer stratum of Jats, with socio-economic power behind them, to gain access to political influence as well.

So far as the caste basis and heavy expenditure in the elections was concerned, the position remained the same even after the 1935 Act. In 1936, the Governor of Punjab observed in a letter to Linlithgow, the Viceroy of India, that the elections under the Provincial Autonomy

---

[73] *JG*, 3 March 1937, p. 1.

[74] Editorial in *JG*, 1 June, 1923. Also see JG 14 November 1923, p. 15; 5 December 1923, p. 3.

[75] Punjab *Census*, 1901, XVII, pp. 324–5.

[76] *JG*, 28 November 1923, p. 14.

would be fought along 'personal and tribal lines rather than on party creed'.[77] The results of 1927 elections confirmed this observation as the electorate of south east Punjab showed preference for their 'own tribal leaders' against the Congressmen. The continued 'heavy expenditure' during the elections was also mentioned by the governor of Punjab.[78] However, it may be underlined that 'Jat domination' in politics could function only under a limited franchise which alone ensured the continuing benefits to the upper strata of Jat peasantry. That is the reason why even a slight liberalization in its property qualification could prompt a strongly entrenched 'Jat leader' like Chhotu Ram to seriously entertain a plan of changing his constituency and contest the 1937 elections from the landholders seat of east Punjab.[79] Significantly, in 1927, this 'Jat leader' did not recommend the extension of franchise to agricultural labourers in the rural constituencies, although he recommended it for urban labourers.[80]

The given account makes it clear that in Rohtak district, the rich stratum of Jat-cum-moneylenders, who constituted an overwhelming majority among the landowners and controlled the socio-economic fabric of the agrarian society, could under a limited franchise, high cost of fighting elections, and dominance of caste factor, be knit together to form a powerful political unit. The slogan of 'Jatism', as raised in this region and exploited for the benefit of the economically dominant classes among the Jats could and did prove successful in this given situation. What was needed was political mobilization of Jats and their identification as a composite class with common interests. This was effected by the British officials with the very able help of 'Jat leaders' of this region.

---

[77] *Linlithgow Collection*, F.125/112: H.W. Emerson to Linlithgow, 16 October 1936.

[78] Ibid., p. 87, H.D. Craik to Linlithgow, 27 January 1939.

[79] *CFDC, Rohtak*, 10/38, the Deputy Commissioner, Rohtak, to P. Marsden, Commissioner, Ambala division, 8 February 1936. Also, *HT*, 6 October 1936, pp. 3–4.

[80] *ISC*, III, Report of the Provincial Committee, pp. 400–3.

3

Contours of Communalism

*Religion, Caste, and Identity in South-east Punjab**

The Hindu-dominated districts of colonial south-east Punjab—Ambala, Gurgaon, Hissar, Karnal, and Rohtak—became notorious for 'tense' and 'strained' relations between Hindus and Muslims during the 1930s of the twentieth century. These frequently escalated into what came to be universally projected, and commonly accepted, as communal riots in official parlance. In their essence, the roots of such confrontations were closely linked to and determined by the socio-economic life of this region. On the one hand, they related to land rights and land relations and, on the other, to the dominance of factors such as caste and growing casteism in this region which was intimately linked to the sharpening sectarian/religious identities. The demands of rising social groups to appropriate crucial indices of status formation in their drive towards upward mobility and enforce recognition on other social groups escalated situations of direct confrontation. These attempts posed a challenge to the traditional structure of authority and the dominance of certain castes and classes in rural society. Yet, the symbols used for the articulation of these demands and the mobilization of wider support for their recognition were religious. They ranged from the construction of places of worship and the celebration of

* This chapter was originally published in 1996, *Social Scientist*, 24 (4–6): 130–63.

religious festivals and taking out religious processions to the widespread
and sporadic cow protection movement.

This chapter investigates the social identity and interests of different
groups and seeks to understand how locally contentious issues between
and within different castes and classes took on wider religious contours
and identity. In the existing context, this identity may have been a
religious or a sectarian identity, though not necessarily a communal
identity—something which was sought to be portrayed.[1] In other words,
the attempt here is to understand the emerging centrality of religion as
a symbol in questions relating directly to wider caste, class, and status
concerns which, under colonial intervention, had been provided with
fresh opportunities.

THE SOCIO-ECONOMIC FOUNDATIONS OF
THE COMMUNAL RIOTS: CASE STUDIES

In order to understand the dynamics of Hindu–Muslim strife in this
region, certain case studies of the most publicized 'communal riots'
have been taken up. The three most notorious riots occurred in a single
district of Ambala division, that is, Rohtak, in the villages of Kanaudha,
Jakholi, and Kharkhoda.

Kanaudha Riot

The Kanaudha riot of 1933 created a great stir in Rohtak.[2] The *Inquilab*
of Lahore, dated 3 October 1933, gave a highly coloured version of the
affair under the caption, 'Grievances of the Musalmans of Kanaudha,
Rohtak District'. The news item accused the Hindu Jats of forcibly
attacking and stopping the Muslims from constructing a mosque on
a piece of land which was reported to have been in the possession of

---

[1] Taking the lead from Gyanendra Pandey, I have used the word sectarian,
even religious, instead of communal for Hindu–Muslim strife. I also agree with
his interpretation that communalism was not the only or logical outcome of
sectarian/religious identities and clashes between Hindus and Muslims. For a
succinct comment on the shortcomings in the analysis of communal situations
and for fresh insights and understanding of this highly contentious problem,
see his, 1983, 'Rallying Round the Cow: Sectarian Strife in the Bhojpuri Region,
C. 1888–1917', in Ranajit Guha (ed.), *Subaltern Studies II: Writings on South Asian
History and Society*, New Delhi: Oxford University Press, pp. 60–129.

[2] *Confidential Files from the Superintendent's Office (CFSO), Rohtak*, 26/51. All
references to this case, unless indicated to the contrary, have been taken from
this source.

Muslims for generations. In the resultant clash between the two, the old mosque was declared to have been demolished by the Jats. The Jats were also accused of carrying away its old woodwork and the newly ordered bricks meant for rebuilding it. The government officials were reported to have arrested and *challaned* (summoned to court) many Muslims. A number of Muslims sent written complaints to the deputy commissioner and even to the viceroy. Outside help was also sought. A petition for help was sent to the Jumma Masjid managing committee of Delhi. The committee, in return, widely exaggerated the incident and inflamed the religious feelings of Muslims everywhere. The danger of outsiders aggravating and exploiting the situation was genuine as Kanaudha was situated on the border of the Delhi and Rohtak districts. Consequently, several arrests were made under the security section of the criminal procedure code.

The two Urdu weeklies published from this district, the *Jat Gazette* and *Haryana Tilak*, commented more or less in the same way, high-lighting the religious identities of the parties involved.[3] Both also noted that the initial cause of quarrel was the desire of Muslims to build a mosque on the village *shamilat* (common) land. Interestingly enough, the deputy commissioner's confidential report and the confidential fort-nightly report of the Punjab government on 'communal matters' also noted, briefly, the attempt of Muslims to build a mosque on the village common land and resistance of the Hindu Jats to it, as the basic cause of the riot in village Kanaudha.[4]

The undivided village common land indeed provided the requisite material for the very frequent quarrels in villages. This was testified to by all the deputy commissioners of this division. The village common land was never one consolidated chunk of land but included several chunks of land, reserved for certain common uses comprising of *chaupal* or *hujra*, shamilat *deh*, *gora* deh, and the *abadi* deh.[5] However, the word

---

[3] *Jat Gazette* (*JG*), Urdu, 1933, Rohtak, New Delhi: Nehru Memorial Museum and Library, 18 October, p. 6; *Haryana Tilak* (*HT*), Urdu, 1933, Rohtak, Private Collection, 6 November, p. 5.

[4] *Confidential Files from the Deputy Commissioner's Office* (*CFDC*), Rohtak, 1934, 2, part 1,'Handing Over Notes' (HO Notes), E.H. Lincoln, Deputy Commissioner (DC), Rohtak, 16 March; and, Government of India, 1933, Proceedings of the Home Political Department (GI: Home Poll), Fortnightly Reports from Punjab (FRRP), 18/10/33, October.

[5] Chaupal or hujra was used as a place where social and cultural functions were held and where other meetings by villagers were arranged; shamilat deh,

'shamilat deh' was used very frequently to include all the area reserved for common purposes. The diminishing reserves of shamilat, the growing demands of the local populace, and the neglect of the proprietors failed to get anything like a just share of it.[6] Quarrels over it occurred mostly between different claimants among the proprietors, as shares in the shamilat land were calculated in proportion to the land revenue they paid; and between the proprietors and non-proprietors, the latter having no share or claim in the shamilat land.[7] It follows, therefore, that those with the strongest objection to encroachments and taking the lead in the matter would necessarily be those with the largest share in shamilat land.

In such cases, the will of the majority of proprietors was effective, specially as they used the power of the village panchayat. Yet, it could be and was challenged by minority through an appeal to the revenue authorities and through civil courts. The claims and contestation came on different grounds. The most effective, both legally and socially, was religion, as it not merely mobilized greater support, it also had a greater chance of success. For instance, although the building of anything could be construed as something which caused 'material and substantial injury to other proprietors', this was not sustainable if the construction was a religious one.[8]

Consequently, recourse to land for the construction of buildings on religious grounds was frequent and expected. In the case of Kanaudha riots, for example, an on-the-spot inquiry held by the deputy commissioner and the superintendent of police disclosed that for the

---

which included the *banjar* (barren) land of the village, was used for grazing of cattle and fetching of wood and grass; gora deh was reserved for further extension of village dwellings; and the abadi deh was the inhabited site of the village which included all the land meant for *dharam-shalas* (rest-rooms), mosques, temples, and gurudwaras; for ghats and graveyards; for tanks, wells, and ponds, and the like, see Paras Diwan, 1978, Customary Law of Punjab and Haryana, Chandigarh: Publication Bureau, Punjab University, pp. 69–70.

[6] *CFDC*, Gurgaon, 10, S/694, p. 7. Also, see S. Wilberforce, 1908, *Agricultural Cooperation in the Punjab*, Lahore: Civil and Military Gazette, p. 7.

[7] 1938, *Report of the Land Revenue Committee, 1938*, Lahore: Civil and Military Gazette, p. 178.

[8] W.M. Rattigan, 1960, *A Digest of the Civil Law for the Punjab Chiefly Based on the Customary Law as at Present Ascertained*, revised by Harbans Lal Sarin and Kundan Lal Pandit (2nd edition), 1880, reprint, Allahabad: University Book Agency, pp. 699–700.

purpose of building a mosque, the Muslims of village Kanaudha had 'usurped' more land in the village shamilat than their share. Their total share in the shamilat land was to correspond to the total agricultural land owned by them. This came to a paltry 20 acres. The Hindu Jat landowners, on the other hand, owned 2,570 acres of land. They had demanded the partitioning of the common land according to the existing rights of ownership before the building work could be undertaken by the Muslims.

The other charges of the Muslim were also pronounced by the inquiry as being highly exaggerated. The quarrel over 5,000 bricks, bought by the Muslims for the mosque, occurred in reality among the Muslims themselves. The quarrel was on the division of bricks which were the joint property of all Muslims who had contributed towards their purchase. A panchayat of Jats which had put a stop to the building of the mosque had also made a suggestion for the division of bricks. This was not accepted by the Muslims. This defiance was clearly born out of their resentment against the interference of the Jat panchayat. Subsequently, the bricks were carried away by the Muslims themselves and the quarrel had begun. Regarding the allegation that the Jats had carried away the woodwork of the century old Badshahi mosque, it was discovered during the inquiry that this particular incident happened long before the present trouble and at a time when the mosque had actually crumbled. The doors and the framework of the crumbled mosque were not carried away by any Jat but by the village *kamins* (menials, both Hindu and Muslim), for being used as fuel.

In any case, passions ran high and several casualties on both sides were reported. Shafru, a low caste Muslim, and his two brothers, Abdullah and Mangla Faquir, filed a case against the Hindu Jats alleging that they had demolished the mosque. Shafru Ranjout was a known *goonda* whose name featured in the surveillance register of the police among *das numbari badmash* (bad character) in the local *thana* (police station). He had collected a large amount of money from the Muslims of the village with the ostensible purpose of rebuilding the mosque. Hard pressed by his fellow Muslims to account for the collected money, he, in the opinion of the officials, took to instigating them against Jats who were resisting the construction of the mosque. The criminal case had no basis and was consequently dismissed.

The other case registered by the police under section 107, CrPC., *King Emperor vs Sri Ram* and *King Emperor vs Shafru*, and such others, sheds light on the fundamental issues involved in what was publicly propagated as the 'worst communal tangle' of Ambala division. The judgement of the court read:

Evidence shows that this plot of land is in the *abadi-deh* and the *abadi-deh* has not been partitioned among the proprietors of the village and nobody may misappropriate a piece of *abadi-deh* to his exclusive possession without a formal partition, and construction of a mosque is certainly to take exclusive possession of land, a possession which can seldom be restored on sentimental grounds. For the Muslims to attempt to build a mosque without the consent of the proprietors of the village was in fact an overt act in a case of this sort. So Jats' objection is within their rights and danger to peace exits. Muslims clearly are the aggressors. The mere building of a mosque is not an objectionable act in itself but is so when being attempted in the face of position held by the muslims in the village and the fact that land is undivided *shamilat*. It is therefore an overt act and must not be attempted.

Jakholi Riot

The other communal riot which also drew a lot of public debate and attention occurred in village Jakholi in 1936–7.[9] The uproar was the same as in village Kanaudha and was, in fact, typical of many such disputes in this division. Some Muslims of the village registered a complaint that Hindus of the village were causing obstruction to the observance of their religion by not allowing them to construct a mosque.

A number of representations were made to the Deputy Commissioner of Rohtak, to the governor, and even to the Premier of Punjab. These representations listed a formidable number of eleven complaints against the Hindu Rajputs, ranging from socio-economic boycott, to the destruction of their crops, molestation of their women, and the horrors of finding pig flesh on their wells. Urgent and frantic overtures to the Muslims of the neighbouring areas were also made. Some Muslims of Delhi responded by establishing a '*khilafat* committee' to campaign against 'the grievances of fellow Muslims'. The committee published a large number of posters dated 12 July 1937, which described in detail the 'untold miseries' suffered by the 'Muslims of Jakholi' and invited the 'Muslims of Delhi' to make a 'common cause' with them to fight the 'Hindu tyranny'. These were widely distributed and also, pasted on the walls of Delhi and Jakholi.

By July 1937, the situation had taken a serious turn. Yet, interestingly enough, the officialdom, five months prior to the eruption of this case,

[9] *CFSO, Rohtak*, pp. 1–22. All references to this case, unless indicated to the contrary, have been taken from this case.

was aware of the brewing socio-economic trouble between the land-lords of Jakholi and their occupancy tenants. An on-the-spot inquiry in February–March 1937 had revealed 'strained relationship' existing between the two. It disclosed that the Rajput landlords were trying to evict their occupancy tenants not only from tenancy but also from their hitherto occupied houses. This was clearly to counteract the severe ero-sion in their landowning status. However, the occupancy tenants were all Muslim by faith and the landlords were Hindus. A communal colour came to be naturally imparted to their relationship.

This quarrel coincided with the fierce disagreement of the land-lords with the buyers of their fruit crop, who were also Muslims, on the question of an increased price settlement. The reluctant buyers were successfully exchanged for those willing to pay enhanced rates. This remedy was apparently not found feasible against the occupancy tenants. Against them, the landlords adopted the familiar weapon of socio-economic boycott. On this, the sub-divisional officer of Rohtak commented: '… in strained relationship economic and social boycott is bound to result.' And since Jakholi was a 'Hindu Rajput village' where they not only constituted a majority in the population but were also in possession of 2,940 acres out of a total of 2,946 acres of cultivated land, they were able to impose collective pressure even on others to participate in this boycott.

The deprived Muslims, whether occupancy tenants or fruit buyers, were unable to retaliate on socio-economic grounds. Totally, this religious minority constituted an insignificant 3 per cent in the village, estimated to be merely seventy-five in number. Numerically so few and economically feeble, the position of the affected Muslims was even legally vulnerable as no legal action could be taken against the offending landlords. This was disclosed by the sub-divisional officer in the report of his investigations dated 19 October 1937, in which he observed that: 'The proprietors had been acting technically within their rights.'

With all doors closed to them, the Muslims took recourse to the only readily available and oft-tried alternative of arousing religious sentiments to gather the support of at least their co-religionists in the rest of the region to their cause. This they attempted by fulminating against the playing of music in the vicinity of what was claimed to be a *kachcha* mosque in the village, on the occasion of the wedding ceremony of the zaildar's daughter. Zaildar Bhopal Singh, a leading landlord, and his relatives reacted belligerently to this new assertiveness. The instigators among the Muslims also went on to convert a kachcha house in the village abadi into a mosque. The landowners, who saw it as an affront to their authority, resisted it. This attempt resulted in a riot in which thirteen Hindus and fourteen Muslims were arrested under 107 CrPC. With certain Delhi Muslims already having joined hands on the issue, the whole affair took a more serious turn. The involved parties resorted to court, and a civil case, *Karim-ud-din vs Bhopal Singh*, followed.

The judgement of the civil court delivered in October 1937, significantly pronounced religion as a non-issue in this quarrel. Instead religion was seen as being exploited in order to challenge the rights of the proprietors; rights which were otherwise not questioned. The judge ruled that the Muslim non-proprietors had attempted to convert the house into a mosque. This would have meant the practical ownership of land under the cloak of religion. He clearly laid down that the non-proprietors could not alienate the houses they lived in without the permission of the proprietors who had full proprietary rights in the village shamilat as well as in the village abadi. The judge maintained that 'in the village the proprietor right in the *abadi* was as a rule vested in the proprietory body.' He also noted that the quarrel was obviously not on building of a mosque but 'on converting that particular spot into an independent holding', as the landowners had offered the Muslims a choice of any one out of the four plots on the periphery of the village which was declined by them. Significantly, the periphery of a village was almost invariably inhabited by low castes and was, thus, considered degraded. The low caste Muslims were clearly being shown their 'place' in the caste hierarchy by the Hindu Rajput landowners.

KHARKHODA RIOT
The third riot, involving Hindu Jats and Muslim Rajputs, blown to grotesque proportions, occurred in 1937–8 in village Kharkhoda.[10] A dramatically worded telegram sent by some Muslims of the village to the Commissioner of Ambala division read 'Kharkhoda situation serious stop Jats attacking Muslims stop immediate intervention essential stop please take necessary action immediately stop'.

A deputation of Muslims also waited on the Deputy Commissioner of Rohtak. Rumours that Jats would hold a big panchayat to stop cow slaughter were spread. The question of playing music before the mosque was also raised. The Muslims declared themselves in 'grave

---

[10] *CFSO, Rohtak*, 1–14, pp. 33. All references to this case, unless indicated to the contrary, have been taken from this source.

danger' from the Hindu Jats. Apprehending further breach of peace, the district authorities posted a police guard at Kharkhoda to meet the much feared outbreak of a 'serious communal riot'. There was no real trouble; and subsequently, authorities owned that their fears had been greatly exaggerated and the local leaders of Muslims had grossly misrepresented things in order to 'effect their self importance'.

The *Haryana Tilak* blamed the entire trouble on 'Muslim Goondas' and their attack on the 'Hindu *kisans*' (tenants).[11] It referred to the 'grievance of Hindus' as regards *gaukashi* (cow slaughter) and also appealed to Hindu panchayat to help stop this practice. According to the weekly, in the fracas that ensued, 235 Hindus and twenty-five Muslims were challaned. The confidential report of the superintendent of police to the deputy commissioner dated 22 February 1938 maintained, 'My information is that there is a party feeling amongst Muslim zamindars of Khakhoda and as their tenants are mostly Hindu Jats of the surrounding villages the mischief is being instigated by some of the Muslims themselves in order to harass their rival Muslims by instigating Hindu tenants against them.'

The Muslim Rajput landowners, like their counterpart among the Hindu Rajputs, were experiencing severe assault on their landowning status due to the rapid alienation and sale of their lands to the Jats of this region (given later). Their differences with their tenants, who were also Jats by caste, could prove serious. The possibility of a riot existed. Yet, for a while, things were patched up. The district officials brought about a compromise between the two sides through the intervention of certain important representatives of Jats and Muslims of the *ilaqua* (region). The much feared trouble at the Moharram celebrations never occurred. The Jat panchayat held after Moharram was also attended by Syed Ayub Ali, one of the Muslim landlords of Kharkhoda. The panchayat made no reference to any religious controversy in the village.

Trouble occurred again in March 1938, when the upwardly mobile Jat tenants joined in the celebrations of the birth of a son to Syed Ayub Ali. Some Muslims resented this greatly. Their attempts at instigation succeeded and resulted in what came to be official described as 'communal riot'. The secret report of the superintendent of police of the district dated 20 March 1938 revealed, 'As they (the other party of the Muslims) could not possibly offer any reasonable protest on any ground

[11] *HT*, 1938, 15 March, p. 4. Also, see 1938, 31 May, p. 4; 7 June, p. 4; 21 June, p. 1.

so they twisted the matter a bit and attempted to convert it into a question of playing music before mosque, on the 18th March 1938.'

The Hindu Jat tenants of Kharkhoda, on their side, were having trouble with the vegetable vendors and *pheri-walas* (hawkers) who were Muslim; they successfully boycotted the latter and brought down their charges. Despite several attempts, the Muslim landlords refused to join hands and make a common cause with their co-religionists, that is, the low caste Muslim vendors and hawkers, against the Hindu Jat tenants.

Some Major and Minor Riots

Several such major and minor outbreaks, termed in the official parlance as well as that of the local media as 'communal disputes' or communal riots, were reported from different villages of Rohtak district. The *Haryana Tilak* mentioned villages of Garhi Brahamanan, Bahadurgarh, Rudhiwas, Gathwal, Gohana, and Sanghi as places where such confrontations occurred most frequently between 'Jats and Muslims'. In May 1935, the Gaud-Brahmin landowners of village Garhi Brahmanan protested against the extension of *Id-gah* (a place of assembly and prayer during Muslim festivals) on the shamilat land.[12] The resulting quarrel was settled by the Sub-divisional Officer of Sonepat, though it was subsequently revived, in the opinion of the district officials, by a Congress leader of Rohtak for political reasons. The Gaud-Brahmin proprietors regained their control over the contested land but only through a court decree.

Similarly, another confrontation occurred in May 1936 in Rohtak for 'ownership of land' where a masjid, it was claimed, had been constructed 'overnight'.[13] The court case which followed dragged on for a year. It was ultimately decided by the district magistrate in favour of the contesting Jats; they were put in possession of the disputed land and rival Muslim party was made to pay Rs 65 towards expenses. In June 1936, another conflict was reported to have taken place in Bahadurgarh where 2,000–3,000 Jats (Hindu) assembled to occupy a site on the shamilat land and clashed with the Muslim claimants.[14] The revenue records

[12] *CFDC, Rohtak*, 1935, 2, part 2, see note by L.P. Addison, Sub-divisional Officer, Rohtak, 25 May. Also see *HT*, 1936, 1 September, p. 7.

[13] *HT*, 1936, 12 May, p. 4.

[14] *HT*, 1936, 30 June, p. 4. *HT* maintained that the land belonged to the Hindu Jats, and the Muslim Pathans had mischievously tampered with the revenue records to show that the disputed land belonged to them.

showed the land to be in possession of Pathans. This confrontation led to several arrests and the matter had to be taken to court.

In September of the same year, the *Haryana Tilak* reported a 'long standing communal dispute between the Muslims and Jats' of village Rudhiawas for possession of a kachcha well on the shamilat land.[15] A similar confrontation between Jats and Pathans was also seriously apprehended in village Gathwal. Here, Jats and Pathans even had a mixed *Pana*, showing perfectly amicable relations between the two.[16] The Hindu Jats objected to the building of a mosque on the shamilat land and went to the extent of stopping the Muslim *kumhars* from supplying bricks for the purpose. A compromise was, however, reached and the apprehended riot was averted. In May 1937, the *Haryana Tilak* reported a 'communal riot' in village Gohana.[17] Once again, a disputed piece of land and attempts to construct a mosque over it provided the combustible material. The matter went up to the district magistrate who decided it in favour of the contesting Hindu Jats.

In June 1937, a similar case, initiated by some Jats, took place over a plot of land situated between the villages of Dighal and Gochchi.[18] In September 1937, the *Haryana Tilak*, once again, gave a great deal of publicity to 200 Jats who had demolished a partially built mosque in village Sanghi.[19] Some Sheikhs had undertaken to build this mosque on a piece of land which the Jat proprietors had refused to give to them. The Sheikhs claimed that they had always held their *namaz* (prayer) at that spot. In the ensuing clash, where firearms were also used, one Hindu was killed and four Hindus and Muslims were injured.

The riot situations were not exclusive to the Rohtak district of this division. In all the districts of Ambala divison, similar cases took place. Karnal district, for example, shows a number of cases from 1926 to 1944. One incident occurred on 27 July 1926, in village Keorah,[20] where a party of 50–60 Hindus beat up ten Muslims who had been offering prayers at

---

[15] *HT*, 1936, 1 September, p. 7.

[16] Ibid. Pana is a compact territorial component of a village named after a common ancestor who had been accepted as an important and influential leader in the past.

[17] *HT*, 1937, 12 May, p. 8.

[18] *GI*: Home Poll, FRRP, 1937, 18/6/37, June.

[19] *GI*: Home Poll, FRRP, 1937, 18/9/37, September; *HT*, 1938, 26 April, p. 4.

[20] *GI*: Home Poll, FRRP, 1926, 112/V/1926, July.

a building which they claimed to be a mosque. In reality, the official report pointed out, the building in question adjoined a shrine where both Hindus and Muslims offered their prayers. In view of the Muslim claims, the Hindus, afraid that the Muslims contemplated converting it to their exclusive use, resisted belligerently.

Two more incidents occurred in the same year at two different places in Panipat itself.[21] The Hindus of Panipat obtained a decree against their Muslim contenders in respect of a property claimed by them to be a mosque. The matter was referred to the High Court. The Hindus appealed for the execution of this decree but the Muslim contenders sent a counter-request demanding that the notice be served on the 'entire Muslim community' on the ground that the mosque was a *waqf*[22] property. It was a clear attempt at involving wider community support in order to strengthen their claims. The matter having become more complicated, stay orders were issued.

In another place, in Panipat, five Muslims and seven Hindus were prosecuted; the cause being the attempt of the Muslim decree holder to execute a civil decree on a Hindu occupant of a shop claimed by them to belong to their religious shrine nearby.[23] Similarly, in village Uplana in Karnal district, in 1937, the Muslim contenders succeeded in getting a building legally recognized as a mosque and set about repairing it.[24] The Hindus who had appealed to the High Court against this decision objected and forcibly stopped all work.

In 1944, the Karnal district witnessed an interesting case in village Pundri.[25] Confrontation occurred when some Muslims opened a window in the back wall of the Masjid Qazia overlooking the house of a Brahmin widow called Mat Chalti. This was seen as the initial step to acquire at least a portion of the compound of the widow's house for the benefit of the mosque. The Hindu owner and her associates succeeded in amassing a lot of support on religious ground to oppose this move. An intense agitation followed and Chowdhri Aurangzeb Khan, the

---

[21] Ibid.

[22] Charitable Islamic trust.

[23] GI: Home Poll, FRRP, 1926, 112/V/26, September.

[24] GI: Home Poll, FRRP, 1937, 18/9/37, September.

[25] *Confidential Files from the Commissioner's Office* (CF comm.), Ambala, 1944, 4–III, 'HO Notes', Commissioner Ambala division; and 1946, 'HO Notes', DC Karnal, 18 April.

Sub-divisional Officer, had to have the window bricked up. This, however, did not satisfy the agitating Hindus as the wooden frame of the window had not been removed from the wall and they were apprehensive that the existence of a wooden frame in the wall may be used, in future, as a proof of the existence of a window. The two parties continued to agitate and make repeated representations to the district authorities and even clashed from time to time over this issue.

The detailed study of the above cited cases links up the rising religious/sectarian situations directly to the socio-economy of this region; land issues emerge basic to the growing claims of different castes and classes. Yet, this understanding fails to answer the widespread use of religious symbols, both Hindu and Muslim; the crucial centrality of mosque and the attempts at building of mosque as a symbol of Islam and Muslimhood. The resultant sharpening of religious/sectarian identities in south-east Punjab, specially during the 1930s and the 1940s, clearly needs a wider explanation.

CASTE AND RELIGION: A WIDER EXPLANATION

An explanation for the sharpening of religious/sectarian identities is to be found in the existing caste structure of northern India. In the cases discussed earlier, caste, as the following account will show, emerges as the most significant peculiarity of this region.[26] In Punjab, caste was the only relevant category for administrative and political purposes. In the Punjab Alienation of Land Act, 1900, which was fundamental to all their policies in Punjab, the colonial masters had rejected the principle of religious distinction regarding the grouping of various castes.[27] The projected rationale behind the acceptance of caste distinction, in the words of Deputy Commissioner of Rohtak in 1900, was:

The Hindu Jat and Mula Jat, the Hindu Goojar and Mohammadan Goojar think more of the common ancestor from whom they have ascended than the fact

---

[26] This central fact, for instance, explains how and why the Hindus involved in the cases cited earlier were mostly Jat by caste. The Jats by virtue of being the largest owners of land in this division came to be involved in most quarrels regarding their right in the shamilat land. So much so that 'communal matters' in this region were frequently referred to not merely as 'Hindu–Muslim affairs' but as 'Jat–Muslim' ones as well. The latter characterization almost reduced the Muslims to yet another social group of caste type seen in contrast to other village castes and not necessarily to the Hindus.

[27] For the major landowning castes created as 'statutory agricultural castes' in this region were see Chapter 2 in this volume, p. 45n27.

that he is a Hindu or the other a Mohammadan and live in the same village with as much peace and good feeling towards one another as if they were members of the same race and religion, instead of being members of the same race but of a different religion. The officers and zamindars with whom I have cultivated freely are also of the same opinion, that any religious distinction would be most unpopular and also unwise. It is with no feeling of uncertainty that I advance this view as it represents the feelings of the district itself.[28]

Such opinions came to be reflected in the voluminous literature which was built upon the operation of caste in Punjab. Denzil Ibbetson, in his famous work, *Punjab Castes*, published in 1916, which incorporates the viewpoint of various district officials of Punjab, similarly maintained:

Conversions in Punjab have had absolutely no effect upon the caste by the convert. The Musalman, Rajput, Gujar or Jat is for all social, tribal, political and administrative purposes exactly as much a Rajput, Gujar or Jat as his Hindu brother. His social customs are unaltered, his tribal restrictions are unrelaxed, his rule of marriage and inheritance unchanged; and almost the only difference is that he shaves his scalplock and the upper edge of his moustache, he repeats the Mohammadan creed in a mosque, and adds the musalman to the Hindu wedding ceremony.[29]

Yet, the caste equations in Punjab were not so simple. They were highly problematic and the conversions had added a more complex dimension to them. For example, the accepted social superiority of the Brahmin did not exist in Punjab.[30] In fact, the census authorities of 1901 had confessed that Punjab defied a systematic classification of castes.[31] In this province, Jat and Rajput were indeed status terms which had assumed almost a 'generic' form used by different caste groups, mostly lower castes, to designate themselves. Significantly, among the converts, the Jats and the Rajputs never adopted different caste names on conversion because their agricultural status was widespread and recognized.[32] Yet,

---

[28] DC Rohtak to the Commissioner and Superintendent of Delhi division, in 1900, *Confidential Files from the Record Room (CFRR)*, Rohtak, I–V, VI, p. 101.

[29] Denzil Ibbetson, 1981 [1916], *Punjab Castes: Races, Castes and Tribes of the People of Punjab*, reprint, New Delhi: Cosmo Publications, pp. 13–14.

[30] For the status of Brahmins, see Prem Chowdhry, 1994, *The Veiled Women: Shifting Gender Equations in Rural Haryana, 1880–1990*, New Delhi: Oxford University Press, pp. 41–4.

[31] *Census of India, Punjab and Delhi, 1901*, XVIII, part 1, Report, pp. 324–5.

[32] R. Saumarez Smith, 1971, 'Caste, Religion and Locality in the Punjab Census', M. Litt. Thesis, Department of Sociology, University of Delhi, pp. 86–8.

the low caste converts in Punjab always changed their names to get a higher social standing. However, the status of Jats and Rajputs varied greatly in different regions of Punjab, specially in relation to each other, with Rajputs superseding the Jats in the north-east and vice versa in the south-east and central Punjab.[33] Similarly, Muslim Rajputs were very high in social status in other parts of Muslim-dominated Punjab but had sunk low in south-east Punjab and had lost their exclusiveness to be recognized as Rajput.

It was also evident that in Punjab, downgrading and upgrading of caste was constantly taking place.[34] This was specially true of the south-east region. For example, there was a noticeable difference, between the condition of a Pathan who took to weaving on the frontier and a Rajput who took to weaving in south-east Punjab. The former fell from his social scale and the better class of the Pathan would not give him his daughter in marriage, but he remained a Pathan. However, in the latter case, the association of caste with occupation was so strong that he would not even be recognized as a Rajput nor his descendants, although he might claim the name.

Similarly, the Muslim Rajputs of Gurgaon had come to be known as Gaurwa Rajputs, as they had begun to practise widow remarriage in its *karewa* (levirate) form. In Karnal also, Muslim Rajputs had become Sheikhs because of poverty and loss of land which made them take to weaving as an occupation. In Rohtak, the Muslim Rajputs were invariably called Ranghars, the cattle lifters.[35] Unlike the Jats, who had both very positive and negative epithets and local sayings attached to them, the Muslim Rajputs in this region had only negative. For example:

Kutta, billi do, Ranghar, Gujar do
jib yeh charon na hon, khule kewaran so
(The dog and the cat are a pair and so are the Ranghar and Gujar.
When those four are not around, open your doors to sleep)[36]

---

[33] Ibid. The Punjab census report of 1901 similarly comments on the differing social status of Jats and Rajputs in different regions of Punjab. For example, in central Punjab, a Sikh Jat did not consider any one his social superior, not even a Rajput, see *Census of India, Punjab and Delhi*, p. 338.

[34] Ibbetson, *Punjab Castes*, pp. 101–2.

[35] 1911, *Rohtak District Gazetteer*, 1910, III-A, Lahore: Civil and Military Gazette, pp. 74, 77.

[36] Ibid., pp. 77–8.

Another local saying considered a Ranghar to be best in a liquor shop, or in a prison, or in the grave. Ranghar had or, in fact, just assumed such contemptuous connotations that it was freely applied to any person considered inferior and low.

In Ibbetson's opinion, the fact of conversion itself effected a change in the status of the Rajputs which came to be degraded to that of Ranghar, specially in the eyes of fellow Hindu Rajputs. The Muslims, by and large, were known in this region as *choti kat*, a term of contempt applied to those who, on conversion to Islam, cut-off the choti or the Hindu scalp lock. Therefore, although they claimed the Rajput status, they were not granted it by the other caste Hindus.[37]

Similarly, the few Jats who got converted to Islam came to be known as Mula Jats (the unfortunate), who had been forcibly circumcized at some point in time. The Meos were also converts, generally believed to be from among the Jats. They, indeed, followed all the major customs of Hindu Jats of this region like the karewa. They also followed the same *Got* (patrilineal clan) system as well as the same avoidance pattern of Got and village observed for marriage alliances as the Hindu Jats.[38] Yet, they frequently claimed Rajput status which did not go uncontested from the Jats who, on occasions, violently contested these claims.[39]

The substitution of caste names or affixation of a qualifying term clearly meant a down-gradation in south-east Punjab. This was noticeable even among the Hindus, for example, the Brahmins were known here as Gaur-Brahmins or Tagas since they had abandoned (*tyag dena*) their priestly functions and taken to agriculture.[40] It is not difficult to see how the socio-economic contradictions played a crucial role, especially among those agricultural castes who could easily claim a higher social status on account of their economic worth and political weightage, or descend socially into a much lower one as a result of their impoverished and economically dependent status. The latter alternative was significantly visible among some of the agricultural caste groups of the Muslims in this region, specially among the Rajputs.

[37] Ibbetson, *Punjab Castes*, p. 139.
[38] Hashim Amir Ali, 1970, *The Meos of Mewat*, New Delhi: Oxford & IBH Pub. Co., pp. 54–68. Also, see Pratap A. Aggarwal, 1976, 'Kinship and Marriage among the Meos of Rajasthan', in Imtiaz Ahmed (ed.), *Family Kinship and Marriage among Muslims in India*, New Delhi: Manohar, pp. 265–96.
[39] Ibid.
[40] Ibbetson, *Punjab Castes*, p. 179.

Among the Muslims in this division, the Rajputs were the largest single owners of land. They owned 5.62 per cent of the total cultivated land and occupied third position among the landowners; with Jats owning 52.74 per cent and Hindu Rajputs owning 8.6 per cent of land.[41] With the rapid alienation of land since 1900, and the emergence of Jat moneylender as a major force in this division,[42] the position of all other castes, whatever their religion, was severely affected. The Muslim agricultural castes, as a rule, were steady losers in all the land transactions. This was especially true of the Muslim Rajputs who saw a severe erosion of their status as landowners during the 1920s and the 1930s of the twentieth century.

The net losses among the Muslim Rajputs would have been sharper had it not been for their recruitment in the army.[43] The resentment and protest were noticeable in riot situation. This loss was shared by Pathans and Sayyeds, but to a much less degree, specially as their ownership of land was considerably less. The figures of land transactions, whether mortgage or sale, between 1926 and 1940 show the heavy and continuous losses incurred by the Muslims in this region.[44] The Hindu caste groups who emerged triumphant were primarily the Jats and, to a far lesser extent, the Ahirs. Significantly, the Jats were involved in confrontations with the Muslims in majority of the cases.

[41] For details, see Settlement Report, Rohtak district, 1879, cited in *Rohtak District Gazetteer* 1910, pp. 767–8; 1876, Settlement Report of Hissar District, 1875, Lahore: Civil and Military Gazette, p. 6; 1884, Settlement Report of Karnal District, 1883, Lahore: Civil and Military Gazette, p. vi, statement no. XXVI.

[42] 1934, *Punjab Legislative Council Debates*, XXV, 1 November, pp. 842–3. For details of the Jats emerging as leading moneylenders among the agricultural castes, see Chapter 2, p. 46, in this volume.

[43] In certain villages like Kalanaur in Rohtak district, 90 per cent of the males of military age among the Muslim Rajputs had enlisted by World War II. See The Board of Economic Inquiry, 1940, *Soldiers' Savings and How They Use Them*, Lahore: Civil and Military Gazette, p. 3. Despite this massive recruitment, Muslims (all castes) supplied 2.6 per cent of the total recruits of the district, whereas the Hindu Jats supplied 50 per cent. See India Office Records (IOR): Punjab Official Records for the Government of Pakistan (POS), 5547, 'War History of the Rohtak District', p. 25.

[44] For details, see statement XXIV appended to the Annual Reports of the Land Administration in the Punjab, 1926–7 to 1939–40. Rohtak is singled out for a detailed study because of the concentration and frequency of the Hindu–Muslim confrontations in this district. For similar details of other districts of this division, see ibid.

The statutory agricultural castes among the Muslims were a little more than half of the total Muslim population, which was a mere 20.78 per cent of the entire population in 1931, scattered all over south-east Punjab.[45] It was only in Gurgaon district that Meos were concentrated. They formed 20 per cent of the population and stood as the single largest caste group. A vast majority of Muslim in this division belonged to the lower castes and pursued the lower professions of their Hindu counterparts. Among them, however, there were large upwardly mobile groups who frequently assumed the title of Sheikh as a means of raising their status.

Denzil Ibbetson explains this by identifying Sheikh as an Arabic word meaning an elder or chief, which corresponded very closely to Chaudhary of Punjab and, in the Hindu caste hierarchy, could be associated with the Kshatriya *varna*.[46] Claims of the Sheikh title meant tracing their descent from the people of the prophet: a foreign origin assumed by tribes of true Arab descent and not converts. The preference of Shiekh was also true of those caste groups which were not so degraded, but who could hardly aspire to the highest, that is, Sayyed, who equated to the priestly class. Sheikhs, therefore, in the opinion of the British, included the so-called 'inferior agricultural Musalman tribes of Indian descent'. A Persian proverb of the period reflected this phenomenon:

The first year I was a Julaha
The next year a Shiekh.
This year if prices rise, I shall be a Sayyed

Commenting on this phenomenon, Ibbetson maintained:

So long as the social position of the new claimant is worthy of the descent he claims, the true Mughal, Sheikh and Sayyed, after waiting for a generation or so till the absurdity of the story is not too obvious, accept the fiction and admit the brand new member into their fraternity.[47]

Most noticeable among such people who claimed the Sheikh title were the Qasabs or Kasai (butchers) as they were locally known. Equated with very low caste, their social position was considered to be the same as that of the Teli or Julaha (both Muslim); and like most low castes,

---

[45] 1933, *Census of Punjab, 1931*, XVII, part II, tables, Lahore: Civil and Military Gazette, pp. 278–9, 283–301.
[46] Ibbetson, *Punjab Castes*, pp. 206–8.
[47] Ibid., p. 10.

they, too, were declared to be 'turbulent and troublesome' by the district administration. For the Qasabs, however, another word, 'upstarts', was also used. This was primarily because many of the Qasabs in the south-east region had emerged as *beoparis* (traders) in meat and beef as also in the export trade in raw hides, and were enjoying an increasing prosperity.[48]

This class of the Qasabs provided the major chunk of lower caste Muslims who claimed the status of the Sheikh. In fact, the very large increase in the number of the Sheikhs of Ambala and Rohtak districts: 41.31 and 76.97 per cent respectively, during 1921 and 1931, can be understood primarily through the remarkable decrease witnessed in the number of the Qasabs.[49] In these ten years, 1921–31, the increase in percentage of Sheikhs in different districts of the Ambala division was as follows: Hissar, 7 per cent; Rohtak, 74.4 per cent; Gurgaon, 12 per cent; Karnal, 17.6 per cent; Ambala, 25.4 per cent.[50]

---

[48] For the growing prosperity of Qasabs and their new professions, see 1933, *Census of India, Punjab, 1931*, XVII, part 1, report, Lahore: Civil and Military Gazette, p. 351. Also see IOR: P/8121/89, 1909, October; The Board of Economic Inquiry, 1939, Canning Industry in the Punjab, Lahore: Civil and Military Gazette.

[49] Total population of the Qasabs:

	1921	1931
Rohtak	8,228	4,829
Ambala	2,363	544

Source: Census of India, Punjab, 1931, p. 351.

[50] Total population of the Sheikhs:

	1921	1931
Rohtak	13,274	23,149
Ambala	22,238	27,886
Hissar	9,776	10,465
Gurgaon	15,093	16,899
Karnal	18,157	21,346

Source: Ibid., pp. 351, 355–6.

In the whole of British Punjab, the Sheikhs increased by 61.4 per cent within a period of ten years, 1921–31. This was primarily because the members of other castes, specially low occupational castes, returned their caste names as Sheikh. Patiala state showed a total disappearance of all its Qasabs running into several thousands.

In south-east Punjab, the Qasabs were increasingly dissatisfied with the noticeable discrepancy between their customary low ritual rank and their newly acquired economic rank. Those upwardly mobile members of the Qasab caste who had received western education and had, consequently, succeeded in raising their economic and political position started a move for abandonment of Hindu customs and practices not associated with high caste/class Muslim style of life.[51] They were also involved in Muslim educational efforts and were major contributors towards building up of mosques and in emphasizing the symbols of Muslim solidarity. The role played by the upwardly mobile groups who called themselves Sheikh can be seen in the local attempts which created a folk hero out of Mughla, a Sheikh of village Sanghi in Rohtak district. Mughla was said to be killing the Hindus out of a feeling of revenge, primarily because of their cow protection movement which challenged the right of Muslims to sacrifice cows as a central part of their religion.[52]

Similar to Qasabs, there were other caste groups who were seeking to carve out fresh social space for themselves. For instance, the Chamars and Lohars of Ambala division, contemptuously termed as mainly 'upstarts' by British administrators. Many among them took to education and joined the professional ranks as pleaders. They sought new status for themselves commensurate with their upwardly thrust in society.[53] They also emerged as rivals and competitors of the traditionally favoured castes and communities in demanding various concessions from the government and recruitment in government departments and public affairs. Similar was the case with Kalals who were distillers by profession and were socially stigmatized. Many members of this caste, who had branched out in trade and commerce, claimed the Pathan or the Rajput origin; but most of them claimed that of the Sheikh.

---

[51] *CFDC, Ambala*, 1924, see 'HO Notes' of Alan Mitchell, DC Ambala, 4 April.

[52] The confidential reports of the DC, Rohtak, disclose that Mughla (like Harphool, local hero of Hindu Jats) was a common murderer who did not differentiate between his victims on Hindu or Muslim grounds. He was a hired assassin who could be hired at Rs 30–40 for committing a murder. Nevertheless, he became a hero of the Qasabs and Sheikhs for targeting the Hindus involved, specially in *gauraksha* movement. See *CFDC*, Rohtak, 1936, 2, part 1, 'HO Notes', M.R. Sachdev, DC Rohtak, 11 May.

[53] *CFDC, Ambala*, 1924, 4, see 'HO Notes' of Alan Mitchell, DC Ambala, 4 April.

In fact, the census reports of Punjab from 1911 to 1931 are full of castes, both Hindu and Muslim, who were claiming higher status in caste terms. Most of them aspired to the statutory agricultural caste category in order to benefit from the Punjab Alienation of Land Act (in terms of buying and selling of land) and to seek recruitment in the army, as agricultural castes, by and large, supplied recruits to the British Indian Army.[54] Most common among the lower castes were: Nai, Lohar, Tarkhan, Darzi, Chhippi, Chimba, and so on. Those specially interested among these castes, as already mentioned, were the 'well to do persons' who were following occupations other than the traditional ones and were successful in hiding their traditional occupations.

In fact, the desire for upward mobility was not exclusive to Punjab but was common to different caste groups in the whole of northern India in the late nineteenth and early twentieth centuries.[55] The decennial census operations recording the social hierarchies of different castes had always led to the upwardly mobile groups from among different caste clusters to seek higher status in terms of caste. This social reality was to have a decisive effect on the shaping or sharpening of religious/ sectarian identities. Once again, south-east Punjab was not exclusive in this respect. Other regions of north India, specially eastern Uttar Pradesh (UP) and Bihar, as Gyanendra Pandey has observed, showed similar socio-religious link ups.[56]

The significance of this connection lies in the caste hierarchy being a relative one. It exists in relation to recognition given by the members of other castes, otherwise its assertion or move for upward mobility remains illusory. In Punjab, there were strong protests by many caste groups who refused to permit the low castes into their caste fold or recognize their status as equal to their own.[57] Their oft repeated demands to be included among the statutory agriculturists created by the Punjab Alienation of Land Act were repeatedly turned down and they were advised not to raise the question of any repeal or amendment of the act as this would evoke the antagonism of the *zamindars*

[54] *Census of India, Punjab, 1931*, p. 324, 352–4.

[55] See, for example, Lucy Carroll, 1978, 'Colonial Perception of Indian Society and the Emergence of Caste(s) Associations', *Journal of Asian Studies*, vol. XXXVII, no. 2, February, pp. 233–50.

[56] Gyanendra Pandey, 1990, *The Construction of Communalism in Colonial North India*, New Delhi: Oxford University Press, pp. 66–108.

[57] *Census of India, Punjab, 1931*, p. 324.

(landowners) against them.[58] In fact, there was a concerted effort of both the Muslim and Hindu landowners at enforcing marks of subordination of lower caste and class, for example, withholding of water from a joint well;[59] or stopping the lower castes from constructing a *pacca* (namely, masonry) well. [60]

Therefore, the attempts of certain Muslims, whether low caste or higher agricultural castes, to enforce recognition through whatever means possible, had to be in relation to both the Hindu castes as well as their own Muslim *biradari* (community). This created its own contradiction in the existing colonial situation of recording caste categories for its census operations because the Muslim identity was being asserted but the caste identity was not being denied. In fact, the attempts were either to enforce the existing one (among the agricultural castes) or claim a higher one (among lower castes). Among the former, the socio-economic exigencies of the colonial situation had been particularly hard, as seen in the case of Muslim Rajputs. Assertion of the Muslim identity by such groups was an attempt to stem this devaluation and remain within the egalitarian fold of Islam which, theoretically, stood above caste fold and its demeaning categorization.

The categorization in the Hindu caste fold was particularly degrading for the low caste Muslims. They perceived a greater dignity in being casteless and in emphasizing their Muslimhood, because Koran explicitly rejects gradation of groups and individuals in terms of birth and the ideology of pure and impure. The only criterion of social evaluation recognized in Islam is religious piety. The lower castes, therefore, showed greater zeal in projecting their Muslimhood.[61] They were also more aggressive in attempting to impose recognition on the dominating Hindus and gain acceptance from the other Muslims on equal terms as Muslims.

[58] *JG*, 1929, 18 September, p. 3; *JG*, 1931, 11 March, p. 4; *JG*, 1935, 15 September, p. 1; *JG*, 1937, 5 May, p. 3; 16 June, p. 4; 22 December, p. 6; *JG*, 1938, 4 May, p. 6; 2 November, p. 3.

[59] For such instances, see *JG*, 1923, 2 May, p. 4; 24 May, pp. 3–4; 23 October, p. 2.

[60] Bhargwa Papers (NMML), see Satyanarayan Saroj to Mahatma Gandhi, 3 August 1940.

[61] Greater Islamization among lower menial classes has a parallel in the effect of change of creed on the lower castes to Sikhism, that is, more emphasis on Sikhism.

In this public assertion of Muslim identity, the building of mosques understandably emerged as crucial. In the face of their scattered reality (excluding Gurgaon district), it was a public espousal of their collective presence in the Hindu majority areas of south-east Punjab. Mosques were to provide the foci of popular social participation of Muslims of all castes, high or low. In the Hindu-dominated area, this need to emphasize the exclusive foci emanated out of the fact that the dominant popular religion of this rural region operated through the shrines, popularly shared by both the Hindus and Muslims. Many shrines had become associated with particular miraculous powers. The Hissar shrine, for example, was renowned for its power of exorcism and another, for sufferers from dog bites.[62] Similarly, other shrines in Rohtak had come to be known for granting boon to childless women.[63] Many of these shrines were in charge of *faquirs*. Generally professing the faith of the prophet, they were considered 'men of low castes' who had 'no definite creed or rules of life'.[64] The scriptural Islamic norms could hardly be emphasized by them. The shrine culture, with its concept of rural biradari which included both the Hindus and Muslims, was a direct erosion of the minority population's Islamic identity in the Hindu-dominated region.

Moreover, by the late nineteenth and early twentieth century, there was a growing emphasis on Islamic traditions in the Muslim-dominated Punjab and attempts had begun to transform these shrines from being the foci of popular devotionalism into centres of Islamic piety and learning.[65] By attacking the religious practise associated with the shrines and by emphasizing personal adherence to the basic tenets of Islam, the reformists were not merely attacking the very foundations of the conceptual system of rural Islam, they were also defining Islamic identity and shaping up public standard of this identity formation.

In this tussle of identity formation, the reformist movements of respective religions to 'purify' their religion played no small a part. For example, the *shuddhi* (purification) movement of the Arya Samaj and its Muslim counterpart of *Ishat-i-Quarran* and *Tabligh-ul-Islam* as well

[62] Ian Talbot, 1988, *Punjab and the Raj, 1849–1947*, New Delhi: Manohar, p. 72.

[63] *Rohtak District Gazetteer*, 1910, pp. 60–2.

[64] Ibbetson, *Punjab Castes*, p. 226.

[65] David Gilmartin, 1989, *Empire and Islam: Punjab and the Making of Pakistan*, New Delhi: Oxford University Press, pp. 54–6, 60–1, 77; also, see Talbot, *Punjab and the Raj*, p. 25.

as *Jamait-ul-Ulema* deepened the consciousness of different classes of people as members of particular religious denomination. These greatly contributed to the rise of movements for social mobility among different groups of Hindus and Muslims.

The movement of shuddhi in this region, for instance, significantly emphasized the purification of the higher caste converts like the Jat, Gujar, and Rajput, and to integrate them into their original Hindu community, specially in view of the fact that Hindu traditions and customs were still followed by the converted rural populace.[66] Despite purification, however, members of these castes were still faced with the humiliation of not being accepted in their original Hindu caste biradari and had to go back to the Islamic fold.[67] This fact was not merely responsible for the failure of the movement but also for the hardening of attitudes among the converted. Moreover, as compared to the above mentioned caste groups, the lower caste Muslim was, more or less, ignored in this region. This fact offers another dimension to the upward mobility drive response of the lower caste Muslims to the powerful movements of religious reform and revivalism. The stigma of Hindu ancestry attached to the Muslims, specially in the days of shuddhi, had to be lived down. This sharpened their awareness and determination to forge a Muslim identity.

The implicit underlining of the social inequality of lower caste groups' existence in the theoretically egalitarian Islamic fold, prompted efforts at greater integration by Muslim organizations. Efforts were renewed to get rid of Hindu traditions and customs and transplant them with Islamic tenets.[68] These attempts were greatly aided by extensive tours of the whole of Punjab by *ulema* to establish mosques in towns and villages, and tapping wealthy Muslims for religious causes and extensive dissemination of religious literature in Urdu.[69] Pressure and systematic attacks from inside and outside the province, the activities of ulema and other religious organizations, journalists and inflammatory biases of the press, all emphasizing new standards of religious

[66] *JG*, 1923, 2 December, p. 3; *JG*, 1925, 28 October, p. 3; *JG*, 1927, 30 November, p. 4. The greatest conflict over shuddhi occurred as a result of the Arya Samaj efforts to reconvert the Muslim Rajputs in this region in the early 1920s. The Muslims retaliated by an effective socio-economic boycott of the Aryas.

[67] See Chhotu Ram, 1923, 'The failure of shuddhi movement in the Jat mainland', *JG*, 2 December, p. 3.

[68] *JG*, 1927, 30 November, p. 4.

[69] Talbot, *Punjab and the Raj*, pp. 74–5.

identity, created great anxiety in this region to show a more personal adherence and observance in Islamic self-identification as part of the larger Islamic community. These considerations were to turn the 1930s into what British officials had termed: 'a period of construction of mosques in this region'.[70]

The move towards Islamic customs and practices is also noticeable in the growing ostentatious celebrations of Muslim festivals and, more importantly, in the growing objections, even violent if necessary, raised to the similarly growing ostentatious Hindu festivals and playing of music in front of mosques. These moves, like that of the construction of mosques, did not go uncontested from the Hindu opponents. They claimed custom, judicial injunctions, moved court, and collected official and unofficial opinion and support against such moves; while all the time making similar moves of their own, which were contested by the Muslims. All moves and counter-moves, not infrequently, led to violent confrontations. In this connection, Chaudhary Ghulam Mustafa, Deputy Commissioner of Rohtak district, insightfully observed that 'the earlier amity when Muslims would hold up the prayers for few minutes to allow the processionists to pass on, who did so hurriedly playing music all the while', or who regulated the procession to avoid the principal mosques at prayer time 'was giving way to hostility'.[71]

The rising new demands also invited a greater role of the state. As regulation of processions and celebration of festivals could no longer be left to mutual agreements and conventions, the state stepped in as the arbiter, creating more confusion through its law and order agency, administrative procedures, and judicial decrees. All accounts of such confrontations are steeped in several restrictions and licences being enforced or lifted by the state agencies, who, apart from being ignorant, had their own biases and prejudices. These often coloured their observations and consequent decisions. For example, Alan Mitchell, the Deputy Commissioner of Ambala, commenting on the rising Muslim protest against Hindu procession that passed through the Muslim living quarters had maintained in April 1924: 'Musalmans have the effrontery to protest against Hindu procession that pass Muslim quarters.'[72]

---

[70] *CFDC, Rohtak*, 1936, 2, part 1, see 'HO Notes', Ghulam Mustafa, DC Rohtak, to Commissioner Ambala division, 10 May.

[71] Ibid.

[72] *CF comm., Ambala*, 1924, A-28, 'HO Notes', DC Ambala, 4 April.

The 'Muslim effrontery' continued to grow till, by 1942, the entire Ambala division had came to be termed by British officials as 'an extraordinary division for a large number of disputes about processions and routes'.[73] For the most part, the city centres of this division were considered the nuclei of these clashes; but a stir on this question even in the rural areas cannot be denied. For example, at village Gharaunda in Karnal district, the hitherto quite and peaceful annual Dussehra celebrations were violently disturbed. In September of that year, certain Muslims were 'suddenly aroused' to the fact that the site of the Dussehra celebration was really a Muslim graveyard.[74] The matter had to be referred to court. From then onwards, the annual religious celebrations and processions of both the communities became an occasion for minor and major clashes.

Similarly, by the late 1930s, the increasing assertiveness of the Muslims, perceived in their collective presence in various fairs and festivals, had come to require 'watching' by the district officials of Ambala.[75] There were two important annual fairs of Lakhi Shah and Shah Quamaris. In popularity and celebrations, both had been growing every year. However, the limited space of the tombs resulted in the spilling over into the adjoining land. In the case of Shah Quamaris, this land was owned by Magh Hindus who resented this and moved court against it. In August 1938, they succeeded in obtaining a court decree that no fair could be held on their land. When this was ignored by the Muslims, the confrontation between them became an annual feature, with both the sides whipping up religious sentiments. An added reason, disclosed by the deputy commissioner of Ambala, lay in the unauthorized utilization of this land as well as claims to the rent charged from the owners of various stalls erected temporarily on the vacant land.[76] Both the manager of the shrine and the landowners claimed this rent. The Lakhi Shah fair was an identical case, except that the adjoining land belonged to the local government. Yet, it provoked protest against its use, as the basic premise of its use and objections to its use remained the same.

---

[73] CF comm., Ambala, 1942, A-4, III, 'HO Notes', Commissioner Ambala division, 24 October.

[74] GI: Home Poll, FRRP, 1937, 18/9/37, September.

[75] CFDC, Ambala, 1941, 4, 'HO Notes', Srinagesh, DC Ambala, 8 September.

[76] Ibid., see a note by DC Ambala, 24 August 1938.

These were not isolated instances. The official records are full of cases in which the Hindu and Muslim festivals provided an occasion for confrontations with unfailing regularity.[77] Religious festivals and religious processions and routes followed by them were potent symbols of religion and were occasions used not only in this region but in major parts of north India to reinforce the identity, self-respect, and self-assertion of the participants.[78] They evoked a kind of emotional response and mobilization which occurred on sectarian lines.

COW SLAUGHTER AND COW PROTECTION: 'COMMUNAL AND POLITICAL ISSUES'

Among the symbols of religion employed which evoked emotional response and mobilization on the one hand, and tension, strife, and confrontation on the other, the cow protection movement was unprecedented. The movement which by the late nineteenth century had emerged as the pivotal rallying point engulfing the whole of northern and central India, stretching up to Bihar in the east, had successfully united members of different castes and classes divided over many different issues.[79] But the kind of violence and aggression seen in eastern UP and Bihar was almost totally absent in Punjab and Central Provinces, where no major clashes occurred. Yet, in Punjab also, the gaukashi (cow slaughter) was an extremely sensitive issue. There were numerous gau-rakhshani sabhas (cow protection association) in this region. Gauraksha was a question which no non-Muslim association or political party could afford to ignore. It was included in the practical programme of all political parties, whether the Hindu Sabha, or the Congress, or the Hindu wing of the Unionist Party, dominated by the Jats.

Interestingly, the Jats were not considered 'very religious minded' by British officials except on the question of cow slaughter. This issue, in their opinion, could arouse the 'communal passions' of Hindu Jats.[80] The wide-scale participation of Jats and their self-perception as the protectors of cows got reflected in the folk songs which hailed Harphool,

---

[77] CF Comm., Ambala, 1943, 4, III, 'HO Notes', Commissioner Ambala division, 31 October; IOR: L/P&J/6/2170, 1978; CFSO, Rohtak, pp. 1–14.

[78] Public processions and ritual displays were widely used in the whole of northern India.

[79] Pandey, 'Rallying Round the Cow', pp. 60–129; Pandey, The Construction of Communalism in Colonial North India, pp. 158–200.

[80] CFDC, Rohtak, 1933, 2, part 1, 'HO Notes', E.H. Lincoln, 4 April.

a Hindu Jat of village Julani, as a heroic figure. Harphool's exploits, as already mentioned were projected to be perpetrated on the Muslim butchers for killing 'the sacred cows'.[81]

Religiously, the sanctity of cow was unrivalled. The use of this symbol of worship is linked up with the enormous importance cattle had for this region's economy, which had remained the most backward and underdeveloped under the British. The needs of imperialism had given very low priority to any improvement of agriculture in south-east Punjab.[82] Throughout the colonial rule, it continued to be seen as a region primarily suited for the supply of draught animals to the rest of Punjab as also to certain other parts of India. Cows in south-east Punjab, in any case, far outnumbered the other cattle as it was more economical to feed them, than a larger animal like the buffalo, specially in the frequent famine conditions prevailing in most parts of this region and the consequent fodder scarcity.[83]

However, this region was not only known for its cattle breeding but also for its flourishing hide and beef trade, which depended primarily on cow slaughter. The Muslims generally involved in cow slaughter were the Muslim butchers. They did not enjoy any official sympathy. In fact, the district officials showed a great deal of prejudice against them. Chaudhary Ghulam Mustafa, the Deputy Commissioner of Rohtak who administered this district from 1936 to 1939, noted in this connection:

The butchers are generally a very unruly and troublesome class of people ... The worst among them have made a regular trade of stealing cattle and slaughtering them in a secret manner. As they generally deal with cattle or are meat-sellers it is not always easy to detect such crime among them.[84]

The butchers were closely aligned with the Muslim Rajputs who were their cattle suppliers. The Muslim Rajputs were also given to cattle

---

[81] These songs titled, *Harphool Jat Julani Ka*, were printed and distributed widely. Many of them were proscribed by the district administration for arousing 'communal passions'. See *CFDC*, Rohtak, 2, part 1, 'HO Notes', M.R. Sachdev, 11 May 1936 and Ghulam Mustafa, 26 June 1939, DCs Rohtak. Also, *GI*: Home Poll, 37/2/35, 1935, pp. 53–4; 37/1/37, 1937, pp. 130–1.

[82] For details, see Chapter 1 in this volume.

[83] The Board of Economic Inquiry, *A Cattle Survey of Rohtak District in the Punjab*, Lahore: Civil and Military Gazette, 1935, p. 30.

[84] *CF comm., Ambala*, 4, III, 'HO Notes', Commissioner Ambala division, 11 May 1939.

lifting.[85] In a state of great economic insecurity, primarily due to the rapid loss of their lands (mentioned earlier), the cattle trade as an alternative source of income had assumed great importance for the Muslim Rajputs. This stealing of cows was considered by the district authorities of Ambala division to be 'the beginning of clash between Hindu and Muslim zamindars which developed into a general communal tangle'.[86]

The stealing of cows was indeed very frequent in this division. The situation, from the point of view of landowners, was irreparable as there could not be any chance of recovery of cows or of apprehending the culprits. Complaints lodged with the police were seldom an effective remedy. On the basis of the religious sanctity of cow, which was a deeply shared religious concern, a bond of unity could be forged by the Hindu landowners among different segments of both rural and urban society. It brought better results than a simple protest lodged with the police against mere thieving. It must also be said that the cattle lifters could be found not only among the Muslim Rajputs and Qasais; Hindu menials also were very frequent culprits. They not only stole and sold the cattle of their landowners to the Muslim butchers but also their own cattle, if any.[87] Stealing of cattle, specially cows by the menials, increased in this region because of increase in the price and export of hides.[88] The menials found that the hide of a slaughtered animal was more valuable than that of a dead animal, fetching the highest price.

The increasing thefts of cows by the menials added to the pre-existing tension between kamins and the proprietors. The landowners were faced with the problem of recalcitrant and even openly defiant *kamins*, who were refusing to render *begar*, give other cesses and

---

[85] *CFDC, Rohtak*, 2, part 1, 'HO Notes', Zaman Mehdi Khan, 4 November 1931.

[86] *CF comm., Ambala*, 4, III, 'HO Notes', Commissioner Ambala division, 31 October 1943.

[87] *GI: Home Poll*, 1937, 37/1/37. *JG* also published news regarding the thefts of the cattle belonging to Jats by the kamins. These kamins were pointedly claimed to be Muslim by faith and not Hindus. *JG*, 1923, 24 October, p. 3.

[88] A.M. Stowe, 1910, *Cattle and Dairying in the Punjab*, Lahore: Civil and Military Gazette, p. 45. The sale price of a dried hide of a slaughtered cow was Rs 40 per maund and Rs 30 per maund for a buffalo.

services; instead they were demanding higher agricultural wages.[89] Apart from this, the kamins had also increased the number of goats and sheep which they maintained for the butchers and grazed them on the shamilat land of the village which was not even adequate for the landowners own growing herd of cattle.[90]

The menials came to be greatly terrorized by the landowners into not having any dealings with the butchers. They were also forbidden to sell even their own cows to the butchers.[91] The chief instrument for making them obey was socio-economic boycott. The recalcitrant village menials sometimes found themselves to be boycotted for months on end. Their appeal to the Muslim landowners was hardly effective, as shown in the case of village Kharkhoda. And it would not be merely the landowners who would boycott the menials. The landowners would also compel their economic subordinates, whether agriculturist or non-agriculturist, to join them in boycotting the menials.

Anti-cow slaughter panchayats were also regularly held to enforce this ban. In fact, the one effective way available to rural Punjab in order to bring about widespread mobilization, which cut across regions, exercised greatest pressure, commanded obedience, specially of subordinate caste/class groups, and imposed unity of action, was to work through the caste and village panchayats. These formed the backbone of the gau-rakhshani (cow protection) movement. The combined strength of the Hindus of different caste groups on this issue was overwhelming. The gau-rakhshani movement provided the landowners as well as their caste men with the much needed opportunity of asserting their dominance in this area and to deal effectively with the defiance and demands of the lower orders as well as the higher ones, as in the case of village Kharkhoda. Religious sentiments were frequently invoked through these panchayats to stop the sale of cows to butchers altogether. The socio-economic boycott imposed by the panchayats also entailed that

[89] JG, 1923, 22 August, p. 6; 12 September, pp. 5–6; 24 October, p. 10; JG, 1925, 10 May, p. 7. For a comprehensive account of disaffection between the untouchables, both Hindus and Muslims, with their landowners, see Prem Chowdhry, 1984, Punjab Politics: The Role of Sir Chhotu Ram, New Delhi: Vikas, pp. 61–86.

[90] IOR: P/8121/1910, see Assessment Report of the Rohtak Tehsil of the Rohtak District, p. 10.

[91] GI: Home Poll, 37/1/37, 1937, pp. 130–1. Also, see CFDC, Rohtak, A-28, pp. 15, 55.

none buy or sell or have any money dealings with the Muslim butchers and cattle dealers.

It is interesting to note that the lower class Hindu Jats of Rohtak district, which had emerged as the centre of gau-rakhshani movement, owed large amounts of money to the Muslim butchers of village Ganaur, who were not only the largest cattle dealers but also the biggest moneylenders of this area.[92] They were undoubtedly providing severe competition to the Jat landowner-cum-moneylender. An effective way was therefore found by an overwhelming number of Hindu Jats to settle their economic difficulties and competition vis-à-vis the comparatively few Muslim butchers and cattle dealers by arousing passions through religious appeal. The ties of caste and kinship further cemented this inter- and intra-caste concerted action; caste and religion providing an ideological binding to sporadic spurts of agitation around the cow issue.

This religious posturing of the landowners in public had a different face in private. Regarding the sale of their own cattle to the butchers, they had, for long, observed a relaxed code of conduct born out of harsh economic realities. H.K. Trevaskis, writing about Punjab of 1890–1925, said:

The Hariana tract is largely Hindu, but the peasants are shrewd agriculturists and rapidly dispose off inefficient stock to the Mohammadan butchers (Qassai) of Panipat, Sonepat, or Rohtak 'asking no question for conscience sake' so that the hide trade flourishes most in the area celebrated for its breed of cattle.[93]

That this practice continued is clear from the secret despatch of Sant Singh, Superintendent of Police, Sonepat, written in October 1937 to R.C. Jeffrey, Deputy Inspector-General Police of eastern range. The despatch read:

The usual practice of Hindu Jats in village Purkhas and about 200 neighbouring villages was to give their old and useless cattle to their Muslim dealers, who were leading butchers also, either in exchange of new ones or otherwise selling to them.[94]

In fact, in the arid south-east Punjab, notorious for its frequent fodder famines, the landowners found it economically more and more

[92] CFSO, Rohtak, pp. 1–23.
[93] H.K. Trevaskis, 1931, The Punjab of Today, Vol. I, Lahore: Civil and Military Gazette, p. 372.
[94] CFSO, Rohtak, I-23, see secret DO, 5 October 1937.

profitable to sell their cattle to butchers than to march them across the River Jamuna for sale to other landowners, or to bring fodder for them from outside at great cost.[95] In fact, some of the landowners of the region were so practical they would themselves kill a *bijjar* (bull) who destroyed their crop by grazing in the fields.[96] In any case, the voluntary sales of cows to the Muslim butchers among the Hindu owners was widely prevalent. This can be seen in the numerous resolutions passed by the Jat and Brahmin sabhas of different districts against such sales.[97]

A difficult situation, officially termed 'communal', arose in Rohtak district in 1937.[98] The Jat landowners decided to call a panchayat of 200 villages at village Purkhas, on 4 October 1937, to stop all cow slaughter. The panchayat was to decide on socio-economic boycott of the Muslim butchers and cattle dealers. Such a decision was bound to lead to widespread law and order problem. Consequently, police help had to be summoned. The district administration asked the local 'Jat leaders' for their 'help' to contain the situation. The pressure of the Jat panchayat, 4,000 strong, resulted in the leading butchers of village Ganaur contributing Rs 200 towards the proposed construction of a *gaushala* (an alm house for sick, aged, or deserted cattle). In return, the panchayat agreed not to effect socio-economic boycott of the Muslim butchers and cattle dealers who belonged mainly to village Ganaur. The panchayat which had aroused 'communal fears', thus, ended up with belligerent Hindu Jats thanking the Muslim butchers for their 'liberal attitude'.

On 18 May 1938, a panchayat was again summoned by the Hindu Jats at village Saya-Khera. It resolved to boycott the Muslim butchers and decided to impose a fine of Rs 100 on those disobeying the panchayat decision. Another panchayat of ninety villages was to be held at village Purkhas on 18 June 1938 to ensure that the decision with regard to the boycott of Muslim butchers was implemented. The so-called 'communal problem' thus persisted, and clearly needed to be negotiated periodically. Three other 'gaukashi cases' of Gurgaon district occurred in the beginning of the 1930s and stretched right up to 1938.

[95] *IOR*: P/11372/1923, 62, p. 6. Also, *Cattle and Dairying in the Punjab*, p. 32.

[96] *GI: Home Poll*, 37/2/35, pp. 53–4.

[97] *IOR*: P/12048/1934. Also, *JG*, 1929, 14 August, p. 9; 28 August, p. 6.

[98] *CFSO, Rohtak*, I-23. All references to this case, unless indicated to the contrary, have been taken from this source.

These add yet another dimension to this complex problem. A perusal of these cases brings out the multiplicity of issues operating behind the gaukashi issue.

A case of cow slaughter which assumed prominence in the early 1930s, in village Agaon in tehsil Firozpur Jhirka of Gurgaon district, reveals certain very interesting facts. The formulation of newer demands under colonial intervention had led to the imposition of restrictions on cow killing in village Agaon in 1891. This move showed the confusion, ambivalence, and even prejudice, mentioned earlier, in the colonial authorities understanding of the local customs. Significantly, Agaon was a 'Muslim village', with Meos controlling 2,573 acres out of a total of 3,579 acres of cultivated land.[99] All this time, cows were definitely being slaughtered though without a licence, but also without any protest form the Hindu population of the village. The protest, in fact, originated from the Meos themselves.

Meos of this arid tract of south-east Punjab were certainly landowners, but their status as landowners was being greatly eroded. They stood impoverished specially when compared to the butchers whose prosperity had increased in the colonial period. In caste terms, butchers were a low caste and Meos, who were included in the statutory agricultural castes, claimed the Rajput status. The non-recognition of the caste superiority of Meos by the rich butchers apparently worked against them as Meos, in order to hit them economically, joined with the other Hindu landowners to take up the cause of cow protection and assert their joint strength.

Even earlier, Meos had initiated a move against cow slaughter. In 1891, they had successfully prosecuted several butchers for operating without a licence and they were, consequently, heavily fined. Even this had not stopped the slaughtering of cows. But since then, repeated efforts were made by butchers to procure a licence in order to regularize their cow slaughter business. Their greatly renewed activity in the 1930s evoked the following comment of the deputy commissioner: 'The Meos themselves brought to the notice of the authorities the high-handed manner in which some butchers killed kine within the boundaries of the village.'

The grant of a licence was made the focal point of this agitation which was, interestingly, not Hindu versus Muslims but Hindus and Muslims

---

[99] *CFDC, Gurgaon*, 23/S/703. All references to this case, unless indicated to the contrary, have been taken from this source.

versus the Muslim (butchers). An appeal made to the Commissioner of Ambala division in April 1930, by some of the Hindus of Agaon, against the grant of such a licence clearly pointed this out:

Any attempt to introduce cow-killing by licence in Agaon will in all probability lead to endless litigation, trouble and breach of peace not only between Hindus and Muslims but between the two sections of Muslims themselves for it is a well known fact that there is a considerable difference of opinion among the Musalmans themselves on this point.

The deputy commissioner also agreed with this; yet, he still penned down: 'threat of communal riot existed'. This 'communal threat' reappeared whenever attempts were made to procure a licence for cow slaughter.

In 1936, the 'communal threat' in the eyes of district officials assumed political dimension. In March of that year, the deputy commissioner confirmed a report of the sub-inspector of police that some village Meos were being instigated by the 'Bania leaders' of the neighbouring village against cow slaughter. The rich Bania traders and moneylenders in urban areas, always in the forefront of asserting their superior status by conspicuous participation in religious activities like erection of temple, celebration of religious festivals, and other activities, were unlikely to miss such an opportunity. Financial help was sent by them from Defhi, Alwar, and even Calcutta. It may be pointed out here that the Congress party in this region, as well as in the rest of Punjab, drew its major support from the urban Hindu middle class and mercantile groups and was notoriously referred to as the 'Bania Congress'. With the involvement of the Banias, therefore, the Agaon trouble came to be officially understood in communal as well as in political terms.

However, certain other factors behind the involvement of the 'Bania leaders' in this trouble may be gleaned from the secret report of the Deputy Commissioner of Gurgaon district, dated 31 August 1931.[100] The report had revealed severe 'Bania disaffection' in this region as a result of the discovery, by the tehsildars of Firozpur Jhirka, of their (Banias) extensive illegal transactions in land. These *benami* (fictitious) transactions had become very common in Punjab in the post-1900 period, when the Alienation of Land Act debarred the non-agricultural castes from purchasing land. Any such discovery, therefore, stood to directly and adversely affect the purchasing rich Banias who were

---

[100] 1931, 'HO Notes', DC Gurgaon, see Report, 31 August.

indulging in widespread benami transfer of land deals through their *banamidar* agriculturist 'friends' in this area, primarily their indebted Meos.

Indeed, by 1928–9, Gurgaon district had become notorious for having a large number of benami transactions.[101] In this impoverished tract, the butchers alone posed a likely economic challenge to Bania moneylenders as potential moneylenders themselves. Apparently instigated, it suited the economically insecure Meos to assert their united voice against the butchers who despite being fellow Muslims, devalued them socially because of their impoverished and economically dependent status. In the official eyes, however, their joining up with the Banias, who were associated with the Congress, was enough to impart political colour to this problem.

One of the most serious and prolonged disputes on the cow slaughter issue, officially identified as communal but, again, understood to have been instigated for political reasons, occurred in village Jharsa of Gurgaon district in April 1930. A detailed discussion of this case will delineate the multiplicity of the issues involved and the consequent apprehensions it aroused. In fact, this case attracted so much of publicity and generated so much of interest that the district office amassed a huge amount of documentary and oral evidence on it.[102] Respective parties sent innumerable telegrams to all officials ranging from the district to the all-India level. The Hindu *Mahasabha* actively propagated on this issue. Frenzied demands for a public inquiry were made. The Hindus of Jharsa village, under the leadership of local pleaders, formed themselves into a defence committee and churned out vituperous and incendiary propaganda in the press.

The deputy commissioner, apprehending breach of 'communal peace' sent for the armoured military reinforcements.[103] These were sent back only after the ringleaders among the Hindus and Muslims had been arrested under section 107 CrPC and several others had been challaned. The case dragged on for a year and was eventually withdrawn by the government as a result of general amnesty following

[101] *Annual Report of the Land Revenue Administration in the Punjab*, 1928–9, p. 29.

[102] Five files were maintained on this case: *CFDC, Gurgaon*, 62, S/703, vol. I, IIa, IIb, III, IV.

[103] *CFDC, Gurgaon*, 62, S/703, vol. III.

the Gandhi–Irwin Pact.[104] The agitation abated for a short while, only to be resumed again; it continued till 1938.

Regarding cow slaughter in village Jharsa, the confidential report of the Deputy Commissioner of Gurgaon district to Miles Irwing, the Commissioner of Ambala division, dated 10 April 1930, stated: 'I must say there is a prime-facie proof that kine-slaughter has been going on in the village for a long time past.'[105] Another report, dated 22 April 1930, traced the origin of this trouble to the severe discord among Hindu and Muslim residents of the village over the possession of a graveyard. This had erupted in an open show of force when the Qassai claimants attempted to construct a hut in the graveyard for a faquir. The Hindu claimants who faced the Qassais' public assertions quickly raised religious objections to the killing of their 'sacred cows', clearly as a means of mobilizing support and showing their collective authority. They demanded total prohibition of such activity in the village with a view to economically hit the flourishing meat trade of their opponents which lay behind such claims and self-assertions. Within a month, the anti-cow slaughter agitation had totally subsumed every other issue at stake. The Muslim butchers, in turn, vigorously resisted the new demands against cow slaughter and succeeded in uniting their religious minority against this threat to their livelihood.[106]

Once the cry of cow protection was raised, and outside help sought, the district officials noted that the local Banias and pleaders quickly established their leadership. The forever 'troublesome Delhi people' took up this 'religious matter' and succeeded in evoking religious frenzy. Regarding this, Sheikh Khurshid Mohammad, the Deputy Commissioner of Gurgaon, noted in his confidential report dated 13 August 1931: 'The movement in Gurgaon is essentially a political one. The local leaders who were at the back of agitation carried on for political ends, otherwise beef had been sold in Gurgaon Bazaar for the last 50 to 60 years without giving offence to anybody.'[107]

Another interesting disclosure was made by a weekly newspaper, *Chhatri Meerath*, published from Meratth district of the adjacent United Provinces. In its issue of 24 April 1930, it commented upon the situation:

---

[104] 1931, 'HO Notes', Sheikh Khursheed Mohammed, DC Gurgaon, 13 May.

[105] *CFDC, Gurgaon*, 62, S/703, vol. III.

[106] Ibid., DC to Commissioner Ambala division, 12 April 1930.

[107] 'HO Notes', DC Gurgaon, 13 August 1931.

'Members of moneylenders classes who preach cow-protection lend money to butchers to carry on their business. We hear that thousands of kine are brought by the butchers from native states at Rs 6 per head.'[108] This accusation stands confirmed by Haji Ghulam Mohammad, one of the big cattle dealers and the Municipal Commissioner of Rohtak district, who in his oral evidence to the Punjab Provincial Banking Inquiry Committee testified that the traders provided the business capital on interest charges to the cattle dealers of this region.[109] Indeed, no attempt was made by the concerned 'Bania leaders' to either squeeze the credit of the butchers themselves or put pressure upon other Hindu creditors to dry up this necessary credit source of the guilty and erring Muslims.

The trouble arose afresh in 1938 when some butchers, in view of the rising demand, tried to procure a licence for a new site for slaughtering cows. The Muslim owners of the existing licenced premises for cow slaughter and some other butchers combined with the protesting Hindus against this demand of a new site.[110] Confronted with overlapping categories of Hindu–Muslim participation, joined on a common platform, the officials chose to project it as merely 'political'.

The third case around the gaukashi issue took place in village Hussainpur of Gurgaon district.[111] Despite having all the outward trappings of an out-and-out 'communal case', the district officials merely projected it in its unidimensional political aspect. An insight into why they did it reveals interesting contours of these confrontations. In 1931, this village suddenly came to constitute a 'danger to peace' on account of the cow slaughter question, despite this practice being legally recognized and socially and religiously accepted by the inhabitants since the inception of the village. This danger arose when a threat to stop this practice was issued by Captain Balbir Singh, Member of the Legislative Assembly (MLA) (Congress), who had built an *ashram* near the village, and Thakur Gaya Singh, his close associate and friend from this region. The former accused the Sayyed of village Hussainpur of killing stolen cows.[112] Balbir Singh was considered by the deputy commissioner to be

---

[108] *Chhatri Meerath in CFDC Gurgaon*, vol. III.

[109] 1930, *Punjab Provincial Banking Inquiry Report, 1929–30*, evidence, vol. II, Lahore: Civil and Military Gazette, p. 980.

[110] 1938, 'HO Notes', Sardar Balwant Singh Grewal, DC Gurgaon, 1 November.

[111] *CFDC, Gurgaon*, 23, S/703.

[112] 1931, 'HO Notes', DC Gurgaon, 13 August.

playing a 'political game by championing certain village grievances' in order to gain 'popular sympathy'.

Indeed, this Muslim village, amidst a large number of Hindu villages, provided the much-needed base to an effective disposal of the stolen cattle of this region. Although legally sanctioned, it could be and was challenged, turning it into potentially combustible 'communal' matter. Yet, this potentially communal matter took a political turn when the 'village grievances' came to be voiced by a Congressman whose ashram was considered 'a source of political danger'.[113] An administrative solution to this apprehended communal-cum-political trouble was found by transferring the concerned village from the Kholl police station to the *sadr* Rewari police station, which enabled the police to 'look after' the village and the Congress ashram more closely.[114] Similarly, the confidential reports of the Sub-divisional Officer of Sonepat to the Deputy Commissioner of Rohtak from 1931 to 1945, go to indicate that strained relations between Hindus and Muslims in a number of villages like Garhi-Sampla, Kundal, and Purkhas were occasioned by political activities of the Congress.[115]

The British administrators believed that Congressmen in Punjab always attempted to divert the aroused communal disposition of the Hindus and Muslims towards an anti-government attitude.[116] In the Haryana region specially, where British administrators were clearly emphasizing the caste divisions as well as the agriculturist versus non-agriculturist division, any intensification of the so-called communal situation had another dimension as well. In any such division, the actual danger, as disclosed by the Deputy Commissioner of Rohtak to the Governor of Punjab and also, recognized by the leaders of this region, lay in the 'Hindu Jat' making a 'common cause' with the 'Bania Hindu' or the urban Hindus, generally recognized as being anti British, against the 'loyal Mohammandans'.[117] Such an attempt would have greatly endangered the entire politics of this region, nurtured so carefully by British administrators with the help of the Unionist leaders. The local Jat and Muslim leaders acted, time and again, to contain the situation

---

[113] *CFDC, Gurgaon*, 23, S/703.

[114] 1931, 'HO Notes', DC Gurgaon, 13 August.

[115] *CFDC, Rohtak*, 2, part 2, 'HO Notes', Sub-divisional Officer, Sonepat, 24 May 1935, 19 April 1935, 29 July 1941, 31 December 1942.

[116] *GI*: Home Poll, FRRP, 1935, 18/11/35, October.

[117] *CFSO*, Rohtak, 1925, N-5, *Confidential Report of DC Rohtak to the Governor of Punjab*, 25 August.

rather than to escalate it, because at the state level, they were together in the Unionist politics. Any breach in it at the local, regional level was to undermine their own public position of a common zamindar biradari, and the zamindar ideology, which was claimed to override religious/sectarian differences.[118]

It is significant to note here that the official characterization of this complex set of social processes as 'communal' or 'political' changed according to the demands and exigencies of the situation. In a similar situation in Rohtak district, the dreaded confrontation between some Jats and Muslims on the question of cow slaughter was projected as communal because no Congress worker was involved. But in certain other cases, for example, in Gurgaon district where the Congress workers were actively taking up these issues, the political epithet was commonly given more prominence.[119]

The colonial master's insistence on the communal or communal-cum political understanding obscured the complexity of the wide-ranging issues. It was not as if they were unaware of them. The wealth of confidential material available at the district level, as the given analysis shows, clearly indicates a far more comprehensive understanding of the issues than the officials were willing to acknowledge openly or publicly. They were, however, unable to correlate social complexities, greatly activated under colonial impact, to the emerging reality of an all encompassing religion which incorporated and articulated these complexities with great success. Moreover, all descriptions and evaluation of riots had to fit in the master narrative of the communal riots, created in official prose of the nineteenth century itself.[120] The district level understanding was, therefore, subsumed under the necessity of the larger colonial projection of an Indian society as mutually divided and inherently communal, in need of the honest brokerage of the British.

---

[118] Prem Chowdhry, 1982, 'The Zamindar Ideology of the Unionist Party: Ideology and Propaganda Tactics of the Unionists in South-East Punjab', *The Punjab Past and Present*, vol. XVI, No. II, October, pp. 317–36.

[119] 1931, 'HO Notes', Sheikh Khursheed Mohammad, DC Gurgaon, 17 August.

[120] For details, see Gyanendra Pandey, 1990, 'The Colonial Construction of Communalism: British Writings in Banaras in the Nineteenth Century', in Veena Das (ed.), *Mirrors of Violence: Communities, Riots and Survivors in South Asia*, New Delhi: Oxford University Press, pp. 94–134.

4

Contesting Claims and Counter-claims

*Questions of the Inheritance and Sexuality of Widows in a Colonial State**

The rising demands of patriarchy and the requirements of the colonial state combined to make certain historically crystallized customs and cultural practices enforceable in law. This had a crucial bearing on the inheritance rights of widows. The present essay seeks to establish the crucial role which the interlinked structures of custom, patriarchy, and state played in colonial Punjab in preventing widows from activating their inheritance rights; rights which, in turn, had an intimate bearing on questions relating to their sexuality. In fact, inheritance and sexuality emerge as two faces of the same coin such that to assert one was to have a direct impact upon the other.

This dual control, that is, of their rights of inheritance and their sexuality, was openly contested by the widows, resulting in prolonged legal battles and open confrontations. On the one hand, patriarchal interests were invoking the aid of the law to get certain highly contentious customs and claims accepted, stretching notions of legitimacy and morality and impinging upon the rights of widows; on the other, the widows were making use of the new legal and public space to counter these moves, activate their inheritance rights, assert their preferences in sexual and marital relationships, and make counter-claims of their

* This chapter was originally published in 1995, *Contributions to Indian Sociology*, 29 (1 and 2): 65–82.

own. In these efforts, whether widows' success in reaching and making use of this new public space was prompted by interested males, natal kin, or others, cannot be fully ascertained on the evidence available to us. On the face of it, the restrictive society in which they lived would hardly afford them this autonomy. It was also very difficult for them to checkmate male counter-claims and successfully assert themselves in the face of the colonial state, which selectively adopted customs and made them legally enforceable through its administrative and judicial agencies.

Crucial to all these attempts was the custom of widow remarriage in its *karewa* or levirate form as the most effective device to control widows. A levirate marriage brought an otherwise relatively autono-mous woman—autonomous in terms of her property as well as her sexuality—once again under male dominance, without endangering established kinship structures. From the widows' point of view, the widespread custom of widow remarriage, which in reality entailed enforced levirate, remained a highly repressive one. For widows, the right of inheritance as well as the desire for relative autonomy, not only economic but also sexual, took precedence over the socially approved married status, which they firmly rejected even at the cost of accepting the charge of unchastity.

However, the situation remained an ambivalent one, with many widows asserting their autonomy and yet others being speedily engulfed in the growing hold of levirate which, as the dominant custom of this region, successfully controlled their inheritance as well as their sexuality.

CUSTOMARY LAW AND WIDOWS: CLAIMING INHERITANCE

The Imperial government had, right from the beginning, adopted the 'preservation of village community' as a settled policy for Punjab. To this end, they advocated 'cohering of tribes' (rather than 'their break up') through the operation of their customary laws as an essential pre-requisite for controlling the province.[1] The general argument of British officials was that the mass of the agricultural population in this province did not follow either the Hindu or the Muslim law. Therefore, a general code of tribal custom was prepared by the settlement officers, who at each settlement had compiled the *riwaj-i-am* (record of customs and

---

[1] C.L. Tupper, 1881, *The Punjab Customary Law,* Vol. I, Calcutta: Government Printing, pp. 17–19.

rights), in consultation with the village headmen of each principal land-owning tribe in the district; those being acknowledgedly 'men of most influential families in the village'. These recordings excluded females, who never appeared before the authorities, and omitted such concerns as may have been accommodating to females.[2] Moreover, the majority of the men who assembled were for depriving women of their say.[3] In fact, the administrators noted down differences between what, according to them, could be termed as 'ideal customs', which the leading caste men wanted to portray, and the 'actual observance of these customs'.[4] Yet, the customs of the landowning class in regard to civil matters like succession, alienation, marriage, tenure of land, and adoption came to be settled primarily by the recorded Punjab customary law, which then became the first rule of decisions.[5]

Under the customary law, the land of the village was seen to belong to the male descendants of ancestors who originally settled and worked on it. Therefore, the male agnatic descendants alone, as members of the localized clan, had reversionary rights in the estate. Land was ordinarily not to be alienated outside this group. This meant basically that daughters and sisters who were potential introducers of fresh blood and new descent lines through their husbands had to be kept legally outside the purview of inheritance rights.[6] This logic, which excluded 'as a rule daughters and their sons, as well as sisters, and their sons'[7] from inheritance, still accommodated the widow. In fact, the right to inherit land as a widow was, to a large extent, almost the only way in which a woman could inherit land directly in the colonial period.

[2] *All India Reporter,* 1940, Privy Council, 17 August, cases from Lahore, Appeal no. 5 of 1939, *Musammat Subhani vs Nawab,* pp. 21–33.

[3] J.M. Douie, 1892. *Riwaj-i-Am of Tehsil Kaithal of Pargana Indri in the Karnal District,* Lahore: Civil and Military Gazette, preface.

[4] G.C. Walker, 1894, *Customary Law of the Main Tribes in the Lahore District,* Lahore: Civil and Military Gazette, pp. iii–iv.

[5] Tupper, *The Punjab Customary Law, Vol. II,* pp. 86–8, 99–100.

[6] David Gilmartin, 1981, 'Kinship, Women and Politics in Twentieth Century Punjab', in Gail Minault (ed.), *The Extended Family: Women and Political Participation in India and Pakistan,* Delhi: Chanakya Publications, pp. 153–73.

[7] W.M. Rattigan, 1960 [1880], *A Digest of the Civil Law for the Punjab Chiefly Based on the Customary Law as at Present Ascertained* (2nd edition), Allahabad: University Book Agency, (reprint), p. 747.

The general custom recognized by the British was that, in the absence of male lineal descendants, the widow came to have a limited right in the property of her dead husband, that is, only a lifetime's interest; ultimately the property passed to her husband's male line. If there were two or more widows, they succeeded jointly. On the death of one of the co-widows, the survivor took by survivorship.[8] In case the widow had children, her sons succeeded to the property and she had right only to suitable maintenance; her daughters and their issue had no right to inherit from the father. The daughters were only entitled to maintenance and to be 'suitably betrothed and married'.[9]

However, even this limited right of the widow was seen as a threat because she could claim a partition of the property on certain grounds, that is, when she could not secure the 'required maintenance' from her husband's heirs.[10] Although the condition of 'required maintenance', as voiced by the rural male population, was understood by the British to be 'a mere expression of opinion as to the custom they would like to enforce, rather than custom itself',[11] it was still accepted as an established custom and became enforceable through the courts. All such attempts of the widows, therefore, came to be challenged in the courts by the collaterals and the onus of proof was on her.[12] This meant that the court either implicitly or explicitly took the position that the required maintenance was indeed being granted to her by her deceased husband's agnates. However, the fact that this view was contrary to reality was even acknowledged by the revenue officials. In their considered opinion, the widow found it difficult to obtain her fair share of produce' as long as the holding remained undivided.[13]

Moreover, the lower grade revenue officials invariably accepted the rural male assumption that 'the widow will only waste the property when she obtains absolute control', and therefore, took the stand that

[8] Ibid., p. 121.

[9] 1907, *Hissar District Gazetteer*, Lahore: Superintendent Government Printing, p. 229.

[10] E. Joseph, 1911, *Customary Law of the Rohtak District, 1910*, Lahore: Superintendent Government Printing, pp. 136–7.

[11] A. Kensington, 1893, *Customary Law of the Ambala District*, Lahore: Civil and Military Gazette, p. 26.

[12] Such cases were very common. See, for example, *Punjab Records*, 1912, Lahore Series, vol. XIII, *Bhag Bhai vs Wazir Khan*, pp. 375–9.

[13] Joseph, *Customary Law of the Rohtak District, 1910*, p. 40.

'women are not qualified to manage their lands themselves'.[14] Although this action was not always considered 'groundless', it was still maintained to be 'untrue' in the case of 'better cultivating castes' like the Jats, Sainis, Rais, Kambohs, and some others whose women were actively involved in the cultivation process. Only after a great deal of scrutiny regarding the 'proper arrangements for the management of [the] holding' were these decisions reversed. There are a few cases in which, although the lower courts had dismissed the suit of the widow for partition, the individual judge accepted it on full scrutiny.[15]

On the whole, the verdicts of the higher court were mixed, but the majority of revenue assistants disallowed partition. Their decisions were thought to be in keeping with the 'very strong feelings among all the tribes against granting a widow separate possession'.[16] Although all claims to the revenue officials and to the higher court were initiated by the widows, such claims, in the opinion of British officials, were 'as a rule at the instigation of her own relations, who wished to get the management of the land'.[17] The validity of this observation is difficult to ascertain, specially in view of the fact that, with separate possession, the widow herself stood to gain enormously. She assumed full control over the estate with the right to get it cultivated through some other person, as she was customarily not allowed to undertake full agricultural operations herself. She could also lease out the land. However, this lease had validity only for her lifetime and lapsed in the event of her death.[18] She was also entitled to the enjoyment of its entire income without accounting to the possible reversioners for her expenditure.[19]

The widow could also alienate the property, though not sell it, for her own maintenance, for her daughter's wedding, or for payment of revenue, that is, reasons dubbed as 'strict necessity'.[20] That many

---

[14] Kensington, *Customary Law of the Ambala District*, p. 26.

[15] C.C. Garbett, 1910, *Riwaj-i-Am of Panipet Tehsil and Karnal Pargana in the Karnal District*, Lahore: Civil and Military Gazette, p. 12.

[16] T.G. Walker, 1885, *Customary Law of the Ludhiana District*, Calcutta: Central Press Co., p. 120.

[17] Ibid.

[18] Paras Diwan, 178, *Customary Law of Punjab and Haryana*, Chandigarh: Punjab University, p. 239.

[19] Kaikhosru J. Rustomji, 1930, *A Treatise on Customary Law in the Punjab*, Lahore: University Book Agency, pp. 52–3.

[20] In the case of widows, 'valid necessity' differed materially from 'necessity' in the case of male proprietors. Under the former, all such 'necessities' were

women had started to utilize this proviso can be seen from the constant
appeals made to the deputy commissioner protesting against widows
who were accused of alienating their property 'without necessity'.[21]
The district level customary law records show extracts of the mutation
sheets as well as lists of the details of cases in which widows of different castes commonly mortgaged or alienated the land for considerable
sums, all of which were challenged by the reversioners. The decisions
of the civil courts were 'always against the widows and in favour
of reversioners'.[22]

CUSTOM OF KAREWA: CONTROLLING THE WIDOW AND HER INHERITANCE

This self-assertion by widows in taking control of economic resources
after their husbands' deaths clearly assumed such proportions that, for
a variety of reasons, government action against it became essential.
J.M. Douie, compiler of *The Punjab Land Administration Manual* of 1908,
advised the revenue officials that the widows' attempts to partition
the land 'should be disallowed'.[23] However, since legally such advice
could not have held much weight, the only solution to the fast-growing
claims to partition was, according to official instruction, to be sought
in 'a firm anchoring of the widow in marriage'. This, the *Manual*
instructed, could be the 'only satisfactory arrangement against which
she had no appeal'.

Indeed, widow remarriage, known as karewa[24] in this region, was the
only effective way in which a widow's right of inheritance could be con-

---

subjected to the overriding restrictions of availability of income from the
estate. She had to prove that it was insufficient to meet the demands of 'legal
necessities'. But an alienation by a male proprietor for a necessary purpose was
valid irrespective of his income and means. If not proved by the widow, this
alienation attempt was invalidated (ibid., pp. 158–62).

[21] H.C. Beadon, 1911, *Customary Law of the Delhi District*, Lahore: Punjab
Government Press, p. 32; C.A. Townsend, 1913, *Customary Law of the Hissar
District* (except the Sirsa tehsil), Lahore: Punjab Government Press, pp. 30–4.

[22] Joseph, *Customary Law of the Rohtak District, 1910*, pp. 70–1.

[23] J.M. Douie, 1971, *The Punjab Land Administration Manual* (2nd edition),
Chandigarh: Government of Punjab, (reprint), pp. 270–1.

[24] For the special features and an analytical discussion of the custom of
karewa followed in this region, see my work, 1994, *The Veiled Women: Shifting
Gender Equations in Rural Haryana, 1880–1990*, New Delhi: Oxford University
Press. See also, Prem Chowdhry, 1989, 'Customs in a Peasant Economy:
Women in Colonial Haryana', in Kumkum Sangari and Sudesh Vaid (eds),

trolled. Karewa, as a rule, was a levirate marriage in which the widow was accepted as wife by one of the younger brothers of the deceased husband; failing him, the husband's elder brother; and failing him, his agnatic first cousin. One of the main reasons for making the marriage arrangements within the family was: (a) to transfer the de facto control of the deceased husband's land from the widow to his brother or to a patrilineal family member in case custom dictated that she retained her property after remarriage; or (b) to acquire full possession of her property in case custom decreed forfeiture of her property after her remarriage. Admittedly, different customs of forfeiture were followed by different caste groups in different regions of Punjab. Yet, the general custom, as operated by the colonial masters, assumed that the widow forfeited her right to property after remarriage.[25] Persons asserting anything to the contrary had to prove the existence of a special custom.

This stand of the Punjab High Court was in direct contrast to the firm stand taken by the Allahabad High Court in which it was consistently held that Section 2 of the Hindu Widows' Remarriage Act of 1856, based upon Hindu law under which a widow forfeited her inheritance on remarriage, was not applicable to castes where customary law permitted widow remarriage prior to its enactment. In a series of cases, it gave the verdict that the castes which followed the custom of remarriage also customarily allowed the widow to retain her property after remarriage. Despite this firm stand taken by the Allahabad Court, the Calcutta, Bombay, and Punjab High Courts continued to maintain that forfeiture was general, and that it applied to all Hindu widows whether the validity of their marriage was derived from the act or not. In Lucy Carroll's opinion, this was clearly an attempt at 'the propagation and imposition of orthodox Hindu values'.[26] In fact, the 1856 Act may

---

Recasting Women: Essays in Colonial History, New Delhi: Kali for Women, pp. 302–36.

[25] For court decisions leading to the forfeiture of property in cases where the widows remarried, see *Indian Cases*, 1930, vol. 129, *Parji vs Mangta*, case no. 767, Lahore, pp. 767–8; Punjab Records, 1893, vol. 8, *Hira Singh and Nathu vs Rani*, case no. 74, pp. 317–21; also, 1883, vol. 18, *Prema vs Pradhan*, case no. 137, pp. 414–19.

[26] For details of court cases and the stand taken by the Allahabad High Court in opposition to the other High Courts and its implications, see Lucy Carroll, 1983, 'Law, Custom and Statutory Social Reform: The Hindu Widow's Remarriage Act of 1856', *Indian Economic and Social History Review*, vol. 20, no. 4, pp. 363–89.

have actually created greater tension in the Punjab society by imposing
the Hindu Brahmanical law of forfeiture of a widow's property on
her remarriage, though remarriage had come to be recognized as the
general custom of Punjab. In Punjab, it was mostly the Sikh Jats who,
by and large, were able to establish their 'special custom' and stay the
forfeiture on remarriage. However, even among them, the exception
was only in relation to the brother; karewa with a cousin or a collateral/
entailed forfeiture.[27]

There are innumerable cases in colonial Punjab centring around the
question of the forfeiture or retention of a widow's inheritance on her
remarriage; the contest in such cases occurring to determine the respective shares or claims of male collaterals in the widow's inheritance. On a
widow's remarriage, the remarried partner of the widow stood to gain
if her inheritance was not forfeited, for he then became the de facto
owner of her inheritance. Thus, if her deceased husband was survived
by more than one brother, or if there was more than one claimant to
the deceased man's property and the widow married one of them, a
quarrel would inevitably ensue. Clearly, a great deal of tension existed
within the rural patriarchal order itself over the exclusive enjoyment of
the widow's inheritance by her second husband. Consequently, there
were numerous cases during the colonial period dealing with collaterals'
claims against the remarried widow which, in their essence, challenged
the exclusive use of her inheritance by one male.

CONTENTIOUS CLAIMS: ENFORCING LEVIRATE

In the process of redefining social norms through recourse to law, the
most disputed question was whether or not karewa included the father-
in-law in its ambit. The opinion of courts regarding the validity of the
remarriage of a widow to her father-in-law differed widely, being based
upon their own biased understanding of the customary law which itself
was not followed uniformly even within caste groups.[28]

In 1934, a case came up involving the validity of the custom of
karewa marriage between a father-in-law and his daughter-in-law. The
original case, initiated in December 1925, involved one Kishan Singh,
a Jat from Ambala district, whose son died leaving his widow, Rali. It
was alleged that Kishan Singh contracted 'illicit intimacy' with Rali

---

[27] *Punjab Records*, 1883, vol. 18, *Prema vs Pradhan*, case no. 137, pp. 414–19.
Also, see Rattigan. *A Digest of the Civil Law for the Punjab*, pp. 203–4, 207.

[28] Ibid., pp. 77–100.

and subsequently, performed karewa marriage with her. Later, a son was born to Rali. The *lambardar* of the village recorded the birth as illegitimate. This was challenged by Rali, who initiated a suit in the lower court for legal recognition that her child was the son of Kishan Singh. This was granted. In 1934, after the death of Kishan Singh, his collaterals moved the court to claim his land on the ground that Rali had no right to succeed to the estate of Kishan Singh as a karewa marriage between a father-in-law and his daughter-in-law was invalid. From the defendant's side, a number of 'important witnesses' deposed that such marriages were 'not uncommon' and gave several instances where the children of such marriages had also inherited the ancestral property.[29] However, the case was decided in favour of the collaterals. An appeal made to the High Court was also rejected. It was maintained that the custom of karewa marriage between a Jat and his widowed daughter-in-law was invalid, being repugnant to the ideas of Jats.

However, this judgment apparently did not lay down a general rule of custom applicable to the entire province. For instance, in another case decided shortly afterwards, in 1936, the Hoshiarpur district judge took a totally opposite view and held, on the evidence, that such a remarriage was valid by custom.[30] This case concerned one Joginder Singh, a Jat of the Garhshankar *tehsil* in Hoshiarpur district, who challenged the sale of 20 *kanals* and 7.5 *marlas* (approximately 10 *bighas* or 2 acres) of ancestral land made by his father, Dalip Singh. He held that the sale which was 'without consideration and necessity' should not be allowed to affect his reversionary rights to his ancestral property. The father resisted the suit on the ground that the claimant did not possess reversionary rights as the land was not ancestral. His plea was based on the contention that he (Dalip Singh) and his two brothers were illegitimate sons being born to Mehr Chand by his marriage with his widowed daughter-in-law, which was invalid according to custom. The case, therefore, hinged on the issue of the validity of the marriage of a father-in-law with his widowed daughter-in-law and whether children of such unions were illegitimate or not. The Lahore High Court upheld the lower district court verdict in 1937 by maintaining: 'The evidence shows that such marriages were attended by the *Biradari* and the sons and daughters have been married with Jat families ... How can

---

[29] *Indian Law Reports*, 1934, Lahore Series, vol. XV, *Jogahar Singh and Chattar Singh vs Sadhu Ram*, pp. 688–93.

[30] *Indian Cases*, 1937, vol. 166, *Joginder Singh vs Kartara*, pp. 719–23.

these marriages be repugnant to the community if the same community attends the marriage.'[31]

Evidence of several similar cases was produced in the court. One such case related to the Rajput Mehtons of Hoshiarpur district, who had availed of the customary law prevailing in the district to validate such an alliance. Documentary evidence in the shape of mutations of property rights in the names of the sons of a father-in-law and his widowed daughter-in-law were also shown where the objections of collaterals had been overruled. In view of this, the judges ruled: 'It may be that such marriages are perhaps not now looked upon with approval and are therefore rare. But that does not necessarily mean that they are invalid.'[32]

Clearly, in the British opinion, it was a recognized practice, even if out of date. On the other hand, it is equally clear that the validity of such marriages was dubious. They were disputed and challenged among those very caste groups which were supposed to accept them. The judges went on firmly to observe that they found the custom of karewa to be repugnant to 'modern notions':

So far as mere repugnancy to modern notions is concerned, a marriage with a deceased brother's widow can scarcely be considered to be less repugnant than a marriage with a son's widow. If the latter marriage is considered to be objectionable because a daughter-in-law stands on the same footing as a daughter, the marriage with a brother's widow would equally be repugnant as the latter stands on the same footing as a sister.

Significantly, it may be noticed that the customs could and were sought to be manipulated by interested parties, specially as they had come to have legal sanction.

Yet, the father-in-law's claim to the karewa custom, like that of the brother-in-law, presents a far more complex picture, varying according to status, region, and caste. For example, the regions of Ambala and Hoshiarpur remained two of the most economically backward regions of Punjab where even bride price was not uncommon.[33] Similarly, the practice of karewa, in the absence of a *dewar* (younger brother-in-law), to the *jeth* (elder brother-in-law), who held a reverential position similar to that of the father-in-law, and in the absence of both dewar and jeth

---

[31] Ibid.

[32] Ibid.

[33] Malcolm Lyall Darling, 1978, *The Punjab Peasant in Prosperity and Debt*, New Delhi: Manohar Book Service, (first edition, 1925), pp. 48–53.

to the father-in-law, seems to suggest that the ideology of a blood bond shared by all the male members of a family and *Got* (patrilineal clan) had at one time even accommodated the father of the deceased husband as a claimant of his daughter-in-law in sexual partnership and marriage. The practice was reinforced by the logic of retaining the widow within the family for reasons ranging from control of property, labour, her sexuality, and reproductive capacity, all of which hinged on the control of her options regarding marriage partners.

Therefore, the widow's right as to whom she could marry was not only severely restricted, but could be settled only by her late husband's family. And although the widow could not be compelled to remarry, she was not free to marry without their consent. If a widow married a stranger against the will of her former husband's family, a caste panchayat would compel him either to give her up or to pay the former husband's family a reasonable price for the woman, underlining their ownership and discouraging anything but levirate marriages.[34] So complete was the control over the woman and the question of her remarriage that it was freely admitted that in practice she was often forced to yield to their wishes.[35]

The British officials also favoured widow remarriage in its levirate form alone, and gave it validity through courts by awarding damages in favour of the former husband's family 'against the stranger who entices the widow away'.[36] Such a move was seen to be consistent with the demands of 'equity' and with the 'custom of many tribes and the idea of the people generally'. However, it was soon discovered that the Widow Remarriage Act XV of 1856 would invalidate such a claim if made through the courts, as Section Y of the act required the consent of a Hindu widow of full age for remarriage in order that the marriage

---

[34] *India Office Records (IOR): MSS.* Eur.D.188, 'Gurgaon district general code of tribal custom', handwritten by J. Wilson, Assistant Settlement Officer, dated 1879. This form of widow remarriage has now been identified as punar vivah, which literally means 'remarriage'. The first choice in remarriage, even now, remains karewa in its levirate form and only 'where none of the brothers accept their widowed sister-in-law as wife, *punar vivah* is performed anywhere in their caste'. See Government of Haryana, 1983, *Haryana District Gazetteer, Bhiwani, 1982*, Chandigarh: Haryana District Gazetteers Organization, Revenue Department , Government of Haryana, p. 67.

[35] Joseph, *Customary Law of the Rohtak District, 1910*, p. 45.

[36] See *IOR: MSS.* Eur.D. 'Gurgaon district general code of tribal custom'.

be construed as lawful and valid under the act.[37] This move had there-fore to be dropped. The officials regretfully recorded that this law had given validity to such marriages which would have been 'illegal accord-ing to native custom' as 'the tribal feeling was very strongly in favour of maintaining the power of the husband's family over the action of the widow in this matter'.[38]

In keeping with these sentiments and their own attitudes and requirements, elaborated upon in one of my earlier articles,[39] the British greatly encouraged the karewa custom, which saw enormous consoli-dation under colonial rule. Wherever possible, they were also known to force karewa upon the unwilling widows. In one of the more revealing accounts, George Campbell, a British official serving in Punjab in the 1870s, delineated his own role in such marriages as follows:

My trouble was quite the other way, to decide adverse claims to women. A special source of dispute was the obligation of widows (under the law, as understood by the men at least), to marry their deceased husband's brothers. They had a contrary way of asserting their independence by refusing to do so. I am afraid the law that I administered was rather judge made law; my doctrine was that if they refuse they must show reasonable cause. The parties used to come before me with much vociferation on the female side, and I decided whether the excuse was reasonable. But if the man seemed a decent man, and the woman could give no better reason than to say 'I don't like him', I said 'stuff and nonsense, I can't listen to that—the law must be respected', and I sometimes married them there and then by throwing a sheet over them after the native fashion for second marriages. So far as I could hear those marriages generally lived out very happily.[40]

REJECTION OF KAREWA: ACCEPTANCE OF UNCHASTITY

Despite the use of force, both patriarchal and state, widows had not always given in easily to levirate marriage. The resistance and revolt of widows to this peasant culture of remarriage, designed to retain them within the families of their deceased husbands, took various forms. For example, the district officials under the colonial administration saw a lot of petitions from young widows seeking sanction to marry men of their own choice, which they were firmly instructed not to

[37] Ibid.

[38] Walker, *Customary Law of the Ludhiana District*, pp. 39–51.

[39] Chowdhry, 'Customs in a Peasant Economy', pp. 307–36.

[40] George Campbell, 1893, *Memoirs of My Indian Career*, London: Macmillan and Co., p. 89.

entertain: 'Often a young widow will present a petition to the Deputy Commissioner for sanction to marry a man of her choice, but with such applications he is wise to have nothing to do.'[41]

Petitions, nevertheless, continued to be made by widows, courts being moved not only for purposes of marriage but also to deny that karewa had taken place. The denial of karewa occurred in two kinds of situations: (a) in the wake of attempts by male claimants to get the widow's property mutated in their names on the grounds of her remarriage; or (b) in case she had petitioned to remarry, when the deceased husband's brother sued for her custody alleging that a karewa marriage with him had already taken place. Widows' resistance to such attempts was apparently quite common. British officials noted in 1921 that criminal proceedings were most frequently resorted to by the deceased husband's brother who would lodge a complaint under Section 498 of the Indian Penal Code to prevent the widow's attempts to escape, asserting that a marriage by karewa or *chaddar andazi* had taken place, a claim that was firmly denied and challenged by the widow in question.[42]

However, it was difficult for widows to disprove the charge of remarriage, as even cohabitation could be, and was, recognized as karewa.[43] This charge could be easily alleged as the widow, in order to avail of her inheritance, had to remain in her deceased husband's house. This acted as a crucial leverage of control because she forfeited her life interest in the latter's estate if she took up residence outside.[44] In fact, it was a 'no-win' situation for her. She could hardly leave the house, or indeed stay in it, without seriously jeopardizing her inheritance rights.

This anomalous situation was most interestingly resolved by the widow denying karewa, even at the cost of accepting *badchalni* (unchastity), because the general customary usage as recognized in Punjab and

---

[41] 1910, *Rohtak District Gazetteer*, III-A, Lahore: Civil and Military Gazette, p. 90.

[42] 1921, *Census of India: Punjab and Delhi*, XV, I, report, p. 244. Also see, *Punjab Records*, 1900, vol. XXXV, *Indi vs Bhaga Singh and others*, case no. 115, Lahore, pp. 447–50.

[43] *Punjab Records*, 1897, vol. XXXII, *Chanda Singh vs Mussammat Kuri*, pp. 334–8; 1900, vol. XXXV, *Chet Ram vs Mussammat Asu*, pp. 197–8; 1911, vol. XLVI, *Har Dial vs Kali Ram*, pp. 249–56; *Indian Law Reports*, 1929, *Sohan Singh vs Kabla*, vol. X, pp. 372–80; *Indian Cases*, 1937, vol. 166, *Joginder Singh vs Kartara*, pp. 719–23.

[44] *Punjab Records*, 1911, vol. XXVI, case no. 65, Lahore, pp. 249–56.

as observed in the courts was against forfeiture of the life estate of a widow by reason of her unchastity, the onus lying with those who asserted a special custom to the contrary.[45] Hindu Rajputs, Brahmins, and Mahajans bracketed unchastity with remarriage, resulting in the women's losing all rights. But all other agricultural caste groups differentiated between remarriage and unchastity; on remarriage alone, the widow lost her rights.[46] These widows might retain life possession of the property of their deceased husbands, even though they were found to be unchaste.[47] In some cases where forfeiture occurred, the special custom was proved by entries in the riwaj-i-am.[48]

Commenting upon the heavy flow of badchalni cases, C.C. Garbett wrote of the Karnal district in 1910:

When the reversioners seek mutation on the ground that the widow had forfeited her estate by remarriage they are opposed by the widow, who, denying that she was married again, asserts that she is merely living in illicit union with her paramour, and that unchastity is no bar to her holding her life estate. These cases are rendered difficult by the fact that formal *karewa* is a ceremony so brief and simple that it is difficult to produce convincing proof, that in some cases ceremonies are not observed at all, and that in the case of *karewa* with the nearest male relative of the deceased proprietor mere cohabitation is generally sufficient proof of marriage. It is therefore difficult for the revenue officer to decide the exact status of a widow who admits cohabitation but denies marriage.[49]

Consequently, in innumerable court cases, the widows chose openly to deny karewa, accept the charge of unchastity, and in British eyes, the notoriety of bearing illegitimate children, rather than forfeit their inheritance by admitting to remarriage.[50]

---

[45] Rattigan, *A Digest of the Civil Law for the Punjab*, p. 201.

[46] Townsend, *Customary Law of the Hissar District*, p. 35.

[47] Beadon, *Customary Law of the Delhi District*, p. 33.

[48] Rattigan, *A Digest of the Civil Law for the Punjab*, p. 201.

[49] Garbett, *Riwaj-i-Am of Panipet Tehsil and Karnal Pargana in the Karnal District*, p. 38.

[50] See, for example, *Indian Cases*, 1931, vol. 29, *Parji vs Mangta*, pp. 767–8; *Punjab Law Reporter*, 1910, vol. XI, *Malan vs Ruia*, case no. 96, pp. 275–7; *Punjab Records*, 1912, vol. 13, *Kuri vs Des Raj*, case no. 102, pp. 315–16; 1893, vol. 28, Hira Singh vs Rani, case no. 74, pp. 317–21; 1883, vol. 18, *Prema vs Pradhan*, case no. 137, pp. 414–19. Also, see R. Humphreys, 1914, *Customary Law of the Hoshiyarpur District*, Lahore: Superintendent Government Printing, pp. 113–18, who gives a large number of cases belonging to different agricultural caste groups.

Here it may pointed out that there were some cases in which 'illicit intimacy' was accepted both by the widow and her paramour, generally her brother-in-law, and karewa denied. This was clearly with a view to preventing the property from being divided among brothers or collaterals. In such cases, the widow had the full public and legal support of the involved male. In other cases, however, the name, occupation, and caste of the lover were not disclosed by the widow. A few of these cases allege them to be of lower castes, such as Teli or Mochi.[51] The involvement of women from cultivating caste groups with men of low castes was not uncommon in the 1920s and 1930s. Not only have British officials written about these, but the exclusive female songs have also celebrated such liaisons.[52] Such liaisons were possibly born out of the close physical proximity enjoyed by the women from agricultural castes with their low caste menials while working together in the fields. In a situation of their continued stay in their deceased husband's home/family and close supervision of their activities, such associations, necessarily short-lived, were perhaps the only ones possible. Such cases were therefore significantly different and it is unlikely that the widow would have had support even from her natal family in such liaisons. Yet, it is equally unlikely that the open acknowledgement of her 'illicit intimacy' and 'illegitimate children' could occur without wider structures of support, whether conjugal or natal, or by other male associates or individual members of her community. However, in view of the paucity of source material regarding this aspect, it is difficult to be categorical on this score.

Analysing the phenomenon associated with badchalni, Humphreys recorded in 1914:

Widows constantly come forward and admit they have had illegitimate children, but deny marriage with the father of the children in order not to lose their estates in their deceased husband's property ... [A]s propertied widows (though cohabiting or remarried) they still had a lot of say in property matters.[53]

[51] For these, see *Punjab Records*, 1900, vol. XXXV, *Indi vs Bhaga Singh and others*, case no. 115, Lahore, pp. 197–8; 1888, vol. 23, case no. 90. *Partabha vs Phango*, pp. 241–2.

[52] These exclusive female songs are generally sung during festive occasions, specially during marriage ceremonies. A number of attempts were made during the colonial period by the reformists as well as the educated elite to put a stop to the singing of these 'indecent songs'. These attempts continue still, but without any success.

[53] Humphreys, *Customary Law of the Hoshiyarpur District*, p. 113.

However, the stand of the widows was due to far more complex reasons than were understood by British officials. The widows' stand becomes comprehensible if we keep in mind the implications for a woman of admitting to 'unchastity'. Acceptance of badchalni implied the woman's freedom from both economic and sexual control. It not only assured her the inheritance, as understood by British administrators, and consequent relative economic autonomy, but also sexual autonomy, by allowing her to retain her chosen partner rather than the imposed one, who was in all probability already married. The presence of a co-wife and the ongoing conflict with her and the husband for various reasons, ranging from his sexual attention to allocation of food, clothes, and other such reasons, were serious problems, which the widow understandably wanted to avoid.[54] From the point of view of inheritance, the coming in of a second wife, even if she brought her inheritance with her, ultimately introduced great tension in the family as their sons (from the same husband) were entitled to inherit equally from their father. All these factors made for an intolerable and humiliating position of women under polygamy. The perception of this experience has been very richly portrayed in the available oral tradition of nineteenth century Punjab.[55]

ACCOMMODATING UNCHASTITY: COMPLEXITY OF A CUSTOM

Though pressurized to cohabit, both by the patriarchal family as well as by the state judicial and administrative apparatus, the resistance of widows recorded by the British clearly emerges as not merely an assertion of her inheritance rights but also of her sexuality and her right to choice of sexual partner. Specifically, the widow's protest indicated her extreme reluctance to become a co-wife. Thus, 'unchastity' obviously had a different meaning for women than it had in the patriarchal construction.

Especially revealing is the fact that even if a woman was acknowledged as 'unchaste', the brother-in-law was willing to take her as his

---

[54] An understanding of women's reactions may perhaps be arrived at from Lynn Bennett's work dealing with polygamy among high caste women in Nepal. Lynn Bennett, 1983, *Dangerous Wives and Sacred Sisters: Social and Symbolic Roles of High Caste Women in Nepal*, New York: Columbia University Press, pp. 187–200.

[55] S.W. Fallon, 1886, *A Dictionary of Hindustani Proverbs*, Benaras: Lazarus and Co., p. 115.

karewa wife because of the benefits of the possession of land and of her productive and reproductive labour. There are recorded instances of brothers-in-law among Gujjars of Sandholi, Rors of Sikri, and Jats of Karnal taking over the widows as wives and their 'illicit' children as their own; or instances of pregnant women being married off to brothers-in law, or to the nearest male collateral, though pregnancy was known to be not due to them.[56] From the widow's point of view, this compromise, after initial defiance, seems to be associated not merely with possible threats of violence or with actual violence, but also with the question of granting legitimacy to the children since the eventual inheritance of property was allowed only to legitimate heirs.[57] A widow could legitimize her child/children only by adopting him/them as heirs to her husband. But she could only do this if she had been expressly allowed by her late husband to do so, or had obtained the consent of her husband's kin. Such consent would hardly be forthcoming unless she agreed to a karewa arrangement.

Quite clearly, widow remarriage and control of her sexuality emerge as contradictory aspects of a complex custom. On the one hand, custom severely restricted a widow's right to marry by enforcing upon her a levirate alliance; and on the other, by tolerating her unchastity, it showed an unusually flexible and liberal attitude to sexuality, albeit to hush up scandal and save the family honour.[58] At this historical point, the hardening of separate gender norms was partially stemmed. Property had scored above notions of chastity and badchalni, even within the given societal constraints. Wider issues at stake had stretched the concepts of legitimacy and morality.

Yet efforts to change matters legally did not slacken, since the landowning male opinion of Punjab was 'unanimous' in wanting to exclude the unchaste widow.[59] The judges also observed 'the universal feelings of the people in favour of forfeiture in case of unchastity of the widow'.[60] The British officials, worried that court rulings which upheld

[56] Garbett, *Riwaj-i-Am of Panipet Tehsil and Karnal Pargana in the Karnal District*, pp. 7–8, 35–8.

[57] Rattigan, *A Digest of the Civil Law for the Punjab*, pp. 239, 750.

[58] Garbett, *Riwaj-i-Am of Panipet Tehsil and Karnal Pargana in the Karnal District*, pp. 7–8, 35–8.

[59] Beadon, *Customary Law of the Delhi District*, p. 33; Garbett, *Riwaj-i-Am of Panipet Tehsil and Karnal Pargana in the Karnal District*, p. 24; Kensington, *Customary Law of the Ambala District*, pp. 17–18.

[60] Ibid.

this 'pernicious custom' could be considered 'subversive of morality in putting a premium on illicit union', specially when remarriage entailed forfeiture, put across a strong case for including badchalni as grounds for the widow's forfeiting her right to her husband's estate.[61] Many of them requested the judiciary to attach the same penalty to unchastity as to remarriage and not to dismiss the charges for lack of precedents, for they felt that it was 'almost impossible that instances should be openly quoted in a matter so intimately affecting the family honour of the people by which the custom is attested'.[62]

Despite this unanimity of opinion, the lawmakers and the administrators found their hands tied. The only solution thought fit was to remove the burden of proof as required in customary law, so that the clauses regarding unchastity could become operative.[63] This, however, could not be done due to the overwhelming 'proof to the contrary'; for, under the rules, the judges had to ask the plaintiff to prove the custom of forfeiture due to unchastity, which could not be done. Thus, notwithstanding the repeated requests of the landowning male populace in consonance with British officials' own predilections, the custom remained, with many widows availing of it. The judiciary regretfully felt its hands to be tied.

As the divisional judge observed in the *Dhan Ram vs Musammat Mari* case in 1889, in which the acknowledged 'unchaste widow' retained full enjoyment of her inheritance rights: 'much as my sympathy is with the plaintiff (Dhan Ram) I regret that I can do nothing'.[64] One apparent result of this practical impotence was to interpret these cases as cases of karewa which, if accepted, would lead to the forfeiture of the woman's estate. It is not surprising therefore that cohabitation was repeatedly equated with karewa, and rural 'laxity' in matters of karewa highlighted by the British, because, once marriage or remarriage status was acknowledged, a Hindu woman could on no account claim release from it.[65] As against this, there was no limit to the number of wives a man could have, either through *shadi* (religious wedding) or by karewa.

---

[61] Humphreys, *Customary Law of the Hoshiyarpur District*, p. 113; Kensington, *Customary Law of the Ambala District*, pp. 17–18, 38–9.

[62] Ibid., pp. 17–18.

[63] Garbett, *Riwaj-i-Am of Panipet Tehsil and Karnal Pargana in the Karnal District*, p. 39.

[64] Ibid., pp. 38–9.

[65] 1911, *Gurgaon District Gazetteer 1910*, Lahore: Civil and Military Gazette, p. 58; Joseph, *Customary Law of the Rohtak District*, 1910, pp. 40–1.

Interestingly, unchastity committed with a brother-in-law or one of the collaterals seemed reassuring, as karewa was, and could be, easily claimed. But, what perhaps caused most heartburn was the 'ordinary unchastity',[66] in which the charge of karewa could not be imposed nor could such an act cause forfeiture.

Quite clearly, the British acceptance of forfeiture on grounds of remarriage but not on grounds of unchastity was also tied up with their primary concern about sustaining the stability of rural society in the region, which the latter did not seem to disturb. In a judgement delivered in 1888 in a case of cohabitation, Partaba *vs* Musammat Phango, this became clear:

A remarriage causes the widow to pass into another family, where she acquires other rights and ceases to require her husband's share for her support; she can not take that share with her for the benefit of her second husband, or introduce new male members into her first husband's family, to whom she would no doubt make over the management of her share, and thus cause a contention which would end in the breaking up of the family. That remarriage would cause a forfeiture is therefore a most reasonable and a very general custom. But ordinary unchastity is a mere personal act of the widow, disgracing herself, but not *prima-facie* causing material injury to anyone else.[67]

The severe moral reservations about the 'premium on unchastity' were therefore ignored. For British purposes, remarriage remained 'an entirely different act' from 'unchastity'. Therefore, unchastity, although denounced vehemently both by the landowning male opinion and the colonial masters, came to be condoned by them for reasons of their own. The case cited earlier was initiated by a widow called Phango (a Hindu Rajput) from village Lohana in Gurdaspur district, who sued the brother of her deceased husband for a half share of the joint estate, sixteen years after her husband's death. Till then she had been given maintenance, which was also stopped on the ground of her 'unchastity', allegedly with a Teli called Shera. The case was decided in favour of the 'unchaste widow' who was self-confessedly 'unchaste', with an 'illegitimate' child of eight months. The property at stake was considerable, that is, 83 *ghumaos*, 5 kanals, and 9 marlas (now altogether equivalent to about 37 acres) of land, certain houses as well as movable property.

---

[66] See *Punjab Records*, 1888, vol. 23, *Fateh Singh vs Kalu*, case no. 107, pp. 306–7; also, 1888, *Partaba vs Musammat Phango*, pp. 241–2.

[67] Ibid.

LIMITED SPACE FOR WIDOWS: CONFORMING TO
THE CUSTOM

Howsoever limited, a certain legal space certainly existed for widows, and some of them sought to enter this space, with differential impact. Yet, it is quite clear that pressure to conform to custom was enormous. In fact, for a self-willed or recalcitrant widow, the situation was one of potential violence. Her last resort to seek release from this system was to run away—to escape violence or enforced levirate, or to enter into a self-chosen marriage or alliance. Although there are no sources in the colonial period which can be cited as instances, at the level of folk consciousness, this phenomenon was reflected in the popular association of running away with a *rand* (widow),[68] as in the phrase, 'rand bhaj gai' (the widow has run away), a phrase commonly used for any female. This 'running away' associated with widows, though not necessarily exclusive to them, is also reflected in local proverbs, for example, 'ughlatiyan nai kise kasar' (a runaway woman gets no traditional farewell),[69] which presumably refers to the fact that those widows who opted for a non-levirate alliance in remarriage stood deprived of even the limited right to land which they had come to possess after their husbands' deaths.

Thus, a widow's liaison outside the family, howsoever difficult, had advantages since, despite her open acknowledgement of the status of unchastity, the charge of cohabitation and consequent karewa could not be laid against her to deprive her of her relative economic and sexual autonomy. Hence, pressure was exercised by local persons to equate cohabitation, whether within the family or with a stranger, with remarriage.[70] Clearly, a certain space, albeit a very limited one, did exist for widows in the colonial period.

Nonetheless, economic hardship and socio-cultural constraints contributed to a wide-scale acceptance of the levirate form of marriage.

---

[68] Personal interview with an Arya Samaj *updeshik*, Ram Singh, 1988, village Bhaproda, district Rohtak, 12 August. Both men and women also maintained that such cases were common in the past and they are still confidentially talked about.

[69] Narrated by Ram Meher Hooda, 1986, Rohtak, 1 June. Hooda, born in 1938, village Makrauli-Kalan, Rohtak district, BA, LLB, Jat College, Rohtak, practising law since 1962 at the district level, has ancestral land in the village. This saying was confined mostly to men who recalled it being voiced by their forefathers.

[70] *Punjab Records*, 1891, vol. XXVI, *Sobhi vs Bhana*, pp. 144–7.

Apart from granting social and cultural approval and acceptance, karewa also allowed the woman to remain in the family into which she was married. And even though her karewa husband became the de facto owner of her land, the land, in many instances, remained in her name; more importantly, she remained on the spot, a full working partner. Moreover, given the realities of rural social conditions, levirate was considered a refuge by the widows for withstanding pressure, threats of violence, and sexual abuse from their husband's other male agnates. In addition, the hold which they had on their inherited land was tenuous when they had no son. A levirate marriage took care of all these constraints. The pressure of facing social ostracism, as against the social and cultural approval which the acceptance of karewa granted to a widow, rooted this system firmly in the soil of colonial Punjab, with many widows opting to remain assimilated in the family through levirate.

Despite deviations, therefore, the operating norm for widows in this region remained a levirate alliance. Yet, it is in these deviant cases, expressed in petitions to partition the land and/or to marry a man of their own choice, in open defiance of levirate alliance, in acceptance of charges of unchastity, and in runaway alliances that the widows' assertion of alternative choices in the face of heavy odds and opposition can be visualized.

5

Fluctuating Fortunes of Wives

Creeping Rigidity in Inter-caste Marriages in the Colonial Period*

Caste endogamous marriages are popularly acknowledged as the cornerstone of the caste system. Yet, inter-caste marriages, both between high caste men and low caste women and vice versa, have existed at various levels of society and in different regions of India in different historical periods.[1] The colonial period shows a serious challenge being posed to such marriages, making them highly contentious. Legally attacked, such marriages bring to the fore the growing contradiction between the needs of the colonial government and certain sections of Indian society. The fluidity noticeable in the colonial policy towards inter-caste marriages closely corresponded to the fluidity existing at the local level. The complexities in the legal processes and its interpretation, in combination with the colonial needs spoke for fluctuating judicial verdicts which either condemned or condoned such cases in different regions of India as well as within these regions in relation to different caste categories.

* This chapter was originally published in 2007, *Indian Historical Review*, XXXIV (I): 210–43.
    [1] Among others, two recent noteworthy works in this connection are: Indrani Chatterjee, 1999, *Gender, Slavery and Law in Colonial India*, New Delhi: Oxford University Press; and Radhika Singha, 1998, *A Despotism of Law: Crime and Justice in Early Colonial India*, New Delhi, Oxford University Press.

In Punjab–Haryana, this essay argues, the colonial government emerges offering legal recognition to inter-caste marriages though not without moral and ethical denouncement, at a time when certain sections were demanding such marriages to be set aside. The colonial intervention had activated conditions that let lose serious challenge to inter-caste marriages that worked towards strengthening the dominant norm of caste endogamy. The court cases taken up for analysis show claims and counter-claims which appropriate and/or invent or re-invent traditions and customs. Such contentious claims reflect on wider social and economic concerns relating to inheritance, widow remarriage, polygamy, bride price, and concubinage, all inextricably tied up with the issue of inter-caste marriages. The competing viewpoints highlight differing social and moral systems vying to gain supremacy and sanctity through colonial procedures. The major fallout in such cases was on the lower caste groups, especially in relation to the status and fortunes of the non-caste wife and her children. The creeping rigidity in inter-caste marriages and concomitant emphasis upon caste endogamy highlight a more dominating and wilful male-oriented social pattern being enforced which defined the structures of social difference and ranking among high caste/low caste, male/male, male/female, and children of different wives, far more sharply and emphatically.

INTER-CASTE MARRIAGES: AMBIGUITY
AND ACCOMMODATION

Inter-caste alliances or marriages in which caste endogamy had not been observed were more often than not confined to a secondary alliance rather than the primary one, both for men and women. In the highly adverse female–male sex ratio[2] of Punjab–Haryana, those agriculturists that were hard pressed economically were known to take recourse to wives from among the lower castes as well. In second alliances, caste groups like the Rajputs, Jats, Ahirs, among others, married women of caste groups other than their own and caste endogamy was not necessarily observed. Malcolm Lyall Darling, the famed writer-cum-civil administrator of Punjab, maintained that a Jat would marry almost any

[2] This region shows enormous difference in the male–female sex ratio—the lowest in the whole of India. In 1931, it was 844 females per 1,000 males and, in 1941, it was 869 females per 1,000 males. See 1991, *Census of India, 1991*, series 1, paper 1, provisional population tables, New Delhi: Registrar-General and Census Commissioner, India, p. 76.

woman he could.[3] In fact, Jats were particularly noted to be marrying women from the lower caste groups such as the Nai, Tarkhan, Mali, Jogi, Jhemar, and, very often, from among the Chamars. However, a faint pretence was kept that the girl was of his caste and an equally faint acceptance followed. A local belief maintains: *Jat ek samunder hai aur jo bhi dariya es samunder mein parti hai who samunder ki bun jati ha*[4] (The Jat is like an ocean and which ever river falls into this ocean loses its identity and becomes the ocean itself).

The emphasis upon question of (separate) identity brings to the fore certain reservations which seemed to have existed around inter-caste marriages even when they were not uncommon. For example, the children of a *Chuhri* or *Chamaran*, accepted in marriage by a Jat, were called Jats, though often they were ridiculed as *Chuhri ke* or *Chamaran ki*.[5] They were considered legitimate and had a right, often a contested one, to inherit land. The man's caste carried sufficient weightage and legitimacy. Use of such epithets, however, points to a process of cultural reproduction which was branding children born of such marriages.

North India is rich in folk tales, still popularly recounted, of low caste women marrying higher peasant caste men, as well as Kshatriyas and Rajas.[6] A popular tale tells of a *bhangan* (a sweepress) who married a *kisan* (cultivator), but being accustomed to receiving *rotis* (unleavened whole gram bread) from the hands of *kisani* (kisan's wife), she was unable to get rid of this habit. She therefore started to put rotis in all the *allahas* (alcoves) of the house and then make loud requests: '*kisani, roti diyo*' (give me roti, kisani). She was soon found out, her low caste stood exposed; but she was happily accepted and told to behave herself.[7] In a recent version of the same story, the woman on being discovered

---

[3] Several instances of inter-caste marriages in second associations were cited by witnesses in *Chanda Singh vs Mela minor through Mussammat Ruri* case. Several of these involved the dominant caste of Jats with lower caste women. For details, see *Punjab Records*, 1987, vol. XXXIV, pp. 334–8. Also, see Malcolm Lyall Darling, 1978, *The Punjab Peasant in Prosperity and Debt*, Delhi: South Asia Books, (first edition, 1925), p. 51.

[4] Personal interview with Khem Lal Rathee, 1986, Delhi, 24 May.

[5] Personal interview with Shamsher Singh, Delhi, 1986, 23 May.

[6] *William Crooke Collection*, MS 124, London, see a tale of the Holi festival narrated by Nathiya Chandu and recorded by Chhajmal Das, teacher of the Rudayar school, Aligarh district.

[7] This tale was recorded in 1886 titled, '*Ala de nivala*', by S.W. Fallon, 1886, *A Dictionary of Hindustani Proverbs*, Benaras: Lazarus and Co., p. 190.

gets beaten and hounded out of the house.[8] The story in both the versions emphasizes culturally two sets of people with differences of caste, culture, custom, belief, and behaviour. Popular among the landowning caste groups, the story highlights the perceived difference between Self and the Other. It identifies the Other and, in one version, accepts it by erasing the difference, and in another, rejects it outright by pretending ignorance of its existence. It highlights values of one group by encountering those of the other. The story retains its popularity in its second version as it justifies the popular rejection of inter-caste marriages that exists today on similar grounds.

By and large, the agriculturist caste groups did not really look down upon lower caste women who became their wives. This is aptly expressed in a local proverb still quoted extensively in Haryana: *beeran ki kai jaat* (women have no caste). It was also clear that social groups who were involved in such duplicity could not afford to and indeed, did not attach undue importance to caste purity if a man breached it. This social practice was rationalized by maintaining that: '*roti to bun jagi, naam to chul jaga, dono ka guzara ho jaga*'[9] (At least the food will be cooked, the family name will be carried on; both will some how manage to live together).

The most significant customary practice in north India that accommodated inter-caste marriages with ease was called *karewa*—a form of marriage, generally though not exclusively, associated with widows. The woman could also be a deserted, abandoned, or a divorced woman. The accommodation of different women, whether widows or not, and of different caste groups, meant the existence of a hierarchy in the custom of karewa, though unacknowledged in practice. For example, at the top of the hierarchy were those popularly and universally accepted higher caste widows who had entered into karewa with the brother-in-law in a levirate alliance or had remained within the clan and essentially formed a caste endogamous remarriage. However, karewa was not only levirate but also non-levirate as a woman could observe karewa with an outsider—a man from different family, clan, and even caste. Karewa, therefore, came to accommodate women of different caste groups, high or low, within its fold. The social status of such inter-caste marriages remained ambiguous. The non-levirate karewa marriage was not only lower in the hierarchy of karewa but also came to be challenged on

---

[8] Narrated by Vidya Vati, 1987, Delhi, 24 December.
[9] Shamsher Singh, 1986, Rohtak, 23 May.

a variety of grounds. Such marriages became highly contentious. The worst attacks came on women from the lower caste groups, as we shall see presently.

Karewa, as a form of marriage had special features of its own. Known as karewa, *karao*, or *chaddar andazi*, the custom is traceable to the old *Rig* Vedic *niyog*, a practice of levirate marriage, which was prevalent in the geographical region of Haryana–Punjab and associated with the early Vedic Aryan settlements.[10] Later, during the Mahabharata times, niyog came to signify cohabitation by the wife with men other than her husband under certain specific conditions like impotency of the husband and the moral and religious duty to beget sons to continue the family line. Eventually, niyog was given up as being inconsistent with increasingly pristinized and Brahmanized standards for marital chastity and devotion. In karewa, the man threw karewa, a white sheet with coloured corners, over the woman's head, signifying his acceptance of her as his wife. Symbolically, this gesture brought the widow once again under male protection; her being given 'his shelter' or 'roof', and with it, receiving colour in her life. With this gesture, he again subordinated a woman who had become relatively autonomous.

This custom represents social consent for cohabitation. There could be certain variations.[11] For example, it could take the form of placing *churis* (glass bangles) on the widow's wrist in full assembly and sometimes, even a gold *nath* (nose ring) in her nose and a red sheet over her head with a rupee tied in one of its corners. The distribution of *gur* (jaggery) or sweets could follow this. Significantly, this form of remarriage was not accompanied by any kind of religious ceremony, as no woman could be customarily married twice, that is, could go through the ceremony of *biah* (religious wedding). After karewa, the widow could wear jewellery and colourful clothes again and discard the drab colours that she had worn since her husband's death. It was said that in Karnal district, these ceremonies in karewa were performed only when the woman was the widow of a member of the family, and hence of the

---

[10] The increasing tendency in the late *Dharm Sutras* was to proscribe such practices. For details, see Gail Hinich Sutherland, 1990, '*Bija* (seed) and *Ksetra* (field): Male Surrogacy or *Niyog* in the Mahabharata', *Contribution to Indian Sociology* (NS), vol. 24, no. 1, January–June, pp. 71–103.

[11] For details, see C.L. Tupper, 1881, *The Punjab Customary Law*, vol. II, Calcutta: Superintendent Government Printing, pp. 93, 123; see also, E. Joseph, 1911, *Customary Law of the Rohtak District*, 1910, Lahore: Superintendent Government Printing, p. 45.

same caste; in all other cases, no ceremony was performed and a man merely took the woman to his house.[12]

In other cases, even cohabitation was considered sufficient to legitimize the relationship which carried all the rights of a valid marriage. The *rivaj-i-am* (record of customs and rights) of the districts and the records of cases decided judicially are full of instances where mere cohabitation as man and wife for a long period without any accepted matrimonial ceremony had been considered sufficient to validate the marriage.[13] However, for cohabitation to be accepted as remarriage, it had to be cohabitation in the man's house. Mere visits to the woman were considered 'adulterous'.[14] Here, it may be noted that though cohabitation was taken to be marriage, it could only be with a widow and not with an 'unmarried woman'. The question of cohabitation, as we shall discuss presently, was to become central to the issue of inter-caste marriages under the British on which a series of such cases were decided.

Karewa as a social practice was widely spread among the agriculturist caste groups in north India. The Jats led in the practice of karewa, and other agriculturist castes followed suit. Even among the Brahmins, reports indicate that karewa in its levirate form was being followed,[15] so that in a far-flung district like Muzaffargarh, the Brahmins had declared their adherence to this custom. Accounts of Brahmins marrying low caste women are also commonly available in folk tales found in Uttar Pradesh (UP) and Haryana.[16] Such appropriation by Brahmins shows a reverse sanskritization taking place through gender. Here, the dictates of land and property nullified the demands of high caste purity and status. The settlement officer of this district pointed out that, 'there

---

[12] J.M. Douie, 1892, *Riwaj-i-Am of Tehsil Kaithal of Pargana Indri in the Karnal District*, Lahore: Civil and Military Gazette, p. 6.

[13] *Punjab Records*, 1897, vol. XXXII, *Chanda Singh vs Musammat Kuri Asu*, case no. 54, pp. 334–8; 1900, vol. XXXV, *Chet Ram vs Musammat Asu*, case no. 54, pp. 197–8; 1911, vol. XLVI, *Har Dial vs Kali Ram*, case no. 65, pp. 249–56; *Indian Law Reports*, 1929, Lahore series, vol. X, Sohan Singh vs Kabala, Lahore: Superintendent Government Printing, pp. 372–80; *India Cases*, 1937, vol. 166, *Joginder Singh vs Kartara*, pp. 719–23.

[14] Joseph, *Customary Law of the Rohtak District, 1910*, p. 46.

[15] Government of Haryana, 1976, *Haryana District Gazetteer, Karnal District, 1976*, Chandigarh: Government of Haryana, p. 85.

[16] *William Crooke Collection*, tale recorded by a teacher of the Bahraich district; also commonly found in Haryana. Personal interview with Khem Lal Rathee, 1986, Delhi, 24 May.

was scarcely a Brahmin there who had even the slightest knowledge of the Hindu books or was acquainted with their names'.[17] The Brahmins of this province, who were not a priestly class but mostly landowners, consequently followed the dominant social custom of the region, in preference to the sanskritic mode of other Brahmins who brooked no remarriage at all and upheld *sati* instead.[18] Among other Hindu castes, the 'low grade Khatris' also followed this practice but others like the Bania and Kayastha did not do so, nor did the Sayyeds among the Muslims.[19] The Sayyeds were the highest caste among Muslims and just like the high caste Hindu, did not follow this practice. The low castes known as *achut* (untouchables) were among its chief followers. It is difficult statistically to calculate the number of people following this practice, but it is clear that an overwhelming majority followed it.[20]

Yet, taking wives from low caste, even in the karewa form, never became a norm as such or was practised on a wide scale. It is not unlikely that such a practice was already under strain in the pre-British period. In the colonial period, the courts offered a space to those who were challenging such marriage norms as well as to those who wanted to retain or enforce them. Such challenges show attempts at moulding or remoulding the existing structure and reflect a society rapidly experiencing shifts as a result of changes in legal and political system as well as in the general climate of opinion.

[17] W.M. Rattigan, 1960 [1880], *A Digest of the Civil Law for the Punjab Chiefly Based on the Customary Law as at Present Ascertained*, revised by Harbans Lal Sarin and Kundan Lal Pandit, second edition, reprint Allahabad: University Book Agency, p. xvii.

[18] Pauline Kolenda argues that widow remarriage in its levirate form is not non-sanskritic. According to her, it appears to have been an ancient north Indian practice, shared by all *varnas*, which higher caste gave up, rather than a 'tribal custom' that has not yet been sanskritized. Over the years, the Hindu law books began to advocate celibacy as preferable and even sati for the widows from the twice-born communities, while widow remarriage was appropriated for servants, the varna of Sudras, and other lower castes. This practice, therefore, has to be looked at as an alternative norm within a north Indian kinship system. For details, see Pauline Kolenda, 1982, 'Widowhood among "Untouchable" Chuhras', in Akos Oster, Lina Fruzetti, and Steve Barnett (eds), *Concepts of Persons: Kinship, Caste and Marriage in India*, London: Harvard University Press, pp. 172–220.

[19] *Karnal District Gazetteer*, 1976, p. 85.

[20] 1911, *Rohtak District Gazetteer, 1910*, III-A, Lahore: Civil and Military Gazette, p. 85.

THE COLONIAL POSITION: SHIFTING STANDS

As a general rule, the accepted stand of the British, enforceable in the courts, was against a legal recognition of inter-caste marriages in keeping with the Brahmanical strictures. Such marriages were considered by the British administrators, ethnographers, and commentators on law and society to have existed in the past but to have been obsolete by the second half of nineteenth century.[21] However, for the purposes of evaluating what constituted caste in judicial terminology, the British adopted the broadest ideological identification associated with the four-fold primary varna category which roughly coincided with the *jati* or occupational category as well. For instance, the Brahmin or the priestly caste; Kshatriya or the warrior caste; Vaishya or the trading caste; and the Sudra or the menials. Consequently, in the judicial view of caste, a marriage between persons belonging to different sub-divisions of a particular varna category was not prohibited and was legally held valid. Marriages between two different varna were declared invalid. However, this was not always so. The judicial decisions prove to the contrary. The general position of the colonial judiciary against mixing of varnas encouraged claims and counter-claims that had detrimental effect on the shifting cultural practices surrounding marriage.

To determine the varna identity, the British applied several tests, differing in different regions, as and when the cases turned up.[22] The result was awarding of different varna status to different caste groups

[21] Cited in *All India Reporter*, 1934, *Suram Chand vs Indar*, Lahore, 1934, pp. 550–3.

[22] Several tests were applied to determine the caste of a person. The study of Vedas and performance of *samskaras* or sacraments, with the exception of the samskara of marriage, were considered to be peculiar to the members of the of the three regenerate caste groups. But this, by itself, was not considered conclusive. The Calcutta High Court applied four tests: the wearing of the sacred thread; the ability to perform the homa; the rules as to the observance of the period of impurity; and the rule as to the right of illegitimate sons to succeed to inheritance. The Patna High Court, however, held that failure to wear the sacred thread or mere non-observance of the orthodox practices could not decide the question of caste. The Madras High Court accepted the principle that the consciousness of a community was a good test of determining caste; its customs and the acceptance of that consciousness by the other castes considered that the test of custom was the only possible test for the courts to adopt in the absence of any principle or rule, see S.V. Gupte, 1981, *Hindu Law*, Vol. I, Bombay: All India Reporter, p. 56.

in different regions as well as within regions. Such an exercise greatly complicated the procedure of judgement. For example, Kayasthas were declared to be twice-born in UP by the Allahabad High Court, but in Bengal, the Calcutta High Court accepted them as a general rule to be Sudras. Similarly, the Marathas (of the former Bombay Presidency) came to be divided into three groups for recognition of their caste ranking: the five families, the ninety-five families, and the rest.[23] The Marathas of the first two categories were declared to belong to the twice-born but the third to the Sudra category. This made the Tanjore branch of the Marathas, descendants from Shivaji, to be Sudras and not Kshatriyas.

In fact, the Sudra category under the judicial view was an all-encompassing one. It included all those who were not or could not be accommodated in the first three regenerate categories of the twice-born. The vast body of the agriculturists who constituted the largest proportion of the rural population belonged to different classes ranging from landowners and tenants of all kinds to agricultural labour, including untouchables and menials. The judicial clubbing meant that the cultural and customary norms of the landowning classes and caste groups were held to be true of all classes and caste categories.

In Punjab–Haryana, the British had adopted a general code of 'tribal custom' prepared by the settlement officers, who at each settlement complied the riwaj-i-am in consultation with the village headman of each principal landowning tribe in the district; these being acknowledged as 'men of most influential families in the village'. Consequently, the customs of the landowning class in regard to civil maters like succession, alienation, marriage, tenure of land, adoption, and the like came to be settled primarily by the Punjab customary law.[24] The opinion of the landowning caste groups entered the legal system and became binding on judicial decisions. Such a system was in keeping with the well-acknowledged social, political, and administrative importance of the landowning caste groups accepted and promoted by the British.[25] These became legally enforceable even for those classes and caste groups like the menials and untouchables who had significantly different norms of custom and behaviour. The operation of different codes

[23] Ibid., p. 58.

[24] Tupper, *The Punjab Customary Law*, Vol. II, pp. 86–8, 99–100.

[25] Denzil Ibbetson, 1916, *Punjab Castes*, Lahore: Superintendent Government Printing, p. 15.

of law simultaneously (customary law in some cases and Muslim and Hindu personal law in other cases), for different categories of people, which were for all purposes overlapping categories, created a great deal of confusion in the judicial decision making. Each case set a precedent for all subsequent cases, even where they contradicted actual practice.

In Punjab–Haryana, for instance, a distinct category defined as 'agricultural tribes' or castes was created by the Punjab Alienation of Land Act, 1900.[26] This was recognized for all administrative, political, and economic purposes and overlapped the 'martial caste' category from which the British drew their recruits for the British Indian Army. Martial castes were considered by the British to have entered the Hindu hierarchy as high caste men and, being warriors, they belonged to the Kshatriya category.[27] In essence, it meant that the administrative and political view of caste as understood and adopted by the British officials was very different from the judicial view enforced by the law courts. This contradiction was never resolved. There was not one dominant classifying procedure or principle that was used for the system as a whole. The British defined caste categories as it suited their requirements. The same caste came to be defined in so many ways. For all judicial purposes, the dominant agricultural caste groups shared the same status as the subordinate agriculturists and menial castes clubbed under the category of Sudras. As Sudras, they were allowed to intermarry. This meant that a marriage between a dominant agriculturist caste like Jat or Ahir with Sainis or the lower castes like Chamars or any other caste group falling under the judicial category of Sudras was valid, unless proved to the contrary by regional or local custom. Clearly, the colonial intervention had introduced complexities in the legal processes and its interpretation. Such a situation spoke for fluctuating verdicts, especially as it was interpreted and implemented by culturally and socially embedded members of colonial society.

[26] For some of the major landowning castes, created as 'statutory agricultural castes', in this region see Chapter 1 in this volume, p. 23n65. Also see Alienation of Land Bill of 1900, *Gazette of India*, 1899, part V. For a comprehensive account of this, see N.G. Barrier, 1966, *The Punjab Alienation of Land Bill*, 1900, Durham: Duke University.

[27] For British viewpoint regarding martial castes, see George MacMunn (Lieut-General), 1979, [1933], *The Martial Races of India* reprint, Delhi: Mittal Publications, p. 12.

UNDERSTANDING CHALLENGE:
WIDER CONSIDERATIONS

The British were offering legal recognition to inter-caste marriages at a time when colonial intervention had activated conditions which let loose serious challenges to such alliances, making them highly contentious. Considerations of material interests, combined with concerns of status, upward mobility, moves towards caste solidarity, and mobilization, necessitating attempts at maintenance of caste purity, all led to make inter-caste marriages highly controversial.

Economically, land emerged as a highly lucrative and marketable commodity in the colonial period. In the period between 1901 and 1931, for which the figures are available, alienation of land in the form of mortgage and sale, mostly by small subsistence landowners skyrocketed and the region came to be dotted with smaller and smaller holdings. The statistical data in a single district, Rohtak, are illustrative enough of this.[28] The figures for these thirty years show an 85 per cent increase in sales of land and a 73 per cent rise in mortgage of land. This prodigious increase in the total number of cases indicates the involvement of so many more agriculturists in land transactions. However, the high price available for land succeeded in limiting the acreage of land under those transactions. And although the annual acreage of land sold or mortgaged during this period did not radically change, the price of land sold or mortgaged rose by five times. Those who lost in these transactions were mostly petty landowners—owners of below five acres of land. The official statistics show that 73 per cent of mortgages in the Jat dominated district of Rohtak belonged to this category of landowners.[29]

Indeed, the steep decline in the lowest category of cultivators is confirmed by the census figures from 1911–51. These categories include not only the petty landowners but also the so called 'ordinary cultivators' (which included petty landowners and tenants) as well as agricultural labourers—all of who saw an enormous increase in their numbers.[30] The resultant fragmentation of landholdings, increase in the number of small holdings and in the numbers of small cultivators,

---

[28] See Table 1.8, Chapter 1, in this volume.

[29] 1930, *The Punjab Provincial Banking Inquiry Committee Report*, 1929–30, vol. II, Lahore: Civil and Military Gazette, 1930, pp. 872–4.

[30] For detailed reference see Chapter 1 in this volume, n99 and n100.

was serious enough for the viceroy to order an inquiry in June 1936. The inquiry was conducted by M.L. Darling, who after taking into consideration the evidence of factors like population growth, irrigation facilities, war and the consequent price rise, and other factors, confirmed that there was indeed a very large increase in the number of very small holdings.[31] The official village surveys of 1936 showed that in the last twenty years there was a decrease in the average area held by individual owners in seven out of eight villages in different districts of Punjab.[32]

These socio-economic changes affecting the landowning classes emerge crucial to their desire to limit the claimants to land, stop its fragmentation, mortgage, and sale. In this, the colonial legal structure came handy. The British courts, representing the higher authority, had opened a way for people to claim certain rights for which they perhaps could not fully rely upon the traditional panchayats. Consequently, attempts came to be made to avail of the colonial court to place a legal bar on the practice of inter-caste marriages, both a second marriage or a secondary or karewa alliance. Here, it may be pointed out that the British, as I have argued at some length elsewhere, who were keen to strengthen the hold of the existing peasant society on land, collect their land revenue, and maintain a constant flow of recruits to the British Indian Army, saw in the institution of karewa a way to maintain status quo as well as serve their interests.[33] More importantly, in the eyes of the British administrators, the enormous work contribution of a woman to the agrarian economy made marriage and possession of a wife an acknowledged 'economic necessity'.[34] So much so that a man's inability to pay revenue dues was put down to his single status. An *akela adami* (single man) was not expected to perform well agriculturally and a widower was considered 'half-paralysed'. The sooner he married, the better it was for the economy of the state and the government dues.

Consequently, despite reservations, the British encouraged karewa. For the colonial masters, karewa signified loose and lax morals and as

[31] *Darling Papers*, Cambridge, Box 5, file no.1, see letter of Laithwait, Private Secretary to the Viceroy, 3 June 1936.

[32] Ibid.

[33] See Chapter 4 in this volume.

[34] Darling, *The Punjab Peasant in Prosperity and Debt*, p. 53.

marriage, was vastly inferior, connoting low level of civilization. The British greatly frowned upon it and declared it 'a kind of disreputable matrimonial agency'.[35] Interestingly, their objections were not necessarily to karewa or cultural practices surrounding widow remarriage in its levirate form, but to an inter-caste association. In such a marriage, the union was generally between a high caste man and a low caste woman.[36] Given to applauding the 'magnificent physique' of the so-called superior agriculturist castes in agrarian and military professions, they actually bemoaned its biological 'deterioration' because of this practice. They were aware that any distinction, however subtle, between caste and non-caste wife under karewa system could hardly be sustained legally. Such a decision was likely to be set aside at the High Court level, as it frequently was.

It was not only the richer peasantry that was behind moves against regularization and acceptance of inter-caste marriages. The major thrust came from the lower ranks of the landowning classes, the small peasantry, whose existence and economic viability was at stake. The hegemonic ideology of rural Punjab–Haryana was that of the self-cultivator.[37] All attempts were therefore made to retain this status and enrich it rather than deplete and join the ranks of the agricultural labourers, which was threatening the peasantry at this time. To derecognize such marriages with other caste groups was one such way to retain the landed property, stem its fragmentation and depletion through mortgage and sale.

Although, karewa (in its levirate form) was encouraged and strengthened enormously in the colonial period, both by the colonial government as well as the landowning groups, the latter had started to make reservations in situations where caste endogamy had not been observed. In this, they were greatly helped by the work of the Arya Samaj which made its own contribution to the practice of karewa in this region. The Arya Samaj provided a justification drawn from the most ancient Hindu texts and offered protection to those who accepted it. In actual practice, the Arya Samaj emphasized the Vedic derived

---

[35] *Census of India, Punjab and Delhi, 1911*, vol. 17, part 1, report, p. 216.

[36] Darling, *The Punjab Peasant in Prosperity and Debt*, p. 51.

[37] Neeladri Bhattacharya, 1983, 'The Logic of Tenancy Cultivation in Central and South-east Punjab: 1870–1935', *The Indian Economic and Social History Review*, vol. XX, no. 2, April–June, pp. 121–70.

niyog, that is, the levirate aspect of it, and widow remarriage per se hardly formed a part of the programme they actually adopted.[38] It was because of its emphasis on the levirate aspect of karewa, which took care of the reigning concerns of the propertied caste groups, that the widow remarriage programme of the Arya Samaj turned out to be such a huge success in this region.

Growing pressure for observing caste endogamy arose not only from concerns of land and property but also on account of upward mobility drive among sections of landowning classes who had come to equate caste endogamy/purity with high status and mobility. This region shared with other regions, the drive among the landowning sections of the dominant caste which were showing a desire for upward mobility initiated by different caste group in north India, like the Kayasthas, the Kashmiri Pandits, and the Kurmis in the late nineteenth and early twentieth centuries.[39] Among the Jats, for example, a combination of factors like land ownership, comparative prosperity, and military recruitment, which emphasized their martial tradition in opposition to, and at odds with their ritual Sudra status, led them to claim Kshatriya status, though not necessarily Rajput status, which was being claimed by Jats of western Uttar Pradesh.[40] The upward mobility not only involved the challenging of existing norms and customs associated with low grade practices, but also meant emphasizing and shaping new ones in keeping with norms of the high tradition.

Significantly, such marriages were common not only among the agricultural caste groups but also the low castes. Indeed, in comparison with high caste Brahmanical notions of marriage as a sacrament and widowhood as an inviolate status, karewa as a social practice came to be associated primarily with low caste groups and compared unfavourably. The British officials recorded a great deal of 'shame and reluctance' on the part of the rural populace in admitting 'the extent to which laxity in

---

[38] For details, see Prem Chowdhry, 1989, 'Customs in a Peasant Economy: Women in Colonial Haryana', in Kumkum Sangari and Sudesh Vaid (eds), *Recasting Women: Essays in Colonial History*, New Delhi: Kali for Women, pp. 302–36.

[39] Lucy Carroll, 1978, 'Colonial Perception of Indian Society and the Emergence of Caste(s) Associations', *Journal of Asian Studies*, vol. XXXVII, no. 2, February, pp. 233–50.

[40] Ibid.

performance of marriage ceremonies in the case of union with widows has [had] become common'.[41] Rejection of cultural practices associated with low and Sudra status, a sense of humiliation and degradation felt by the practitioners, and its condemnation by the colonial masters made sections among many caste groups opt for a high-tradition norm which guaranteed social acceptance and recognition.

Moreover, in the first two decades of the twentieth century, extensive mobilization of different caste groups with differing results was taking place. This was done by using both the help of newly found caste associations and by strengthening the traditional caste panchayats and *Mahasabhas*. Both these modern and traditional forms of caste associations hinged upon claiming and maintaining a separate identity, with its separate history and culture for its caste followers. In this region, for instance, the Hindu Jats were mobilized and knit into a strong social and political force and successfully laid claims to all spheres ranging from political to appointments in the administrative and educational services.[42] In the days of high competition for jobs and other favours from the colonial government, the claimants, drawing their strength from their caste status, attempted to guard this status from encroachments. This was specially so, as 'Jat' along with 'Rajput' had emerged as 'a status term with widespread occurrence', embracing not just a locality but the whole province.[43] Since 'Jat' had assumed almost a 'generic' form, used by different caste groups to designate themselves, it is not difficult to see how they, along with other peasant castes groups like Ror, Gujar, and Ahirs, accelerated the move towards reforms to get rid of what they considered to be social and caste anomalies.

Under severe attack, the inter-caste marriages came to be contested both by the upper caste and lower caste groups for entirely different reasons. Colonial intervention had introduced discussions and claims about the status of such marriages, prompting some to deny and yet others to claim it. In the later category fell low caste women and the children of such marriages. They saw in the British regulated courts a way to claim legitimacy and inheritance denied to them by the

---

[41] R. Humphreys, 1914, *Customary Law of the Hoshiayarpur District*, Vol. XXVII, Lahore: Superintendent Government Printing, p. 40.

[42] For extensive mobilisation of Jats, see Prem Chowdhry, 1984, *Punjab Politics: The Role of Sir Chhotu Ram*, New Delhi: Vikas, pp. 40–60.

[43] R. Saumarez Smith, 1971, 'Caste, Religion and Locality in the Punjab Census', M. Litt. thesis, Deptartment of Sociology, University of Delhi, pp. 86–8.

collective power of the higher caste husband's male collaterals making counter-claims, and in certain cases, by the caste panchayats dominated by similar vested interests.

CHALLENGING KAREWA: VARIED GROUNDS

The existing judicial records suggest that from the late nineteenth century onwards, all sorts of grounds were being used by different sections of society to challenge karewa. These attempts especially concentrated upon those cases of karewa where caste endogamy had not been observed. One of the first cases to be adjudicated involved marriage between two different varnas. The decision of the court went against the professed general stand of the colonial government. In *Bai Gulab vs Jivanlal Harilal* case of 1888, *anuloma* marriage (of a high caste man with a low caste woman) of a twice-born man with a Sudra woman was held valid. The judge in this case was unable to accept the view that 'because such marriages are obsolete, they are illegal or prohibited by law', and held that 'the prohibition must be found in the law books or the usage having the force of law, and such usage must be proved like any other fact'.[44]

Recalling this case, the Bombay High Court in a later 1931 case of *Natha Nathuram vs Chhota Lal Daj Bhai Mehta*, upheld a similar marriage of a Brahmin man with a Sudra woman, Koli (Chamar) by caste, as valid and her son legitimate though entitled to one-tenth of his father's property. The judgement, citing Justice J. Shah in Bai Gulab case, maintained:

[T]he attitude of the caste as prohibiting inter-caste marriages is generally indicative of nothing more than the disapproval of such marriages according to the rules of practice of each different caste. It does not afford a sufficient justification for treating as illegal what has not been prohibited but in terms contemplated and allowed by law.[45]

In an exactly opposite *pratiloma* case (marriage of a high caste woman and a low caste man), the courts again took a stand which went contrary to their professed legal position. The British had taken a stand against such marriages and declared them as invalid throughout India on the basis that a higher caste woman could not contract a legal marriage

---

[44] Cited in *Indian Cases*, 1931, Bombay series, vol. 30, pp. 17–24. For similar cases, see Gupte, *Hindu Law*, Vol. II, p. 582.

[45] *Indian Cases*, 1931, Bombay series, vol. 30, pp. 17–24.

with a low caste man.[46] In *Sespuri vs Dwarka Prasad* case from UP in 1912, the former brought a case against his kins who had deprived him of his inheritance by declaring him an illegitimate son of one Sidha. Sidha, a Thakur by caste, had married a Brahmin woman. Sespuri was their son. The court of first instance as well as appellant and the higher court declared this as a pratiloma marriage and hence illegal. Sespuri was declared illegitimate.[47] This was a landmark judgement that came to be cited in most such pratiloma cases.

Yet, in the Punjab case, the colonial masters legally accepted marriages across varna divisions as well as pratiloma marriages valid, and children born of such unions as legitimate.[48] The resultant cases were born out of this ambiguity of situation and contradictory judicial decisions. The attempts in colonial Punjab to invoke the Hindu law applicable to the female status to refute the customary law which was the operable norm did not find favour with a government anxious to enforce karewa. For example, in the case of *Sahib Ditta vs Musammat Bela*, 1900, the reversioners challenged a karewa marriage between a Jat and a Brahmin woman and sought to deprive her children of their inheritance on the ground of illegitimacy.[49] The petitioners contended that 'if a Brahmin widow cannot marry a Brahmin, why should it be held that she can marry a Jat'. The ideology of the 'purity of caste', as in the Brahmanical structure, was being claimed as a tradition and cultural norm. The case for invalidating such a marriage was made from the point of view of the higher status considerations of a woman who could not make a pratiloma marriage. Legally, however, this was untenable

---

[46] For pratiloma marriages, see *Indian Cases*, 1926, vol. 97, *Munilal vs Shyama Sonarin*, pp. 347.

[47] *Allahabad Law Journal*, 1912, vol. 10, *Sespuri vs Dwarka Prasad*, pp. 181–2.

[48] In an early 1890 case from the Ambala district, marriage presumed from long cohabitation between a Brahmin woman and a Rajput man was held valid by custom and the issue of such a union legitimate. The case was considered important as it showed relaxation of prohibition against inter-caste marriage between two varnas, even by the Brahmins. By and large, inter-varnas marriages not recognized legally, were considered against religious texts of the Hindus, and set aside. Case cited in *Punjab Law Reporter*, 1908, vol. IX, *Haria vs Kanhaya*, pp. 137–46. For other similar cases, see All India Reporter, *Suram Chand vs Inder*, pp. 550–3.

[49] *Punjab Record*, 1900, vol. XXXV, case no. 50, pp. 184–46; 1910, vol. XLV, *Musammat Kaur vs Sawan Singh*, pp. 232–4; 1897, vol. XXXII, *Chander Singh vs Musammat Mela*, pp. 334–8; *Indian Law Report*, 1929, Lahore series, vol. V, *Sohan Singh vs Kale Singh*, pp. 372–80.

as after the Widow Remarriage Act of 1856, all widows, regardless of their caste, had the right to remarry.

However, in delivering the verdict, the judges opted to view the case from the point of view of the Jat agriculturist man. They rejected the plea on the ground that marriage between Jats and Brahmins, although the later belonged to a higher caste, was recognized by the Jat *biradari* (community) and the children of such unions were considered legitimate heirs. This judicial stand not only negated the colonial government's general principle of refusing to grant recognition to a pratiloma alliance but also the fact that marriage alliance between two different varnas was prohibited as a general rule. Both these practices were considered to be firmly against the Hindu law. Yet, in Punjab–Haryana, where custom was given precedence, both these norms were ignored repeatedly.

The same position was held in a series of cases involving lower castes like Chamars and others.[50] It was acknowledged that any Hindu widow, from a Brahmin to a Chamar, could be married to a man of agriculturist caste by karewa.[51] The coupling of these two caste groups, high and low, is significant. In Haryana region of Punjab, the norms were dictated by the dominant agriculturist castes—the chief being the Jats. Consequently, the higher ritual ranking of the Brahmin dropped when confronted with the harsh reality of existence in which the Brahmins were an agriculturist rather than a priestly caste. Moreover, in relation to the Jats, they were numerically and socio-economically far inferior.[52]

Interestingly, the landowning Jats, well recognized for establishing secondary alliances with low caste women, emerged as major challengers of such marriages. One of the principal contentions of Jats was to lay claim to higher status within the Sudra varna category. They challenged the British position on the use of Sudras as an umbrella category. They contented that Jats as a 'touchable caste' could not be equated with the 'untouchable' castes groups such as Chamars, Jhimars, Kori,

[50] *Punjab Record*, 1897, *Musammat Kaur vs Sawan Singh*, pp. 232–4; vol. XXXII, *Chander Singh vs Musammat Mela*, pp. 334–8; *Indian Law Report*, 1929, Lahore series, vol. V, *Sohan Singh vs. Kala Singh*, pp. 372–80.

[51] Douie, *Riwaj-i-Am of Tehsil Kaithal of Pargana Indri in the Karnal District*, p. 4. The Jats of Indri in Karnal district quoted a case in which a man was turned out of the biradari for marrying a Brahmin woman by karewa.

[52] For the status of Brahmins in this region, see Prem Chowdhry, 1994, *The Veiled Women: Shifting Gender Equations in Rural Haryana, 1880–1990*, New Delhi: Oxford University Press, pp. 110–11, 225.

Koli, and others. Sections of upwardly mobile Jats sought to argue that they were a higher caste among the Sudras. The claim was based upon gaining recognition of the existence of stratification and hierarchy among the Sudras as accepted by the British rule for other varna categories. In *Sohan Singh vs Kabla Khan* case of 1929,[53] the male collaterals of one Khushal Singh, a Jat Sikh of village Sawan ke in Sheikhpur district, sued for the ownership of land on the basis that the two minor sons of Khushal Singh by Isher Kaur were illegitimate as Isher Kaur was from untouchable caste and her marriage to a Jat man was illegal. Such a marriage was challenged on the ground that a general rule which validated all marriages between different sub-divisions of the Sudra caste could not be extended to inter-caste marriages of males of the pure Sudra caste like the Jats with woman of the 'unclean' classes, 'touch with whom was pollution'. The judges negating this claim, upheld the marriage while noting that 'such marriages were not of recent innovations but seem to have been recognised as valid long before the British occupation.'

In certain cases where Rajputs were involved, such challenges to karewa were perhaps more pronouncedly towards an upward mobility move than those among the Jats, who were not so sharply divided and hierarchized as the Rajputs. In Punjab, for instance, the inheritance of one Jangi, son of a Rajput man by karewa marriage with a Tarkhan woman, was challenged in 1911 by the male collaterals of his deceased father on the ground that marriage between a Rajput man—a high caste Kshatriya man—and a Sudra woman was illegal and their son illegitimate.[54] Clearly, the status of a low caste woman and her son was devalued and challenged after the death of her husband. In a society where children, particularly sons, were highly valued and hardly considered illegitimate, there emerged attempts to delegitimize them. This was not merely to limit the claimants to land, but more importantly, a shiftage of kin and family solidarity from the mixed blood son to the 'pure' among the kins. The caste of the father was no longer sufficient to grant a child his status. The move was towards adoption of the concept of blood purity by observing caste endogamy.

In this case, the challenge emanated from a section of Rajputs called Jhabra Rajputs, who, as the court observed, were held in 'very

---

[53] *Indian Law Reporter*, 1929, Lahore series, vol. X, pp. 372–80.
[54] *Punjab Record*, 1911, vol. XLVI, *Hardayal vs Kali Ram*, Lahore, pp. 249–56.

low esteem and category among Rajputs in general'. In an attempt at upward mobility, they denounced karewa as a customary social practice in order to be at par with other Rajputs and claimed kshatriahood. The judges dismissing the case maintained:

No doubt high class Rajputs are Kshatriyas as a Tarkhan is a Sudra; but Jangi was a Jhabra Rajput and we are inclined to think that he was not a Kshatriya ... there are five classes of Rajputs, each class being much subdivided and we find that the Jhabras are almost lowest in the fifth class, and is said that even the forth class (the Rathis) are hardly to be regarded as true Rajputs as they practice karewa and do not marry into the higher class. Further the marriage customs of the higher and lower kinds of Rajputs are by no means the same.

In Punjab, the Jhabra Rajputs were agriculturists and were categorized among the Sudras by the British and marriage between two sub-castes of Sudras was held valid.

Yet others took recourse to challenging the 'nature' of marriage or remarriage itself. In *Musammat Kishan Dei vs Seo Paltan* case of 1925,[55] the plaintiffs argued that 'a *karao* marriage being contracted by the consent of the parties, would be identified with the *gandharva* form of marriage mentioned by Manu ... *Gandharva* is one of the most primitive, and is nothing more than unregulated indulgence of lust.' They sought to declare it invalid on the basis that 'in widow remarriage there is no giving by the father and the widow herself is a principal in the transaction'. This was very much the ground accepted by the colonial government, as I have argued elsewhere,[56] in relation to unmarried girls who made runaway marriages, without the consent of their male guardians. In such marriages, there was no formal giving of the maiden in marriage.

This was a construction of the notion of marriage on the basis of Hindu *Dharmasastra* as recognized by the colonial system. Within this ambit, the attempt was to declare that karewa was not a 'proper marriage'. The Dharmasastra of Manu, as well as the majority of jurists, recognized eight forms of marriage arranged in a hierarchy of esteem.[57] In this, the four forms under the *kanyadan* (gift of a virgin) marriage

---

[55] *Indian Cases*, 1925, vol. 90, *Musammat Kishan Dev vs Sheo Paltan*, Allahabad, pp. 358–64.

[56] See, for instance, Prem Chowdhry, 2004, 'Private Lives, State Intervention: Cases of Runaway Marriage in Rural North India', *Modern Asian Studies*, vol. 38, no. 1, February, pp. 55–84.

[57] Thomas R. Trautmann, 1981, *Dravidian Kinship*, Cambridge: Cambridge University Press, pp. 288–91.

called *Brahma*, *Daiva*, *Arsa*, and *Prajapatya* were the highest forms. Considered an act of religious charity, the associated ideology in kanyadan marriage deemed that nothing could be taken in exchange for the bride. The non-kanyadan marriage forms included *Asura*, *Gandharva*, *Rakshsa*, and *Paisaca*, condemned and degraded as inferior forms, and were not considered worthy of recognition. In the non-kanyadan marriage, the Gandharva form was particularly contemptible as it was considered to be 'the voluntary union of a maiden and her lover...which springs from desire and has sexual intercourse for its purpose.'[58] The self-regulation of sexual activity by a woman under Gandharva form of marriage turned it lower in scale than Asura form that rested on the payment of bride price.[59] Consequently, it was being argued that such alliances were not deserving of legal recognition of the status of marriage at all.

The large number of cases suggest a clear move towards observing caste endogamy in karewa marriages by declaring those cases as invalid, where caste endogamy had not been observed. In Punjab, by and large, these attempts failed at the high court level, though they generally succeeded at the lower courts. In UP however, the Allahabad High Court recognized such contentions, thus opening floodgates of similar claims elsewhere too. In *Balraj vs Jai Karan* case of 1931 from Meerut, the male collaterals usurped the land of one Balraj Singh on the basis that the karewa marriage of his grandmother, who was a hill woman from the tribe of Naiks, to his grandfather, who was Gujar by caste was not valid. This marriage had taken place forty years ago and the biradari (community) had recognized the marriage. The daughters and sons of the two had married into Gujar families, which were attended by a large number of caste men and relatives. More

---

[58] Ibid., p. 289.

[59] Most caste groups, whose lower class members were well known to charge bride price, roundly assailed it. Legally recognized by the British as a customary practice among many of the agricultural caste groups, it, however, came close to the *Arsa* form of marriage, considered one of the inferior forms among the kanyadan marriage. The lowest form in the kanyadan marriages decreed in the Dharmasastra was the Arsa marriage, which comes very close to the Asura form, designated as a non-kanyadan marriage. In the former, the emphasis is on 'gift' of cattle by the groom to the father of the bride in accordance with the scriptural injunction, and in the latter, the emphasis is on purchase by the groom of a 'sale' by the father. Even the jurists were hard put to differentiate these two forms. For details, see ibid., pp. 290–1.

than a hundred persons of his father's Gujar biradari were said to have participated in celebrations. Yet, the judges ruled:

We are satisfied that for a valid *karao* it is necessary that there should be a caste marriage and not an inter-caste marriage. In a caste-ridden Hindu India it is almost inconceivable that a man of one caste could marry a woman of another caste, with out infringing the caste rules. Even Mr Crooke refers to non-caste women kept by Gujars as 'concubines' and not as '*karao* wives'. In the *wajib-ul-arz* of village Bhawapur and Baklana, there are clear statements that *karao* marriages would be made only with caste-women and not with non-caste women…There is a large number of witnesses examined by the defendants who have proved that all the *karao* marriages take place among the caste-people only.[60]

The case was decided in favour of the male collaterals. The dead grand-mother, after nearly half a century, was reduced to the position of a 'prostitute' and a 'concubine' and her descendants illegitimate.

COHABITATION AS KAREWA: CONCUBINE OR WIFE
The attack on karewa (whether inter-caste or intra-caste) as a form of marriage was taking place at a time when cohabitation was legally recognized as marriage. In karewa, the lack of ceremonies and acceptance of cohabitation as marriage opened up space for claims and counter-claims leading to both denial of karewa and its reiteration by interested parties. There were discussions in the colonial period in judicial and executive agencies, whether specific forms of unions could be called marriage or mere cohabitation.[61] The western notions of marital relationship and union combined with the Brahmanical categorization of marriage to make adverse judgements about cultural diversity existing in India. These discussions and value judgements were undoubtedly used by the colonized to claim or deny their marital relationships on the basis of their own inclination, interests, status considerations, and upward mobility moves.

Recognition of cohabitation as marriage was both accepted and challenged by interested parties. It came under attack not only from upwardly mobile male sections of rural society but also, as I have argued elsewhere at great length, from a section of women themselves.[62] In order to protect their relative economic and sexual autonomy, these

[60] *All India Reporter*, 1931, *Balraj Singh vs Jai Karan*, Allahabad, pp. 107–111.
[61] Chatterjee, *Gender, Slavery and Law in Colonial India*, pp. 78–85.
[62] See Chapter 4 in this volume.

widows accepted the charge of *badchalni* (unchastity), even notoriety of bearing illegitimate children, but refused karewa and cohabitation as karewa. On the other hand, their brothers-in-law were willing to accept such illegitimate children as their own by claiming cohabitation as marriage to appropriate the land. Such challenges, however, were well within the fold of caste endogamy.

The landowning caste groups, however, frequently denied the status of a wife to a non-caste karewa woman by declaring her a concubine who had merely 'cohabited' with the man and was not married to him. Once such a woman became a widow, perhaps for a second time, she was disinherited and her children were declared illegitimate. Although this was mostly done in cases where caste endogamy had not been observed in a karewa marriage, even the caste marriages were not outside this challenge. Such moves were especially noticeable where low caste women were involved.

One of the reasons why low caste women were under special attack may well have been because such a woman, for all purposes, was purchased from her parents and generally made to terminate all connections with them after marriage. This was essential to keep the myth of her belonging to a higher caste. This, however, meant that kinship network normally available to a caste endogamous/equal status marriage was denied to the lower caste woman. The weakness of a lower caste woman's natal family may well have accounted for the large number of such attempts made by the higher caste male collaterals of her husband. The inferior kinship networks in terms of class/caste/status could not act as avenues of social sanction and support. The low caste woman, without the security of her natal family network and support system, was vulnerable as a widow. Even her children could be denied their rights, as attempts were made to do so.

In *Askaur vs Sawan Singh* case of 1910,[63] the karewa woman moved the court to legally claim her widowhood and her property which had been appropriated by the male collaterals of her deceased husband. The male collaterals rejected that karewa between Natha Singh, a Jat, and Askaur, a Koli by caste, had taken place and insisted that 'the Chamari' had merely lived as the man's concubine. As such, neither she nor her children had any claims to the property. Natha Singh had purchased

---

[63] *Punjab Record, Musammat Kaur vs Sawan Singh*, pp. 232–4.

Askaur from Karachi through an intermediary. Upholding the karewa marriage, the judges maintained:

The agreement executed by Prabhu Dial, who brought the plaintiff from Karachi and by plaintiff herself, shows that she was being made over to Natha Singh for the purposes of being married to him by *chaddar andazi*. Jats do procure women in this way, and it is prima facie more likely that the customary marriage by karewa took place between Natha Singh and Musammat Askaur than that the latter lived as concubine of the former.[64]

In case after case, the court was moved by the woman and her heirs to seek recognition of cohabitation as karewa form of marriage, as these associations, after the death of the husband, were not being honoured by his male collaterals. In *Fateh Muhammad Khan vs Abdul Rehman Khan* case of 1931 from Hoshiarpur, the former moved the court to deny the status of concubinage imposed upon his widowed mother, to assert his legitimacy to be the son of late Shah Nawaz Khan and to seek possession of the inheritance appropriated by his father's collaterals.[65]

The acceptance of cohabitation as karewa was clearly under strain. In 1913, for instance, Kalu, a Sikh Jat from Chak Kota, district Gurdaspur, felt it necessary to perform the ceremony of chaddar andazi with Budni, after a son was born to them. After Kalu's death, his male collaterals refused to recognize his son. They declared him illegitimate, contending that he was born before the ceremony of chaddar andazi was performed. The judges, however, dismissed their claim by observing: 'We can not force standards of morality observed by high civilised countries upon Punjab villages.'[66]

The non-acceptance of cohabitation as karewa reduced a married woman to the position of a concubine. Indeed, the charge of concubinage could very often stick even in the case of a karewa marriage as, in many instances, karewa was not a levirate marriage and the wife was a purchased one. This was because there was a thin line between purchase or sale of a woman, as wife or for immoral purposes, that is, concubinage or prostitution. When concubinage was insisted upon and children declared illegitimate, such innovations claimed an alternative social and moral system. These attempts can be seen as legitimizing the

---

[64] Ibid.

[65] *Punjab Law Reporter*, 1931, vol. XXXII, *Fateh Muhammad Khan vs Abdul Rehman Khan*, pp. 68–71.

[66] *Punjab Law Reporter*, 1913, vol. XIV, *Ishar Singh vs Budani*, pp. 595–8.

exploitation of a woman's productive and reproductive potential without any moral strictures and responsibility. These claims were based
upon, and in return reiterated, the claims of higher caste male members
to the bodies and services of lower caste women. They reinforced the
stereotypical perceptions of low caste women as sexually available and
morally lax. There is a strong association of untouchable women with
prostitution all over India and not necessarily in the north alone.[67] An
extension of such a negative perception also meant that in relation to a
high caste man, a low caste woman could hold no better position than
that of a concubine and produce illegitimate children. These protesta-
tions, in return, reflected upon low caste morality and masculinity. This
evaluation was premised on the fact that low caste men made their
women available to men of higher castes for purposes of concubinage.
It underlined the high caste male prerogative to keep such women
as concubines.

Clearly, a more dominating and caste-oriented social pattern was
being enforced which defined the structures of social differences and
ranking among high caste/low caste, male/male, male/female, and
children of different wives, far more sharply and emphatically. Also,
considerations regarding status were changing. Status that could be
determined by man alone now came to include his wife, including a
karewa wife. As a wife, she came to serve as an agent of upward and
downward status mobility. A low caste woman brought down the
status and an endogamous marriage maintained it, if not helped to
upgrade it.

Reduced to concubinage, the low caste woman's wifehood/widow-
hood as well as the legitimacy of her children, if any, were at stake.
In many instances, low caste woman moved the court to retrieve her
status, resisting it being pulled down. The courts came handy in dealing
with situations of status inconsistency and conflict. They gave a voice
to women which the traditional panchayat denied to them—a voice to
make demands and to bring the machinations of male collateral's of the
deceased husband under scrutiny.

The question of sale or purchase of wife got intertwined with wider
questions. Its overlap with issues of concubinage, traffic in women,
and slavery found reflection in the official debates of early nineteenth
century and there was apparent confusion about adopting a uniform

---

[67] Harshad R. Trivedi, 1977, *Scheduled Caste Women: Studies in Exploration*,
New Delhi: Concept Publishing Co., pp. 70–130.

policy about them.[68] The uncertainty got reflected in their policy and judicial decision making. In the region of Punjab–Haryana, for example, the purchase of a wife by an agriculturist and even sale of his land in this connection was recognized as 'legal necessity' by the British.[69] For this, the colonial government relaxed its own legal strictures regarding sale of ancestral property. Although the British, reflecting their own racial–cultural bias, considered the practice of 'selling daughters [or buying a wife] for a consideration' as a 'bad custom' even a 'barbarous' one,[70] the legal enablement provided by them to sell land to procure brides obviously sanctioned such a practice. The British administrators noted the consequent noticeable increase in the sale of brides.[71] Recognizing the absolutely essential nature of women's labour, both productive and reproductive, as pointed out earlier, the British were keen on granting recognition to these marriages rather than withhold it. Therefore, unlike in Bengal, as argued by Indrani Chatterjee, the recognition of marriage rather than its denial was of concern to the British.[72] The politico-cum-economic and military logic of the colonial masters which made them recognize even cohabitation as karewa and who compelled widows to observe the levirate form of karewa,[73] could hardly refuse to entertain the claims of karewa legally made by the non-caste women/widows to regain legitimacy and inheritance.

However, the question of purchase of wife, legally recognized, though morally and ethically condemned by colonial masters, turned the issue of marriage more complex. For one thing, the wide acceptance of the custom of sale/purchase of brides prevalent among the economically distressed peasantry included both higher agricultural as well as the lower caste groups. Such sale/purchase was not only inter-caste, that is, between higher and lower caste groups but also within the higher caste groups, that is, endogamous alliance between higher and lower classes. This was not necessarily a karewa alliance but could well be a primary association for both or one of them. Bride price was accepted, in a caste

[68] Singha, *A Despotism of Law*, pp. 121–39.

[69] *All India Reporter*, 1931, Lahore series, *Bhan Singh vs Ram Singh*, pp. 599–600.

[70] Rattigan, *A Digest of the Civil Law for the Punjab*, p. 78.

[71] *Rohtak District Gazetteer, 1910*, p. 85. Also, see A. Kensington, 1893, *Customary Law of the Ambala District*, Vol. X, Lahore: Civil and Military Gazette, p. 5.

[72] Chatterjee, *Gender, Slavery and Law in Colonial India*, pp. 75–85.

[73] See Chapter 4 in this volume.

endogamous marriage, for marrying a daughter into a lower ranking lineage that was probably a 'mixed lineage' or an inter-caste one. Many such marriages lay behind the acceptance of bride price. In the official perception, the custom of bride price was looked down upon by the rural populace as a 'disgraceful custom' and admitted with a certain amount of apology and an obvious sense of shame.[74] Yet, the officials perceived this practice to be gaining ground everywhere in the first decade of the twentieth century. Some of these came to be challenged. The growing local adverse reactions to bride price were not merely an attack on bride price per se. These may be understood in relation to the violation of the principle of caste endogamy in marriages, showing inter-caste marriages to be under a great deal of strain.

In most such cases, however, the property considerations emerge prominent. Frowned upon by the British administrators, the custom of bride price came handy to move the court. Ambiguity inherent in the sale/purchase of a wife was used in these cases, to challenge a 'purchased bride's' status. In such a case, the sale of land, even ancestral land (in order to purchase a wife), permitted under the law, could be invalidated. In *Bhan Singh vs Ram Singh* case of 1931, the sale of 1 *kanal* and 14 *marlas* of land for Rs 1,000 was challenged by the reversioners on the ground that such a sale for the purchase of a woman (not wife) was against public policy.[75] Refusing to accept this contention, the judges ruled:

As regards the question of necessity it appears that a sum of Rs. 700 was borrowed to secure a wife for one of the vendors. The learned counsel for the appellants argued that the purchase of a woman was against public policy and this item should not have been allowed. But the payment of such a sum is, I believe, customary amongst Jats and the transaction was not really in the nature of a 'purchase' in the sense urged by the learned court.[76]

STATUS OF CO-WIVES: CASTE ENDOGAMY
AND POLYGAMY

It was not merely the status of the wife but also that of the co-wife that came to be legally challenged and tested in the colonial period. Very frequently, in a polygamous situation, endogamy was observed in the first marriage but not in subsequent marriages. Wives other than the

[74] Darling, *The Punjab Peasant in Prosperity and Debt*, p. 49.
[75] *All India Reporter, Bhan Singh vs Ram Singh*, pp. 599–600.
[76] Ibid.

first could, and very often did, belong to a different caste group. In such a situation, customarily, the children of the co-wives also inherited land, sometimes in equal proportion, at other times less than the son/s of the first wife. The community recognized such marriages, showing the flexibility observed in caste matters. In the colonial period, a second or any subsequent marriage/s outside one's caste group, same as the karewa marriage, came under tremendous strain. Attempts were made to declare such wives as concubines and their children illegitimate. It may be noted that objections were raised only in cases where caste endogamy was not observed. In such cases, the caste endogamous first wife was very much an active participant.

In *Fateh Muhammad Khan vs Abdul Rehman Khan* case of 1931 from Hoshiarpur cited earlier, the judges had noted the pressure exercised by Shah Nawaz's first 'lawful wife' not to recognize Fateh Muhammad Khan as his son from his second association. They noted in their judgement:

It appears that the putative father intended to acknowledge him (Fateh Muhammad Khan) as his son, but was prevented from carrying out his intention by his wife Mussammat Khadija who had given birth to a son two years before the birth of the plaintiff, and who naturally desired that the whole of the estate of her husband as well as that belonging to her father should devolve upon her son.[77]

Revolving around questions of inheritance, the hostility and reservations of both males and females, in such cases, were not towards polygamy as such but towards caste exogamous marriages. The situation in colonial Punjab was quite contrary to the one observed in colonial Sri Lanka, where the move was towards monogamy, as a superior marriage system, in emulation of the western pattern.[78] Yet, in a different context, the female objections to polygamy in this region, were also crystallizing. The objections of women to polygamy are available in abundance in the popular sayings of this region.[79] In such

---

[77] *Punjab Law Reporter, Fateh Muhammad Khan vs Abdul Rehman Khan*, pp. 68–71.

[78] Carla Risseeuw, 1996, 'State Formation and Transformation in Gender Relations and Kinship in Colonial Sri Lanka', in Rajani Palriwala and Carla Risseeuw (eds), *Shifting Circles of Support: Contextualising Gender and Kinship in South Asia and Sub-Saharan Africa*, New Delhi: Sage, pp. 79–109.

[79] Polygamy disadvantages both the wife and the co-wife. Folk literature is extremely rich in portraying the intolerable and humiliating position of women

cases, there was a neat dovetailing of polygamy with caste endogamy, for the first wife—the caste wife.

The spate of cases that followed from the early twentieth century onwards sought to declare such marriages invalid in retrospect. The judges in case after case noted how the changing attitudes towards inter-caste marriages were denying the legitimacy of marriage to the second wife and her children. In *Haria vs Kanhaya* case of 1908, regarding the legality of marriage of a Rajput with a Khatrani woman, the judges noted:

We have certain indications from the evidence that although Rajput society looks on such marriages with disfavour, it does not absolutely refuse to recognise them. Now Haria's mother clearly lived with Desu as his wife and Haria had been recognised as Desu's son in most respects, if not all, by the brotherhood. He was recorded as Desu's son in settlement record, which he could not have been had he been universally treated as illegitimate. In the next place he was allowed the place of honour as a bridegroom when his marriage took place, and the brotherhood sat and ate in the same row with him. He is given the *huqqa*, but the bulk of defendants witnesses and some of his own say he is not allowed to smoke from the same pipe. The case being somewhat novel, the brotherhood do not treat him with absolutely equality with the son of a Rajput wife, but it is equally clear he is placed above a *sartora* (illegitimate) son. This treatment does not show that by custom the marriage is invalid and Haria illegitimate, but rather the contrary. Such a custom would require clear evidence or definite and specific instance, which are not forthcoming ... Some witnesses for defendants had admitted that daughter of Rathi Rajputs could be married to families such as that of Haria (i.e. Rajput and Khatrani)—an important indication of the caste flexibility in the Kangara region—well known for marrying below the caste groups.[80]

Inter-caste marriages were clearly under enormous pressure, and hierarchy among children born from different wives was surfacing. The creeping reservations of the community are highlighted in the hierarchy claimed between issues of 'pure blood' and 'mixed blood'. In social ranking, absolute equality with representatives of pure blood was denied to a male of mixed parentage. He was denied a smoke from a common pipe—the final test of acceptance by the biradari.

---

under this. To quote just one popular proverb, commonly quoted by women in the villages: *saukan choon ki bhi buri* (even a harmless co-wife is intolerable). For several such proverbs common in the colonial period, see Fallon, *A Dictionary of Hindustani Proverbs*, pp. 115, 141, 156–8, 190, 211–16.

   [80] 78 *Punjab Law Reporter*, 1908, *Haria vs Kanhaya*, pp. 137–46.

Several such cases followed in which the male collaterals or the son born of a caste endogamous alliance appropriated the property of the son of an inter-caste marriage or denied recognition to the second wife belonging to a different caste group. A Sahswal Rajput of Fatehpur tehsil of the Attock district challenged the widow of one Mehr Khan Sahswal on the ground that she belonged to the Maliars caste group. As an inferior caste group to the Sahswal Rajputs, her status as second wife was illegal. She therefore could not avail of her husband's property. The case was dismissed in 1908.

In another case from Jullunder tehsil in the same year, the Rajputani widow and her son refused to give land to the sons of the deceased man's second wife, a non-Rajputani—a Pathani by caste—and had the land mutated in their favour.[81] Ten years later, in 1918, the heirs of his second wife moved the court to claim their inheritance. They lost the case in the trial court but won in the High Court. In the verdict given in 1934, the judges refused to give any recognition to the oral testimony of the witnesses who claimed that customarily the sons of a non-Rajput wife did not get any share. In this case, the court refused to recognize the inter-caste marriage and denied the status of a widow to the second wife. This meant that her material rights were also not recognized. Yet, her children were accepted as legitimate. The male children were also deemed entitled to inherit their father's property. In such cases, the sons were valued but the mother was devalued.

The flux of court cases in the colonial period shows a growing anxiety around issues of sexual liaison/marriages with caste groups other than their own. A court judgement, accepting or setting aside such liaisons/marriages, ended up by focusing attention and passing moral judgement based upon western concepts of what was inferior or superior. The court cases, therefore, had the effect of strengthening the hands of those sections of society that were challenging the existing social flexibility.

It was emerging clear that a 'misguided' marriage alliance, outside the caste, could inhibit absorption within the much-sought-after higher status caste groups. It could also adversely affect the marriage of their daughter into an equal or higher status group family within the caste. The existing evidence, as is made clear later, suggests that children, both male and female, of such marriages were facing difficulties in getting married in high status, 'pure' caste families. Also, the betrothed

---

[81] *All India Reporter*, 1934, *Chirag Din vs Dilawar Khan*, Lahore, pp. 465–7.

couples, in which one party was of ambiguous caste status, were either not allowed to get married or, those who were already married, were denied conjugal life. This is clearly evidenced in a large number of cases dealing with breach of the promise of betrothal.

The British had introduced a novel legal right in which such a breach was enforceable in courts. For example, when a girl's side broke off the betrothal, they could be sued through the courts, though not vice versa. J.M. Dunnett, in 1911, recorded a series of such cases in Ludhiana district in which damages were awarded and decrees of money were given to the boy's side.[82] Ambala district judge similarly recorded several instances where decrees varying from Rs 40 to over Rs 300 were given by the courts for breach of betrothal contracts. The British reading of the situation was as follows:

If it was not for the fear of law courts, the girl's people would often keep the money paid at betrothal and then sell the girl elsewhere. It is clear that all tribes in giving their replies to the question are divided between their sense of right, which prompts them to say that betrothals cost nothing and should not involve liability to damages and their fear of the consequences if they make the admission too clearly. It is recognised that the custom of wife-purchase is deplored, but under stress of the system growing up around them the people are becoming more prone to invoke the dangerous aid of the law courts and save themselves the risk of losing money.[83]

This illustration speaks of almost a market-like situation as depicted by Jonathan Parry about the Rajputs of colonial Kangra, which allowed fathers to dispose of their daughters to the highest bidder.[84] In colonial Punjab, the father was frequently accused of reselling his daughter.[85] However, it is equally likely that in some of the cases, the peer pressure would not allow the sale of brides from the lower classes of the higher caste groups to boys of 'half-caste' families (for example, see *Munni Lal vs Shyama Sonarin*, case cited later). As such, this move may be looked upon as denouncing inter-caste marriages by refusing marital alliance with such families, and an attempt at strictly enforcing caste endogamy in marriage.

---

[82] J.M. Dunnett, 1911, *The Customary Law of the Ludhiana District* (revised edition), vol. V, Lahore: Punjab Government Press, pp. 16–22.

[83] Kensington, *Customary Law of the Ambala District*, pp. 4–5.

[84] Jonathan P. Parry, 1979, *Caste and Kinship in Kangra*, New Delhi: Vikas, pp. 243–6.

[85] *Punjab Law Reporter*, 1933, vol. XXIV, *Nathu vs Sarnun*, pp. 282–3.

It was also a way to limit or eliminate the competition for the small number of brides. This also explains why and how the panchayat which would have normally taken up such cases, was perhaps not evoked by the concerned parties and recourse was taken to British introduced law. We cannot therefore fully agree with Parry that the British, by providing a legal recourse to seek a compensation for a broken promise, destroyed the curb of customary violent retribution to the avarice of a calculating father.[86] It was not necessarily the avarice of the father at work, but the convenience and aspirations of certain members of the community. However, such a step certainly negated the violent retribution that customarily followed the breach of such a promise.

Along with the legal enforcement of the breach of promise in betrothal cases, the colonial government introduced the restitution of conjugal rights (made available to the husband, though not to the wife). Under this, a series of cases came to be registered. Apart from throwing significant light on various aspects of Punjab rural life, as I have discussed elsewhere,[87] these cases also point to the pressures exercised over the girl's family regarding caste affairs. In *Munni Lal vs Shyama Sonarin* case, Shyama, a Sonarin (Vaishya) by caste, got married in 1923 to Munni Lal who was of 'mixed blood'.[88] His father was a Sunar but mother was a Mallahin. Apparently, under the pressure of the wider Vaish community, the girl was kept back and not sent to her husband. Munni Lal instituted the restitution of conjugal rights case, demanding his wife back. Moving the court suggests that he did not expect justice from a community which had taken a stand against him and declared him an inferior caste. The Allahabad court ruled that being of 'mixed blood', he was illegitimate and a Sudra and no legal marriage could be contracted between a higher caste girl and a lower caste boy.

Although uncertainty reigned supreme as differing decisions were given, cases such as this suggest that status considerations had come to be pegged on to the concept of caste endogamy/purity which determined matters such as marriage, land, and material rights. Wives and children born of inter-caste marriages could not expect the same rights

[86] Ibid.

[87] Chowdhry, *The Veiled Women*, pp. 116–18.

[88] *Indian Cases*, 1926, vol. 97, *Munni Lal vs Shyama Sonarin*, p. 347. See also, *Punjab Law Reporter*, 1914, vol. 15, *Budhu Mal vs Mansh Ram*, pp. 259–61; *Punjab Law Reporter*, 1934, vol. 35, *Santu vs Har De*, pp. 480–1.

as the 'pure' ones. Customs and traditions were being redefined. Their rights had become challengeable in courts.

⋆ ⋆ ⋆

This study signifies a hardening in the colonial period of what was essentially a fluid social condition. It argues that there was a creeping rigidity in the inter-caste marriages, performed with the participation and consent of the society, which were being challenged and denounced by sections of the same community. The court cases show sections of different communities accepting and rejecting such marriages, as well as attempting to challenge them retrospectively. Attempts were made to declare children of low caste women as illegitimate. It emphasizes social hierarchy between high and low ranking caste groups and growing resentment against mixed lineage groups.

The colonial-cum-patriarchal concerns as well as the attitudes of the British in India, which found favour with certain sections of society, made way for such a social approach to become ascendant. The legal shifts, with their contradictory and highly ambiguous judicial pronouncements, prompted rather than negated the emergence of such conflictual social attitudes in relation to inter-caste marriages. The emerging rigidity in marriage matters was especially noticeable among the landowning classes spread over different caste groups. Even the space allowed to high caste men in making caste exogamous marriages was restricting. For women of this class, this space had hardly existed. Their marriage to suitors born of inter-caste marriage was also under strain as seen earlier in cases regarding restitution of conjugal rights as well as in cases around the breach of betrothal contract. The lower caste women in such inter-caste alliances found their conjugal status being challenged and their children's legitimacy in question, suggesting especially hard time for low caste groups, particularly the women. The sharpening caste hierarchy was shaping and reshaping the hierarchy of gender and patriarchy afresh.

It is clear that British courts representing higher authority had opened a way for both men and women, to claim certain rights that perhaps could not be claimed through the traditional panchayats. More importantly, the decisions of the panchayat could be challenged in courts. In several instances, the decisions of panchayat were reversed by the high court.[89] Although these were statutory panchayats, it was

---

[89] See, for instance, *Punjab Law Reporter*, 1931, vol. XXXV, *Kundan Lal vs Ram Chand*, pp. 140–2.

legally possible to challenge the caste/community panchayats' decisions as well. The British courts reserved the power to correct the local indigenous adjudication procedures, if and when brought to notice. There is a possibility that not finding 'justice' in the caste panchayat, the aggrieved party reopened the case in the local courts for a different verdict. Panchayats generally worked to affect a compromise among different parties and to maintain a status quo. In the colonial period, they may or may not have necessarily reflected the changing aspirations of certain sections of the biradari.

The large numbers of court cases in the colonial period around marital practices indicate the changes taking place in the attitude of the biradari. These attitudes tended to get reflected in the decisions of lower courts. Depending upon the oral testimony and opinion of the important personages of the locality and region, these courts frequently gave adverse verdicts against inter-caste marriages. Such decisions were not infrequently diluted or set aside by the higher courts, operating certain set norms based upon wider political and financial considerations of the colonial masters. It is also likely that due to the long drawn out and highly expensive litigation in the court of law which may well have left the litigants penniless, many of the cases never reached the high court level.[90] Yet, the existence of large number of cases underlines the importance of the issues at stake. They indicate the rapid changes taking place in cultural practices which were to crystallize noticeably into maintenance of caste purity and caste endogamy in the postcolonial period.

---

[90] On the extremely prohibitive cost of pursuing legal cases, see the judgement of Justice Agha Haider in *Umra vs The Crown, Punjab Law Reporter,* 1931, vol. XXXII, pp. 104–8.

Caste, Community, and Gender:
The Post-colonial Constraints

6

High Participation, Low Evaluation
Women and Work in Rural Haryana*

Haryana's post-colonial socio-economy comes in sharp contrast to the colonial times when it had remained one of the most backward and underdeveloped regions of British India.[1] The needs of imperialism had given very low priority to any improvement of agriculture, and British irrigation policies had kept this region starved of this basic requirement which is the crucial determinant of agriculture. In this hard subsistence level economy with total dependence on family labour for cultivation, women had emerged, as we have shown elsewhere,[2] as economic asset and were even popularly acknowledged so. Except for ploughing, digging, and driving a cart, there was no form of agricultural labour which the women did not perform. This was common among the dominant cultivating castes as well as the lower castes, and could be seen to operate regardless of social divisions.

The six decades of independence have, however, situated the rural women of Haryana in a different rural set-up. The introduction of wide-reaching agro-economic changes has successfully catapulted this region from a backward subsistence level economy to be

---

* This chapter was originally published in 1993, *Economic and Political Weekly*, XXVIII (52): A 135–A 148.

[1] For details, see Chapter 1 in this volume.

[2] See Prem Chowdhry, 1989, 'Customs in a Peasant Economy: Women in Colonial Haryana', in Kumkum Sangari and Sudesh Vaid (eds), *Recasting Women: Essays in Colonial History*, New Delhi: Kali for Women, pp. 302–36.

the second richest state in India. This study seeks to locate the Haryanavi women with all their regional, class, and caste differentiation, in the new political economy of independent India. It correlates different aspects and levels of this region's economy with the extent and nature of women's work in twofold work spheres: agriculture as well as agriculture processing and animal husbandry work. For this, the work spheres of two categories of women are investigated, that is, female family workers from landowning households and female agricultural wage earners from landless as well as cultivating households. An analysis of agriculture and agriculture-related work under the heightened demands of a changed socio-economy reveals an increased and extensive use of female family labour which generally cuts across class and caste divisions. Similarly, in animal husbandry, the second most important sector of rural economy in this state, almost all work from intensive labour to supervisory is performed by females regardless of divisions of class and caste. This analysis highlights the dominant socio-cultural and ideological factors which have made for this continuing high participation rate of Haryanavi women, along with a cultural devaluation which considers their work to be inferior/secondary/supplementary to that of men. The conspicuous emergence of a dominant man in control, especially in the aftermath of not only the green revolution but also the white revolution, has only strengthened this devaluation. This contradiction has had the effect of redefining gender equations in rural Haryana to the detriment of its women.

Workwise this analysis also shows that the green revolution has not hit the female family workers but the second category of females, that is, the agricultural wage earners. The enormous increase in labour requirement in the wake of green revolution, being primarily in male recruitment, has left female agricultural labour totally marginalized; and statistically, a mere fraction of male agricultural labour. They have lesser number of days of employment and draw less than their male counterparts for the same tasks. The capitalist thrust in agriculture leading to severe segmentation of agricultural work has resulted in reservation of the so-called 'inferior jobs' for women, with lower payments and much lower annual earning capacity. A growing intrusion of females thrown from lower categories of cultivating households into the wage market and calculated preference of employment shown to them on caste/community basis has had its own socio-economic fallout in terms of reinforcing caste, intra-gender, and status/hierarchy differences. It has also had a more dramatic gender implication as distinct proletarianization of certain sections of females, though not necessarily of males, is visible in pockets of Haryana, closely identified with the green revolution and its heightened prosperity.

This extensive work participation of females of both categories has been analysed finally to explore the reasons which have not allowed women to gain any status and recognition. This highlights the existing dominant cultural work ethics which appropriate her work application without allowing her any economic or social worth. This ideology of work ethics based on high moral values and hard work has succeeded in making rural women accept and internalize the downgrading of their own contributions and the imposing of their own subalternism.

GREEN REVOLUTION: NEED OF FEMALE FAMILY IN A SKEWED ECONOMY

Agriculturally, the independent state marks a sharp break with the colonial past, bringing in phenomenal transformation of contemporary Haryana from a pastoral and, predominantly, subsistence level economy into one of the major grain producing surplus states of India.[3] This unprecedented prosperity, however, has not been evenly distributed. The green revolution, being a highly selective capital-intensive strategy was concentrated in certain well-endowed areas and within these areas, to the advantage of well-endowed peasantry. This resulted in growing regional disparities, with irrigated areas advancing steadily, dry areas languishing, leading to severe economic disparities and accentuation of inequality. This dif-

---

[3] From a deficit food producing state and an importer of food grains, Haryana, by 1976–7, was contributing 6,41,000 tonnes of rice and 9,07,000 tonnes of wheat to the central food pool. The other cash crops like sugar cane and cotton, scantily present earlier, show an abundance with 5,24,000 tonnes and 6,90,000 bales (170 kgs each), respectively, being produced per year according to 1987–8 figures. The production of bajra, on the other hand, which was once the primary crop in the colonial period, was reduced to a mere 2 per cent of the total wheat produce in the region. See Government of Haryana, 1979, *Statistics of Economic Development Haryana, 1977–78*, Chandigarh: Government of Haryana, pp. 1–2; and Government of Haryana, 1989, *Statistical Handbook of Haryana 1988–89*, Chandigarh: Planning Department, Economic and Statistical Organization, pp. 35–6.

ferential impact, as will be shown in the succeeding pages, was to have profound effects on rural women belonging to different classes, castes, and regions within Haryana.

Agro-economically, the green revolution, as described by economist Sheila Bhalla, has etched Haryana predominantly into three regions and two other small sub-regions.[4] The richest tract consists of the Karnal district and its adjacent area. Its gross irrigated area is nearly 70 per cent of the total cropped area and is mainly irrigated by tube wells. This is the region to which the green revolution came first and was consolidated. It has 26 per cent of the total cropped area under high yielding variety (HYV) seeds. The second most prosperous area runs in a broad west to east belt across the middle of Haryana covering most of Hissar and parts of Rohtak district. Although 62 per cent of its total cropped area is irrigated from the agricultural point of view, this irrigation is not available to the farmers in the quantity and at the time it is wanted, with the result that only 14 per cent of the total cropped area is under HYV crops. The third ranking region in terms of agricultural richness and prosperity is the rain desert region in which the returns from cultivation are meagre. This arid region borders Rajasthan, its gross irrigated area is only 12 per cent of the total cropped area and less than 6 per cent of it is under HYV seeds. This region continues to be poor and technologically backward. For all practical purposes, the green revolution has simply bypassed it.

The other two small agro-economically identifiable regions are widely separated from the rest of Haryana. Of them one is the second poorest region of Haryana in terms of cultivator's income. It lies in the north, constituting the high rainfall, hill, and 'cho' area, covering much of the Ambala district; the high rainfall, being ruinous to its crops. Now, both HYV wheat and some rice are grown in this region, more usually on the strength of rainfall rather than irrigation, and labour-intensive methods of production are used. A part of the poorest of all regions lies in the south-east of the state. It is an area defined by a large

[4] For fivefold division and full description of Haryana's agro-economic regions, see Sheila Bhalla, 1981, 'Islands of Growth: A Note on Haryana Experience and Some Possible Implications', *Economic and Political Weekly*, vol. XVI, no. 23, 6 June, pp. 1022–30. For similar information, also see her other articles, namely, 1976, 'New Relations of Production in Haryana Agriculture', *Economic and Political Weekly*, vol. XI, no. 13, 27 March, pp. A23–30; 1977, 'Changes in Acreage and Tenure Structure Landholdings in Haryana 1969–72', *Economic and Political Weekly*, vol. XII, no. 12, 19 March , pp. A2–15.

arc adjacent to the west of Delhi, including parts of Rohtak and a large part of Gurgaon. Now, HYV wheat grows here but on an extremely limited scale and low cash value crops like bajra, jowar, and maize are the main crops.

On the whole, the south-western part of Haryana still suffers from recurrent droughts and near famine conditions because it continues to lack both canal as well as well-irrigation. Digging of wells is not a simple process in this region as the sub-soil water level is very low, being available only at the depth of 150–250 feet.[5] In most parts, the water is also not very suitable for irrigation. The existing crops are drought resistant, but are nevertheless prone to damage.

Thus, in many cases, cultivators continue to live on a subsistence economy, just about managing to feed their families and their cattle, with hardly any surplus to sell. The pattern of landholdings in the drought-prone areas shows them to be larger than elsewhere so as to be economic but even then, mechanized farming has not been possible due to non-availability of water. Consequently, cultivators can hardly be expected to make use of inputs like fertilizers, insecticides, pesticides, and the like. Major inputs in agriculture in these areas are traditional ones such as family labour, wooden ploughs, cattle, organic fertilizer, and seeds. Significantly, the plough mainly used continues to be wooden, as relatively few cultivators use the steel plough or any accessories; levellers are rare and even Persian wheels are very few in number.[6] Here, the mode of cultivation has not undergone any radical change. Farming remains the least capital intensive. This continuation of a hard subsistence level economy cultivated traditionally with total dependence on family labour, naturally also continued to cast the role of women mainly as economic assets, as under the colonial economy. In certain areas of Haryana, where nothing seems to have changed substantially, women continue in their assigned roles.

---

[5] 1971, 'Economic Impact of Drought in Haryana—A Survey', Mimeograph, Marketing and Economic Research Bureau, New Delhi, 1971. The survey noted that the farmers required eight bullocks for irrigating one bigha of land per day. Thus, not only was the cost of digging a well prohibitive, but even irrigation from such deep wells proved very expensive.

[6] The figures relating to 1982 show that there were 5,49,855 wooden ploughs as against 1,90,373 iron ones in Haryana. See Government of Haryana, 1990, *Statistical Abstract of Haryana, 1988–89*, Chandigarh: Planning Department, Economic and Statistical Organization, p. 241.

The strategy of the green revolution did not confine itself only to selecting certain regions, it also selected, within these areas, the so-called 'progressive farmers' for the distribution of inputs. Initially, these were usually the larger farmers with superior capital at their command necessary for acquiring the requisites of the green revolution.[7] Slowly, as the profitability of growing HYV was well demonstrated, the small farmers, helped with yet greater incentives by the state, progressively adopted the same strategy.[8] Yet, compared to the big cultivators, their investment was modest. They tried to make up this deficiency by making use of family labour or, in some cases, by hiring labour. However, for a capital-intensive strategy, this could hardly succeed. Labour, family or not, could not be a substitute for chemical fertilizers.[9] What needs to be emphasized here is the lack of capital investment which was sought to be made up by the use of family labour. In such a case, female labour did not, in fact could not, be withdrawn from agriculture. For all purposes, its application became more intensive.

In fact, the green revolution, whatever the size of the holding, shows an increase in demand for all kinds of labour.[10] Barring a reduced demand in ploughing and threshing, there has been an increase in the labour requirement in all other tasks such as, multiple cropping, greater care in sowing, transplanting, weeding, pesticide control, and irrigation. This is specially so if some of these operations like harvesting and threshing are not simultaneously mechanized. Given the still incomplete mechanization in this region, the additional labour requirement was

[7] The rationale behind this strategy was to make intensive use of the limited modern inputs into areas by those who were in a position to make optimum use of them rather than spreading it thinly over a large area and among many farmers, with hardly noticeable returns. See Biplab Das Gupta, 1977, 'India's Green Revolution', *Economic and Political Weekly*, vol. XII, nos 6, 7, and 8, pp. 241–60.

[8] M. Prahladachar, 1983, 'Income Distribution and Effects of the Green Revolution in India: A Review of Empirical Evidence', *World Development*, vol. 11, no. 11, November, pp. 927–44.

[9] B.D. Talib and A. Majid, 1976, 'Small Farmers of Punjab', *Economic and Political Weekly*, vol. XI, no. 26, 26 June, pp. A42–6.

[10] For details, see Bina Agarwal, 1985, 'Women and Technological Change in Agriculture: The Asian and African Experience', in Iftikhar Ahmed (ed.), *Technology and Rural Women: Conceptual and Empirical Issues*, London: George Allen and Unwin, pp. 67–114; and Anne Whitehead, 1985, 'Effects of Technological Change in Rural Women: A Review of Analysis and Concepts', in Ahmed (ed.), *Technology and Rural Women*, pp. 27–64.

seen to be rising noticeably in the early phases of the green revolution and still remains very real, despite having reached a plateau by the late 1970s and the early 1980s under the impact of accelerated mechanization.[11] In realistic terms, this demand, the concomitant escalating labour costs, and efforts at maximizing the output have meant that the family women must continue to work. Hiring expensive labour to do what could be done by family labour is observed to be a waste of hard-earned money not only by men but also by women.[12] Consequently, women continue to perform, more or less, every kind of field labour except ploughing: they help men in preparing the fields for sowing, breaking clods with mallets, making embankments on the fields, following the plough, dropping seeds during the sowing season, managing water application in the fields, hoeing, weeding, harvesting, threshing, winnowing, and transplanting of all produce. They also personally carry food for the men working in the fields and bring back green fodder for the milch cattle. In fact, mechanization has lightened the work load of men; for example, the use of the tractor which has replaced the plough and the oxen. But the women continue to load the tractor, as she had once loaded the cart. Significantly, the work load of women has only been recast, not reduced.

FEMALE FAMILY LABOUR: CASTE AND CLASS
The extensive use of female family labour in Haryana has generally cut across caste and class divisions. It holds true for dominating cultivating caste groups like the Jats, Gujars, Ahirs, and Bishnois, among other

[11] For accelerated mechanization, see Sheila Bhalla, 1989, 'Technological Change and Women Workers: Evidence from the Expansionary Phase in Haryana Agriculture', *Economic and Political Weekly*, vol. XXIV, no. 43, 28 October, pp. WS67–8. Also, see A.V. Jose, 1988, 'Agriculture Wages in India', *Economic and Political Weekly*, vol. XXIII, no. 26, 25 June, pp. A46–58. However, the recent government statistics show relatively low figures of different mechanical devices adopted in this region in 1980–1 as compared to the total number of operational holdings estimated to be 1,01,200 in number, with 3,56,200 hectares area under cultivation. For these holdings, there were only 21,626 tractors and 3,318 sugar cane crushers worked by power as against 8,464 worked by bullocks. The preponderance of wooden plough (see Note 6) also indicates the low level of technology in this region. The other sophisticated devices are also not readily available. See Government of Haryana, *Statistical Abstract of Haryana, 1988–89*, pp. 241–2.

[12] Ursula Sharma, 1980, *Women, Work and Property in North-West India*, London: Tavistock Publications, p. 23.

cultivating castes, as also among the lower castes. It has also been seen among those who have been the major beneficiaries of the green revolution and have seen an enormous rise in their incomes. In fact, the dominant cultural norms do not consider the participation of women in manual work outside the house as lowering to family prestige. However, this manual work must be in the fields of the family as those who work for themselves enjoy a higher status in rural society. Working for others is considered to bring about a lowering of this status.[13]

This attitude towards agricultural work is reflected in the folklore of this region. One popular tale shows the queens assisting the king in sowing the field. The folk tales goes back to the days of the Mahabharata. It tells of a time when the land of Kurukshetra had been suffering from twelve years of prolonged drought. It rained only when its ruler, Raja, Kuru, performed the rain *yagna* (ritual sacrificial rites). However, by that time, the cultivators had forgotten how to plough. Balram, the elder brother of Lord Krishna and a well-known '*haldar*' (ploughman), reached Kurukshetra at this time. The king told him about his problem and requested his help. Balram, being a '*paidaishi kisan*' (a born farmer), agreed. He ploughed the land and so did the king. The queens followed the golden plough wielded by the king and sowed the seeds. The cultivators learnt how to cultivate again and prosperity reigned in the region.

The folk tale was narrated to me when I was exploring the reasons behind the famed excellence of Haryanavi cultivators.[14] Being performed by kings and queens, the folk tale underlines the idea that agriculture can never be a demeaning task. In keeping with this tradition, Haryana continues to show the active involvement of women in cultivation. As symbolized through the tale, the plough, seeds, and the earth are semiotic terms which, in the popular cosmos of the inhabitants, are equated with reproductive and agricultural activity. The vocabularies of production and reproduction can be seen to overlap and blend. Moreover, as both are difficult, involving hard labour, they are used interchangeably. In the still existing arid, drought-prone areas of

[13] T.K. Dak and M.L. Sharma, 1988, 'Social Framework of Female Labour Participation in Rural Sector', in T.M. Dak (ed.), *Women and Work in Indian Society*, New Delhi: Manohar, pp. 26–48.

[14] Narrated in village Bandh of Karnal district. This folk tale is also included in the collection brought about by Indu Roy Chaudhury, 1974, *Folk Tales of Haryana*, New Delhi: Sterling Publishers, pp. 43–4.

Haryana, where all hands are needed to eke out their meagre agricultural gains, the female family members cannot afford to be withdrawn. In the areas, 'technologically most advanced' and considered the 'richest regions' of Haryana, the involvement of female family members in agriculture is comparatively lower than in other regions. Table 6.1 shows this to be 19.21 per cent less for holdings with operated acreage of 2.5 acres and above. However, this difference cannot be related either to the rise in status and prestige considerations, as made clear later on, or to the rise in income levels. The given figures for the richest region show an increasing involvement of family females with agriculture as the operated holding increases in size.

TABLE 6.1   Unpaid Female Days as Percentage of
Unpaid Family Person Days

Operated Acreage	All Haryana	Richest region
0–2.5	13.9	0.00
2.5–5	27.9	26.7
5–10	21.5	12.5
10–15	16.5	14.4
15 or more	23.7	18.7
All average	21.9	16.2

Source: Sheila Bhalla, 'Technological Change and Women Workers: Evidence from the Expansionary Phase in Haryana Agriculture', *Economic and Political Weekly*, October 28, vol. XXIV, no. 43, 28 October 1989, pp. WS67–89.

In fact, the table emphasizes a continued association rather than any systematic withdrawal of family females from work as the operated average holding increases. For example, the females with holdings from 5 to 10 acres seem to be putting in a lower percentage of work than those from 10 to 15 acres or 15 acres and above. In the lowest acreage group of 0–2.5, the agricultural wages being far more remunerative in the richer regions of Haryana and their labour being surplus in their own uneconomic holding, the contribution of family females remains nil.[15]

My own field observation and oral information gathered from the villages also reflects an extensive use of family labour. By and large, even

---

[15] Sheila Bhalla, 1976, 'New Relations of Production in Haryana Agriculture', *Economic and Political Weekly*, vol. XI, no. 13, 27 March, pp. A22–30.

women from 'well-to-do families' contribute fully to all agricultural tasks.[16] Both men and women agree on this. Some men even opine that family females are doing 'much more work' as a result of the agricultural changes than they did before. As an example, it is pointed out that where a small *zamindar*'s wife may bring only one *bharota* (a head load of fodder) from the fields, a bigger zamindar's (landowner's) wife will have to bring back four or five bharote.[17] Similarly, it is claimed that she does more work in the fields involving weeding, sowing, transplanting, and so on, in view of the greater intensity of cropping and use of fertilizers. This observation is corroborated by a recent study of Punjab which points out that as a result of the green revolution, there has been an increase in the per hectare utilization of female family labour, wherever utilized, by 22.52 per cent between 1971–2 and 1980–1.[18]

Yet, undoubtedly, there are women who have withdrawn from agricultural work; for example, in Karnal district, which is the richest green revolution area. Here, the women maintain that this work is now being done by their '*naukars*' (servants).[19] Keeping naukars to do agricultural work is almost entirely a post-colonial phenomenon. However, the number of naukars continues to be fairly limited despite having increased from 5 per cent of the permanent or attached agricultural labourers (figures given later) in the 1950s to 38.66 per cent in 1972–3.[20] Moreover, this increase cannot be directly related to the withdrawal of family females from agricultural work. Whatever withdrawal that is noticeable, however, seems to be on account of the very great amount

[16] Interview with Chhotu Devi, 1986, village Dujjana, district Rohtak, 6 June; born 1911, her late husband was a big landowner of Dujjana.

[17] Interview with Dheer Singh, 1988, village Asodha Todran, Rohtak district, 21–7 December; 50 years old, owns 2 *kilas* or 10 bighas of land. His wife, Gyano Devi, confirmed the observations of her husband.

[18] Ramesh Chand, D.S. Sidhu, and J.L. Kaul, 1985, 'Impact of Agricultural Modernisation on Labour Use Pattern in Punjab with Special Reference to Women Labour', *Indian Journal of Agricultural Economics*, vol. XL, no. 3, July–September, pp. 252–9.

[19] Fieldwork in 1990 in villages Lapra, Kaith, and Kalanaur in Yamuna Nagar district, 9–10 August; and 1988, village Bandh in Karnal district, 21–2 August.

[20] Bhalla, 'New Relations of Production in Haryana Agriculture'. Interestingly, in the three regions delineated by the author according to the richness and technological advancement, the number of permanent agricultural labour is calculated to be only 25.52 per cent of the total agricultural labour force; out of these, the percentage of naukars was as follows: region A, 44.1 per cent; region B, 43.3 per cent; and region C, 28.6 per cent.

of agricultural processing work which has so increased due to increased output under the green revolution, as well as due to the extra cooking for hired agricultural labourers and naukars in some of the villages. The fact that in certain cases, naukars have taken over does not necessarily mean a withdrawal of work for women but a shift of her work from the field to the *ahata* (courtyard), where her supervision and active participation is considered to be more valuable though not necessarily more prestigious.

Yet, in view of the virtual absence of relevant material, it is not possible to know what percentage of female family members have withdrawn from active agricultural work. There is also no caste-wise study to indicate the participation or withdrawal of women belonging to different caste groups. A recent study[21] suffers from the severe handicap of following the present Haryana government's criterion of designating high castes by clubbing the Brahmin, Rajput, Bania, and Khatri, who have been known in this region traditionally to keep their women away from agricultural activities, together with landowning castes like Jats, Ahirs, Gujars, Bishnois, Sainis, and the like, whose women always worked in the fields! This severely limits and dilutes the actual participation rate of women from the so-called 'cultivating castes'. However, despite this shortcoming, the same study shows caste differences to be severely cut across, and women of all caste groups playing a dominating role in agriculture-related tasks such as processing and storage of farm produce and making of farm yard manure; all of which are, however, home-bound tasks.

Similarly, class-wise data given in the same study shows that females from different land size categories, ranging from below 2.5 acres to above 15 acres, do not really show any significant difference in respect to their participation in most of the listed agricultural activities; which

[21] Dak and Sharma, 'Social Framework of Female Labour Participation in Rural Sector', pp. 26-48. This study uses the classification of castes used by the Department of Social Welfare, Government of Haryana, as follows:

1. High castes: Brahmins, Rajputs, Bania, Khatri, Jat, Ahir, Gujar, Bishnoi, and Saini.
2. Medium castes: Sunar, Khati, Darzi, Kumhar, Nai, Jhimar, Lohar, Jogi, and Dhobi.
3. Low castes: all scheduled castes, Chamars, Balmiki, Sansi, Bawaria, Khatik, Julaha, Mazhabi Sikhs, and others.

This classification is not specified in the book, but was personally communicated to me by the author and editor of this work.

means that those activities are being generally performed or avoided by all females irrespective of the landholding and irrespective of adoption of green revolution strategy.[22] This is specially noticeable in activities like weeding, inter-culture, and harvesting.

However, certain traditional high castes, with the exception of Brahmins, like Rajputs, Banias, and Khatris, who have never allowed their women to work in the fields, continue the same practice. Leading a more restricted and secluded life, akin to being in *purdah*, the green revolution and its gains have reinforced women's seclusion among such families, and also, in the minor ones among these castes who tend to emulate their caste superiors. Yet, those women who do not perform any agricultural work are by no standards considered 'superior' but only 'different' as 'their menfolk do not allow' or 'have never allowed them to work outside the house'. This observation is widespread in all the villages I visited. A woman in village Chhara of district Rohtak aptly remarked, '*na kabhi karamte, na kiya, na karti*' (women have not been asked to work in the fields, nor have they ever worked, nor do they want to work). On the other hand, even their own active involvement in agricultural work is not hailed as being 'superior' or as affording them any freedom because they work with men.

As far as utilizing female family members goes, the Haryana pattern is more closer with Rajasthan's than the Punjab, Madhya Pradesh, or Maharashtra patterns, where the employment of female labour is negatively related to the size of the holding and adoption of new production technology.[23] In the green revolution or HYV technology adoption

[22] It may be noted here that Dak and Sharma make a tentative suggestion about the correlation of land size and mechanization of farm with use of female family labour. A bigger landholding and high mechanization, according to them, led to women playing a 'less dominant role' in the productive process. On the other hand, the high adoption of other farm technologies is shown to promote greater utilization of women in agriculture and allied areas notwithstanding their economic status. Although not mutually contradictory, this analysis along with the given statistical data, does not show a clear picture. My own observations have therefore been utilized to reach a sharper focus on women's involvement than made available by these two authors.

[23] For the above mentioned states, see C.K. Joshi and H.R. Alshi, 1985, 'Impact of High Yielding Varieties and Employment Potential of Female Labour—A Study of Akola District (Maharashtra)', *Indian Journal of Agricultural Economics*, vol. XL, no. 3, July–September, pp. 230–4; D.K. Malhotra and S.K. Sharma, 1985, 'Female Labour Participation in Rice Farming System of Chhatisgarh Region', *Indian Journal of Agricultural Economics*, vol. XL, no. 3, July–September,

areas of Rajasthan, for example, there is a very sharp increase in the absolute level of utilization of female family labour time.[24] In this case, a comment here on the Punjab situation as a counterpoise to Haryana, specially in view of the latter having been part of Punjab, may not be irrelevant. The general consensus of opinion is that Punjab has amongst thè lowest rural female participation rate, attributed to the increased prosperity in that region consequent on the success of the green revolution.[25] An analysis of employment during different stages of modernization on sample farms in Punjab showed that in those farms, using only bullocks for cultivation, 56 per cent of female family labour was employed. With the introduction of tube wells and farm machinery, female family labour was reduced to 46 per cent, and when tractors were also used, it was further reduced to 24 per cent.[26] Other studies have similarly suggested women's withdrawal from work, specially among the new class of capitalist landowners, a decreasing role among middle peasant households and continued participation only at the lower end of the social scale.[27] This change is attributed partly to the different social values and traditions of the dominant Sikhs who do not favour the participation of women in farm work.[28] However, the reasons behind this apparent difference between the two states of Haryana and Punjab need to be investigated more fully, specially in view of the fact that the dominant norms of the two states were and continue to be set by the Jat peasantry.

---

pp. 235–9; J.S. Sisodia, 1985, 'Role of Farm Women in Agriculture: A Study of Chambal Command Area of Madhya Pradesh', *Indian Journal of Agricultural Economics*, vol. XL, no. 3, July–September, pp. 223–30.

[24] A.K. Ray, I.V. Rangarao, and B.R. Attari, 1985, 'Impact of Technological Changes on Economic Status of Female Labour', *Indian Journal of Agricultural Economics*, vol. XL, no. 3, July–September, pp. 244–52.

[25] Rohini Nayyar, 1987, 'Female Participation Rate in Rural India', *Economic and Political Weekly*, vol. XXII, no. 51, 19 December, pp. 2207–16; Krishna Dutt Sharma, 1973, 'Female Participation in Rural Agricultural Labour in North India: A Spatial Interpretation, 1971', *Man Power Journal*, vol. VIII, no. 4, January–March, pp. 52–67.

[26] Cited in Robert O. Whyte and Pauline Whyte, 1982, *The Women of Rural Asia*, Boulder: West View Press, p. 186.

[27] Ursula Sharma, 1982, 'Women's Participation in Agriculture in India', *Current Anthropology*, vol. 23, no. 2, April, pp. 194–6.

[28] Martin M. Billing and Arjan Singh, 1970, 'Mechanisation and the Wheat Revolution: Effects on Female Labour in Punjab', *Economic and Political Weekly*, vol. V, no. 52, 26 December, pp. A169–74.

WHITE REVOLUTION: ECONOMICS OF
ANIMAL HUSBANDRY

The class and caste barriers which are generally cut across in performance of certain agriculture-related tasks are specially noticeable in animal husbandry work. The relevant statistics, given in the same study cited earlier, show a much clearer assessment of this work in comparison to the confused and imprecise picture of agricultural work. For example, the figure of 96 per cent relating to high caste females engaged in tending farm cattle with the corresponding figures of 95 per cent from low castes, and 97 per cent for females from bigger holdings of 15 acres or more, as also for those up to 5 acres, are expressive enough of this work.[29] In an interesting reversal, the same figures may be used to show the very insignificant amount of animal husbandry work left to the males.

Animal husbandry has gained a new importance in view of the intense commercialization of milk. The Operation Flood Project, initiated in the wake of the 'white revolution' in 1970–1, has created a virtual milk bowl out of Haryana. For example, the 283.5 lakh litres milk procurement in 1978–9, only through societies, excluding individuals and private efforts, more than doubled itself in five years.[30] There has also been corresponding increase in the milch animal strength in Haryana. In a decade, between 1972 and 1982, their numbers have increased by 39 per cent.[31]

Most of the big dairies with their high milk yielding, cross-bred cattle are concentrated in the green revolution areas. This is primarily because the cross-bred, though far superior to the indigenous cows, are far more expensive to maintain, which only the more affluent landowners-cum-dairy farmers can afford.[32] On account of the fairly lower cost of maintenance, indigenous cows are kept by the economically weaker sections and tend to be concentrated in the dry zones. They provide an

[29] Dak and Sharma, 'Social Framework of Female Labour Participation in Rural Sector'.

[30] Government of Haryana, 1987, *Statistical Abstract of Haryana, 1985–86*, Chandigarh: Planning Department, Economic and Statistical Organization, p. 285.

[31] Government of Haryana, *Statistical Abstract of Haryana, 1988–89*, p. 267.

[32] For a similar cross study of cattle in Andhra Pradesh, see Uma Shankari, 1989, 'What is Happening to Cows and Bulls of Sundarapalli?', *Economic and Political Weekly*, vol. XXIV, no. 21, 27 May, pp. 1164–70.

inexpensive source of milk and returns from the sale of calves.[33] Clearly, animal husbandry and dairying in Haryana is both class and caste based. Bullocks continue to have an enormous importance in Haryana. Not only do the dry farming areas show a preponderant use of animals for draught power as against less use of costly machinery like tractors, but the high technology green revolution areas continue to use bullocks for field operations like levelling and seeding. In fact, Surendra Mohan Batra shows that crops requiring intensive inputs of bullock labour covered 91 per cent of the total cultivated area in a green revolution village in Haryana.[34] Bullocks also remain the most important and inexpensive means of transport, carrying up to 96 per cent of the produce to the markets, which is specially due to the poor condition of village roads. Even agro-industrial equipment like sugarcane crushers are operated by bullocks.

The significance of animal husbandry for this region has not only made it the second most important sector of rural economy in this state, it has also emerged as the mainstay of life for the weaker sections of the rural community.[35] The large areas of Haryana adjacent to Delhi though poor in terms of farm labour earnings, are rich in terms of supplementary income from dairying and poultry keeping among landless households.[36] Significantly, keeping of livestock such as sheep, goats, pigs, and donkeys for food and sale, as also poultry keeping, is mainly restricted to the lower classes and castes of rural society.[37] However, in the recent years, keeping poultry, having emerged as an income-generating activity, is rapidly being established on commercial lines among

[33] Surendra Mohan Batra, 1981, 'The Place of Livestock in the Social and Economic System of a Village in Haryana', PhD thesis, Department of Sociology, Delhi University, p. 297.

[34] Ibid., pp. 214–16. Also, see Shanti George, 1985, *Operation Flood: An Appraisal of Current Indian Dairy Policy*, New Delhi: Oxford University Press, p. 85.

[35] 1978, 'Integrated Rural Development, Hissar (Haryana)', Mimeograph, vol. III, Directorate of Project-cum-Plan Formulation, Haryana Agricultural University, Hissar, March, p. 27.

[36] Sheila Bhalla, 1977, 'Agricultural Growth: Role of Institutional and Infrastructure Factors', *Economic and Political Weekly*, vol. XII, nos 45 and 46, November, pp. 1898–1905.

[37] The poultry stock increased between 1972 and 1982, from 9,600 to 2,01,400. Government of Haryana, *Statistical Abstract of Haryana, 1988–89*, p. 267.

landowning groups in the areas encircling Delhi, along with subsistence farming and vegetable gardening for the city markets.[38]

This reinforced importance of animal husbandry, livestock, and poultry keeping has therefore meant an increase in the work of family female members, regardless of divisions of class and caste. For animal husbandry, the bigger and richer milch animal owners have started to engage some help. Yet, an overwhelming 82 per cent of work continues to be contributed by the family members, specially females and children.[39] In the arid zone, covering the districts of Hissar, Bhiwani, Sirsa, and Mahendergarh, there are fewer cattle than in the green revolution zones, but it is calculated that more work is involved due to the paucity of fodder and lower monetary returns.[40]

Even here, the lot of women from economically weaker households is worse both in the dry zone as well as in the abundance of green revolution areas. They are faced with the difficulty of finding free fodder like grass which was earlier available in the village common lands or on fallow lands which are now considered the private property of the landowners. With more and more fallow land under cultivation and landowners themselves having taken to dairy farming, the work load of women has increased enormously as they have to go to far-flung areas for fodder for the animals.[41] The milking of animals is a female task, though sometimes undertaken by men; the milk processing, whenever done at home, which includes the making of curd, butter, and *ghee* (clarified butter), is done exclusively by women. In all other tasks, children often help the women. The animal-related tasks are: bringing fodder from the fields, chaff cutting, preparing feed-mix for the cattle, giving

[38] Stanley A. Freed and Ruth Freed, 1976, 'Shanti Nagar: The Effects of Urbanisation in a Village in North India', Anthropological Papers of the American Museum of Natural History, vol. 53, part I, Social Organisation, New York, pp. 7, 13–15. Also, see M.S.A. Rao, 1968, 'Occupational Diversification and Joint Household Organisation', *Contributions to Indian Sociology* (NS), Vol. VII, No. 11, December, pp. 9–111.

[39] Government of Haryana, 1987, *Family Budgets of Cultivators in Haryana, 1984–85*, Chandigarh: Planning Department, The Economic and Statistical Organization, p. 26.

[40] George, *Operation Flood*, p. 152; also, see Mahesh Lalwani, 1987, 'Effects of Technological Change in Dairy-Farming: A Case Study of Haryana', PhD thesis, Department of Economics, Delhi School of Economics, University of Delhi, pp. 39-49.

[41] Maria Mies, 1986, *Indian Women in Subsistence and Agricultural Labour*, Geneva: ILO, p. 81.

water and feed, bathing and cleaning the cattle, cleaning the cattle shed, treating the sick cattle, making dung cakes, preparing *bitora* (a structure for storing dry dung cakes, and compost making). Men have taken over from women only where technology has substituted electricity for manual operations, as, for example, in chaff cutting.[42] Yet, all the tasks left to women remain intensive.

A parallel study on animal husbandry in a Punjabi village in Pakistan shows that an average rural woman spends one hour and forty-five minutes everyday caring for the animals and an additional three hours and forty-five minutes, collecting, carrying, and chopping their fodder.[43] Field observation shows that these figures for time consumption may be considered more or less accurate for this region as well.

Yet, despite all this work, so far as the recognition of their contribution to dairy farming is concerned, women again remain invisible. A 1973 inquiry into the dairy development programme in Ambala district reported that no female was declared to be a worker in the animal husbandry work.[44] In fact, till the 1980s, the cost of human labour involved in the general tending of milch animals was not included in evaluating cost of milk production, as milk production was considered a 'subsidiary industry [being] carried on in spare time, there being no extra expenses incurred for labour employed for this work' .[45] Moreover, the white revolution resulting in the industrialization of dairying has had the severely adverse effect of eroding a woman's value in terms of her economic contribution. This is due to a shift away from the traditional primacy of women in the processing aspect of dairying.[46] For example, the manufacturing of ghee was a task performed by the rural women which showed the economic return of her labour. Now, the household

[42] P. Rangaswamy, 1981, 'Economics of Dry Farming in Drought-prone Areas: A Case Study of Hissar in Haryana', Unpublished research study no. 81/1, Agricultural Economic Research Centre, University of Delhi, p. 17.

[43] Seemin Anwar and Faiz Bilquees, 1978, 'The Attitudes, Environment and Activities of Rural Women: A Case Study of Jhok Sayal', in Ruth B. Dixon, *Rural Women at Work: Strategies for Development in South Asia*, Baltimore and London: John Hopkins University Press, p. 50.

[44] S.S. Tyagi, 1973, 'Evaluation of the Small Farmer's Development Agency: A Pilot Study of Ambala District', Unpublished research report, Agricultural Economics Research Centre, University of Delhi, p. 56.

[45] Government of Haryana, 1976, *Family Budgets of Cultivators in Haryana, 1972–73*, Chandigarh: Planning Department, The Economic and Statistical Organization, p. 17.

[46] George, *Operation Flood*, pp. 196–7.

production of ghee has declined in houses supplying milk for dairying, thus affecting a change in her economic worth, whilst her work has only increased in terms of catering to the increased demand for milch animals. So, although in dairy keeping women perform intensive labour and supervisory work, the man, whose work is marginal compared to that of woman, is the key controlling authority in the crucial sphere of marketing and collection of income as well as sale and purchase of livestock. This fact hardly leaves the woman an integral part of the dairy system as such.

Specially significant in the increased work load of the woman in animal husbandry, is dung work, particularly in the white revolution areas with their high concentration of cattle. Women from a wide range of social classes can be seen spending a great deal of time performing tasks related to dung. Sometimes, low caste women are employed, at a nominal charge of 50 paise to one rupee per day, to help out the family females, due to the enormity of work. This dung work is essential to the economy due to its use as cooking fuel which has become more significant than before. In fact, dung occupies the second most important source of energy for cooking, next to firewood and chips, to the extent of 35.57 per cent.[47] The rapidly dwindling sources of firewood, due to diminishing common property resources and *shamilat* land (common land), have been exacerbated by the effects of the green revolution technology with their HYV crops yielding a lower crop residue per unit weight of grain which is not necessarily made up by higher per crop output.[48] This fact has put a further premium on the use of dung.

Besides, the role of dung as a fertilizer of the major crops still remains crucially important and profitable. Yet, men's evaluation of '*gobar-ka-kaam*' (dung work) as being a source of contamination to them and fit only for women has not changed. Men are reluctant even to consider handling it.[49] The religio-cultural sanctity of dung in which the image of Govardhan made out of dung is worshipped by men and women,

---

[47] *National Sample Survey, Thirty-eighth Round*, January–December 1983, no. 336: *Report on Sources of Drinking Water and Energy used for Cooking and Lighting*, 1988, Department of Statistics, New Delhi, p. 9, Table 3.

[48] Bina Agarwal, 1986, 'Under the Cooking Pot: The Political Economy of the Domestic Fuel Crisis in Rural South Asia', Paper no. E/122/86, Institute of Economic Growth, Delhi.

[49] Roger Jeffery, Patricia Jeffery, and Andrew Lyn, 1989, 'Taking Dung-Work Seriously: Women's Work and Rural Development: Northern India', *Economic and Political Weekly*, vol. XXIV, no. 17, 29 April, pp. WS32–7.

signifying animal prosperity as a part of ancient peasant ritual has still not lifted the gobar work to the level of a man's work.[50] Part of this explanation lies in the logic of inferiority attached to the 'private'/inside space being the domestic/female space where gobar is brought in the form of *uple* or *gose* (dung cakes) for cooking or as part of covering the *kachcha* (mud) floor and walls of the house. This devaluation has only highlighted its 'dirty' and 'demeaning' aspect rather than giving it the kind of sanctity which it might otherwise have evoked. This is an ambivalent aspect of pollution ideology in rural areas, as gobar along with *ganga jal* (water of the Ganges) remains one of the major ingredients of purification in the Brahmanical/peasant ritual world.

MIGRATION OF MEN AND CULTURAL WORK ETHICS
An important factor which has kept the ranks of female family workers swollen and a sustained involvement in agricultural work is the migration of men for work outside their villages and, in many cases, outside the state. Haryana has also had, for a variety of reasons, a very deep-rooted tradition of men seeking work outside the agrarian sector.[51] In fact, the need for economic security had attracted many towards the much coveted government jobs in the otherwise insecure agricultural conditions under the British. The social recognition this security afforded came to be associated with general *izzat* (honour/prestige). Its post-colonial popularity may be explained by the great increase in population,[52] and pressure on land due to limited expansion in

[50] This popularly observed festival of Govardhan, celebrated in most parts of rural north India, comes after Diwali. Marriot traces the village etymology for Govardhan to gobar + '*dhan*', that is, cow dung wealth. It is perhaps a significant fact that the image of Govardhan is made by women alone. See McKim Marriot, 1955, *Village India: Studies in the Little Community*, Chicago: The University of Chicago Press, pp. 177–222.

[51] See Chapter 1 in this volume.

[52] The post-1947 Haryana saw an alarming rate of population growth between 1951 and 1981. Between 1951 and 1961, it rose by 34.17 per cent; 1961–71 by 31.53 per cent; and 1971–81 by 28.75 per cent. See Government of Haryana, 1970, *Statistical Abstract of Haryana, 1968–69*, Chandigarh: Govt of Haryana, Economic and Statistical Organization, Planning Department; Government of Haryana, 1972, *Statistical Abstract of Haryana, 1970–71*, Chandigarh: Govt of Haryana, Economic and Statistical Organization, Planning Department; Government of Haryana, 1987, *Statistical Abstract of Haryana, 1985–86*, Chandigarh: Govt of Haryana, Economic and Statistical Organization, Planning Department.

commerce and industry in the province.[53] The overburdening of agrarian sector has created severe unemployment in the state. The statistical figures of job seekers waiting for jobs through employment exchanges, calculated until December 1987, is of 6,00,000 people in Haryana.[54] In the still existing *barani* (dependent on rainfall) areas, with subsistence or even below subsistence living, the need for an outside job is self-evident. In the green revolution areas, the young educated boys are generally known to be averse to agriculture and keener for an outside job.[55] There is, therefore, a great scramble for any employment, high or low, by all, whatever the social status.

The drive for an outside job is however not exclusive to the land based. A recent study of the villages of Karnal and Bhiwani districts shows a great desire among the rural populace belonging to different social categories to move out of the villages motivated by the desire to leave their traditionally polluting work in the villages.[56] Also, many traditional artisans have been unable to face the competition with cheap factory-made goods, and consequently, have been shifting towards urban semi-skilled and unskilled occupations.

Interestingly, most of those out-migrants from the villages have been men only. Although there are always exceptions, specially for the higher income jobs and among the low caste–class households, the migration in and from Haryana has essentially been male migration only. The total rural male migration within the state has been calculated in the 1981 census to be 54 per cent, and to the other states of India, 37 per cent. As compared to this, rural female migration to other states of India has

---

[53] Government of India, 1969, *Employment Trends and Manpower Situation in Haryana,* Chandigarh, p. 5. Despite industrial growth in the last twenty-two years, that is, 1968–9 to 1989–90, this evaluation has hardly changed. The recent official figures show that the share of secondary sector, including manufacturing, construction, and the like, has indeed stagnated. At current prices, it was 19 per cent in 1980–1 and 19.2 per cent in 1988–9. See Government of Haryana, 1990, *Economic Survey of Haryana,* 1989–90, Chandigarh: Planning Department, Economic and Statistical Organization, p. 1.

[54] Ibid., pp. 15–17.

[55] The increased income in those areas and its commercialization has given the young boys a taste for urban life. They are not willing to settle down to an agriculturist's life in the village. Income generation of the green revolution areas has driven away, rather than attract, the younger generation to agriculture.

[56] Sarita Mehra, 1980, 'Social Mobility in Rural Haryana', PhD thesis, Rural Sociology, Haryana Agricultural University, Hissar, pp. 147–247.

been only 4 per cent.[57] Within the state, the migration figure of rural female, though 80.29 per cent, is accounted for by the marriage patterns followed in the state which completely forbid marriage within the village itself. Among the lower castes, the migration of families is more noticeable, as even in the urban centres, their women become earning members and full contributors to the support of the family.[58] For the land based, any such contribution is not expected or acceptable. Taking women along raises problems, and could also involve finding of alternative ways of getting agricultural and other work done. Moreover, the petty, poorly paid urban job occupations of most men have meant that women have had to be left behind because of the enormous expense of city life.

The dominant socio-cultural factors behind the male-only migration which focus the fallout on women can perhaps best be seen in a popular Lord Krishna's lyric,[59] in which Krishna's motive for leaving behind his wife Radha, when going off to Dwarka, range from her looking after the household, animals, milking the cows, making curd, churning the butter, making ghee, and looking after the children. And Krishna's insistence on '*donu chale na sare*' (it will not do for both of us to leave) underlines the work culture of women, left at home by the migrating male, which requires her essential presence.

Another popular folk song recorded in 1984 emphasizes her agricultural work.[60] In this, the woman while beseeching her husband to take her with him, complains that although he goes away to do a *naukri* (job), she is left behind to work with a hoe and a sickle in her hand. Indeed, a work culture in which women cannot even be spared to visit their natal homes for a few days, could hardly acquiesce to her going off with her husband.[61] Very clearly, the care provided by a woman of the land, cattle, and the household, alone has allowed a man to avail of the job opportunity outside. The family females taking over the entire agricultural work left untended by

---

[57] 1983, *Census of Haryana, 1981*, series 6, part II, Special Report and Tables, Chandigarh: Directorate of Census Operations Haryana, pp. 47–61.

[58] Mehra, 'Social Mobility in Rural Haryana'.

[59] Nadan Hariyanavi, 1962, *Haryana Lokgeet Sangrah* (Hindi), Delhi: Dehati Pustak Bhandar, pp. 107–8.

[60] Ibid., p. 80.

[61] Government of Haryana, 1983, *Haryana District Gazetteer, Gurgaon, 1983*, Chandigarh: Haryana District Gazetteers Organization, Revenue Department, p. 121.

their menfolk has led to yet greater intensity of work for women. Men do come back frequently due to the close proximity of their work and village, specially during the peak agricultural seasons, but their coming has never meant the withdrawal of women from agricultural work.

Another factor which has kept a high rate of female participation in agricultural work intact is the dominant cultural work ethics for women. Culturally, a woman has always been an equal work partner in agriculture. However, this only becomes demanding and operative after her marriage. In Haryana, marriage not only underlines the wife and mother roles but also her responsibility for agricultural and animal rearing work. Her active agricultural work participation is born out of the cultural understanding that this is 'their work' and they are bound to do it.

Even when leading questions are asked about their attitude to agricultural work, the women almost unanimously reply: '*hamare ghar (khet) ka kaam sai kaisi sharmindgi*' (there is nothing to feel ashamed of about doing your own work).[62] The concept of '*hamara khet*' (our land) is very apparent. The woman looks upon the land as not belonging only to the man but as a family property. And the reigning ideology insists that those who own it must work at it as the *kheti* is known to give best results when worked at by those who own it.

Several proverbs recorded in the nineteenth century, which continue to be popularly cited even now, make this point:

jis kheti per khasam na jawe
wuh kheti khasam nu khawe[63]
(If the owner does not work on his farm the farm swallows him up.)

Another one pronounces:

sari kheti uski jo apu bawe hal
uski adhi jis ki bail by ka hal
uski adhi na sari jo kai baithe pucche
kahan chalen mhare hal[64]
(One who ploughs the land gets everything
One who has seeds and bullocks gets half

---

[62] This was the general comment of all women, young and old.

[63] A commonly cited proverb both by men and women. Also included in the nineteenth century collection of R. Maconachie, 1870, *Selected Agricultural Proverbs of the Punjab*, Delhi: Imperial Hall Press, p. 180.

[64] Ibid., p. 181.

One who sits back and wonders who is working
gets nothing at all.)

This sentiment is fully shared by women. Most acknowledge the personal satisfaction derived from working in their own fields. This feeling is pervasive among nearly all the cultivating castes because traditionally, even the wealthy never decried working on one's own land. An old proverb from Ambala emphasizes:

kheti, pali, bandgi, aur ghore ka tang
charon ap hi kijiye chahe lakho log ho sang[65]
(Even if you have thousands of attendants
you should do four things yourself: farming,
letter writing, worship and harnessing a horse.)

Confirming this proverb, the women declared, *'beshak paisa ho jave, sab kaam karti hain'* (all women work despite the availability of money).[66] The women play an integral role in the rural economy without really being conscious of it. Therefore, it is not looked at as a financial proposition and, in fact, it is not even considered to be income generating. The concept of *'hamara kaam sai'* (it is our work) makes it a moral duty rather than an economic contribution.

It is a fact that women are spending more time today in doing both agricultural and domestic work, specially with the coming of the green and white revolutions. Their economic participation is undisputed, yet, what seems to be crucial is not the work done by women but its evaluation, which shows no signs of change. An increase in their work load makes no difference to the way their economic contribution and work is valued. Paradoxically, the family females in particular, perceive only 'male work' as income generating and not their own, although they are, and have always been, conscious of the hard work which they put in. This could be evidenced even earlier. A nineteenth century proverb, for example, maintained:

jeore se nara ghisna hai[67]
(Women as cattle bound, working and enduring all.)

---

[65] Ibid.

[66] Opinion voiced in village Jhojho Chamani in district Bhiwani, and village Chhara in district Rohtak.

[67] S.W. Fallon, 1886, *A Dictionary of Hindustani Proverbs*, Benares: Lazraus and Co., p. 114.

Women's own perceptions come out vividly in this saying, which is still remembered and cited to illustrate the 'back-breaking' work which the women put in the fields and at home. In most of the villages I visited in my fieldwork, the young and old were more than willing to catalogue their day-to-day work.[68] Women's awareness in Haryana of being heavily overworked has been recorded by another scholar as well.[69] Yet, the strong cultural and ideological hold has conditioned them to internalize it to such an extent that women accept the burden of work as their moral duty—just a part of the numerous duties to be performed. Therefore, women consider their own work as being supplementary to the main work of man. The males, on their side, consider this work as being essential for women's health. The general refrain heard is *'kaam karne se aurat tandrust rahe sai'* (a woman who works, remains healthy).

By equating health with work, the male reasoning has made the work ethos more rigorous. This logic is also used to deny any advantage that technology might provide to women in the household to lighten her work load. If, on the other hand, women attempt to subvert this logic refraining from work, their behaviour is vehemently and even violently condemned and dealt with. This work ethos is constantly subverted by men, who can be seen with ample leisure time on their hands, smoking their *hukkas*, playing cards, or just hanging about, and shows that the work ethos applies only to women. This is ironical when it is accepted that men notionally are not idle beings, but bread winners.

FEMALE AGRICULTURAL LABOUR:
INCREASING MARGINALIZATION

In sum, as far as work is concerned, the green revolution has not really affected family female workers from cultivating households who continue to contribute greatly in Haryana, both in the green revolution and non-green revolution areas. The work-hit are really the female wage earners who are becoming increasingly marginalized.

---

[68] The feeling among rural women that it was 'hard life' for them was universal. A few, like Moorti Devi, 1986, village Mokhra, 7 August, said it in comparison with the city women.

[69] Madhu Kishwar, 1986, 'Nature of Women's Mobilisation in Rural India: An Exploratory Essay', *Economic and Political Weekly*, vol. XXIII, nos 52 and 53, pp. 2754–63.

In the initial phases of the introduction of HYV and mechanization, Haryana underwent what has been described by economists as the expansionary phase of labour absorption, that is, roughly till about 1977.[70] It is only in the last decade or so that labour absorption could be seen to have stagnated, though not diminished. This is due entirely to the post-expansionary phase developments in states like Haryana, Punjab, and northern Uttar Pradesh (UP), concentrating on intensification of mechanization and utilization of labour-saving devices. In the expansionary phase, more intense cultivation and multiple cropping coupled with increased costs demanded additional labour for better cultivation, harvesting, and handling of the greater output. This resulted in the increased use of both casual as well as permanent or attached labour. The former category of agricultural labour shows an increasing male dominance and the latter an almost male monopolistic condition. Economic data from Haryana shows that in the most advanced green revolution area, the permanent male agricultural labour force comprises 48 per cent of the total labour force, that is, permanent plus regular casual, as compared to less than 1 per cent of the female permanent agricultural labour (Table 6.2). In fact, one can say that all female labour in varied regions of Haryana is really casual labour, that is, either regular or seasonal labour only. Among the casual labour also, the full time agricultural work has invariably been for the male labour, as female labour tends to get employed at peak agricultural seasons like harvest time.[71]

It is significant that in the backward areas, the total demand for agricultural labour is low and in that also, the share of female labour is lower still. For example, those areas of Mahendergarh and parts of Gurgaon, Jind, and Hissar which have dry land agriculture have significantly more male agricultural labourers willing to do extra work, if available, at wages even slightly lower than prevailing wages,[72] a situation where, if men are willing to underbid their own labour, the women will naturally lose out. Table 6.2 shows female labour to be a mere 15 per cent of male agricultural labour in the most advanced

---

[70] Bhalla, 'Technological Change and Women Workers', pp. WS67–78. Also, see Jose, 'Agricultural Wages in India', pp. A46–58.

[71] Billing and Singh, 'Mechanisation and the Wheat Revolution'.

[72] A.C. Ganwar and M.V. George, 1973, 'Rural Unemployment in Haryana', *Eastern Economist*, vol. 16, no. 4, 27 July, pp. 159–63.

Table 6.2 Agricultural Labourers, Permanent and Casual, by Sex (1972–3)

	Region A			Region B			Region C		
	Total	Casual	Permanent	Total	Casual	Permanent	Total	Casual	Permanent
Male agricultural labourers	1,26,975	54,735	72,240	1,25,873	88,129	37,744	56,633	49,683	4,820
Casual and permanent male agricultural labourers as per cent of total male agricultural labourers		93.1	56.9		70.0	30.0		91.2	8.8
Female agricultural labourers	22,599	21,146	1,453	23,251	23,251	—	5,084	5,084	—
Casual and permanent female agricultural labourers as per cent of all agricultural labourers	15.1	27.9	15.6	15.6	20.9	—	8.5	9.3	—
Per cent of female agricultural labourers from landless labour households	51.8	45.3	6.4	32.5	32.5	—	81.3	81.3	—

Source: Calculated from Sheila Bhalla, 1976, 'New Relations of Production' in Haryana', *Economic and Political Weekly*, vol. XI, no. 13, pp. 1923–30.

Notes: Region A: High technology richest agricultural area with 70 per cent of total cropped area under irrigation and 26 per cent under HYV.
Region B: Moderate technology agricultural area with 62 per cent of total cropped area under irrigation and 14 per cent under HYV.
Region C: Low technology agricultural area with 12 per cent under irrigation and less than 6 per cent under HYV.

green revolution areas. This percentage dips to 8.5 per cent in the least green revolution affected area.

For this small per cent of female agricultural labour, the number of days of employment is also much lower than for male agricultural labour. For example, the female average for days employed as a percentage of male days employed in 1969–70 were as follows: 30.35 for sowing; 58.9 for harvesting; and 32.00 for other activities.[73] On the whole, the female, on an average, was employed for only 30.6 per cent of male days only. In fact, the average number of days that female agricultural labour is employed in a year has shown a steady decline. For example, the average annual full days of agricultural work in 1964–5, or in a pre-green revolution period, was calculated to be 173 days in the then combined Haryana and Punjab; this declined within a decade in 1974–5 to 131 days, a decline of 24.27 per cent.[74] Moreover, the average annual days not worked due to want of work increased from fifty-nine days in 1964–5 to eighty-eight days in 1974–5, an increase of nearly 50 per cent.[75] Both these factors combine to reduce severely the total annual earning capacity of female agricultural labour. In fact, the average number of wage earners among the female agricultural labourers declined from 0.52 persons in 1974–5 to 0.34 persons in 1977–8, that is, a decline of 34.61 per cent.[76]

It is noteworthy that of the total female agricultural labour force in 1970–1, those from agricultural labour households were 17.80 per cent as compared to 19.20 per cent of those from small cultivating households.[77] This greater intrusion of the agricultural labour, both male and female, from landowning households may very well account

---

[73] G.S. Bhalla, 1974, *Changing Agrarian Structure in India: A Study of the Impact of Green Revolution in Haryana*, New Delhi: Meenakshi Prakashan, p. 97; Geeta Sen, 1982, 'Women Workers in Green Revolution', in Lourdes Beneria (ed.), *Women and Development*, New York: Praeger Publication, pp. 29–64.

[74] Government of India, *Rural Labour Enquiry, 1974–75*: 1981, Final Report on Employment and Unemployment of Rural Labour Households, Chandigarh: Labour Bureau, Ministry of Labour, pp. 140, 143, Tables 3.3(a), IM and 3.3(a) LW.

[75] Ibid., see Tables 3.6(a), 1.W.

[76] Government of India, 1988, *Rural Labour Enquiry, 1977–78: Report on Wages and Earnings of Rural Labour Households*, Shimla: Labour Bureau, Ministry of Labour, Tables 2.9(a) 1; Government of India, *Rural Labour Enquiry, 1974–75*, pp. 80–1, Table 2.9(a) 1.

[77] Sen, 'Women Workers in Green Revolution'.

for the growing marginalization of agricultural labour from landless agricultural labour households who, in Haryana, are primarily derived from the scheduled castes. In fact, a 1968 study highlighted the fact that labour offers from the small uneconomic cultivator's households were keeping out the landless labour families from employment.[78] This has obviously increased. The increasing involvement in agricultural labour of the families from landowning households is specially noticeable in the high and moderate technology-rich agricultural areas, but shows a decline as the impact of the green revolution diminishes; it further dwindles in the dry zones (Table 6.3).

TABLE 6.3   Female Labour from Households Whose
Main Income Source is Cultivation

	Region A	Region B	Region C
Total female labourers (casual, there being no permanent ones).	22,599	23,251	5,084
Those from cultivating households (female)	8,782	11,386	952
Percentage	38.9	49.9	18.7
Total male labourers (casual only)	26,975	1,25,873	54,683
Those from cultivating households (male)	29,021	27,602	13,804
Percentage	22.9	21.9	25.2

Source: Sheila Bhalla, 'New Relations of Production in Haryana Agriculture', Economic and Political Weekly, 27 March 1976, vol. XI, no. 13, pp 1923–30.
Note: For details of the three regions see Table 6.2.

Taken together, the two most advanced regions in terms of technology, irrigation, use of HYV, and agricultural output (regions A and B) show 44 per cent of females from cultivating households performing casual agricultural labour. This 44 per cent concentration in the green revolution region, as compared to the 19 per cent in the low technology area, clearly relates it to the new agricultural changes associated with the green revolution and technological changes which increased the demand for agricultural labour. Moreover, the increased money capital investment required for the new technology put a premium on money incomes in small farm households, so that women started to be sent out

[78] B. Sivaraman, 1968, 'Problems of Agricultural Labour', paper presented at the conference on Agricultural Labour, The National Commission on Labour, December, pp. 182–5.

increasingly for agricultural labour not only at seasonal peak times but also on a more regular basis.[79] The high agricultural wages undoubtedly worked as an incentive. An examination of the total number of productive working days of women workers among small and marginal farmers and among landless labourers, who primarily subsist on the wage earnings alone, shows that whereas the former worked on an average for 110 days a year, the latter worked only for seventy-nine days in a year, that is, a difference of 28.13 per cent.[80]

The supply of this agricultural labour force is traceable to the increasing fragmentation of landholdings, due to a variety of reasons. In fact, the green revolution has coincided with an enormous increase in the number of holdings below 5 acres from 16.14 per cent in 1961 to 45.49 per cent in 1971.[81] For the very small, under 2.5 acre holding, there has not been enough work to go round. Even in the next category, 2.5–5 acres, the draft on unpaid family labour is not enough to exhaust its availability and willingness to undertake additional field crop work.[82] Although the main agricultural labour available for hire comes from small landholders downwards, the size of the landholding alone does not determine this factor. Other crucial factors like the number of family members, income from agriculture or other sources, the fertility of landholding and inputs, also contribute to the family members hire-out as agricultural labourers. For example, a government survey of 1973–4 showed that in village Mirch of district Bhiwani, a household with 10.92 hectares of land earned Rs 210 per year from agricultural labour work.[83]

These observations were confirmed by my own field trips in which, in the green revolution areas like village Bandh of Karnal district, Pawan Singh, a Jat zamindar, owner of two-and-a-half *bighas* of land, and his wife Bimla, perform *mazdoori* (agricultural wage work) in their

[79] Ibid. Also, see Bhalla, 'New Relations of Production in Haryana Agriculture'.

[80] 'Integrated Rural Development', vol. III, pp. 79–80.

[81] For these reasons, see Bhalla, 'New Relations of Production in Haryana Agriculture'; and also, Bhalla, 'Agricultural Growth'.

[82] Bhalla, 'Technological Change and Women Workers'.

[83] Government of Haryana, 1976, *Family Budgets of Cultivators in Haryana, 1973–4*, Chandigarh: Planning Department, Economic and Statistical Organization, pp. 46–51, Appendix VII. The disaggregated (family level) data are not available for all of these annual reports. In fact, after 1975–6, these were totally discontinued.

neighbour's and kinsman's *khet* (field).[84] Similarly, in village Dujjana of Rohtak district, many women are known to work not only on their own land but also as wage labour to supplement the money incomes of their households.[85]

The involvement of a fairly large number of families from cultivating households is therefore obvious. What is less obvious is how many of them come from castes other than scheduled castes, as this has social significance. However, in the whole of Haryana, the total number of scheduled caste households among cultivators is calculated to be 5.18 per cent only.[86] Even if all of them are considered to be working as agricultural labourers, overwhelming numbers from other castes are still included. This female involvement for agricultural wage work shows a considerable modification in the old behavioural patterns and prejudices among the cultivators. They were known to frown upon their family females working as agricultural wage labourers considering this as affecting and compromising their status. Clearly, status considerations have been superseded by others. With land units too small to employ all family members or to provide full subsistence for all of them, it is the male, by and large, who continues to operate his own holding, sending out the female for wage work, while he himself might explore the possibility of outside employment, preferably in the urban centres.[87] Table 6.2 clearly shows that as compared to female, the male agricultural labour from cultivating households is significantly less, that is, 21.55 per cent less in the first two highly developed green revolution affected regions; only in the least green revolution affected region do the male outnumber the female agriculture labourers by 6.5 per cent.

[84] Pawan Singh and his brother Abhay Singh inherited 2½ bighas of land each from their father. Abhay Singh, however, does not do any mazdoori as his grown-up sons periodically remit money to him. One son is employed in the Delhi Constabulary and the other in the Delhi Transport Corporation.

[85] Chhotu Devi, village Dujjana, cited a number of instances where women were 'pocketing as much as Rs 20 per day' as their wages. Similar cases were reported in Karnal district. Interestingly, the fact that 'Brahmini' or Brahmin women were working as wage labourers in the fields was reported by many.

[86] *Census of Haryana, 1981*, series 6, vol. I, part III, A and B, General Economic Tables, pp. 156–7 and part IX, Special Tables for Scheduled Castes, pp. 6–7.

[87] For the integration of the small uneconomic landholders and their families into the labour market instead of product market, see Alain de Janvry, 1975, 'The Political Economy of Rural Development in Latin America: An Interpretation', *American Journal of Agricultural Economics*, vol. 57, no. 30, August, pp. 490–9.

Crucially, it is the land management along with labour which has always remained in man's hands leaving labour alone to women. It follows that to sustain itself under pressure, the family would preserve the traditional role pattern and not necessarily effect a reversal in it. Therefore, a woman continues to labour but the man retains his production management-cum-labour role on his own land. The female economic participation as wage labour from cultivating households without the male underlines her subjugation; and shows the power equation in the rural households which makes a male work on his own holding while he sends out the women for wage labour. So, while men participate in the dominant capitalist mode of production, this participation has important repercussions for women, whose proletarianization is distinctly visible. This also underlines the man's possession and control of land and other means of production, rendering him a member of a different class from that of the woman who is absorbed in the system as an agricultural wage labourer.

This compromise by men of cultivating households with regard to their family females working as agricultural labourers has been for casual and seasonal labour only, and not attached, even though attached labour admittedly has certain advantages like assurance of continuity of employment and regular wages, and so on. Tom Brass shows the strong dislike of this attachment status and a corresponding preference for non-bonded casual employment due to reasons ranging from maltreatment, long working hours, low wages, and the lack of freedom experienced by the attached labourers.[88] Required to perform full agricultural as well as domestic jobs, the attached labourer is, in reality, no more than a servant of the landowner. Consequently, members from cultivating households and agricultural castes are reluctant to work as attached labourers considering it below their dignity.[89] The attached workers—male or female—are, therefore, mostly drawn from the scheduled castes.

[88] Tom Brass, 1990, 'Class Struggle and the Deproletarianisation of Agricultural Labour in Haryana (India)', *The Journal of Peasant Studies*, vol. 18, no. 1, October, pp. 36–7. According to the information coming from different parts of India, the number of permanent agricultural labourers is on the decline. Haryana also shows a similar trend, though much less than in other parts of India. This information has been communicated to me by Sheila Bhalla.

[89] Government of India, 1975, *Report on Intensive Type Studies on Rural Labour in India: Hissar, 1967–68*, Shimla: Labour Bureau, Ministry of Labour, pp. 7.2–7.8, 12.6.

Females from cultivating households taking outside employment is not entirely new. Yet, the form it has assumed and the vast numbers now involved is certainly a new phenomenon. The earlier practice revolved around a custom called *dhangwara*, where two cultivating households, including their females, helped each other during the crucial peak season.[90] The capitalist thrust in agriculture has made this practice almost invisible; and changed it from voluntary mutual help to a hard transaction of a cash and kind arrangement. The other features of dhangwara are however still visible. For example, labour during special peak periods continues to be provided but preferably from one's own kinsmen or caste fellows within the village precincts. Regarding this change, the local male opinion in village Bandh of Karnal district stated: *'sharminda to mahsus karte hain per ab bura nahin mante'* (they do feel embarrassed, but no longer frown upon it). Another interesting fact discovered was that there is a great deal of kinship feeling which makes an employer engage his fellow caste man or caste woman for mazdoori in preference to the scheduled castes. Apart from kinship, a hard pragmatism seems to be operating in terms of gaining a more satisfactory work output, behind the acceptance and even encouragement of this practice. One of the more revealing reasons can be found in the following comment: *'doosari mattar gashti karti hai, yeh sharmati kaam zada karti ha'*[91] (acute embarrassment, for having to work on other's fields, makes the woman work harder. The low caste women while away their time).

Clearly, members of the landowning strata see their fellow caste women working for them on wages as needing much less supervision than scheduled caste women, which for the cultivating owners, becomes an important practical factor behind such employment in preference to others. Also, on account of their poor physique, the scheduled caste women are less strong than the upper caste women, and lose out in the competition for wage work, where hard physical work is required.

[90] Interview with Harpal Singh, Ratan Singh, and Ram Chander, 1988, village Bandh, district Karnal, 21–2 August. They are three brothers in their late forties who together own 33 bighas (11 bighas each) of land in the village. For the existence of a similar system of labour exchange in Rajasthan, called *Deelavari*, see Tulsi Patel, 1987, 'Women's Work and Their Status; Dialectics of Subordination and Assertion', Social Action, vol. 37, no 2, April–June, pp. 126–49.

[91] Fieldwork, 1988, in village Bandh of Karnal district, 21–7 August.

The landowners believe that upper caste women perform a great deal more work in a given time than scheduled caste women. Yet another reason given for employment of upper caste women involves the managing of the pollution aspect in the rendering of small services, such as in providing drinking water. In the case of a scheduled caste labourer, the stored water taken from the *ghara* (earthen pot) would have to be poured so as to be drunk in cupped hands. But a non-scheduled caste person would take the water out for herself or himself. Here, kinship and caste binding on women can be seen to operate both as exploitation and protection given to them in the context of the forces of market economy and other forms of harassment. The green revolution, instead of breaking down caste norms has not only adopted them but has also reinforced classes within castes and differing statuses within the hierarchies, between men and women, and has actually pitted the scheduled caste women against other caste women. What emerges is a peculiar reinforced mix of patriarchy, caste, and class.

WORK AND WAGES: GENDER DIFFERENTIALS

Gender differential has determined both work and wages in rural areas. Basically, this difference emanates from the ideology operating behind the evaluation of the work of male as compared to female agricultural labourers, their capacity to perform certain tasks, and the awarding of this performance in terms of wages. The existing differential has been further affected by the differing effects of green revolution technology which has mechanized certain jobs performed by males and females, all of which have proved detrimental to the latter. For example, wherever mechanization has occurred, making the task easier, men have taken over those activities traditionally performed by women, like threshing and fodder cutting. Thus, hand threshing is mostly done by women, but when power threshers or electricity operated fodder and chaff cutters are used, men take over, with the women as active helpers. Moreover, men's work has been greatly simplified and the time spent on it reduced by machines, for example, in the case of ploughing. Men drive tractors and harvest and thresh with a combine. This is so much so that all skilful jobs, and those associated with machinery introduced under the green revolution package programme—like stocking and distribution of fertilizers, seeds, or insecticides or management of the measured water supply—are a close preserve of the male.

A woman, who is generally regarded as inferior to a man, is considered specially handicapped in matters of acquiring mechanical skill.

The male who considers *aurat ki mat to guddi ke peeche ho sai*[92] (a woman is brainless), can hardly trust her with machines. Most men tend to ridicule a woman's intellect; a few passed crude remarks about her intellect being between her thighs. Consequently, jobs like transplantation, weeding, sowing, interculture, and the like, requiring much less skill and generally stereotyped as purely female tasks have come to be reserved for females. The green revolution has, therefore, brought out a more severe division of agricultural work. The explanations regarding this range from the biological, with its consideration of a woman's body being suited only for certain agricultural operations, to the existence of 'sex-differences' in performance between male and female, specially in connection with mechanization.[93]

More important has been the effect of this division of work on wages. Not only do all the jobs reserved for men carry higher wages, but men also get paid more for those jobs which they share with women. The sharp difference in wage rates for male and female agricultural labourers in Haryana in the so-called female specific and dominated tasks as well as in an average day's labour earnings can be seen in Tables 6.4 and 6.5.

TABLE 6.4 Average Daily Earnings of Male and Female Agricultural
Labour Belonging to Agricultural Household in
Different Agricultural Operations

(in Rupees)

	1974–5		1977–8	
	Male	Female	Male	Female
Transplating	4.93	2.70	5.76	4.16
Weeding	5.23	4.67	5.50	3.50
Harvesting	5.56	4.41	6.26	4.56

Sources: Rural Labour Enquiry, 1977–78: Report on Wages and Earnings of Rural Labour Households, Labour Bureau, Ministry of Labour, Government of India, Shimla, 1988, pp. 193–4, Table 3.3(a) 1 and pp. 181–2, Table 3.3(a) lM.

[92] This local saying was popular and in use even much earlier. Recorded in the nineteenth century as *'aurat ki aql guddi peeche hoti hai'* (a woman's sense always lies in the back of her neck). See Fallon, *A Dictionary of Hindustani Proverbs,* p. 22.

[93] Sunanda Krishnamurthy, 1988, 'Wage Differentials in Agriculture by Caste, Sex and Operations', *Economic and Political Weekly,* vol. XXIII, no. 50, 10 December, pp. 2651–7.

TABLE 6.5   Agricultural Wages in Haryana, 1970–1 to 1984–5

(in Rupees)

Year	1	2	3	4	5	6
1970–1	6.44	3.96	59.64	100.00	6.64	3.96
1971–2	6.84	4.17	60.97	105.67	6.47	3.94
1973–4	7.40	4.26	57.55	140.72	5.25	3.02
1974–5	8.58	5.02	58.53	173.71	4.93	2.88
1975–6	8.55	5.22	61.01	158.76	5.38	3.28
1976–7	8.75	6.32	72.25	157.21	5.56	4.02
1977–8	10.44	6.68	63.99	171.13	6.10	3.90
1978–9	11.17	6.61	59.20	173.19	6.44	3.81
1979–80	11.89	8.35	70.27	192.78	6.16	4.33
1980–1	12.41	9.62	77.54	225.25	5.50	4.27
1982–3	16.14	13.81	85.55	247.42	6.52	5.58
1983–4	18.15	14.40	97.35	264.94	6.85	5.43
1984–5	19.35	14.99	77.47	291.23	6.00	5.14

Sources: Columns 1–3, A.V. Jose, 'Agricultural Wages in India', *Economic and Political Weekly*, vol. XXIII, no. 26, 25 June 1988, pp. A46–58; Columns 4–6, calculated from Government of India, *Indian Labour Journal*, vol. 28, no. 12, December 1987, p. 103. The basis of these calculations follow the same norms as laid down by A.V. Jose.
Notes: 1. Money wage rates for male agricultural labourer; 2: Money wage rates for female agricultural labourer; 3: Ratio of female to male agricultural money wages; 4: Agricultural Labourer's Consumer Price Index (April 1970–1 prices); 5: Real wages of male agricultural labourer; and 6: Real wages of female agricultural labourer.

The figures show that even for the same work, there are considerable differences in the wages of male and female agricultural labourers. In fact, this difference increased within a span of three years from 10.70 per cent in 1974–5 to 36.36 per cent in 1977–8 for weeding; and from 20.68 per cent in 1974–5 to 30.57 per cent in 1977–8 for harvesting. In transplanting alone, there was a narrowing of this difference, but then here also, a female in 1977–8 was drawing 15.6 per cent less than a male.

Table 6.5 shows the continuing difference between male and female agricultural wages from the latter being 40 per cent less in 1970–1 to 23 per cent in 1984–5. These figures certainly have a positive aspect which shows a narrowing of the gap between their wages over a period of 14 years, though never reaching equality. The narrowing of the gap has occurred due to the increase in the female agricultural wages in absolute terms which has been 279 per cent to 191 per cent for the male during this period. Yet, the real wages of both show a decline. Female wages show an increase only from 1979–80 onwards; by 1984–5, a 30 per cent rise is visible in the rate of real wages. The real wages of male agricultural labour, on the other hand, tended to stagnate almost throughout. For the stagnation in male agricultural wages, various reasons are offered. These range from the migration of agricultural labourers, predominantly male, into Haryana and Punjab from the neighbouring states of UP and Bihar, and the combined effect of technological changes leading to stagnation in labour absorption in the preceding decade, to demographic pressure on land, the vast unemployment, and segmentation in the labour market in which hiring of attached labour at cheaper rates significantly depresses male agricultural labour wages.[94]

Regarding the increase in the real wage rate of women agricultural labour, a topic which undoubtedly needs more research,[95] two factors, among others, may perhaps be held responsible. One is the in-migration of labour which has been 96 per cent male,[96] and second, the segmentation of the labour market in which operation-specific division of labour has kept the demand for female agricultural labour high. For example, primary agricultural work like weeding, interculture, and transplanting which have increased enormously due to a greater intensity of cropping and use of new technology, are nevertheless jobs associated and biologically explained and determined for females. So firm is this stereotyping that women are not only preferred but many women consider themselves as performing these tasks better than men and at considerably cheaper rates of wages. It is not unusual to find some of the men echoing the same opinion. Moreover, men are not always readily available to work at these jobs. Not only have these jobs come to be seen

[94] H.S. Sidhu, 1988, 'Wage Determination in the Rural Labour Market: The Case of Punjab and Haryana', *Economic and Political Weekly*, vol. XXIII, nos 52 and 53, 24–31 December, pp. A147–50.

[95] One can hardly agree with A.V. Jose's suggestion of the substitution of male workers by female workers as an explanation of increase in the real wage rate of woman. See Jose, 'Agricultural Wages in India'.

[96] S. Mukhopadhyay, 1987, 'Inter-Rural Labour Circulation in India: An Analysis', Asian Employment Programme Working Paper, ILO-ARTEP, Delhi; A.S. Oberoi and M. Singh, 1980, 'Migration Flows in Punjab's Green Revolution Belt', *Economic and Political Weekly*, vol. XV, no. 13, 29 March, pp. A2–12.

in many instances as *auraton ka kaam* (female work), but they are also lower paid.[97] Both these factors militate against a general acceptance of these jobs by males. Yet, whatever the improvement in the female agricultural wage rates, the reality of the significant lower earnings of the daily as well as yearly earnings of women being much less than their male counterpart continues to exist.

A research study on conditions in north India[98] reveals that women do not regard the wage differential as unjust and also, feel the man's work as 'harder and more strenuous'. Further, they also feel that 'if they receive wages equal to men's wages they would be getting equal wages for unequal work'. It is interesting that I found this perception of women's work shared by employees, their family members, as well as the wage earners themselves, both male and female. Maria Mies explains this qualitative difference in evaluation in terms of the tools women use which depend upon women's own physical energy. For example, women use their hands for most agricultural operations like sowing, transplanting, weeding, harvesting, threshing, grain processing, and the like. But a man's tools usually depend on other sources of energy like hydraulic, animal, mechanical, chemical, and electrical energy. So, although women's tools require more labour-intensive work than those of men, it is an energy relatively less efficient than that of draught animals and machines and therefore, considered less 'productive' than man's work and also, less valued.[99]

In view of the greater value being placed upon men's work, women show a kind of self-imposed subalternism under patriarchal norms. Such a self-image clearly stands in the way of forging a democratic movement to voice a united demand for better and equal wages. A not infrequent refrain of the landowners in some of the villages was, 'if we have to pay the same wages to women, then why not take a man who'll do better and more work'.[100] Although this seems to contradict the opinion that in certain agricultural tasks women perform better, the payment to, and acceptance of lower wages by women, even for the

[97] General opinion summed up in 1990 in villages Lapra, Kaith, and Kalanaur in Yamuna Nagar district, 8–10 August, voiced by landless agricultural labourers as well as landowners.

[98] Leela Kasturi, 1981, 'Poverty, Migration and Women's Status', Unpublished report, ICSSR (pages not numbered).

[99] Mies, *Indian Women in Subsistence and Agricultural Labour*, p. 55.

[100] General opinion of the landowners in 1990 in villages Lapra, Kaith, and Kalanaur of Yamuna Nagar district, 8–12 August.

same task, reinforces and sustains the ideology that female labour is less valuable. Therefore, despite the work involved, women do not acquire the status which a man receives in return for agricultural labour on the land. For, even in a household of labourers, the female's earnings are meant to supplement the male's earnings. This is notwithstanding the fact that the male earnings often go towards liquor and tobacco and the women's earnings actually support the family.[101] The not so infrequent cases of households headed by females where female earnings are no longer a mere supplement, still remain exceptional, with the implications unregistered even among women earners themselves.

This ideological situation, resulting in low evaluation of female labour in a restricted market for agricultural labour displaying a high degree of unemployment and underemployment, leads to women not only being thrown out of work but to a self-withdrawal by women from the labour market as well, in order to give the males an opportunity of finding work first. Termed as 'sexual dualism', the major cultural premise is that man is the breadwinner and a woman, therefore, accepts subordination in the face of this basic fact.[102] This coupled with traditional social prejudices about the nature of women's work and her inferior biological capacity to work has resulted in restricting her work options during non-peak seasons and keeping her wages comparatively lower. Consequently, one of the most deprived rural sections of female agriculturists, that is, wage earners, have remained adversely affected, despite the enormous rise in productivity and income levels of landowners of Haryana, specially of the green revolution regions.

[101] For similar observations, see V. Shobha, 1987, *Rural Women and Development: A Study of Female Agricultural Labourers in Telengana*, New Delhi: Mittal Publications, pp. 84–9.

[102] See Guy Standing, cited in Rohini Nayyar, 1987, 'Female Participation Rate in Rural India', *Economic and Political* Weekly, vol. XXII, no. 51, 19 December, pp. 2207–16.

7

Persistence of a Custom
Cultural Centrality of Ghunghat*

The rural ethos of work presents a contradictory visual image of women in Haryana: full participation of women in the dominant economic activities albeit in a *ghunghat* (veil). This dual image signifies a dual reality which serves patriarchal needs. On one hand, it retains women as full working partners of men, showing the genuine seclusion of women to be clearly uneconomical, and on the other, the retention of ghunghat, refashioned to accommodate their intensive work involvement, imposes efficacious constraints upon women, leaving them ineffective in all crucial spheres. Ghunghat effects the most cogent control on married women which extends from their private and public conduct in purely domestic and familial sphere to the outside social and political structures of the wider village community.[1] These constraints

---

* This chapter was originally published in 1993, *Social Scientist*, 21(9–11): 91–112.

[1] A large number of scholars have provided comprehensive analysis of ghunghat or *purdah* observance. For a wide-ranging resume of this scholarly work across societies in South Asia and the ideology behind its observance, structuring sexual, social, economic, and political relations, see David G. Mandelbaum, 1988, *Women's Seclusion and Man's Honour: Sex Roles in North India, Bangladesh and Pakistan*, Tucson: University of Arizona Press; Hanna Papanek and Gail Minault (eds), 1982, *Separate Worlds: Studies of Purdah in South Asia*, New Delhi: Chanakya Publications; Ursula M. Sharma, 1978, 'Women and Their Affines: The Veil as a Symbol of Separation', *Man*, vol. 13, no. 2, June, pp. 218–33; Ursula M. Sharma, 1980, 'Purdah and Public Space', in

impose social distance and patterns of avoidance which regulate the behaviour and limit the interaction of women with those who control economic resources, wield power, and make decisions inside and outside the house, especially the senior males and some of the senior females. This essay seeks to analyse the persistence of the custom of ghunghat and the wider factors operating behind its reinforcement and inordinate acceptance, especially in the rapidly changing social milieu of post-colonial Haryana. Ghunghat emerges as an outward symbol of patriarchal control which has retained its hold over women despite dramatic internal politico-legal and socio-economic shifts, and, in fact, as a result of those shifts.

This analysis highlights women in ghunghat as being central to what is projected as the *dehati* (rural) culture'. It investigates how and why the veiled woman, with the attendant ideology of plain living and austere eating, is perceived by the rural people as the sole custodian of their culture. The stripping away of this veil is imagined as leading to the collapse of the entire rural social fabric. This rural culture is necessarily seen as opposed to the 'other' or 'urban culture', which attracts all the pejorative epithets with urban women as its symbolic target.

In the wake of the green revolution prosperity, the affluent sections of the rural population have taken over the externals of 'urban culture' in a big way. The change has not helped women in any positive manner and, in fact, it has tended to intensify its more negative effects for them. The newly acquired wealth spent on modern consumer durables has created yet greater nuclei of male control, confining women more and more in ghunghat. The growing urbanization has similarly separated a section of Haryanavis from the socio-cultural collective of the villages. With their life styles and cultural patterns necessarily imitative and derivative of the consumerist culture in metropolitan cities, they are far removed from the ideals of a simple and austere life. Yet, it has become incumbent, even upon them, to keep the symbol of their 'village culture', that is, their women, as 'safe' as the others do. These compulsions have, in fact, imposed an ideological barrier, inhibiting the spread of certain influences beneficial to women. This is evident in the successful negation in this region of the often catalytic, even liberating

---

Alfred de Souza (ed.), *Women in Contemporary India and South Asia*, New Delhi: Manohar, pp. 213–39.

effects of the partition of Punjab on its women. Moreover, the apprehension generated in the wake of drastic changes in the politico-legal structure granting equal rights of inheritance, marriage, and divorce, open defiance of the practice of levirate, remarriage of widows in the form of *punar vivah*, and increasing instances of runaway marriages have greatly contributed to male anxiety and increased the attempts to control women, leading in part to the strengthening of the custom of ghunghat.

The strength of this custom is ultimately based on social approval and its imposition lies in the hands of women themselves. On their side, women of Haryana, too, continue to support a 'rural culture' which is highly constrictive for them. Internal hierarchy among women has its own logic, with senior women enforcing this custom which ultimately safeguards the hold of patriarchy as well as their own control. Ably supported by women, the patriarchal stakes in the cultural centrality of ghunghat will not allow this norm to be breached.

EXIGENCIES OF WORK: REFASHIONING THE
WEARING OF *GHUNGHAT*

An ubiquitous sight in rural Haryana are the veiled women who cover either the whole face or just permit the eyes to show. This sight is somewhat incongruous set against the high visibility of women in Haryana involved in all sorts of field work, working alongside the men, from preparing the fields to irrigating and harvesting the crop. Visible, too, are women in processing agricultural produce at home, tending the animals, fetching and carrying water with heavy *ghara*s (earthen water pots) on their heads, or involved in numerous other domestic chores. The few uncovered faces that may be seen are those of the daughters of the village, yet to be married or visiting their natal homes, or those of older women, the exposure of whose face is socially sanctioned. Except for the very young, even these women invariably cover their heads.

Accepted as a symbol of seclusion, ghunghat or purdah, the two words being used interchangeably in this region, is generally explained as having created a spatial boundary between the private and the public domain; the latter being the exclusive preserve of men. Yet, in Haryana, ghunghat or purdah has not prevented rural women, despite their veiled faces, from working alongside men in the fields nor has it obliged them to observe any kind of seclusion. For many of them, the fields, although ostensibly a public space, are in reality a mere extension of private space. The need for women's participation in agricultural work, and the precedence given to agriculture as an economic activity, not only shows that this qualified seclusion is economically prudent but it has also refashioned the mode of wearing the ghunghat. The unhampered movements of arms and shoulders needed for field work, as also the danger of the ghunghat moving from its place accidentally while working, and exposing the face to view, has created its own compulsions. The form which ghunghat has had to adapt is known as *dhhattha* in which the face and head are wrapped up in a way that leaves the eyes unveiled. This also leaves the bosom unveiled as the *odhni* (a long scarf) is thrown back well behind the shoulders, closely hugging the neck. Some women can be seen to observe this form of ghunghat even while fetching water or while tackling domestic chores. On all other occasions, ghunghats of varying lengths covering the entire face are generally worn. Special care is also taken to cover both the face and the bosom in the presence of senior male affines.

The custom of ghunghat is perceived by the local populace to offer *izzat* (honour) to those before whom it is observed and to indicate a woman of *sharm-lihaz* (modesty and deferential behaviour). A woman's modesty is defined as '*ankh ki sharm*' (eye modesty). She is not expected to make direct eye contact with the senior village males. Her unveiled eyes in the work space are accepted not only due to the exigencies of work but also because, at best, her interaction is really with other women or with low caste and class men.

Yet, some men frown upon the dhhattha observance, while not denying its utility during work, considering it inadequate to preserve female modesty. They say: '*jab ankh ki sharm nahin rakhti to kya rehta hai*' (if eye modesty is breached, all is lost), and regret its growing usage. Significantly, the local perception, both male and female, rates the practice of ghunghat higher than dhhattha. Moreover, it is the somewhat older women who have been married for some years and have children who are given to observing dhhattha. The younger ones remain enveloped in a ghunghat nearly all the time, specially as in their early year or years of marriage, their domestic chores and animal husbandry and agricultural processing work are mostly performed at home and they are not required to tackle field work. These two differing practices of veil observance emphasize not merely the sexual but also the communicative dimension of ghunghat. In fact, the ghunghat, as a symbol of sexual control of women which operates by separating women from men among whom sexual relations are regarded with great disapproval,[2] offers only a partial explanation of this widespread practice. It also cannot be accepted as a mere symbol of feminine sexual modesty because often the ghunghat may cover the face but not the bosom. It is indeed a common sight in the villages to see women at work and in the house breastfeeding their infants with veiled faces.[3] However contradictory the image of a bared breast and veiled face may seem to us, local opinion, both male and female, perceives no contradiction in this. Paul Hershman explains this in terms of different compartments of behaviour: one of mother–child relations of mutual nurturance and the other of woman–senior man relation of mutual avoidance.[4] There is no transgression of the norms and values in either or even a defiance of the symbolic order. The breasts being primarily symbolic of nurturance may perhaps partially explain the popular acceptance and usage of the dhhattha version of ghunghat in which the bosom is exposed to view.

ENFORCING GHUNGHAT: HIERARCHICAL CONSIDERATIONS

Socio-economic consideration may have remoulded the wearing of ghunghat but it is nowhere being given up. In fact, it is estimated that an overwhelming 72.61 per cent of Haryana women observe ghunghat.[5]

---

[2] For the veil as a symbol of sexual control of women, see Paul Hershman, 1981, *Punjabi Kinship and Marriage*, New Delhi: Hindustan Publishing Corporation, pp. 158, 174–5; Mandelbaum, *Women's Seclusion and Man's Honour*, p. 1; Sharma, 'Women and their Affines', pp. 218–33. In the context of 'sexual modesty', Veena Das's article is helpful in understanding how purdah observance marks a different kind of sexual reality, operative, recognized, and understood by all, but denied outwardly. Veena Das, 1976, 'Masks and Faces: An Essay in Punjabi Kinship', *Contributions to Indian Sociology* (NS), vol. 10, no. 1, pp. 1–30.

[3] As a visual illustration of this, see a photograph published in the *Indian Express*, 1991, New Delhi, 8 September, p. 3. It shows a group of women who, among others, attended the sarv khap panchayat of 360 Bahadurgarh villages which met at Brahi village in Haryana on 7 September 1991, to protest against the stripping of some Brahi men before their women in a police station on 31 August 1991. The photograph shows a veiled woman with a dhattha feeding her infant at a public rally.

[4] Hershman, *Punjabi Kinship and Marriage*, pp. 74–5.

[5] Government of India, 1975, *Towards Equality: Report of the Committee on the Status of Women in India*, New Delhi: Department of Social Welfare, Ministry of Education and Social Welfare, pp. 61, 141.

A woman who does not observe or is reluctant to observe ghunghat is called *nangi* (nude) or *besharm* (shameless) and even *badmash* (loose character). Older women are particularly vocal and vehement in condemning any such lapse. The allegation made is '*chhati dikhati phirti hai*',[6] literally, she goes about exposing her bosom or breasts, rather than her face. The sexual references are explicit. The language used reaffirms the ideology of seclusion-cum-control and passes judgement on its non-observance. The male logical response to this, within the prevailing ideology, may very often be aggression, verbal or physical, and even indecent behaviour.

Clearly, senior women's vehemence and prejudice in favour of ghunghat emanates out of their own position in the family hierarchy which stands to be affected by its non-observance. Ghunghat in this region is observed by married women not only in the presence of their husbands and husband's affines, including most of the senior men of the village, but also notably in the presence of mothers-in-law or classificatory mothers-in-law. A ghunghat imposes upon women a passive and deferential mode of behaviour in her encounters not only with senior males but also with senior females; it affords women much less chance to disrupt this hierarchy.

The family hierarchy within the household itself is dominated by the older female, specially the mother-in-law, symbolized in the veiled younger women and unveiled mother-in-law. Indeed, there is a noticeable weakening of the observance of ghunghat among older women, which they observe much less and before fewer people in the village, indicating the weakening of the patriarchal hold to some extent. Significantly, this change in the wearing of odhni without ghunghat is accompanied with bolder and much less restrained behaviour. Ethnographic evidence similarly suggests that as women age and reach menopause, they tend to use the hitherto tabooed language of the male, often indulging in sexual banter or so-called 'obscene' comments with men listening indulgently and amusedly.[7] This kind of a behaviour is not uncommonly observed in Haryana. All this speaks for an hierarchy in the family unit itself; with the older woman, specially the mother-in-law, enjoying much more personal freedom herself and firmly in control

---

[6] Observations of Moorti Devi, a school teacher in village Mokhra, and several other women, 1986, village Mokhra, district Rohtak, 7 August.

[7] Mahadev L. Apte, 1985, *Humour and Laughter: An Anthropological Approach*, Ithaca: Cornell University Press, pp. 79–81.

of the younger women. She lays down norms of behaviour, dress, and speech; controls domestic life; and imposes the same oppressive regime on others which she had been forced to follow. It is she who allocates jobs in agriculture or the household; with heavy and difficult jobs in agriculture, animal husbandry, and household going to the daughter-in-law and lighter supervisory jobs remaining with her.

Apart from asserting and maintaining her own dominance, the mother-in-law is most effective in channelizing the institution of patriarchy in the household by confirming male dominance, including that of her sons' dominance over their wives and children.[8] In fact, at a very crucial stage of the young wife's life, the mother-in-law controls her contact and interaction with her husband knowing fully the 'dangers' involved to her own position. Here again, ghunghat comes in handy as the wife observes, and the mother-in-law ensures that she observes, ghunghat from her husband in the presence of others. Her potential influence is thus most effectively controlled through the strict observance of ghunghat. Once this is lifted, the reverse effect is significant and obvious.

Any attempt to avoid ghunghat even slightly is therefore severely criticized. Such attempts have become the subject of jokes among women themselves who negotiate it through an often double-edged humour. An interesting story told by a woman is illustrative of this:

In village Chatwal, a very small village, a father brusquely instructed his son to tell his *bahu* (daughter-in-law) to wear a proper *ghunghat*. The *bahu* quipped 'bhai keh de mere susre se ke jaisa tera Chatwa sai, utna to kadhe rahi sun aur Baroda-Batana ho to ek gaz ka kadh lun', i.e., 'tell my father-in-law, my *ghunghat* is as befits his village Chatwal; if it were Baroda-Batana (a big village), I would have worn a yard long *ghunghat*.'[9]

The ghunghat may be lifting higher or may already be lifted higher, but it is far from being given up. As the story indicates, the woman would lift her veil this far and no further. Attitudes are clearly marked with ambiguity, arising out of an acceptance of subordination, and therefore compliance, along with some resistance.

---

[8] For similar observation on Rajasthan, see Tulsi Patel, 1987, 'Women's Work and their Status: Dialectics of Subordination and Assertion', *Social Action*, vol. 37, no. 2, April–June, pp. 126–49.

[9] Narrated by Shakuntala, 36 years old, 1988, village Mokhra, district Rohtak, 3–4 August.

LOCAL PERCEPTIONS: DEHATI VS *SHEHRI* CULTURE

Despite the widespread acceptance of ghunghat, a few disgruntled voices do exist. Some women do privately complain of ghunghat.[10] Yet they, along with village men, justify its retention on the basis of their 'culture' and 'tradition'. This culture, defined as dehati (rural) culture, at the heart of which is the woman in ghunghat, is necessarily seen against the other, that is, shehri (city) culture.[11] A combination of factors, both historical as well as contemporary, are needed to explain this perceived sharp dichotomy that is linked to the persistence of this custom in Haryana. Part of this explanation lies in the abject poverty and stunted agrarian economy of the British days in Haryana which were responsible for certain historically determined social and cultural norms inherited by the rural populace even after independence. The subsistence level economy of this arid and deficit region had come to be reflected in the austere, simple food habits, dressing, and living standards.[12] The necessarily limited, coarse diet meant that anything apart from a barely adequate and economical vegetarian meal was considered extravagant; a virtue was made out of sheer necessity; coarse, rough, and multipurpose ordinary household requirements made up the austere life style, while any ostentation was ridiculed. Since lifestyle, dressing, and cuisine are general accepted barometers of civilization and culture, Haryana came to represent a region severely lacking in these so-called 'fine aspects'.

On the whole, Haryanavis, in general, have come to be ridiculed as uneducated, uncouth, unrefined, and witless fools. Generally denigrated, they have been dismissed as 'dehatis' (a rough translation of this word in its pejorative form is 'country bumpkin'). This stereotype of a 'crude dehati' or 'crude Jat' has been accepted by Haryanavis

---

[10] Many women complained of the physical confines of ghunghat when at home, specially in the smokey kitchen, where, also, they are required to keep their faces covered.

[11] Incidentally, the Hindi cinema has contributed a great deal in reinforcing ghunghat which is romanticized in order to highlight a woman's coyness, beauty, and obedience. In the end, it is the *ghunghatwali*, with her head covered, projecting a symbol of 'traditional India' and 'Indian culture' who wins and the independent woman who looses. It may be noted that covered head with a sari is nothing but a raised, shortened ghunghat. See Beatrix Pfleidrer and Lothar Lutze, 1985, *The Hindi Film: Agent and Reagent of Cultural Change*, New Delhi: Manohar, p. 74

[12] See Chapter 1 in this volume.

themselves. However, this acceptance is not merely self-deprecating but, as pointed out by social scientists, has to be looked at as a class phenomenon, specially as a means of attacking and perhaps controlling the lower classes.[13] These derogatory charges are openly voiced by better-off Haryanavis, both rural rich and urban-based educated ones, and have increasingly become a part of popular usage, specially after the newly found prosperity of the green revolution and rapid urbanization. On their part, the not-so-privileged and underprivileged rural sections always joke among themselves, about the upwardly mobile higher class who try in their language, behaviour, and self-conception to over-distance themselves from the rural masses.

They judge urbanites, whether Haryanavis or non-Haryanavis, as 'greedy', grasping, and given to a great deal of ostentatious living. Delhi and its inhabitants, who signify an epitome of this culture, have been and continue to be described as:

Dilli ke dilwaali
munh chikna pet khali[14]
(Flaunting girls of Delhi,
stomachs empty, faces slick)

Any one projecting an image different from the 'rural' ideal is dubbed as shehri (townsman), and given to false pretences. Some popular proverbs ridicule the urbanites as:

joru chikni, miyan majur[15]
(Wife bedecked, husband a labourer)

---

[13] For a consolidated view, see Lawrence W. Levine, 1977, *Black Culture and Black Consciousness*, London: Oxford University Press, pp. 339–40.

[14] A commonly heard proverb in the villages. See also, Jai Narayan Verma, 1972, *Haryanavi Lokoktiyan: Shastriye Vishleshan* (Hindi), Delhi: Adarsh Sahitya Prakashan, p. 114. The oral tradition used in this essay is based upon my extensive interviews and fieldwork in Haryana. Some of the oral sources used here may also be found in the published works of certain Hindi literati and folklorists of this region, based on their field observations. I have taken care to record such instances, as they underline the popular usage of this tradition. Here, I also wish to point out that in translating the local dialect, the emphasis is on conveying the mood and the message rather than its literal meaning.

[15] A commonly quoted proverb. Also, in the collection of Ram Naresh Tripathi, 1952, *Gram Sahitya, Vol. III* (Hindi), Delhi: Atma Ram and Sons, p. 247. This work is a collection of proverbs collected by the author from north Indian villages from 1925–50.

and

shaukeen budhiya, chatai ka lehnga[16]
(Fashionable hag, in a skirt of woven straw.)

Significantly, women have not only been singled out as a symbol of the unnecessary ostentation of urban life, but are also being warned against making any such demands. That such demands do exist is clear from a large number of local songs which express women's desire for cosmetics, clothes, and the like.[17] Greatly frowned upon by rural men and older women, the longing and wish to acquire such things was confirmed by the younger ones among them.[18] The attraction of 'shehri things' among certain sections of women, although ambiguous and indeterminate, cannot be denied.

At the same time, it is interesting that the rural rich and the urban-based Haryanavis are able to join the others in voicing the popular sentiment which ridicules and condemns 'shehri' culture, despite sharing significant aspects of the same culture. This projection of a united rural voice transcending any class distinctions, that is no doubt fuelled by a more general resentment over the disparity in urban–rural standards of living, consumption, expenditure, and access to social services such as roads, communications, health, and education,[19] emerges repeatedly in relation to various issues. Based on the traditional egalitarianism of caste *biradari* and *bhaichara* systems as well as the peasant proprietorship ethos prevailing in Punjab and Haryana, a collective voice and action is allowed to emerge in a variety of different political contexts,

[16] Ibid., p. 270.
[17] As heard in the villages, these songs make demands ranging from high-heeled shoes, cosmetics, foreign clothes to cars and electronic gadgets. Newer additions keep on getting made as knowledge about these things spreads. In all this, the impact of urbanization—radio, cinema, television, video, and education—plays a part. However, the impact of these factors on rural women's consciousness, dress, behaviour patterns, and attitudes still awaits scholarly investigation.
[18] The younger ones like Meena, 18 years, from village Akopur, district Rohtak; Shakuntala, 24 years, and Santosh, 24 years, from village Bidhan, district Sonepat, all showed their preference for cosmetics and clothes.
[19] One of the recent jokes illustrates this brilliantly: during Asiad 1984, a peasant from Haryana happened to visit Delhi. On seeing the vast network of construction, lighting, road building, and the beautification drive being carried out, he very perceptively commented, 'Now I know where all the money goes'.

as seen in the recent incidents at Brahi village in Rohtak district.[20] Yet, on the other hand, as far as women are concerned, the same collective acts unite to reinforce patriarchal ideology to control women, crucially here, in retaining her in a ghunghat. So what perhaps is the 'united rural male strength' acts as a united repressive force and exercises ideological pressure on women.

This united ideology representing 'all ruralites' and advocating 'rural interests', opposed to 'urbanites' and 'urban interests', had been the foundation of highly successful Unionist politics in this region from 1923–45.[21] The opposition between the values of the rural and urban has had its basis in the centuries old exploitation experienced by the peasant groups and debtors at the hands of urban-linked or urban-based creditors mostly, though not entirely, belonging to non-peasant castes like the Banias. This antagonism was used and exploited by the colonial government which gave it a constitutional and legal status in the form of the Alienation of Land Act, 1900, which divided the population of Punjab into agricultural and non-agricultural categories, and the Reforms Act of 1919, which divided the legislative seats between rural and urban areas.[22] Socio-politically, these divisions continue to have some relevance and can be successfully used even now. This can be exemplified by Devi Lal's public assertions, significantly only in the rural constituencies, in the May 1991 Lok Sabha and Assembly elections that 'once in power' he'll make *chhutti* (do away with) of shehris and Banias.[23] The fact that this assertion did not succeed in the 1991 elections, even in the rural constituencies, is another matter altogether.

[20] As stated earlier in note 3, the incident in Brahi village, involved stripping of certain village men before their women by the local police. This led to a huge stir in Haryana, galvanized by the sarv khap panchayat of 360 Bahadurgarh villages. For details, see *Indian Express*, 1991, New Delhi, 8 September, p. 3; *Times of India*, 1991, New Delhi, 7 September, p. 4; 8 September, p. 10.There are several such examples, which can be cited about the role of the panchayat and the use of its collective voice.

[21] Prem Chowdhry, 1982, 'The "Zamindar Ideology" of the Unionist Party: Ideology and Propaganda Tactics of the Unionists in South-East Punjab', *Punjab Past and Present*, vol. XVI, no. 2, October, pp. 317–36.

[22] For details of colonial polity, see Prem Chowdhry, 1976, 'Social Basis of Chaudhri Sir Chhotu Ram's Politics', *Punjab Past and Present*, part 1, vol. X, no. 19, April, pp. 156–75.

[23] Narrated by Shamsher Singh, 1991, who followed Devi Lal's election campaign in Haryana on 10–18 May. Shamsher Singh is the owner of 12½ *bighas* of good cultivable land in Haryana.

Yet, one can see that in the popular rural perception, 'urban interests' and their value system, even when admittedly shared by their rich rural counterparts, can be successfully pitted against 'rural culture', and the former may continue to be referred to with a fair amount of contempt and ridicule.

IDEOLOGICAL BARRIER: REJECTION OF 'URBAN CULTURE'

This social attitude was severely to compromise the positive liberating effects of the Partition in relation to women, specially seen in the lifting of purdah for the women of Pakistan[24] and that of ghunghat for the women of Punjab sans its Haryana region. The partition of Punjab in 1947, displaced a very large number of persons, both Hindus and Sikhs, many of whom came to settle down in Indian Punjab which then included the Haryana region. The total number of Hindus and Sikhs who came to Haryana was as follows:[25] Hissar, 1,27,657; Rohtak, 1,23,644; Karnal, 2,50,471; Ambala, 1,88,892; Gurgaon, 84,587; and Mahendergarh, 4,944.

Commonly referred to as 'refugees', they were forced to start life afresh, and women emerged as major contributors towards the rebuilding of their lives.[26] These women refugees included a number of widows and single women, from across class affiliations; and many had to remain single despite efforts to get them married. Several among them, specially in the lower classes, went on to become the sole supporters of their families, sustaining and educating the male members, until they were ready to start work on their own. The Government Rehabilitation Centres acknowledged the ability of women to work. Sheer economic reasons made these women come out of their houses/purdah/ghunghat and enter a public space. In the rural areas, however, the 'public field' of work for a woman, from the cultivating households, is actually an extension of her 'private' area and her status declines once

---

[24] See Hanna Papanek, 1982, 'Purdah: Separate Worlds and Symbolic Shelter', in Papanek and Minault (eds), *Separate Worlds*, pp. 3–53.

[25] 1951, *Census of India, Punjab*, vol. VIII, part I-A, Simla: Controller of Publication, p. LXVI.

[26] The account which follows is based upon a discussion with Urvashi Butalia who, along with Sudesh Vaid, extensively interviewed persons dislocated by the Partition, focusing on hitherto untouched social aspects of dislocation and rehabilitation. Significantly, the social effects of the Partition still remain unresearched by scholars.

she starts to work on another's field. She then enters a 'public space'. This venturing out on the part of 'Punjabi women' into a public space, as was to be expected, aroused a hostile and defamatory reception. Many of these women working in 'public spaces' came from urban and semi-urban areas of the united Punjab. Some were already educated enough to undertake lower clerical and similar jobs. Even the illiterate, either from rural or urban backgrounds, found work as domestic helps, cleaners of utensils, and general factotums. Those from more affluent backgrounds went on to finish higher studies and take on professional jobs.

This forced entrance into the public sphere was to revolutionize the lives of these women, who before the Partition, had been mostly enclosed within the fold of a religious ethos with its purdah ideology. Giving up this custom triggered off an unimaginable level of emancipation for the displaced Punjabi women. Significantly, this had a positive fallout not only in the urban centres but also in the rural areas of Punjab leading to a gradual acceptance of lifting of the veil. The sociological background to its acceptance was provided by the progressive elements in Sikhism and the reformist Arya Samaj. In the latter, there was also a coalescing of reformist zeal with the construction of the powerful image of the modern Indian woman, urban based; this provided a positive atmosphere for the dropping of ghunghat.[27] It is interesting to note, however, that while ghunghat is on its way to being almost totally lifted in Punjab rural areas, its ideological hold over women, for a variety of reasons, has remained and, in fact, has somewhat tightened.[28] For example, ideologically, the Punjab women may have given up ghunghat, partially or wholly, yet the behavioural patterns connected to its observance, that is, the sharam-lihaz (code of behaviour) and deference to senior affines, specially male, continues to be expected and even demanded. Moreover, the lifting of ghunghat in the Punjab rural areas has been accompanied by the withdrawal of women from working in

[27] For the details of the construction of this image in Punjab, see Madhu Kishwar, 1986, 'Arya Samaj and Women's Education: Kanya Mahavidyalaya, Jallandar', *Economic and Political Weekly*, vol. XXI, no. 17, 26 April, pp. WS9–24. Also, see her article, 1989, 'The Daughters of Aryavarta', in J. Krishnamurthy (ed.), *Women in Colonial India: Essays on Survival, Work and the State*, New Delhi: Oxford University Press, pp. 78–113.

[28] In the early 1970s, 44.65 per cent observed ghunghat in Punjab as compared to 72.61 per cent in Haryana. See Government of India, *Towards Equality*, p. 141.

the fields, strikingly evident among the richer cultivators, specially in the wake of the green revolution. [29]

In Haryana, notwithstanding the Arya Samaj's influence, which has always been partial,[30] the ghunghat remains and so has women's active participation in agriculture. Here, it should be remembered that Haryana's population, by and large, had not shared the displacement from Pakistan, and therefore the direct impact on its population cannot be expected to be the same as that of Punjab. Haryana seems to have closed its ranks even to the indirect influence of this displacement on women. An ethos which regarded 'urban values' as artificial and superfluous was not going to accept this Punjabi 'refugee' influence. Significantly, even forty-five years after the Partition, the former displaced and now fully rehabilitated population continues pejoratively to be called 'refugee' and 'Punjabi'. A popular proverb, possibly coined during this time and still in popular use, voices this sentiment:

Desi gadha, punjabi raink[31]
(Local donkey, brays like a Punjabi.)

The single status of Punjabi women, if widowed or unmarried, and their lifting of ghunghat and being openly seen working in public was received most negatively by Haryanavis, both men and women. The 'Punjabans' came to be denigrated as 'besharm' (shameless) who did not respect their elders; the utter shamefulness of one who *'susre ko munh dikhati phirti hai'* (shows her face to the father-in-law) was cited as an example; and those among Haryanavi women who attempted to reduce the size of the ghunghat, have been condemned as *'nangi punjabano ki terhan'* (without clothes just like the Punjabi women).

---

[29] The general consensus of opinion is that Punjab has amongst the lowest rural female participation rate, attributed to the increased prosperity in that region consequent on the success of the green revolution. See Rohini Nayyar, 1987, 'Female Participation Rate in Rural India', *Economic and Political Weekly*, vol. XXII, no. 51, 19 December, pp. 2207–16; Krishna Dutt Sharma, 1973, 'Female Participation in Rural Agricultural Labour in North India: A Spatial Interpretation, 1971', *Man Power Journal*, vol. VIII, no. 4, January–March, pp. 52–67.

[30] For the partial influence of Arya Samaj, see Prem Chowdhry, 1984, *Punjab Politics: The Role of Sir Chhotu Ram*, New Delhi: Vikas, chapter V.

[31] A very commonly voiced proverb, also included in the collection by Tripathi, *Gram Sahitya*, p. 174.

This severe condemnation voiced in support of what is widely termed 'dehati culture', which does not allow its women to go unveiled into the bazaar or public domain, is made with an air of smugness and superiority over 'urban culture' which is said to 'expose' its women, who then become fair game for sexual harassment.[32] To this estimation of the 'urban woman' may be added the fact of a large number of rural men leaving their wives in the villages, both in the colonial and post-colonial period.[33] This has always meant a demand for the sexual services of willing women in towns. The post-colonial, specially the green revolution, prosperity, urbanization, and growing consumerism has also had its effect in increasing this demand. Male opinion is unanimous in maintaining that prostitution, not noticeably visible in colonial times, has now come to be firmly and openly established in urban centres (though still not in rural areas), catering to the ever-growing number of male patrons from different sections of the rural community. This results in a lack of respect for urban women as a whole, and a consequent sharpening of suspicion of their 'influence' on rural women.

Clearly, in Haryana, there has existed, and continues to exist, a definite ideological barrier, as posited by Richard Lambert, between urban and rural value systems, which inhibits the spread of urban influence in the villages.[34] This barrier, however, remains a selective one. Such selective adoption of other customs is most clearly visible in the adoption of the Punjabi dress, *salwar-kamiz*, but not in the lifting of ghunghat. For rural Haryana, the symbol of its culture is the veiled woman, and the attempt is to maintain this custom or cultural practice at all costs. This may explain the anomalous behaviour pattern of the educated, urban Haryanavi women who observe ghunghat on their visits to the villages, a practice also commonly observed in Rajasthan. Such women also observe ghunghat when their husband's male relatives from the village visit them in the cities. These educated, urbanized women represent it as a loud declaration of remembering their cultural moorings and of not having been 'corrupted' by 'urban culture'.

[32] Significantly, a number of eve teasing and rape cases in Delhi involve bus drivers and conductors, who are frequently drawn from the rural areas of Haryana. See *Indian Express*, 1991, New Delhi, 30 May, p. 1.

[33] For details, see author's work, 1994, *The Veiled Women: Shifting Gender Equations in Rural Haryana, 1880–1990*, New Delhi: Oxford University Press.

[34] Richard D. Lambert, 1962, 'The Impact of Urban Society Upon Village Life', in Roy Turner (ed.), *India's Urban Future*, Bombay: Oxford University Press, pp. 117–40.

Their gesture provides further legitimacy to this custom and underlines and perpetuates its ideological hold. And although such educated and urban-based women may really not be expected to observe ghunghat, observing it evokes social approbation and applause from all. This special approval clearly acts as a double-edged weapon. On the one hand, it acts as a complementary gesture towards those who show token observance of this custom and, on the other, severely condemns those who do not.

However, this praise is not given to the non-literate, semi-literate, or rural-based women. For them, it is simply taken for granted. It is, therefore, not surprising that even educated men and women in Haryana have not raised their voice against this observance. In fact, neither the Arya Samajis nor any other social reformers or leading intellectuals have paid any significant attention to this major anomaly which continues to pervade rural society.[35] For the ideology which ghunghat or purdah projects, that is, man's domination over and control of woman or the inferiority and seclusion of woman from certain crucial spheres, suits both the urban and the rural male. Ghunghat or purdah, therefore, is not a mere symbol of male authority and power over women, but represents a persisting reality, even in the changed socio-economic milieu.

URBANIZATION AND CONSUMERISM: GROWING NUCLEI OF MALE CONTROL

Despite an apparent successful positing of the two cultures, rural and urban, as being distinct, there is also a perceptible ambivalence here as the distinction between urban and rural has never been and is not watertight. There is a massive overlap of the two.[36] Haryana itself has

[35] Khem Lal Rathi, 1986, New Delhi, 24 May. Born in 1912, village Rajlugarhi, district Sonepat, he has been practising law in the Supreme Court. An avowed Arya Samaji, he is familiar with its work in the rural areas of Haryana since colonial days. His wife, Khazani Devi, 70 years old,also confirmed this. Raghbir Singh, 1988, village Singhpura, district Rohtak, 6–7 August, voiced the same opinion. Born in 1933, Raghbir Singh, an ex-*sarpanch* of his village, is currently the President of the Singhpura Gurukul and an active Arya Samaji.

[36] It is estimated that from inside the rural and semi-urban areas of Haryana, more than one lakh of people commute daily to Delhi. For example, trains from Rohtak, Gurgaon, Palwal, and Panipat are scheduled to leave in the morning and return in the evening, keeping to the work schedule of the Haryanavi workers from different villages employed in various capacities in the metropolis. These

been greatly urbanized, drawing heavily from the rural areas. The post-colonial urbanization of Haryana is directly connected with the major capitalist thrust in its economy through the adoption of a green revolution type of highly selective strategy resulting in unprecedented growth in the agrarian sector.[37] The recipients of the newly found prosperity, although differentially distributed within Haryana, show new patterns of expenditure and consumption which has had a crucial effect on the strengthening of the custom of observing ghunghat.

Much of this expenditure and consumption is connected with a new kind of consumerism in the villages. Consumerism is directly linked up with the steady progress of urbanization in Haryana as well as an enormous increase in the number of very large villages. Within twenty years, that is, between 1961–81, the total number of towns in Haryana has increased from sixty-one to eighty-one. During this time, the urban index of growth of the urban population has more than doubled.[38] At

---

trains are not only full to capacity but are overflowing. What shall these urban workers, with their families in the villages, be called: urban or rural? Moreover, the very large number of army recruits, specially the so-called 'other ranks', all drawn from rural areas, still have to leave their families in the villages as only 14 per cent of them are provided with family accommodation. Information given by Lt General B.T. Pandit, Adjutant-General, Adjutant-General's Branch, Army Headquarters, 1991, New Delhi, 1 April. Are these rural or urban? Rural affluence has added its own complications. The children of the rural rich with their urban education, behaviour, dress, and living styles can hardly be placed in the rural slot. Even Devi Lal, the Deputy Prime Minister of India from December 1989 to June 1991, and the former Chief Minister of Haryana, with his emphasis on 'ruralites', has been hard put to define them.

[37] This new agrarian strategy introduced in the mid-1960s, achieved a major breakthrough in less than a decade. This new agrarian strategy introduced in the mid-60s, achieved a major breakthrough in less than a decade. From importer of food grain, the state not only made up its shortfall but by 1976–7 also started to make very substantial contribution of both wheat and rice to the Central food pool. Crops like sugar cane and cotton, meagerly present earlier, started to show profusion. For figures, see Government of Haryana, *Statistics of Economic Development, Haryana, 1977–78*, Chandigarh: Government of Haryana, 1979, pp. 1–2; Government of Haryana, *Statistical Handbook of Haryana 1988–89*, Chandigarh: Planning Department, Economic and Statistical Organization, Haryana, 1989, pp. 35–6. Also see Chapter 6, n3 in this volume.

[38] *Census of India, 1981*, Haryana, Series 6, Part II-A, and Part II-B, General Population Tables and Primary Census Abstract, Chandigarh: Directorate of Census Operation Haryana, 1986, pp. 26, 28.

the same time, Haryana witnessed a remarkable drop in the number of very small villages and witnessed a corresponding rise in large and very large villages. By 1981, there were fifty-seven villages which were fully incorporated into the towns and eighteen villages which were partially incorporated.[39]

This increase in the size of the average village has been accompanied by the introduction of a much wider variety of 'modern' goods and services. The number of retail shops selling consumer goods has increased and the number of articles for sale has greatly expanded. In the large villages, the variety and quality of goods offered is indistinguishable from that available in very small shopping centres of metropolitan cities.[40] Moreover, a total of 835 villages in Haryana lie within a radius of 15 kms from the neighbouring town; in fact, many of them are within a radius of 3–5 km only. This distance, within the existing infrastructural facilities is negligible, specially in commercial interactions, which are no longer a 'casual phenomenon'.[41] Therefore, this combination of factors, namely, increase in urbanization; growth of service sector, specially trade and banking; improvement of the infrastructural facilities; increasing marketing agencies; better literacy; spread of television network; and better awareness about industrial products, has resulted in a shift of consumption expenditure in rural areas towards consumer and luxury goods. According to the 1991 study by the Birla Economic Research Foundation, consumer products, after remaining somewhat stagnant during 1960–1 to 1973–4, have undergone a major increase, specially in the last years of the 1980s.[42] This is held to be specially true of the agriculturally advanced states like Punjab and Haryana. Clearly, a variety of factors have been active, resulting in a popular spillover of urban consumerist culture into the rural areas, spurred by a desire for acquisition as well as emulation.

[39] Sheila Bhalla, 1981, 'Islands of Growth: A Note on Haryana Experience and Some Possible Implications', *Economic and Political Weekly*, vol.XVI, no. 23, 6 June, pp. 1022–30.

[40] Ibid.

[41] S.P. Sinha, (n.d.), *Processes and Patterns of Urban Development in Haryana, 1901–1971*, ICSSR, Project Report, Geography Department, Kurukshetra University, Kurukshetra, pp. 331–3.

[42] See 1991, 'Rural Market on the Rise', *Hindustan Times*, 18 February, p. 16. For the newly acquired socio-economic and political importance of the small town, see Chandan Mitra, 1991, 'Rise of the Small Town', *Sunday Observer*, New Delhi, 27 January–2 February, p. 5.

One such spillover is visible in the phenomenal increase in the number of common entertainment places from sixty-nine in 1970 to 113 in 1980–1, as well of common eating places whose number can hardly be estimated, accompanied by an increase in the numbers of their users. [43] This has added another dimension to the spending of income in ways which exclude women. The vast increase in the number of users of these places of entertainment, which in the rural areas are almost entirely monopolized by men, can be seen in the increase of entertainment tax collection (partly due to increase in tax) from Rs 10,54,000 in 1970–1 to Rs 7,01,89,000 in 1984–5; and increase of show tax from Rs 10,03,000 in 1970–1 to Rs 51,44,000 in 1984–5. [44] This means an increase of 534.96 per cent and 412.86 per cent, respectively, within fourteen years. Significantly, the trade, hotels, and restaurant sector, according to the official figures, has emerged as second in importance to the agricultural sector. The 1988–9 figures show its share in the state domestic products, at the current prices, to be 16.9 per cent and the manufacturing sector to be 15.2 per cent. [45]

What is more significant is that these new norms in consumption patterns extending from tea, cold drinks, liquor, and non-vegetarian food in *dhabas* and other eating places, to entertainment venues including the cinema houses and a few video parlours that have opened up in some of the villages, have contributed to the already existing all-male social practices like hukka smoking, sitting round the fire, card playing, as well as an increasing numbers of *sharab ke adde* (drinking places). [46] The available figures of liquor consumption, whether country

---

[43] Government of Haryana, 1987, *Statistical Abstract of Haryana, 1985–86*, Chandigarh: Planning Department, Economic and Statistical Organization, p. 514.

[44] Ibid., pp. 515–16. There are no separate figures for urban and rural Haryana.

[45] Government of Haryana, 1990, *Economic Survey of Haryana, 1989–90*, Chandigarh: Planning Department, Economic and Statistical Organization, p. 2.

[46] The dhabas as centres of predominant male gatherings can be seen in a Punjabi proverb which maintains: 'dhabha is like a courtesan, the more you decorate it, the more customers it will attract'. The functions of dhabas range from serving food (both vegetarian and non-vegetarian) to liquor and pimping. The majority of its clientele does not consist of vehicle drivers (mostly trucks) as popularly believed, but rural men. See Pranav Kumar, 1991, 'Dhabhas of Ambala', *Hindustan Times*, New Delhi, 13 February, p. 13.

liquor, Indian whisky, or wine and beer, show an enormous increase between 1966 and 1985 and are said to be growing every year.[47] It is true that not all of this alcohol is consumed in Haryana itself, as the state is an exporter of spirits and beer to other states. But even if we take only the figures for country liquor known locally as *tharra*, the percentage increase in eighteen years is 745 per cent, whereas the population growth has been less than 30 per cent during this period. This excludes the enormous illicit distillation carried out in the state.[48] The growing liquor consumption in the rural perception and in the eyes of the academics is entirely due to the increased paying capacity of the consumer, particularly in the rural areas.[49] This huge network of *sharab ke theke* (licenced liquor shops) has become a continually growing problem in the whole of northern India.[50] Liquor is a significant factor in the deteriorating quality of women's lives and cuts across region, caste, and class lines.[51]

[47] For details of consumption of country liquor, foreign liquor, wine and beer in proof liters in Haryana (1966–7 and 1984–5) see Chapter 8, n93 in this volume.

[48] 1989, *Haryana District Gazetteer,* Sirsa District, 1988, Chandigarh: Govt of Haryana, Haryana District Gazetteers Organization, Revenue Department, pp. 303–4. The illicit distillation has increased so much that police raids have had to be carried out on different occasions to discourage it, but this has not been of much help.

[49] Ibid.; also, see 1987, *Haryana District Gazetteer,* Hissar District, 1987, Chandigarh: Govt of Haryana, Haryana District Gazetteers Organization, Revenue Department, p. 233. John Peter Dorschner also shows that the lower castes as well as higher castes hold the availability of money with the higher cultivating castes, as being responsible for this habit. See his, 1983, *Alcohol Consumption in a Village in North India*, Michigan: UMI Research Press, p. 46.

[50] The existing practice shows the licencing and setting up of one sharab ka theka within a radius of every 10 kms and the opening of small retail shops every 3 kms. This has resulted, according to the 1990–1 government figures, into a formidable number of 820 country liquor vends and 370 Indian-made foreign liquor vends in this small state. Information supplied by Yushvir Singh Thekedar, born 1960, a liquor thekedar and brick kiln owner in village Dulhera; lives in village Chhara of district Rohtak. Interestingly, his caste name 'Thakran' has been changed to 'Thekedar', in view of his profession. Also, see a report from the Tribune Bureau, 1990, 'Rum, Gin through Thekas in Haryana', *Tribune,* Chandigarh, 13 February.

[51] For similar opinion and observation of women of different classes on liquor in Rajasthan, see Miriam Sharma and Urmilla Vanjani, 1989, 'Women's Work is Never Done: Dairy Development and Health in the Lives of Rural

It is these strictly male-oriented aspects of the capitalist consumerist economy which have tended to enlarge the nuclei of male assemblage in the public sphere, thereby controlling women's mobility more strictly and confining women more and more to the private and work domain. Although, in Haryana, women are conspicuously visible out in the fields and streets, they are never seen loitering around, as only mobility which is part of a sanctioned purpose is recognized. Therefore, the constant presence of so many men merely reinforces the ghunghat ideology and practice.

FEARS REINFORCED: SOCIO-LEGAL CHANGES AND NEED FOR GREATER CONTROL

Just as the drastic post-colonial changes in the socio-economy of Haryana, leading to a capitalist consumerist thrust, have had a most inhibiting effect on women, so also have the socio-legal changes. The independent state's intervention on behalf of women through the enactment of the Hindu Code Bill 1955–6, relating to the question of inheritance and marital affairs, has exacerbated the need and urgency for control over women. Immediately after independence, the Indian government attempted to bring about certain structural changes to remove the disabilities experienced by women in these spheres. The Hindu Succession Act, part of the Hindu Code Bill, was enacted and brought into force on 17 June 1956.[52] It amended and codified the law relating to intestate succession among Hindus and brought about fundamental and radical changes in the law of succession, breaking violently with the past. Section 14 of this act applied to women and granted them equal inheritance rights along with male members. The act enabled, for the first time, daughters, sisters, widows, and mothers to inherit land with full proprietary rights to its disposal. The earlier limited ownership right awarded to the widows was converted into full and absolute ownership.

As a direct and absolute beneficiary, it is the widow rather than the daughter or sister who emerges as a major threat in the post-colonial

---

Women of Rajasthan', *Economic and Political Weekly*, vol. XXIV, no. 17, 29 April, pp. WS38–45. Also, see Mukul, 1987, 'Sharab Virodhi Andolan', *Navbharat Times* (Hindi), Delhi, 18 May, p. 3; 19 May, p. 3; 20 May, p. 3.

[52] For details of this act and its comparison with the earlier situation existing in British India, see the Hindu Succession Act, No. XXX of 1956, in Sunderlal T. Desai, 1966, *Mulla Principles of Hindu Law* (13th edition), Bombay: N.M. Tripathi Private Ltd.

situation. It is significant that women as daughters and sisters have been customarily denied all proprietory rights. Even now, the long established custom, alongside cultural and ideological constraints continues to make nonsense of the legal enactments.[53] For daughters and sisters, ghunghat does not exist while unmarried or while on a visit to their natal home. Here they are allowed comparative freedom, visibly noticeable in different body movements, and consequent freedom expressed in informal behaviour, when they no longer have to observe ghunghat, without evoking the charge of immodesty or causing dishonour to anyone. Only as a married woman she comes to have a stake in her husband's property, which she considers as her own to work upon. Moreover, as a widow, she gains full and absolute control over it, a control which in colonial time also had been substantive, although limited to her life time. Ghunghat for a married woman therefore ensures that her effectiveness is most circumscribed in an area where it is most dangerous, that is, where she is a wife rather than a daughter or sister. It renders women unable either to assert themselves or to intervene effectively in any relationship between those men who are the controllers, whether in the family matters or matters of property. The ghunghat effectively averts what could be a major threat from a married woman to the control of the affinal male kin over economic resources and decision making.

The unambiguity of the 1956 Act has also meant that as a widow, she cannot be deprived of her property by any counter-claim. The changed situation was highlighted when a series of court cases brought by the male collaterals challenging the widow on a variety of grounds, were decided, according to the 1956 Act, in favour of the widows.[54] It was therefore found necessary to retain her within the family through the established practice of *karewa* (levirate), which, as mentioned elsewhere, had been used to control even her limited right of inheritance in the British Punjab.[55] Consequently, pressure upon her to enter into levirate marriage has increased in the post-colonial period. However, the institution of widow remarriage in this region has no longer remained in

[53] See 1993, 'Conjugality, Law and State: Inheritance Rights as Pivot of Control in Northern India,' *National Law School Journal*, vol.1, special issue on Feminism and Law, pp. 95–116.

[54] For details of these cases, see ibid.

[55] Prem Chowdhry, 1989, 'Customs in a Peasant Economy: Women in Colonial Haryana', in Kumkum Sangari and Sudesh Vaid (ed.), *Recasting Women: Essays in Colonial History*, New Delhi: Kali for Women, pp. 302–36.

its levirate form, as it had primarily been under the British. There has been a growing popularity of punar vivah, that is, literally, remarriage of widows anywhere in the caste.[56] In recent years, breaches in levirate have occasionally occurred, as the young, issueless widows, in many cases, go back to their parents and get married again. The cases of widows defying all norms to make their own choice of partner in remarriage have always existed. But for a widow to marry of her own choice still means a runaway marriage. The popular rural belief continues to equate running away with a *rand* (widow); '*rand bhaj gai*' (the widow has run away), is a phrase commonly used for any absconding female.[57] It emanates out of widows' self-assertion in marriage. All villages have several such cases to recount, but only in confidence.[58]

Those sanctioned or unsanctioned breaches in levirate through punar vivah, or the growing runaway matches, have increased the male anxiety to control women, married or widowed. Ghunghat, in this case, remains an effective means of controlling a woman's interaction with other males who might fall prey to her 'fatal attractions'. In the local perception, the widows 'bereft of any control' (that is, the husband's) are known to improve in 'health and wealth'.[59] Moreover, the inheritance rights of widows have certainly increased the value of their assets in the remarriage market. As a widow's remarriage no longer means her being deprived of her inheritance, she seems to have acquired, superficially at least, a greater freedom to marry outside the former levirate practice. It is partly the anxiety faced by a patrilineal rural society which has reinforced and tightened customary practices like ghunghat and karewa.

---

[56] *Haryana District Gazetteer, Bhiwani, 1982*, 1983, Chandigarh: Government of Haryana, Haryana District Gazetteers Organization, Revenue Department, p. 67.

[57] A common observation heard in all the villages.

[58] The forced levirate practice and the repression of women can be estimated from these runaway cases. Some of these cases take place even after the levirate alliance has been effected. In many instances, these matches are between much older widows and their very young *dewars* (brothers-in-law). All such cases which have come to my notice have requested anonymity.

[59] Interview with Vidya Vati, 1997, Delhi, 24 December (several other women confirmed this observation); born 1918, married to Hardwari Lal, ex-member of Lok Sabha from Rohtak; she has kept a very close touch with rural life despite having lived in different urban centres from the age of sixteen.

This anxiety was further underscored by the Hindu Marriage Act of 1955 that legalized the idea of divorce.[60] The passage of this Act created severe rancour among rural males. It is not as if divorce did not exist in the past. However, such cases were few and far between and they always emanated from the side of the man. Although informal, this divorce was binding and socially recognized. In such a divorce, unchastity was the major ground for activating a practice called *tyag* (renunciation) which resulted in a virtual divorce as the wife was left at her parental home and never brought back.[61] Unlike the man, a Hindu woman, on the other hand, could never claim release from her marriage, once her marriage or remarriage status had been accepted. Clearly, the anger and opposition in the aftermath of the Act of 1955 originated, apart from other socio-economic reasons, out of the cultural bias of the rural males.The right to divorce given to a woman was perceived to seriously assail the respect for the husband as also the male authority itself. Despite the legal enactment, the customary practice of tyag or chhordena (having left) as it is popularly known continues to be observed and socially accepted.[62] It is sanctified by any of the traditional panchayats that exist, whether that of the family elders or *kunba* (joint family) or of the village elders or the caste council itself.

Interestingly , post-1955, many women , unable to bear the marriage situation , for what ever reason, are known to have used the customary practice of chhordena. Under this, a woman takes the initiative to leave the husband on her own, return to her parents and refuse to return

[60] Government of India, 1956, *The India Code*, Vol. II, Part IX, New Delhi: Ministry of Law, pp. 149–56. A few changes have been made under the Marriage Law (Amendment) Act 1976, which by introducing categories of divorce by mutual consent, has further facilitated the granting of divorce by either party.

[61] E. Joseph, 1911, *Customary Law of the Rohtak District*, Lahore: Superintendent, Government Printing, pp. 35, 40; also, see Government of Punjab, 1911, *Gurgaon District Gazetteer*, 1910, Lahore: Civil and Military Gazette, p. 58.

[62] Several people highlighted the chhordena form of socially accepted divorce. This customary arrangement had been considered by the rural populace as essentially different from the divorce instituted by law. That is the reason why till the late 1960s, almost all denied the existence of divorce in the rural areas Divorce was considered to be an anomaly of urban life and education. Now the fact that even informal arrangement means a divorce in reality seems to have dawned upon people. Interview with R.M. Hooda, 1986, Rohtak, 17 June.

to the husband. This initiative was unthinkable before 1955 Act.[63] This 'defiance ' has therefore come to be associated with the after effects of the Act itself.

The legislation of 1955, unlike what was feared and projected, has not made substantial difference to the number of divorces taking place in Haryana. Even after close to three decades, less than one per cent of married couples have gone through the legal divorce.[64] These are generally from the urban educated classes of society, who are well aware of the illegality of a polygamous marriage.[65] So much so that in the popular perception divorce and the breach of established norms has come to be firmly associated with the urban based educated sections of society, specially urban, educated women. Whether formal or informal, separation or divorce are perceived to be inimical to the rural ethos, its norms and cultural practices. It is considered to be activated by state power dominated by urbanites who are accused of not understanding rural problems[66]

Such a reversal of rural societal norms and customary practices challenges patriarchal and patrilineal interests, thereby enhancing the need and the stake to control women more strictly, specially when these rights are to operate within the growing prosperity of the region. The introduction of 'modern' and 'progressive' elements has proved to be its opposite, that is, 'conservative' and 'non-progressive' for rural women. This subversion of the 'modern' has been effective because of

[63] The rising cases of such divorces in the rural areas are not directly related to the 1955 Act, but to the changed society and its consumerist demands. Among these, dowry has emerged as the foremost cause for the practice of 'chhordena'. Or the woman is tortured so much that she leaves the husband voluntarily. This was the consensus of opinion among both men and women. Among the other reason included was the beating of women.

[64] 1986, *Census of India, Haryana, 1981*, Series 6, Part IV-A, Social and Cultural Tables, Chandigarh: Directorate of Census Operations Haryana, chapter 1.

[65] *Haryana District Gazetteer, Rohtak, 1970*, 1970, Chandigarh: Government of Haryana, Haryana District Gazetteers Organization, Revenue Department, p. 48.

[66] In Punjab and Haryana, the general feeling in the rural areas after the passage of Hindu Code Bill, was one of sharp condemnation of the Indian National Congress. The reigning Brahmin and Bania Congress*wallas*, mostly urbanites, were accused of not understanding the rural problems. Interview, Hardwari Lal, 1985, Delhi, 19 March; born 1912, he is a well-known educationist and politician of Haryana.

the successful projection of 'rural culture' against 'urban culture', at the centre of which stands a woman shrouded in ghunghat. So far, the persistence of ghunghat practice shows the triumph of patriarchal and patrilineal interests in containing the mounting pressure of internal threats and external demands. But for how long? The challenges of a changed society with its varied demands, patterns of behaviour, expectation, and different reference points of culture, both for men and women, are becoming more and more visible.

8

Ideology, Culture, and Hierarchy
*Expenditure–Consumption Patterns in Rural Households**

The power structure within the household operating through specific gender hierarchies is closely related to the wider socio-economic structure and derives its legitimacy and acceptance in the ideological and cultural matrix of a society. The dynamics of the wielding of power lie not only in the highly visible forms of domination and control but also in the more subtle and somewhat invisible equations which, in the domestic sphere, relate specifically to the expenditure of income, its allocation, and consumption. This study of expenditure–consumption patterns in rural households of Haryana shows how gender articulates with other socio-cultural structures not only to reinforce but to further tighten existing gender inequalities.

The present essay explores the insignificance of women's opinion and voices in the evolving expenditure–consumption patterns as seen in the domestic sphere, extending from food, housing, clothes, and fuel, to entertainment and expenditure on social and cultural occasions, on which 91 per cent of the total domestic expenditure of the cultivating

* This chapter was originally published in 1999, Uma Chakravarti and Kumkum Sangari (eds), *From Myths to Markets: Essays on Gender,* Shimla: Indian Institute of Advanced Studies, Shimla and Manohar, New Delhi, pp. 274–311.

households is spent.[1] It highlights how women of all classes, with hardly any socio-cultural recognition of a right to a share of resources face gender-based and intra-household inequalities. They emerge deprived and discriminated against, resulting in severe malnutrition and impaired health. The new and vastly changed expenditure–consumption patterns, specially in the wake of the green revolution and based upon male priorities, emphasize status symbols and give low priority to women's needs even in the crucial domestic sphere. Such patterns can be seen becoming more and more male oriented, creating yet greater nuclei of male control. The old cultural constraints, which have been determinedly kept alive, have not only ideologically conditioned women's non-participation in decision making but have physically inhibited them from decision-making fora with detrimental repercussions. Considered inferior in morality, knowledge, and wisdom, and unfit even to tender advice, women's role and effectiveness is circumscribed by ridiculing those who may accept their advice.

[1] In 1984–5, the expenditure on food, housing, clothing, entertainment, fuel, social and cultural occasions covered 90.68 per cent of the total domestic expenditure of the cultivating households in Haryana; the remaining 9.32 per cent was spent on health, education, transport, lighting, religion, and other miscellaneous items. For an in-depth analysis, the major heads of expenditure are being taken to determine the decision makers behind domestic expenditure and consumption. See Government of Haryana, 1987, *Family Budgets of Cultivators in Haryana, 1984–85*, Chandigarh: Planning Department, Economic and Statistical Organization, 1987, pp. 14–15. The Economic and Statistical Organization, Government of Haryana, ran annual surveys of farm family budgets for cultivators from 1966–7 onwards (last available report is for 1984–5). A multi-stage stratification random sampling technique with the village as a primary unit and the holding as an ultimate unit was adopted for conducting these annual surveys. The farmers were selected randomly with probability proportional to the net area cultivated. While selecting the holding, due representation was given to the entire district. The sample families covered all the agro-climatic regions of the state. The survey did not select a completely new set of farm families every year. Rather it tried to retain all or the maximum number of families included in the previous year in the next year's sample. When new families had to be included, care was taken to keep the same representational character of landholdings throughout. However, between 1966–7, when the survey began, through 1968–70 to 1984–5, it remained fairly large, fluctuating between sixty-one to eighty-one. See Satya Paul, 1989, 'Green Revolution and Income Distribution among Farm Families in Haryana, 1969–70 to 1982–83', *Economic and Political Weekly*, vol. XXV, nos 51 and 52, 23–30 December, pp. A154–8.

Ideologically and culturally socialized right from birth to accept their own inferiority, women actually help to tighten the reins of patriarchy, reinforcing its ideology and becoming a willing party to their own marginalization and exploitation. This is even given a moral sanctity and legitimacy, leading to a self-imposed subaltern-ism. Women's complicity with the patriarchal order also operates through the intra-gender differences within the household based upon life cycle status, and age, seniority, and gender relationships.

The new social set-up, however, is not lacking in potentialities for change. This is signified by men's attitudes and reactions, as also in certain departures from what was considered customary. It can be seen in resistance and defiance, however limited, offered by women, as well as in the preservation of individual interest and self-help without openly confronting the set hierarchies of power and authority. Outwardly and more openly, however, legitimated cultural and ideological practices continue unabated in the new socio-economic milieu, internalized by women themselves.

CONTROL OVER EXPENDITURE: FOOD ALLOCATION AND CONSUMPTION

The drastic change in Haryana in the wake of the green and white revolutions, as shown elsewhere, has resulted in the increase and not the decrease of women's agricultural-cum-animal husbandry work, specially in the areas benefited by these revolutions.[2] Yet, hardly any economic value is placed on this productive work and it is universally acknowledged as 'inferior', 'secondary', or 'supplementary'. As its value is entirely invisible, it grants women no economic worth or social stand-ing which might give them a deciding voice in the public and private domain, or offer a woman a role in the control of income which she produces or helps to produce.

This raises the crucial question of a woman's control over cash income. The woman does get to handle money now and then; in fact, it is generally in her safe keeping.[3] But its use is strictly controlled—its allocation being a man's special preserve and prerogative. An old Ambala proverb, recorded in the nineteenth century, shows how a full

[2] See Chapter 6 in this volume.
[3] Khazani Devi of village Sherjabad, aged 50 years; Kalawati, 42 years; and Shanti, 40 years, of village Bandh, among other women, testified to this practice.

account is taken from a woman even in the case of very small amounts; the reality today is very similar:

lekha mawan dhianda
bakhshish lakh lakheti[4]
(Even if one gives away lakhs in charity, a wife and a daughter must be held accountable.)

Confirming this, some of the men in Haryana expressed the view:

'*aurat apni marzi se kharach nahin ker sakti,*
aurat ki chalat ko galat mante hai'[5]
(a woman cannot spend money as she wishes to, this is considered wrong.)

The women when asked replied:

randi mange repaiya, le le meri maiya
main mangu paisa, chal be sali kaisa[6]
(When the whore demands a rupee, it is given so promptly, when I want a paisa, I am abused soundly.)

Even those women who earn wages as agricultural labourers have no control over the cash and how it is to be spent. Money is almost automatically handed over to the man and becomes his property, except in cases of households headed by women.[7]

Yet, most rural men insist that women set aside some money and produce, and make money on the sly by stealthily selling the household grain when their menfolk are not at home. The modus operandi adopted is said to be through a *tokni* (brass water carrier), full of grain, which is taken to the house of a known or a potential buyer and sold off at half its price.[8] A recent work similarly observes how the 'wise men' in Haryana village store their grain in their *baithak*, a room which is an

---

[4] R. Maconachie, 1980, *Selected Agricultural Proverbs of the Punjab*, Delhi: Imperial Hall Press, p. 209.

[5] Comment by Harpal Singh and Ratan Singh, 1988, village Bandh, 20–1 August, endorsed by many in different villages.

[6] Daya Kaur, 1988, Sonepat, 12 October; born 1929, her three sons are well employed in various government services; the land in the village is being looked after by her brother-in-law and his wife.

[7] In conversation with female agricultural labourers, mostly from scheduled castes, in village Dujjana, district Rohtak. Similar observations were made in village Bandh of Karnal district.

[8] Interview with Surendra Pal Singh, 44 years, and Dharam Pal Singh, 47 years, 1986, village Dujjana, district Rohtak, 6 June. The two brothers together own 25 *bighas* of land.

exclusive male preserve, so that women of the household may not sell it to vendors in order to get some spending money for themselves.[9] Such sales have been observed to be widespread even in the rural areas of Uttar Pradesh (UP).[10] Elsewhere in rural India also, women from households producing a surplus are often known to sell their grain without the knowledge of their husbands.[11] The male members are sometimes aware of this practice but prefer to feign ignorance of it as the family income is not greatly affected by it, and outwardly, their hold over the produce and its income goes unchallenged.[12] Although the Haryana women vehemently deny it, they probably do the same thing too. Such a practice certainly highlights the total lack of control over produce and money as well as the extent of women's needs leading to their limited defiance against the men's absolute control in surplus producing households. In households where the subsistence level economy dictates expenditure, whatever cash is available, is not likely to be given to women, nor would they be given a say in its disposal.

Income and its expenditure being out of a woman's control, it is the consumption patterns which assume importance. Women's opinion and voice in the evoking consumption patterns is closely intertwined with the concept of 'entitlement' enunciated by Amartya Sen and further developed by him and by Hanna Papanek.[13] This concept refers to the socially and culturally recognized entitlements of specific categories of persons to particular resource shares. Based on the relative value of different categories of persons, entitlement ideas constitute part of a

[9] S.K. Chandhoke, 1990, *Nature and Structure of Rural Habitations*, New Delhi: Concept, p. 235.

[10] Mildred Stroop Luschvinsky, 1963, 'The Impact of Some Recent Indian Government Legislation on the Women of an Indian Village', *Asian Survey*, vol. 3, no. 12, pp. 573–83.

[11] T. Padmasini and A. Sun, 1975, 'Farm Women and Home Management', *Indian Farming*, vol. 25, no. 8, November, pp. 55–6.

[12] See Luschvinsky, 'The Impact of Some Recent Indian Government Legislation on the Women of an Indian Village'.

[13] See Amartya Sen, 1981, *Poverty and Famines: An Essay on Entitlement and Deprivation*, New York: Oxford University Press, pp. 1–8; Hanna Papanek, 1990, 'To Each Less Than She Needs, From Each More Than She Can Do: Allocations, Entitlement and Value', in Irene Tinker (ed.), *Persistent Inequalities: Women and World Development*, New York: Oxford University Press, pp. 162–81; Amartya Sen, 1990, 'Gender and Co-operative Conflicts', in Irene Tinker (ed.), *Persistent Inequalities*, pp. 123–49.

system of beliefs about distributional justice in which women occupy a very low position.

The concept of 'entitlement' is most conspicuously noticeable in the sphere of food, its allocation, and intake. This becomes specially glaring not only because the women of the family universally and exclusively deal with it, there being no tradition of employing domestic help,[14] but also because a very large portion of the household budget is spent on it. A government survey of the family budgets of a cross-section of cultivators of Haryana from 1969–70 to 1984–5 shows anything between 56–60 per cent of the domestic expenditure being spent on food.[15] The details given for 1973–4 show that, on an average, the yearly food expenditure incurred ranged from Rs 9,858.04 by a landholding family owning 16 hectares in village Sondh of district Gurgaon out of a total domestic expenditure of Rs 18,343.04, to Rs 1,609.00 out of a total expenditure of Rs 3,195.00 by another family in village Furlat in Karnal district, owning 1.76 hectares of land.[16] However, in terms of percentages, this difference is not so wide ranging, that is, 53.74 per cent in village Sondh and 50.35 per cent in village Furlat. Clearly, on an average, more than half of the total expenditure in the rural areas is devoted to food.

The richer peasantry with greater incomes at their command is obviously spending more on food, and some of them are able to have what they boastfully assert to be 'the food of city people'.[17] This boast is not without some justification. The number of the mobile men from

[14] Employment of a domestic servant was considered a sign of affluence in the past. Only the upper classes in towns and some landlords in the villages used to engage servants for domestic work. Now, in the urban areas, they are being more commonly employed, although the tradition has hardly changed in the rural areas. See 1986, *Haryana District Gazetteer: Jind District, 1986*, Chandigarh: Haryana District Gazetteers Organization, Revenue Department, p. 140.

[15] See Government of Haryana, *Family Budgets of Cultivators in Haryana, 1969–70 to 1984–5*.

[16] Government of Haryana, 1976, *Family Budgets of Cultivators in Haryana, 1973–74*, Chandigarh: Govt of Haryana, Economic and Statistical Organization, Planning Department, Appendix VII, pp. 46–51.

[17] General opinion summed up by Ram Chander, 1988, village Bandh, 20–1 August; and Dheer Singh, 1988, village Asodha Todran, 21–7 December. Ram Chander, with his two brothers, Harpal Singh and Ratan Singh, ages ranging from late forties to early fifties, owns 33 bighas (11 bighas each) of land in village Bandh, district Karnal. Dheer Singh of village Asodha Todran in Rohtak district, born 1938, owns 2 *kilas* or 10 bighas of land.

rural backgrounds who, despite their totally vegetarian upbringing, have taken to eating eggs, meat, and chicken is significant. Yet, by and large, non-vegetarian food is still not cooked at home except among the lower castes. It is the rapidly multiplying restaurants in the cities and *dhabas* (eating places) in most of the villages, specially on the fringes of townships and in the towns, which cater to these newly acquired tastes. Significantly, the percentage of households reporting consumption of meat and eggs in rural Haryana was only 5.18 per cent and 3.39 per cent as compared to 12.42 per cent and 11.17 per cent in urban Haryana in 1975–6.[18] These rural households were calculated to spend a mere 0.27 per cent of their total food budget on meat and poultry products.[19] Although a major change, non-vegetarian diet is confined to a very small section of the rural society and is consumed almost totally by men.

The primarily vegetarian nature of the diet of Haryana in 1984–5 can be seen in the 80 per cent of the total household expenditure on food being spent on milk, cereals, pulses, and sugar.[20] Only a few amongst the very rich and smaller sized families are known to afford an expensive diet containing vegetables, fruit, animal products, and vegetable fat. Moreover, the vegetable and fruit consumption is relatively higher in villages located close to urban centres, whereas their consumption is confined only to a few rich families in less favourably located villages. An overwhelming 90 per cent are calculated to subsist on a relatively poor and moderate diet of *rotis*, eaten with a variety of *dals* (legumes) such as chick peas, *urad*, *moong*, *arhar*, and *masur* which provide the main protein requirement of adults and children.[21] Recent studies point out that even this diet is no longer so assured under the impact of the green revolution as the growing of low-yield dals faces tough competition from high-yield food grain and other commercial crops, resulting

[18] *National Sample Survey, Haryana,* Thirteenth Round, no. 281/10, July 1975–June 1976, pp. 9–10.

[19] Government of Haryana, 1977, *Family Budgets of Cultivators in Haryana, 1975–76,* Chandigarh, Govt of Haryana, Economic and Statistical Organization, Planning Department, p. 12. Even in 1984–5, this percentage rose to only 0.30 per cent.

[20] Government of Haryana, *Family Budgets of Cultivators in Haryana, 1984–85,* pp. 20–1.

[21] Surinder K. Aggarwal, 1986, *Geo-Ecology of Malnutrition: A Case Study of the Haryana Children,* New Delhi: Inter-India, pp. 103–6.

in the severe shrinkage of acreage under the former.[22] The nutritional health of Haryanavis—both male and female—is severely affected, though more severely for the latter, as will be shown presently.

In spite of a major part of the household budget being spent on food, one of the common problems accepted as ubiquitous in India is the still 'mal-nourished and exhausted reality of women'.[23] In Haryana, the crucial factor for women remains a very basic one: the access to food itself, which also determines its nutritional content. The women continue to be the last to eat in Haryana as elsewhere in rural India, with the choicest bits in quality and quantity having already been consumed by the men. Man and wife or, for that matter, men and women eating together has no acceptance in rural areas, mainly because the ideology of the man eating first and the best, as befitting his role of *karmadata* (doer), has not changed. The woman, on the other hand, is expected to be satisfied with whatever she gets. As an ideal, women are frequently told:

dekh biranni chaupri, keyon lalchawe jee,
rukhi sukhi kha ke, thanda pani pee.[24]
(Be content with your dry crust woman, don't hanker for another's feast.)

Culturally, the intra-household distribution of food which favours men over women cuts through caste and class barriers. Even among women themselves, there exists a power hierarchy in eating, operating from the mother-in-law and *jethani* (older sister-in-law) downwards. In fact,

[22] In fact, cultivation of dals shows a distinctly shrinking acreage. For example, the total harvested area for chick peas (the principal legume) and other pulses, declined from 34 per cent before the green revolution to 18 per cent during 1970–3. In eastern Haryana, the acreage devoted to mixed cropping of wheat and grain has almost dropped to one-third of the previous figures due to the single cropping practice for wheat alone. The cultivation of pulses is being pushed to the marginal lands, where water is at a premium and the soil is of poor quality. In fact, the general observation is that as irrigation, one of the most important inputs of the green revolution, increases, the cultivated area under pulses declines. See Aggarwal, *Geo-Ecology of Malnutrition*, pp. 104–6; also, see Jasbir Singh, 1976, *An Agricultural Geography of Haryana*, Kurukshetra: Vishal Publications, pp. 289–93.

[23] Rajammal P. Devdas, 1975, 'Role of Women in Social Transformation', *Indian Farming*, vol. 25B, no. 8, November, pp. 15–17.

[24] Frequently heard in the Haryana villages; also, see Jai Narayan Verma, 1972, *Haryanavi Lokoktiyan: Shastriye Vishleshan*, Delhi: Adarsh Sahitya Prakashan, p. 26.

the differential distribution of food reflects and creates social division and conveys hierarchies of power and status within the household. A present-day proverb describes this very aptly:

sas gai gaon, bahu kahe main ke ke khaun[25]
(With the mother-in-law away what all shall I eat, says the daughter-in-law.)

Even children have to follow a feeding hierarchy. A jethani's son, for example, may be given more by the jethani. A proverb used exclusively by women expresses this:

jethani ka bhainsa asar dhann dhann.[26]
(The sister-in-law's son is always fat.)

Despite this hierarchy among women, all women, whatever their status or age, are discriminated against in relation to men regarding food intake.

It is not as if women do not attempt to break these set norms. In fact, women's attempts to stealthily eat better are the theme of many jokes and stories which are very revealing. The following story is extremely popular, familiar to both men and women.[27] It depicts a *lugai* (woman) who, while cooking roti (unleavened whole grain bread) would save up the best ones for herself by hiding them in her *ghaghara* (long skirt). A man observing this remarked, '*dadi, ann sankat to mit jaga lekin chutad par ka daag na mitega*' (grandmother, you'll be rid of your hunger, but not the mark left on your buttocks). Equally well known and universally popular is another story, generally known as '*kuein jhere mein*'.[28] It is usually narrated where women are suspected of eating the choicest food on the sly. A woman repeatedly invited by her husband to join him while eating, an unheard of thing, replied: '*mein to kuein jhere main pad lungi*' (I shall eat the leftovers). The husband, having got suspicious

---

[25] Popular among women of all ages. Heard in village Chhara of Rohtak district; also included in the nineteenth century collection of S.W. Fallon, 1886, *A Dictionary of Hindustani Proverbs*, Benaras: Lazarus and Co., p. 211.

[26] Heard in village Bandh, district Karnal; also, see Fallon, *A Dictionary of Hindustani Proverbs*, p. 120.

[27] A very popular story, it was narrated to me by several men in different villages, more or less in the same manner except that the word lugai was substituted for by a Brahmini, a jatni, a kisani, or a zamindarni. Also, included in Bhim Singh Malik, 1981, *Haryana Lok Sahitya: Sanskriti Sandarbh*, Pilani: Chitra Prakashan, p. 111.

[28] Heard first of all from Hardwari Lal in my childhood. Born 1911, Hardwari Lal is a well-known educationist and politician of Haryana.

in the meanwhile, spied on her and saw her eat what she had hidden. Next day, he again invited her and elicited the same reply as before. To this he said: '*ari kha le, tere kuein jhere me to mein pad chuka*' (woman, now eat, as I have already finished your leftovers).

These jokes and stories show that, over the years, women have tried to outsmart the men's cornering of the largest shares of food. However, because of practical difficulties, the cultural milieu, and priorities in eating observed in rural areas, these jocular tales can be seen as only partial attempts by women to find a clandestine space which may have been foiled by the tight security maintained by the family hierarchy. They are also an expression of women's resentment but since such tales and jokes belong to a predominantly male discourse, they ultimately reinforce the patriarchal order by subtly stereotyping a woman who does not conform.

In fact, in matters of food, a woman is generally considered to be a thief, and her association with a cat is very pronounced all over northern India where the cat is considered to be a thief. The association between the two is based on an old myth, the roots of which go back to antiquity, saying that the cat was actually a Brahmini. Her present degradation is the fate to which she has been doomed by the curse of her saintly husband. The husband pronounced the curse in a fit of anger aroused by his wife's habitual pilfering. Since then, the house cat has always been considered a thief just as a woman is.[29] The tale also reveals the resentment against the ritual hierarchy of the high caste Brahmin, by stereotyping their women as 'greedy'.

These folk tales also indicate men's internalized acceptance of women's exact position regarding food allocation in the family as the question of 'stealing' is directly linked to the question of entitlement. The question as to what compels women to 'steal' in their own house is something no one wants to recognize or venture to answer. The endeavour is either to laugh it out of existence or dismiss it as the result of women's basic thieving nature. So ingrained is this belief that attempts to control women's behaviour begin very early. Therefore, if a girl is found eating out of turn or, as generally interpreted, to be stealing food, swift and severe punishment is meted out to act as a

---

[29] *William Crooke Collection*, MS. 131, Museum of Mankind, London; see note from Ram Gharib Chaube on the rural areas of UP. A few people in Haryana villages, mostly belonging to the age group of 70 years and above, remember this story.

future deterrent. But a boy's similar behaviour is justified by recalling tales of the God Krishna who was a notoriously loveable thief in his childhood.

The insistence of rural men that *lugai chhup chhupa ke khati hai*[30] (a woman eats stealthily), or the allegation that she eats better than her husband and children, arises out of the fact that she not only does the cooking but, what is more important, in a primarily vegetarian Haryana, has control over milk and *ghee* (clarified butter). This allegation is not very convincing, specially in view of the social behaviour of joint families in the villages where each keeps a strict eye on the behaviour patterns of others and where set norms of gender and hierarchy are being strictly observed.[31] Specially in the case of milk, the opportunities to keep some for themselves are much less for women. The highly commercial remuneration of the white revolution attracts a great deal of milk from many of the villages to the urban centres, leaving that much less for the family. For example, the percentage of expenditure on milk out of the total expenditure on food in Haryana was 63.08 per cent in 1971–2, which fell to 55.96 per cent in 1975–6 and further to 50.17 per cent in 1984–5.[32] This declining percentage of expenditure is substantiated by the decline in the daily adult male consumption of milk and milk products which fell from 789 grams in 1971–2 to 778 in 1975–6 and to 512 grams in 1984–5. Linking the two percentages, it becomes apparent that in the rural areas, consumption lessened significantly in the wake of commercialization of milk, with its products being diverted to urban consumers through an expanding market network covering procurement, processing, and distribution.[33]

[30] Interview with Shamsher Singh and his wife, Angoori Devi, 1986, Rohtak, 23 May. A Jat agriculturist, Shamsher Singh is the owner of 12½ bighas fertile land in Haryana.

[31] The joint families are still the dominant norm in most villages of Haryana. See, *Haryana District Gazetteer: Jind District*. Also, see T.M. Dak and M.L. Sharma, 1988, 'Social Framework of Female Labour Participation in Rural Sector', in T.M. Dak (ed.), *Women and Work in Indian Society*, New Delhi: Manohar, pp. 25–47.

[32] For consumption of and expenditure on milk, see Government of Haryana, *Family Budgets of Cultivators in Haryana, 1971–72*, p. 7; *1975–76*, pp. 12–14; *1984–85*, pp. 20, 23.

[33] For the milk drain from rural to urban centres in the wake of 'Operation Flood Programme', see S.N. Misra and R.K. Rishi, 1989, *Livestock Development in India: An Appraisal*, New Delhi: Vikas, pp. 135–6.

Consequently, milk has become even more valuable than before in view of its economic return. This commercialization has meant a great deal of cash income accruing to the rural households. In 1984–5, income from milk and milk products was calculated to be 5.69 per cent of the total average annual income among Haryana's landowners.[34] But, all this money is controlled by men. Whereas previously when milk was not sold, women used to drink it and use its products, albeit within the limits of the family hierarchy, as admitted by some of the older ones. Women of an older generation in Haryana and Punjab nostalgically remember their own milk drinking days when milk was not sold but kept entirely for home consumption. In the changed circumstances, women are marginalized as far as milk consumption is concerned and do not even control the proceeds of its sale. What does remain for them is the labour-intensive care of animals, the extraction of milk, and making of milk products. This reinforces the division of labour and status hierarchy within rural society. It also establishes what has been described by Miriam Sharma and Urmila Vanjani as a 'gender based internal colonization',[35] not only in the functioning and capital accumulation of the modern dairy system, as represented by the male-controlled processing and marketing centres in the city which depend upon the cheap labour and intensive work of women, but also at home and at an individual intra-personal level.

Commercialization has therefore meant a certain calculated quality of milk being reserved for home consumption, in which women come last of all. Here, it may be pointed out that culturally, consumption of milk and milk products such as *lassi* (buttermilk) and ghee is usually higher among certain caste groups such as Jats and Rajputs than with other castes.[36] Among these castes, cultural factors would dictate that even women would be better fed, and might not be so deprived as those from other castes, including higher castes like Bania and Brahmin, and lower ones, including scheduled castes. In fact, for the scheduled castes, a disruption of the old *jajmani* (institutionalized hierarchical service between families of the dominant castes and families of various

[34] Government of Haryana, *Family Budgets of Cultivators in Haryana, 1984–85*, p. 4.

[35] Miriam Sharma and Urmila Vanjani, 1989, 'Women's Work is Never Done: Dairy Development and Health in the Lives of Rural Women of Rajasthan', *Economic and Political Weekly*, vol. 24, no. 7, 29 April, pp. WS38–45.

[36] Aggarwal, *Geo-Ecology of Malnutrition*, pp. 45–6.

artisan and servicing castes) system due to commercialization of milk, among other factors, has meant withholding of the buttermilk as well as food traditionally given on a yearly basis by the landowners. This has caused severe malnutrition among the scheduled castes, specially women and children.[37]

Women's failure to benefit from the increased milk production in terms of consumption is not confined to Haryana. A study from Rajasthan reaches the same conclusion.[38] In fact, it is an all-India picture that on the question of access to milk and milk products, women and female children are always relatively deprived, even within households where there is a high milk consumption.[39] Moreover, the family power hierarchy and gender roles also determine milk distribution. For example, in many of the rural households in Haryana, this distribution can be seen to be firmly controlled by the *sas* (mother-in-law), and as the saying goes, it is reserved for *bete* and *jamai*, that is, sons and son-in-law.[40]

A combination of all these factors explains the current general marked preference for *cha* (tea) among rural women.[41] When questioned closely, most women insisted that they actually preferred tea to milk. A few even went to the extent of saying that they could no longer digest milk. The older ones accuse the younger ones of taking tea as a camouflage for milk by brewing tea leaves in milk. Moreover, tea is declared to have medicinal qualities, particularly for common coughs and colds. A recent study corroborates this and points out how tea has become a staple in the diet pattern of not only adults but young children as well, across most villages in Haryana.[42] Not counting those who are breast fed, it is held that tea is consumed by more than 90 per cent of children (gender not specified) over two years old as a full or partial substitute for milk.

[37] Government of Punjab, 1974, *Punjab Nutritional Development Project*, Chandigarh, CARE Project, p. 54.

[38] See Sharma and Vanjani, 'Women's Work is Never Done'.

[39] M. Chen, K. Mitra, G. Aitreya, A. Dholakia, P. Low, and A. Rao, 1986, *Indian Women: A Study of their Role in the Dairy Movement*, New Delhi: Shakti Books, p. 13.

[40] Heard in village Jhojho Chamani, district Bhiwani.

[41] Angoori Devi, 1986, wife of Shamsher Singh, summed up this general preference for tea among women, Rohtak, 23 May.

[42] This was the general observation of rural women. Also, see Aggarwal, *Geo-Ecology of Malnutrition*, p. 104.

Nevertheless, it is certainly possible that women eat and drink between meals since they cook the food. The fact that some do so is evidenced in the folk tales given earlier. But, by and large, cultural and ideological conditioning, which includes certain taboos regarding food, seems at least to limit it. The dominant trend of this ideology is summed up in an old folk saying:

nar sulkhni kutumb chhikawe
ap tale ki khurchan khawe[43]
(A good housewife feeds the household well and eats the leftovers herself.)

This local proverb is not only currently in use but the purport is clear in the working of its ideology. The fact that women's behaviour is directed towards the well-being of the family as a whole, with special attention for its male members, and that women have no clear perception of individual welfare or personal interest has been amply commented upon by sociologists, and has been used as a justification for inequality. Yet, as pointed out by Amartya Sen, inequality not only in food but also in the allocation of other resources cannot be denied.[44] My study also shows that women's own perception of discrimination in matters of intra-family food allocation remains unacknowledged, at least in public.[45] The interviews revealed the contradictory and often problematic nature of women's own feelings towards food. But the fact that they could manage with much less compared to other family members was a universal feeling among them. The frequent answer elicited from the older women about the food intake of the younger women is, *'khub khavain sain'* (they eat a lot), while the younger ones merely say, *'theek khavain sain'* (we eat enough). Clearly, ideological and cultural norms have made women complicit in the system by conditioning them to accept this marginal allocation or even to justify it. The women were quite aware of the differences in the food being eaten by men, specially when out of the home, or the changed and

---

[43] A common folk saying often quoted by women when accusing others, mostly younger women, of food pilferage; or, more frequently, as a piece of advice to young girls or to the newly married. Also, recorded by Fallon, *A Dictionary of Hindustani Proverbs*, p. 171.

[44] Veena Das and Ralph Nicholas, cited in Jocelyn Kyuch and Amartya Sen, no date, 'Indian Women: Well Being and Survival', Unpublished paper, ICSSR, New Delhi. For a full critique of their point of view, see Sen, 'Gender and Cooperative Conflicts'.

[45] Chowdhry, *The Veiled Women*, pp. 216–43.

fast changing food habits of many of their menfolk, but attached no significance to it, either in terms of quality or nutritional value.

It is clear, therefore, that custom and actual conditioning may rule out the women's eating the food despite their realization that there may not be an opportunity later. In fact, there are even rules against tasting food during its actual cooking that exist in Punjab, Haryana, and UP, when even salt is not to be tasted but smelt.[46] All these factors which affect their behaviour culturally may not be so important when there is enough food to go around, but become crucial when it is limited, and work against women and girls.

INEQUALITY, NUTRITION, AND HEALTH

The subtle indoctrination regarding acceptance of this discrimination and control of women's food intake begins early, in fact right from birth. The nursing of the infant girl by the mother has always been minimal. It is not an uncommon sight in the villages to see boys of four or five years of age demanding and succeeding in getting a suckle from their mothers, back home from working in the fields. The early weaning of the infant girl is also prompted by the desire to conceive a male child as soon as possible by removing a traditionally accepted natural deterrent to conception, that is, breastfeeding. Culturally, feeding and weaning practices vary among the cultivating castes, who breastfeed their children for better health, whereas early weaning is usual among the rich business castes of Haryana.[47] Among the scheduled castes and other lower classes, on the other hand, poverty is one among several limiting factors in choosing breastfeeding for a longer time. Yet, class and caste conjoin in breastfeeding the boys for a much longer time than the girls. The inadequacy or failure of breastfeeding has been accepted as the main cause of death among children. Breastfeeding is known to make a significant difference to the chances of the child's survival as it not only transmits nutrients but also certain immunity creating elements which help fight the risks of infection from the environment.[48]

---

[46] Vidyavati, 1987, Delhi, 24 December; Raj Kumari Chopra, 1990, Calcutta, 5 February.

[47] Aggarwal, *Geo-Ecology of Malnutrition*, pp. 45–6, 109.

[48] Leela Visaria, 1988, 'Determinants of Regional Variations in Infant Mortality in Rural India', in Anrudh K. Jain and Pravin Visaria (eds), *Infant Mortality in India: Differentials and Determinants*, New Delhi: Sage, pp. 67–126.

A tendency to give preferential treatment to a male over a female child in matters of food is a well-accepted reality of Haryana and Punjab.[49] Gradually, throughout childhood, girls are brought up to believe that in the organization of serving and distributing food within the household, the leftovers are to be eaten by the women and not by the male members. This is a kind of inculcation of the ideology of self-denial, as can be noticed in the story of the woman given earlier who talks about her eating the leftovers. This ideological conditioning which a girl child imbibes from her mother and grandmother, makes it almost unthinkable for her to behave otherwise when grown up. Daughters are always made aware of this difference, specially by the mother, in day-to-day references to her future *sasural* (conjugal home) and its demands and expectations, specially in matters of work and food.

A recent study showing data on the allocation of food in Punjab among girls and boys substantiates the given observations. It shows that while girls are given more cereals, the boys are given more milk and fat with their cereals.[50] This is because all over north India, milk and fat are the most valued and expensive foods that are considered to be of high nutritional value, and reserved for male children. Girls' inferior position in this connection was brought home by a very telling common occurrence reconstructed by a woman. It relates to a common practice of boys to drink the milk straight from the family buffalo or cow as it is being milked. Yet, when a girl child demands the same privilege by asking, '*bapu* give it to me too', she is frightened off by the man who says: '*bhajja tere moochch jum jagi*'[51] (run away or you'll grow a moustache).

Girls' eating habits have always been sought to be controlled. There is a long list of 'hot' and 'cold' foods over which a precautionary taboo

[49] Omi Manchanda, an urban highly educated Punjabi, born in 1927, recalls her youth in the mid-1940s, when the cream from the top of the milk was always given to the boys and not to the girls. Also, see Government of Punjab, *Punjab Nutritional Development Project*, pp. 38–9. In Haryana, dal, etc., is served to the boys with dollops of ghee, but never to the girls.

[50] Monica Das Gupta, 1971, 'Selective Discrimination against Female Children in Rural Punjab, India', *Population and Development Review*, vol. 31, no. 1, March, pp. 77–100.

[51] Narrated by Ratni, 38 years old, 1988, village Chhara, district Rohtak, 5 December. It was confirmed by the men in the family who treated it as a joke.

exists in rural Haryana.[52] The *garam* or hot foods range from sour, spicy, fried, and over-sweet foods, butter and ghee, to red chillies and tamarind-based snacks and food. There is another list of '*thanda*' or cold foods, like buttermilk, curd, and cold drinks. The concept of garam and thanda foods does not relate to temperature but is defined as generating either 'heat' in the body or cooling it. These categories, supposedly meant for all, are specially observed for children but are primarily enforced for girls. When asked about this strictness on girls alone, the answer given was, '*laddke ke manne sain?*'[53] (do the boys listen?). The fears for girls range from irregularities in the menstrual cycle and consequent barrenness to acceleration of emergent sexuality, which would invite undue masculine attention and lead to girls being maligned as bad characters.[54] Once again, the older women can be seen as privy to the control of younger ones here, regarding sexuality. The accepted need for control also rationalizes the offering of a regulated and limited diet to women.

This cultural and ideological bias regarding food has severe consequences for the health of rural women. Here, it may be well to point out that it is difficult to calculate the extent of this due to the lack of data on nutritional status and morbidity in rural Haryana. Also, there are significant differences in the intake of energy giving foods, proteins, and the like, between women of different socio-economic classes within the same region and even districts, with corresponding differences in the quality of diet. And, although discrimination against women exists, cutting across caste and class lines in rural areas, it is also a fact that the richer women from agriculturist families are still nutritionally better fed than the poor low caste/class women as well as men. An east Punjab study, for example, shows that the nutritional status of girls among Ramdasias and other low castes was much lower than that of boys. Among the wealthier Jats, however, despite discrimination in

[52] For details, see Aggarwal, *Geo-Ecology of Malnutrition*, p. 112; and Ministry of Health and Family Planning, North Zone, 1990, *Diarrhaoea in Rural India: A Nation-wide Study of Mothers and Practitioners*, New Delhi: Vision Books, see 'Haryana' section, pp. 33–73.

[53] Remark of Ratni and other women, 1988, in village Chhara, 5 December.

[54] For the control of emergent sexuality among female children and prospective motherhood through a special diet for the female child, see Leela Dube, 1981, 'On the Construction of Gender: Hindu Girls in Patrilineal India', *Economic and Political Weekly*, vol. 22, no. 18, 30 April, pp. WS11–19.

feeding practices against girls, the difference was less and the nutritional status higher.[55]

In Haryana, the problem of malnutrition and mortality among female infants and small children can be seen in the distinctly higher rate of deaths among females in all the age groups except those above forty-five years of age.[56] In this age group, the female death rate in 1981 was 7 per cent less than that of the male. Yet, even in this age group, an in-depth study of households belonging to a lower economic category, ranging from small cultivators downwards to landless labourers in Hissar district in 1978, shows no such advantages for females.[57]

For women, a very high incidence of mortality is noticeable during their high fertility period between 14 and 44 years of age. It is during these years that 96.84 per cent of children are born. These deaths occur due to many factors ranging from neglect, lack of medical facilities, multiplicity of child births, frequent conceptions, general weakness, and other factors such. But an important reason is nutritional, specially in view of the very high fertility rate. The minimum average number of children born per married woman in rural Haryana is 5.3.[58] This excludes those pregnancies ending in miscarriages, abortions, or infant deaths. The very frequent pregnancies result in maternal malnutrition which is largely responsible for the high maternal mortality rate. The woman has to draw heavily on her own bodily resources to supply the needed nutrients for the baby in her womb. Childbirth is continuing

[55] F.J. Levinson, 1972, *An Economic Analysis of Malnutrition among Young Children in Rural India*, Cambridge and Ithaca: Cornell University Press, pp. 91–2.

[56] Percentage of deaths by age and sex in rural Haryana in 1981:

Age group	Male	Female	Difference (percentage)
0–4	19.3	22.7	+3.4
5–14	19.1	19.5	+0.4
15–44	15.4	18.6	+3.2
45 and above	59.2	52.2	−7.00

Source: Registrar-General, India, 1984, *Vital Statistics of India 1981*, New Delhi: Ministry of Home Affairs, p. 19, statement XVII.

[57] For figures, see 1978, 'Integrated Rural Development', Mimeograph, vol. III, Directorate of Project-cum-Plan Formulation, Hissar Agricultural University, Haryana, March, pp. 52–3.

[58] 1983, *Census of Haryana, 1981*, series 6, part II, Special Report and Tables, New Delhi, p. 36.

to be a common cause of women's deaths, as noted in all the recent district gazetteers of Haryana.

In any case, pregnant and lactating women are considered to be nutritionally the most vulnerable group. A clinic in the green revolution area of Karnal district vouched for the dangerously below-normal haemoglobin level of pregnant women, directly attributable to nutritional inadequacies, leading to a high incidence of spontaneous abortions, premature births, and miscarriages.[59] It also vouched for the fact that nearly two-thirds of pregnant women from even well-to-do homes showed very low haemoglobin counts and doctors were surprised that there were not more miscarriages.[60] Clearly, the problem is not only a medical one but also of health and nurtrition. However, this malnutrition of women is not specific to Haryana, but is a harsh reality of the entire 'third world' and has been well documented.[61]

It is possible to assess the nutritional intake of the diet of pregnant and lactating women, the more so because of the ways they themselves perceive and determine their nutritional levels. Since the woman is associated with the cooking, the male presumption, as described earlier, is that women feed themselves well. This may explain men's indifference towards women's food intake, as men assume they can take care of themselves. No worry is shown on account of women's diet at least. At best, their requests for a few special foods now and then may be fulfilled, but attention is never given to regular meals.[62] The general

[59] Information given by Kama Puri who has been closely associated with clinics in rural Karnal, specially in the Madhuban village and the charity hospital wing established by the Arpana Ashram in this village. For a cross reference to low haemoglobin level among women due to nutritional inadequacies in third world countries, see Perdita Huston, 1979, *Third World Women Speak Out*, New York: Praeger Publications, p. 68.

[60] Anaemia is one of the important causes of morbidity and mortality among mothers and children. See Government of India, 1990, *Annual Report, 1980–90*, New Delhi: Ministry of Health and Welfare, p. 218.

[61] See S.P. Hamilton, B.B. Popkin, and D. Spicer, 1984, *Women and Nutrition in Third World Countries*, New York: Praeger Publications; Janet H. Morrison and Janet Townsend (eds), 1987, *Geography of Gender in the Third World*, New York: State University of New York Press.

[62] A comparative study undertaken in western UP points out that a pregnant woman is never given a special diet in the rural areas and highlights some of the reasons why such attention to her is culturally not feasible. See Patricia Jeffery, Roger Jeffery, and Andrew Lyn, 1989, *Labour Pains and Labour Power: Women and Child Bearing in India*, New Delhi: Manohar, pp. 77–81.

opinion of rural women is that such indulgence is shown only during the first pregnancy; women may even continue to eat well for a short while in case it is a son. The rest of their pregnancies are treated as a matter of common occurrence as 'all women bear children, what's so special about her' is the general refrain.

However, even though the 'poorly fed' and malnutritional reality of rural women of UP, highlighted by some recent studies,[63] may not be true of certain sections of Haryana's women belonging to households which have adequate or plentiful resources, there are ever-growing numbers of households where the women often go hungry to feed men and children. Significantly, an official sample survey of 1979–80[64] of fifteen selected villages of Gurgaon district shows 37.7 per cent of the population living below the poverty line according to the criterion adopted for the survey. The number of households below the poverty line varied from the lowest of 21.6 per cent in one village to the highest of 69.8 per cent in another village. This included not only the unemployed and agricultural labourers but also small cultivators with uneconomic holdings, whose per capita income fell well below the poverty line. Another more recent survey of 1981–2[65] in the Ambala district, covering 168 villages, identified an overwhelming 71 per cent of the families surveyed to be below the poverty line. Caste wise, 42.3 per cent of them were from the scheduled castes and 57.3 per cent from among other castes. Class-wise, those from among the small farmers, that is, owners of 2.5 to 5 acres were 14.41 per cent; those from the marginal farmers, that is, owners of 2.5 acres and below were 14.15 per cent; and from the landless agricultural labourers, 28.26 per cent; the remaining 43.18 per cent were from the non-agricultural labour households. On the whole, the official figures given for population below the poverty line in Haryana rural areas was calculated at 15.2 per cent in 1983–4.[66]

[63] Studies cited in Govind Kelkar, 1981, 'The Impact of the Green Revolution on Women's Work Participation and Sex Roles', Tripartite Asian Regional Seminar on Rural Development and Women, Mahabaleshwar, April.

[64] See Government of Haryana, 1981, 'Area Potential-cum-Poverty Line Survey of Sohna Block in Gurgaon District', Mimeograph, Chandigarh.

[65] District Rural Development Agency, 'Income Generation Plan for Families below Poverty Line in Selected Cultivators of Villages, 1981–82', (n.d) Mimeograph, Ambala District, New Delhi, pp. 10–11.

[66] Directorate of General Health Services, 1989, *Health Information in India, 1989*, New Delhi: Ministry of Health and Family Welfare, p. 289, Table 17.1.

Other scholars have put the below poverty line figures roughly at 45 per cent of the cultivating population.[67] The reality of these households, in terms of what it means for the women, needs no comment.

CONSUMERISM AND URBANIZATION AS NUCLEI OF MALE CONTROL

Expenditure on clothes is the second largest item, next to food, for the rural household. Between 1967–8 and 1984–5, it fluctuated between 11 per cent and 13.54 per cent of the total household budget.[68] This general heading of 'clothes' includes not only clothes for ordinary and special occasions but also expenditure on toiletry, bathing and washing soaps, hair oil, combs, cosmetics, footwear, and other miscellaneous requirements. A 1973–4 breakdown of this expenditure shows that those with higher incomes spend a great deal more per year on clothing.[69] For example, in village Jawa in district Bhiwani, a family owning 3.64 hectares land spent Rs 151 or 4.16 per cent of its total expenditure of Rs 3,628.35 on clothes. Another family with 16 hectares of land in village Bandh of district Gurgaon, spent Rs 2,271 or 12.38 per cent on clothing out of a total expenditure of Rs 18,343.04. In the expenditure on 'clothing', a substantially large portion is spent on garments. In 1984–5, for example, 63.44 per cent was being spent on garments out

---

The given estimate is calculated by using the poverty line of Rs 49.09 per capita per month at 1973–4 prices corresponding to daily calorie requirement of 2,400 calories per person in rural areas.

[67] Utsa Patnaik, in calculating these figures for Haryana, has considered estimates of minimum levels of subsistence from three different sources: (i) The Planning Commission figures of Rs 43.60 per capita at 1972–3 prices; (ii) The Indian Council of Medical Research Classification by age and sex-wise calorie requirements to arrive at the monthly equivalent of minimum nutrition of Rs 43.06 per capita at 1972–3 prices; and (iii) The Dandekar-Rath estimate of Rs 15 per capita per month, as an index of absolute rock bottom level of existence. See Utsa Patnaik, 1987, *Peasant Class Differentiation: A Study in Method with Reference to Haryana*, New Delhi: Oxford University Press, pp. 152–8.

[68] Government of Haryana, *Family Budgets of Cultivators in Haryana, 1967–68*, p. 5; 1984–85, p. 15.

[69] Government of Haryana, *Family Budgets of Cultivators in Haryana, 1973–74*, p. 8.

of the total expenditure on 'clothing'.[70] Yet, the ideal of simplicity and austerity is specially extended to unmarried girls as:

baap he ghar betti gudar lipti achchi[71]
(In her father's house, a daughter is best
clad in simple and rough rags.)

It is true that those who can afford it are visibly spending money on clothes and looking better dressed, and also, it is true that most men use just a thick *khes* (rough handwoven cotton wrap) in winter. A common saying is *'dolre ke ratch sai, odheye chahe bichhaye'*[72] (*dolra*, a thick cloth, can be worn as well as used as a blanket at night). Yet, none of this expenditure can be decided by women as it is mostly the male member's prerogative to do the marketing. One extreme opinion maintained that a woman generally has to make do with the clothes she brings in her dowry or what her parents give her as gifts on different occasions; clothes are bought only for children and men and very rarely for women.[73] Although clearly far-fetched, this observation is very telling; again, even in the purchase of clothes women come last. Moreover, whether the clothes are brought as part of the dowry or brought later, it is the mother-in-law as the senior woman who has the greatest say in their distribution.[74] The priority observed in this distribution can perhaps be visualized from the tradition in which *nanande* (sisters-in-law) are ritually allowed to pick up a set of clothing of their choice for themselves from among the personal clothing brought as dowry by the bride, thus repeating the hierarchy among women even in the matter of clothes.[75]

Another important head of expenditure reserved by the male head of the household is for housing. In fact, apart from the acquisition of farm machinery, his priority lies in acquiring a *pacca* home. The two important aspirations of men in Haryana are summed up in a common

---

[70] Government of Haryana, *Family Budgets of Cultivators in Haryana, 1984–85*, p. 26.

[71] This is a very common utterance in the villages. Also, included in Verma, *Haryanavi Lokoktiyan*, p. 57.

[72] Ibid., p. 27.

[73] Voiced by Dheer Singh and his wife, Gyano Devi, 1988, village Asodha Todran, 27 December.

[74] Renee Hirschen, 1989, *Women in Property—Women as Property*, London: Croom Helm, pp. 62–73.

[75] A commonly observed tradition in Haryana and Punjab.

utterance, 'pucci roti aur pucci haveli' (a well-cooked meal and a well-built house). On an average, a peasant proprietor's family between 1969–70 and 1984–5, has been calculated to spend 4–5 per cent of its domestic budget on housing.[76] Despite this allocation of money indicating the desire to possess a pacca house, and setting aside money for it, not everyone can possess one. Two-thirds of the cultivators with holdings of 5 acres and below, still live in kachcha houses which are expensive to maintain.[77] Among the landless labourers, the percentage of those living in kachcha houses is an overwhelming 87 per cent. In fact, only households of marginal farmers and those above take the lead in constructing pacca houses, though often part of them is still kachcha.[78]

For the paucca houses, the most popular ground plan has a baithak (a large outer apartment for men). Standing as a 'symbol of masculinity', this baithak is exclusively a male preserve completely out of bounds for women.[79] This emphasis on the acquisition of a baithak, distinct from the ghar (inner quarters for women), is not only symbolic of the new male-oriented pattern of expenditure but also further underlines the social organization of space leading to a yet greater physical exclusion of women based on the segregation of sexes. Those who now can afford it among low caste and class groups, have also started to emulate the construction of a baithak as a 'male space', a practice contrary to their earlier sharing of space in single or two-room units. However, in practice, even for landowning groups, a baithak remains a 'luxury', reserved for cultivators with holdings above 5 acres; below that, only 13 per cent are calculated to possess a baithak.[80] This baithak has a new look, as the earlier design which accommodated milch animals along with a charpai (cot) for the men of the family and guests is now seen less often. The emphasis today is on an urban-style furnishing with cushioned chairs and side tables, a table fan if possible, and a transistor radio. All these are symbols of modernization and therefore, denote the prestige and social status of the households. Among those households

[76] Government of Haryana, *Family Budgets of Cultivators in Haryana, 1969–70*, p. 5; 1984–85, pp. 14–15.

[77] 'Integrated Rural Development', p. 85.

[78] Ibid., pp. 82–4. The number of rooms in the house depends on financial status. The majority of small farmers and below have a maximum of two rooms.

[79] S.K. Chandhoke, 1990, *Nature and Structure of Rural Habitation*, New Delhi: Concept, pp. 168–78, 223–5.

[80] 'Integrated Rural Development', pp. 82–4.

which have now built baithaks, 76 per cent possess chairs and tables.[81] A transistor radio is also fairly common and it is considered the major source of entertainment. Television ownership is more recent, and is still restricted to a few of the most affluent families in the villages. In 1984–5, only four families out of the eighty surveyed, possessed a television set. Moreover, it is only recently that the television set has become a part of the dowry, and has replaced the radio as a status symbol in the richer families of rural Haryana.

Other status symbols include a bicycle, a wrist watch, a sewing machine for women, and even the kerosene oil stove. Yet, the priority observed in the acquisition of these status symbols, as given earlier, show them to be male oriented and male dictated. Being in their custody, they (excluding the sewing machine and stove) are kept in spaces specially reserved for men and are out of bounds for women, who have no access to them even though they may well have been part of their dowry items. Even where access is possible, the women are not allowed to use those facilities. For example, they cannot switch on the radio, but may listen to it from the women's quarters.[82]

This expenditure has direct relation with growing consumerism which followed the green revolution and urbanization in Haryana. In twenty years time (1961–81) the total number of towns in this state increased from 61 to 81, leading to the doubling of urban population.[83] This period also saw a remarkable drop in the number of very small villages and increase in the number of large and very large villages. So much so that by 1981, 57 villages were fully absorbed in the growing townships and 18 villages became extensions of towns being partially absorbed.[84]

Incorporation of villages into towns also brought many of the villages close to the urban centers. As many as 835 villages in Haryana are easily approachable from the neighbouring towns as they lie with in

[81] Government of Haryana, *Family Budgets of Cultivators in Haryana, 1984–85*, p. 37.

[82] Malkit Kaur, 1982, 'Emerging Status Role of Rural Women in the Context of Changing Technology in Haryana', PhD Dissertation, Haryana Agricultural University, Hissar, p. 161.

[83] *Census of Haryana, 1981*, part II-A and part II-B, General Population Tables and Primary Census Abstract, pp. 26, 28.

[84] See Sheila Bhalla, 1981, 'Islands of Growth: A Note on Haryana Experience and Some Possible Implications', *Economic and Political Weekly*, vol. 26, no. 23, 6 June.

a radius of 15 kms. In fact, several villages are located within just 3 kms. of a town's periphery. This has accelerated the commercial interaction between towns and villages, which was earlier casual and infrequent.[85] Larger villages have attracted the sale of modern goods and services. The increasing numbers of retail shops selling a variety of consumer goods are now a conspicuous presence in these villages. Indeed the variety of goods available in these shops is no different from that available in small shopping centers of metropolitan cities.[86] Clearly, certain factors like growing urbanization, consumerism, increasing retail marketing, easy availability of goods and services, augmentation of service sector, especially trade and banking, and improvement of infrastructural facilities, along with growth in education and better awareness of industrial and commercial products, extensive advertisements and enormous growth in entertainment sector have gravely impacted the consumption patterns in rural areas. There is a noticeable shift towards consumer and luxury goods. A study on expenditure on non-food consumer products in rural areas brought by the Birla Economic Research Foundation in 1991 shows a distinct increase in this expenditure in the 1980s.[87] This is noticeably true of states like Punjab and Haryana. The prosperity of the green revolution has led both these states to take enthusiastically to urban consumerist culture.

The urban consumerist spillover in to rural areas is conspicuously visible in the entertainment sector. The number of cinema theatres, for example, increased from 69 in 1970 to 113 in 1980–1, as did the eateries and the number of patrons they attracted.[88] In the rural areas, these are almost exclusively patronized by men. The spending in this sector has further added to the male oriented expenditure pattern which excludes women. The increase in the entertainment tax collection, (including the rise in income tax) from Rs 10,54,000 in 1970–1 to Rs 7,01,89,000 in 1984–5; and increase of show tax from Rs 10,03,000 in 1970–1 to

---

[85] Ibid.

[86] S.P. Sinha, *Processes and Patterns of Urban Development in Haryana, 1901–1971*, ICSSR Report, Kurukshetra: Kurukshetra University, pp. 331–3.

[87] See 'Rural Market on the Rise', *Hindustan Times*, 18 February 1991, p. 16. For the newly acquired socio-economic and political importance of the small town, see Chandan Mitra, 'Rise of the Small Town', *Sunday Observer*, 27 January–2 February 1991, p. 5.

[88] Government of Haryana, *Statistical Abstract of Haryana, 1985–86*, Chandigarh: Economic and Statistical Organization, 1987, p. 514.

Rs 51.44,000 in 1984–5 has meant an increase of 534.96 per cent and 412.86 per cent respectively in four years.[89] According to the official figures the trade, hotel, and restaurant sector has emerged as second in importance to the primary agricultural sector. In 1988–9, for example, the agricultural sector contributed 16.8 per cent to the state domestic products at the current prices and the manufacturing sector contributed 15.2 per cent.[90]

More importantly, the new consumption patterns involving drinking, whether tea or liquor and partaking non-vegetarian food in dhabas and other eating places, or going to entertainment places like the cinema houses or video parlours that have opened up in some of the villages, have added immensely to the all-male social assemblages that already exist in the villages.[91] The existing practices range from hukka smoking, card playing, or sitting around the fire in winter months, as well as in liquor drinking in *sharab ke adde* (a place where people gather routinely to drink liquor). With the increase in the gathering places of males in the public sphere, female mobility has become more constricted. They are being confined more and more to the private and work domain. Although it is true that in Haryana women have a visible presence in the fields and streets, it is a mobility which is socially sanctioned and recognized. Women are never seen to be just hanging or going about purposelessly. The growing public presence of men, specially in the increasing leisure activities, has a controlling effect on the mobility of women. It reinforces the practice and ideology of *ghunghat* (veil).

A special mention may be made of the growing liquor consumption in the rural areas. Its growth in the local perception and in the opinion of academics is directly related to the increased income generation of

---

[89] Ibid., pp. 515–16. There are no separate figures for urban and rural Haryana.

[90] Government of Haryana, *Economic Survey of Haryana, 1989–90*, Chandigarh: Planning Department, Economic and Statistical Organization, 1990, p. 2.

[91] The *dhabas* as centres of predominantly male gatherings can be seen in a Punjabi proverb which maintains: 'a dhaba is like a courtesan, the more you decorate it, the more customers it will attract'. The functions of dhabas range from serving food (both vegetarian and non-vegetarian) to liquor and pimping. The majority of their clientele does not consist of vehicle drivers (mostly trucks) as popularly believed but rural men. See Pranav Kumar, 'Dhabhas of Ambala,' *Hindustan Times*, 13 February 1991, p. 13.

the consumers.[92] The united figures of country liquor, Indian whisky, wine and beer, show a tremendous growth between 1966 and 1985 and is estimated to be on the upward swing every year.[93] Not all this liquor is consumed in Haryana as the state is also an exporter of liquor. However, even if we take the figures for *tharra* (country liquor) consumed primarily in the state itself, the increase in these 18 years has been stupendous 745 per cent, where as the population growth was less than 30 per cent.[94]

It is this aspect of the capitalist consumerist economy, symbolized in alcohol consumption, which affects women emotionally, physically, and economically. Alchohol consumption—an important aspect of capitalist economy—is well known to adversely affect women in emotional, physical, and economic spheres. Yet, the sharab ke theke (licensed liquor shops) in Haryana have been constantly on the increase.[95] The women of Haryana and UP openly complain that their men spend their

---

[92] *Haryana District Gazetteer: Sirsa District, 1988,* Chandigarh, 1989, pp. 303–4. Also see *Haryana District Gazetteer: Hissar District 1987,* Chandigarh, 1987, p. 233. According to Jon Peter Dorschrer lower as well as higher castes hold that the availability of money with the higher cultivating castes is responsible for this overriding habit. See his *Alcohol Consumption in a Village in North India,* Michigan: UMI Research Press, 1983, p. 46.

[93] *Consumption of Liquor in Haryana:*

Year	Country Liquor (proof litres)	Foreign Liquor (proof litres)	Wine and Beer (proof litres)
1966–7	14,20,345	50,785	1,46,994
1984–5	1,19,97,529	50,44,105	67,83,549

Source: *Statistical Abstract of Haryana,* 1984–5. p. 514.

[94] *Sirsa District Gazetteer,* 1988, pp. 303–4. The illicit distillation has increased so much that police raids have had to be carried out on different occasions to discourage it, but this has not been very successful.

[95] The existing practice shows the licensing and setting up of one *sharab ka theka* within a radius of every ten kilometres and opening of small retail shops every two miles. This has resulted, according to the 1990–1 government figures, into a formidable number of 820 country liquor vends and 370 Indian made foreign liquor vends in this small state. Information supplied by Yashvir Singh Thekedar: born in 1960, he is a liquor *thekedar* (contractor) and brick-kiln owner in village Dulhera who lives in village Chhara of district Rohtak. Interestingly, his caste name 'Thakran' has been changed to 'Thekedar' in view of his profession. Also see, 1990, 'Rum, Gin through Thekas in Haryana', *The Tribune,* Chandigarh, 13 February.

incomes on alcohol and ruin their health.[96] They consider the spread of liquor and intoxicants as the cause of tension in homes, leading to shortage of money for family expenses, frequent quarrels, and violence. Indeed, regional, caste and class differences cease to count so far as the impact of liquor in contributing to the deterioration of the quality of women's life is concerned.[97] In fact, the greater the poverty, the worse its impact on women and children. The growing menace of liquor consumption provided the one occasion on which woman came together to demonstrate in 1985. In village Nahiri in the Sonepat district, a few women along with several men successfully demonstrated against the liquor theka, which had to be closed down.[98] Along with village Nahiri, village Ferozepur Boangar in Sonepat district and village Bhor Saidan in Kurukshetra district emerged as important centres of this protest. The protest movement, despite great optimism, and yet greater efforts of several interested organizations, did not catch on.[99] However, under the Chief Ministership of Bansi Lal in 1996, as a part of populist election-oriented measures, the government first introduced prohibition and then dropped it using pro-women arguments in both cases!

TECHNOLOGY AND DOMESTIC WORK:
A CASE OF LOW PRIORITY

A crucial point which emerges out of the given discussion is that the income received from the greater output of agriculture has not been

[96] Unanimous opinion expressed in Haryana. Also, the same view was heard in the fieldwork around Bagpat district region of UP, 1990, 9–18 July.

[97] For a similar opinion and observations by women of different classes on liquor in Rajasthan, see Sharma and Vanjani, 'Women's Work is Never Done'. Also see Mukul, *'Sharab Virodhi Andolan,'* *Navbharat Times,* 18–20 May, 1987 p. 3 on all days.

[98] For detailed information and comprehensive coverage, see ibid. Also, see Bharat Dogra, 1985, 'Village Women vs. Liquor Contractor', *Economic and Political Weekly,* vol. 20, no. 48, 30 November, p. 2112; and his article on thekas in Haryana in *Times of India,* 1989, 2 October, Section 2, p. 6.

[99] Several men from Rohtak and Sonepat districts felt that women, by themselves, could never achieve anything in the protest against liquor consumption. They insisted that the real force behind women were their family men. As an explanation it is pointed out that not all men drink and some stand to be adversely affected by the drinking habits of other male members of the family. The movement could hardly take off because, according to local opinion, the thekedars, despite their thekas being closed, continued to supply liquor under cover at a premium.

used either for or by women. For example, hardly any relief is provided for women by purchasing time and energy-saving household devices, readily available in the market, in order to reduce their domestic chores. Several recent studies have indicated that for rural women, traditional tools and implements are still primarily in use and the level of technology introduced is still 'very unsatisfactory'.[100] Modern household equipment has hardly entered rural households and peasant women still work with little or no mechanical aid. In 1984–5, out of the eighty families surveyed,[101] only eight possessed pressure cookers; twenty-four used coal irons, the use of electric irons being extremely restricted; and three families had refrigerators. However, an overwhelming number had sewing machines, which were invariably brought as a dowry item. The survey also showed 50 per cent as possessing kerosene cooking stoves. However, possession does not necessarily mean its use. My fieldwork shows that earthen *chulhas* (hearths) are in overwhelming common use, despite the possession of kerosene stoves; and even portable *angithis* (braziers), smokeless chulhas, and *gobar* gas are hardly used.[102]

Kerosene is used in rural areas primarily for lighting purposes, as only 35.58 per cent of households use electricity; the remaining 60.03 per cent use kerosene oil and 1.39 per cent use other methods.[103] Kerosene for cooking purposes is used by less than 1 per cent of rural households. The use of different sources of energy for cooking in rural Haryana confirms my own fieldwork. The percentage distribution of cooking energy in rural Haryana is as follows: firewood and chips, 47.76 per cent; dung cake, 35.57 per cent; kerosene, 0.78 per cent; coke coal, 0.66 per cent; gas, coal, or oil, 0.23 per cent; gobar gas: 0.50 per cent; charcoal, 0.07 per cent; and others, 14.43 per cent.[104] With basic technology for cooking being unavailable, women continue to spend time and energy in the work of fuel collection. The landed rural households may depend upon obtaining firewood (often with the help of hired labour)

---

[100] Arti Dutt, 1980, 'United Nations Conference on a Decade of Women', *Social Welfare*, vol. 27, no. 7, p. 22; I. Grover and S. Sharma, 1981, 'Technology to the Aid of Rural Women', *Kurukshetra*, vol. 29, no. 17, p. 26.

[101] Government of Haryana, *Family Budgets of Cultivators in Haryana, 1984–85*, pp. 36–7.

[102] 'Integrated Rural Development', p. 83.

[103] *National Sample Survey*, January–December 1983, Thirty-Eighth Round, no. 336, report on Sources of Drinking Water and Energy used for Cooking and Lighting, New Delhi, 1988, pp. 15, 23, Tables 5 and 9.

[104] Ibid.

from trees located on their own land, residues from their crops, and dung from cattle they own as fuel; but the women from poorer households have to face shortage of firewood and other fuels, specially as a result of the green revolution technology.[105]

The low level of technology can only be explained by the disinclination of men to invest in it, although it is true that women's knowledge about improved home technology is very meagre. A recent study shows only 1.9 per cent of women who have this knowledge.[106] Yet, even when it comes to using those things about which she knows and which are available at her door step, a woman does not have any deciding voice. This can be illustrated by the failure of attempts in certain villages of Haryana to introduce the new smokeless chulha.[107] The new chulha would have been far less dangerous and injurious to women's health and would also have saved time spent on cleaning smoke-blackened cooking pots. Subsidized at a price of only Rs 25, the chulha sale was unable to take off due to the refusal of husbands to give permission for its purchase.[108] A case has been cited regarding a retired army officer, now farming in Rohtak district, with a wide-ranging career in West Asia during the World War II behind him, in which he insisted that his wife had refused his offer to buy her a cream extractor.[109] Whether true or not, the case illustrates not only the low priority afforded to women's needs and convenience by men but also the internalizing of such attitudes to labour-saving technology by the women themselves.

Moreover, work ethics for women equates hard work with good health. This is used to deny them the advantages of modern technology,

[105] Bina Agarwal, 1986, 'Under the Cooking Pot: The Political Economy of the Domestic Fuel Crisis in Rural South Asia', Institute of Economic Growth, paper no: E/22/86, Delhi.

[106] See Kaur, 'Emerging Status Role of Rural Women in the Context of Changing Technology in Haryana'.

[107] Madhu Kishwar, 1988, 'Nature of Women's Mobilisation in Rural India: An Exploratory Essay', *Economic and Political* Weekly, vol. XXIII, nos 52 and 53, 24–31 December, pp. 2743–54.

[108] The initial success in the sale of chulha was because the sale coincided with the marriage season in which this new chulha assumed a status symbol for men; a symbol which projected a family's progressiveness. See Madhu Sarin, 1986, 'Some Insights into Rural Women's Lives', *Manushi*, vol. 35, p. 26.

[109] Shanti Chakravarti, 1975, 'Farm Women Labour: Waste and Exploitation', *Social Change*, vol. 5, nos 1 and 2, March–June, pp. 9–16.

on the plea that even overwork is good for women's health. Some men go to the extent of suggesting that women were far healthier in olden days when even *atta* (flour) and dal had to be ground at home.[110] Here, it may be pointed out that flour continues to be ground at home by the hand-operated *chakki* (stone grinder), not only in remote villages but even in certain villages enjoying a developed agricultural technology. In 1977, 15 per cent of flour was still being ground at home in such villages.[111] The situation is only marginally changed now. My own fieldwork shows that those households which have taken to purchasing the atta processed in the market still use the chakki for grinding *dalia* (porridge), dal, and the like.

Another glaring example of failing to provide basic technology to women is in the realm of water collection which also consumes a lot of their time and energy. In rural Haryana, the wells are still the primary source of drinking water. In 1973–4, as much as 65.41 per cent of water was supplied by wells and tube wells; taps supplied only 7.06 per cent and other sources contributed 27.53 per cent. Ten years later, in 1983, wells were still supplying 50 per cent of water, taps 23 per cent, and other sources 27 per cent.[112] Other sources include ponds, tanks, reservoirs, canals, rivers, and springs. These are mainly used by the underprivileged but since they are also used by animals, they constitute a serious health hazard. Although the taps may provide 23 per cent of water to the villages, there are no individual or domestic connections. Public hydrants are installed at focal points which provide water at scheduled times, with no facilities for turning them off. This factor leads to water stagnating in the open drains and is a severe health hazard, with both sides of the *nali* (drain) being used as defecating places.[113] The predominant use of wells, on the other hand, means that women continue to trudge long distances to draw water for domestic or other uses and carry it in heavy headloads.

---

[110] Khem Chand, a 65 year old *sangi* (singer of local folk songs), in 1988, in village Govad, district Sonepat, summed this up as a popular male feeling, 15 October. Several others echoed the same opinion.

[111] M. Sharma, 1977, 'Science and Technology for the Betterment of Rural Women', *Kurukshetra*, vol. 25, no. 12, pp. 4–5.

[112] *National Sample Survey*, January–December 1983, p. 21, Table 8; p. 7, Table 1.

[113] This can be commonly observed in the villages of Haryana.

DECISION MAKING: SPHERES OF CONTROL
AND ITS LIMITS

Clearly, the crucial sphere of expenditure which might afford women some relief is not even considered to be under their purview. Yet, expenditure on social and cultural obigations, most affected by urban consumerist culture, is generally considered to be women's preserve where men claim they have a free hand.[114] This expenditure on celebration of festivals, weddings, births, and funerals, and giving of ritual gifts on religious and social occasions occupies the third highest item on an average peasant proprietor's budget. In 1977–8, it was calculated to be 4.47 per cent of the total household budget and considered to have doubled in four years' time.[115] By 1984–5, it was occupying 10.72 per cent of the total household budget.[116] The fact that more and more money is likely to be spent on this item is revealed by a recent field enquiry studying expenditure behaviour. More than half of the sample households said that in case of an increase in their incomes, they would spend it on social purposes.[117] A family's reputation, within its own village and caste group in the surrounding countryside, is built on the magnificence of the feasting and entertainment at such functions; display at life cycle ceremonies is taken as an index of wealth—an expenditure considered essential for image and status building by men. Given a chance, women may very well prefer to lay out this money elsewhere rather than to give it away to the husband's relatives or spend so much on guests and celebrations on different social occasions. Although women do not acknowledge it, this sphere of expenditure, according to men, remains one of the major causes of frequent quarrels between them. Whatever the contention, even here, women hardly have a free hand as it is the men who determine and supply the capital for such obligations.

Interestingly enough, despite the exercise of power and authority by men, and decision making being concentrated in their hands, rural men continue to insist upon the 'aggressiveness of women' and their

---

[114] Harpal Singh and Ratan Singh, 1988, village Bandh, district Karnal, 20–1 August.

[115] Government of Haryana, *Family Budgets of Cultivators in Haryana, 1978–79*, compared to that of 1974–5, see Tables 2.3(a) and 2.3(b).

[116] Government of Haryana, *Family Budgets of Cultivators in Haryana, 1984–85*, Table 3.1.

[117] Among others, one-third opted to spend it on food and 15 per cent on social purposes-cum-food. See Aggarwal, *Geo-Ecology of Malnutrition*, pp. 94–5.

'domination' in household matters. When questioned closely, the replies have been evasive and have boiled down to the following list: her hostility towards guests; her open preference, as mentioned earlier, for her 'bhai and jamai' (brother and son-in-law); her 'interference' when the husband wants to make a grain donation for some cause or the other, or give presents and ritual gifts to his sisters or other relatives; frequent sulks and constant nagging and refusals to work, and so on. This informal influence and 'power' that men attribute to women is difficult to evaluate. It does not lie in the realm of concrete evidence which may show their authority or right to take a particular decision and command obedience or exercise 'power', as alleged, over other persons. In other words, there is no evidence forthcoming which might indicate a change in their subordinate status. The men's assertion hardly finds an echo in the realities of rural women's lives.

It is however an undeniable fact, though difficult to ascertain, that some women do indeed wield some authority at least in the household matters. But even these women have to work their way up for a considerable period to time before they acquire some measure of authority. The position and status of younger women and the daughters–in-law has been traditionally low. They are permitted little power till they reach the status of a mother-in-law. There are certain situations in relation to the family with in which they may acquire some measure of power. For example, as a mother she comes to acquire influence over her children. This is especially true in relation to her sons who are wielders of power and authority. Then as a mother-in-law she controls domestic life. As such she may impose an oppressive regime on younger females which she herself had been made to follow when young. In control of domestic life she lays down norms of behaviour, speech, dress, and exercises general control geared to maintain her dominance. More importantly, she is instrumental in keeping the male dominance and female subordination in the household. She reinforces her sons' dominance over their wives and children and thereby provides an important channel to maintain the institution of patriarchy in the household.[118] Within the household, it is she who has access to the immovable property and the custody of cash, jewellery, and grain.[119]

[118] Tulsi Patel, 1987, 'Women's Work and Their Status: Dialectics of Subordination and Assertion', Social Action, vol. 37, no. 2, April–June, pp. 126–49.

[119] Ibid. Also, see Ursula M. Sharma, 1978, 'Women and their Affines: The Veil as a Symbol of Separation', Man, vol. 13, no. 2, June, pp. 218–33.

Reserving the lighter supervisory role to herself, she assigns different jobs to the daughter-in-law, whether in agriculture, animal husbandry or the household maintenance. Knowing the 'influence' that a young wife may come to wield over her husband and the consequent threat this may pose to her own position, the mother-in-law controls her daughter-in-law's contact and interaction with her son. Interestingly, when the young rural woman is at the height of her productive and reproductive powers, her own power in the domestic group is at the lowest.[120] For older women, patriarchal control becomes less strict to some extent. It may be noted that older women are under far less patriarchal control than the younger ones. This can be distinctly noticed in the observance of ghunghat by the former. There is a noticeable weakening in its observance by the older woman—an observance which tends to get restricted towards fewer and fewer elders of the village, as she ages.

Indeed, ethnographic evidence confirms that women become bolder as they age and reach menopause. Much less restrained, these women are given to use the hitherto tabooed language of men, which is often sexual and 'obscene' in nature, within the hearing of men who listen indulgently and amusedly.[121] Enjoying much more personal freedom, the older woman's behaviour, specially that of the mother-in-law, firmly in control of younger women, demonstrates the existence of hierarchy in the family unit. However, since men hold positions of authority, women in their roles of wife, mother, sister, or daughter may influence men's decisions. But the strategy revolves around 'working through men', be they husband, sons, brothers, or fathers.

CULTURAL AND IDEOLOGICAL CONSTRAINTS

The marginalized position of women in decision making is confirmed by the generally accepted view which considers women unfit to offer

[120] Tulsi Patel, 1982, 'Domestic Group, Status of Women and Fertility', *Social* Action, vol. 32, October–December, pp. 363–79. Patel also shows the mother-in-law exercising extreme pressure on the young wife to have a large family, which the latter may not want. For cultural factors operating behind the lack of any controlling authority in the hands of a young woman, despite her crucial role in rural society, see also, Sharma, 'Women and their Affines'.

[121] Mahadev L. Apte, 1985, *Humour and Laughter: An Anthropological Approach*, London and Ithaca: Cornell University Press, 1985, pp. 79–81. This kind of behaviour is commonly observed in Haryana.

advice. This region abounds in local sayings and proverbs which frequently voice this:

naukar setti matta upave, ghar triya ki challe seekh, kah Ghaghaji, teen chutiya, gaon gorve bove ikh[122]
(Those who consult servants, those who are guided by women, those who sow sugar cane near the village, are great fools, says Ghaghaji.)

This only evokes the traditional advice still given to men nowadays:

aurat ki salah per jo chale voh chutiya[123]
(The one who acts according to his wife's advice is a fool.)

In fact, those men who heed a woman's advice, where giving advice is equated with superiority, wielding of power, and authority, are considered to be *chutiya* (used as an abuse, literally it means a man with a vagina instead of a penis, therefore a weakling and a coward like a woman). This is perceived to lead to '*aurat ka raj*' (a household ruled by a woman), and such an impression is enough to damn that household forever. Explaining this, local male opinion maintains that '*jis ghar main aurton ke chalti hai us main rishta bhi nahin karte hain, kahten hain ki us main mard ki moonchh nahin hoti*'[124] (no one wants to enter into a marriage in a family where the woman dominates and the husband is henpecked).

A cultural system which considers a woman to be no better than a man's shoe ('*lugai admi ki juti ho sai*'),[125] inferior to him in morality, knowledge, and wisdom, must naturally consider women's advice, if acted upon, to be anomalous and disruptive. In fact, the most frequent advice is, '*lugai ne sir per na charhya karern*' and '*lugai ke akal te kaam na chale*', both saying that a woman's advice should not be heeded.

Any woman who asserts herself even slightly and voices an opinion rather than meekly accepting the advice or orders of a man invites ridicule and denigration. Taken as a challenge, the man's sarcastic com-

---

[122] A commonly cited folk saying. Also, see Shankar Lal Yadav, 1966, *Haryana Pradesh Ka Lok Sahitya*, Allahabad: Hindustan Academy, 1966, p. 445.

[123] Also, given in Fallon, *A Dictionary of Hindustani Proverbs*, p. 22.

[124] A comment by Sita Ram, 1988, 5 December, which found its echoes everywhere. Sita Ram, 45 years old, owns 8 kilas or 40 bighas of land, village Chhara, district Rohtak.

[125] R.S. Mann and K. Mann, 1988, 'Status Versus Work and Role of Jat Women', in Dak (ed.), *Women and Work in Indian Society*, pp. 155–90.

ment is found in the proverb: '*nangi boochi sam to unchi*'[126] (a shameless, literally a naked woman is always superior, as you cannot shame her any further). The only way to deal with an argumentative woman is '*bhonkne do*'[127] (literally, let her bark or allow her to have her say). What is implicit in the statement is, do not listen to her. The other way to deal with such a woman is: '*rand ke maar*' (beat up the shameless hussy). In fact, the consensus of men was: '*jo zada bolti hai wohi pitati hai*'[128] (the one who talks too much gets beaten up). Beating of women is an effective way of silencing their opinions.

Apart from the direct physical control, there are certain cultural constraints which not only control woman ideologically but also assure their non-participation in decision making, and in a curious way, even physically inhibit them from making the attempt. The custom of purdah is foremost among them. Non-observance of ghunghat by women leads to sexual innuendoes and obscenities being hurled at them. Frequently referred to as shameless and of loose character, she is also denounced as *nangi* (nude)[129] Her exposed face is taken to be akin to an exposed body. The alleged nudity is met with aggression and indecent behaviour from male members. The male reaction, the language used and behaviour reaffirms the ideology of control and seclusion of women and acts as a warning to others against any such 'disobedience' or breach of this cultural practice.

Estimated to be observed by 72.61 per cent of this region's rural women,[130] ghunghat is not merely a symbol of male authority and power over women. In very practical terms it renders a woman ineffective in dealing with the decision makers and holders of economic resources. Neither can these women voice their opinions effectively nor can they influence decision making inside the family or outside. Required to observe ghunghat in the presence of a wide category of senior males and females, at home and in the village,[131] this observance

[126] Verma, *Haryanavi Lokoktiyan*, p. 116.

[127] Surendra Pal Singh, 1986, village Dujjana, 6 June.

[128] Khem Chand, 1988, summing up the opinion of a lot of rural males, 15 October.

[129] Observations of Moorti Devi and other women, 1986, village Mokhra, 7 August.

[130] Government of India, 1975, *Towards Equality: Report of the Committee on the Status of Women in India*, December 1974, New Delhi: Ministry of Education and Social Welfare, p. 61.

[131] Sharma, 'Women and their Affines', pp. 218–33.

has the effect of confirming social hierarchy at both these places. As decision making remains both gender and hierarchy based, it leaves them totally out of reckoning.[132]

It is because of the cultural and ideological realities and consequent public censure that women also want to avoid giving the impression that they may wield authority in their families, even if they actually do so. This attitude makes a correct reading of the situation difficult. In all situations, women *appear* most subservient. For example, even a 'dominant' woman continues to conform to the 'submissive woman' stereotype, who walks three paces behind her husband and carries the heavier load.[133]

This attitude also moulds and restricts men's behaviour. For example, a husband who takes his wife's side in a quarrel against his mother is dubbed 'henpecked'. Similarly, if a woman is seen to be assertive, it is the husband who is declared to be weak. Culturally valued authority and decision-making power continues to reside with men; both the woman who usurps it, and the man who allows her to do so, are ridiculed and condemned. An extremely popular joke repeated all over Haryana insists, with obvious falsity, that women hold the decision-making power and exercise influence over men. The variation goes as follows:

A man sitting in a group of men asked all those who acted according to the wishes of their wives to raise their hands. All but one raised their hands. Everyone wanted to know how this man resisted his wife's dictates. The odd man out replied that he indeed did what his wife told him to do. When asked as to why he did not raise his hand he said, 'Let me go and ask my wife, whether I should raise my hand or not'.

This joke never fails to evoke uproarious laughter among men. It ridicules even the idea that such a thing could ever happen.

The male assertion of female domination projected so vociferously, and often caricatured, nevertheless has to be understood and contextually placed among certain historical realities. Post-independence changes seem to suggest that this assertion is born out of men's

[132] David G. Mandelbaum, 1988, *Women's Seclusion and Men's Honour: Sex Roles in North India, Bangladesh and Pakistan*, Tucson: University of Arizona Press, p. 74.

[133] For a similar observation for other rural areas, see Robert O. Whyte and Pauline Whyte, 1982, *The Women of Rural Asia*, Boulder, Colorado: West View Press, p. 138.

consciousness of women's potentialities as well as by their attempts to control women, whether directly or indirectly or through ridicule. These changes range from changes in women's dress—the 10–40 yards heavy *ghaghra* (a long skirt) being substituted for a much lighter *salwar-kamij*—to their frequent demands for consumerist articles.[134] To these surface changes, may be added the education of women, however limited, which has been highly suspect. Closely intertwined with this are the far more serious changes noticeable in the countryside. These relate to highly individualized assertions such as the runaway marriages and elopements, either inter-caste or between those belonging to the same village, both traditionally tabooed alliances. Almost all the villages have such alliances to report, with many resulting in violence and physical elimination of the girl. Even widow remarriage is no longer strictly in its levirate form, with some widows asserting and opting for outside alliances in their second marriage. To these social changes may be appended the legal rights which women have come to enjoy through the Hindu Code Bill, 1955–6, such as the right to divorce and equal inheritance rights. These cumulative changes have created a sense of insecurity in men who have taken to projecting a bizarre future filled with dominating females. Whatever the dominant male opinion, this image hardly conforms to the role which rural women play in determining expenditure–consumption patterns in the domestic sphere. Any self-assertion, protest, and resistance remain covert strategies which do not necessarily pose a challenge to the ideological and cultural hold of patriarchy even as they may have contributed to the insecurity felt, and projected, by men.

[134] This demand has also become reflected in folk songs. See Yadav, *Haryana Pradesh Ka Lok Sahitya*, p. 180.

9

A Matter of Two Shares

*A Daughter's Claim to Patrilineal Property in Rural North India**

'Why should we take two shares,' questioned the women.
'Why should we give two shares,' asserted the men.

Voiced in relation to female inheritance in rural areas, I discovered this predominant opinion neatly summing up the crux of the problem of female inheritance in northern India. The Hindu Succession Act of 1956 granted to females' inheritance rights equal to those of male members of the family, for the first time in independent India.[1] Yet, its failure in this respect is a well-acknowledged fact. My fieldwork in Haryana during 1985–90, and more recently in 1992–5, enabled me to analyse and understand this problem within the rural structure. I found

---

* This chapter was originally published in 1997, *The Indian Economic and Social History Review*, 34(3): 289–320.

[1] For details of this act and its comparisons with the earlier situation existing in British India, see the Hindu Succession Act, No: XXX of 1956, in Sunderlal T. Desai, 1966, *Mulla Principles of Hindu Law*, Bombay: N.M. Tripathi Pvt. Ltd, thirteenth edition; also *Hindu Law*, Vol. II, Nagpur: All India Reporter, A.V. Chitaley, third edition, 1981.
The equal right of inheritance, that is, intestate succession, however, did not extend to the concept of joint family property where a son's share in the property is calculated to be five times that of the daughter's share. For details, see Lucy Carroll, 1991,'Daughter's Right of Inheritance in India: A Perspective of the Problem of Dowry', *Modern Asian Studies*, vol. 25, no. 4, October, pp. 781–809.

that in a curious way, rural society sees this legal enablement of females as a right to inherit two shares: as a daughter and as a widow. It is this 'dual inheritance' which the patriarchal forces have been determined to curb. However, this attack has been on the share of the daughter and not on that of the widow. The latter has always customarily enjoyed the right to inheritance, albeit a limited one. Daughters, on the other hand, had been kept outside the purview of inheritance rights. The daughters could not be given shares in land because they were potential introducers of fresh blood and descent line through their husbands. Customarily, the land of a village was deemed to belong to the male descendants of ancestors who originally settled and worked at it. Therefore, the male agnatic descendants alone, as members of the localized clan, had reversionary rights in the estate.[2] Land was obviously not to be alienated outside this group.

In this essay, I concentrate on the daughter's right of inheritance whose legal enablement has created a greater sense of unease in the rural society than that of a widow. The ability of patriarchal forces to control a widow, as argued elsewhere,[3] was never the same in relation to a daughter. For purposes of analysis, I use my field observations and case studies, along with the study of a variety of popular cultural forms[4]

[2] C.L. Tupper, 1881, *The Punjab Customary Law, Vol. II*, Calcutta: Government Printing, pp. 86–8, 99–100. Also, W.M. Rattigan, 1960 [1880], *A Digest of the Civil Law for the Punjab Chiefly Based on the Customary Law as at Present Ascertained*, second edition, revised by Harbans Lal Sarin and Kundan Lal Pandit, reprint, Allahabad: University Book Agency, p. 747.

[3] See Chapter 4 in this volume.

[4] The oral tradition used in this essay is based upon my extensive fieldwork and interviews of widows; see ibid. The folk songs, tales, proverbs, and the like, which have been cited in this work are still current, specially among the landowning classes of Haryana. Wherever possible, short biographical sketches of the informants containing their age, sex, and socio-economic status has been provided. Although most of the cited oral tradition has been in use for a long time, there is no adequate way in which it can be dated. Some of it can be traced to the nineteenth century colonial compilation of oral tradition. Where it has been possible to trace the tradition, it is pointed out in the notes. Some of the oral sources that I have cited are also published in collections of the Haryana government, as well as by the literati and folklorists. Where my field collection overlaps with the published collections of other individuals or government agencies, it has been indicated in the notes. I also wish to point out that in translating the local dialect, my aim is to convey the mood and the message rather that the literal meaning.

surrounding wedding ceremony, *rites-de-passage*, folk songs, proverbs, and festivals, all of which show several socio-cultural constraints preventing a woman, specially in her relationship of a daughter, from claiming and using a share in property that is legally hers.

These constraints operate by mobilizing a variety of selective cultural and ideological controls which result in: underlining the tradition of the daughter as a transit member of the natal family which does not allow a share in its property; in strengthening the sister–brother bonds of love which, in the vastly changed realities of the post-colonial period, can be nurtured only by the sister relinquishing her inheritance rights; in invoking customary norms and prejudices to prevent any breaches and even using force to forestall any such attempts, leading to conflict and violence; and in substitution of inheritance claims by dowry, notwithstanding its inherent contradiction. Even the newly bestowed marital rights, including divorce and the tradition of remarriage, have come handy in reinforcing the norms rather than in breaking them. All these have successfully prevented daughters from activating their inheritance rights.

Ideologically and culturally socialized to accept her exclusion from property matters since birth, what emerges in this study is that the woman's best chance of survival rests on her accepting the cultural and societal bonds rather than in breaking them. It is small wonder, therefore, that women acknowledge the 'ideal pattern' of inheritance of land and property by males from males. Whatever the legal position, she does not voice or appears to have accepted her own equality of right of inheritance with other claimants. Though the patrilineal principle of transmission of property and descent may have been given up by the 1956 Act, the patrilineal ideology continues to hold sway.

Yet, breaches have occurred and limited challenges thrown. Wherever these have occurred, they have been primarily male inspired. Built into the patriarchal system, these challenges and female rights are ostensibly appropriated by male counterparts. The consequence is that the patrilineal and patriarchal hold over women is tightened. Nevertheless, certain subversive methods have remained. The equal rights law may help women as their potentiality to assert power and rights clearly exists, even within this frame. Visible now and then, such assertion has made men more anxious to control women, even if it has meant making futile attempts at reversing the legal enactment, as in 1979, and again, in 1989.

IDEOLOGY: NEGATING FEMALE INHERITANCE

A woman right from her childhood has been and continues to be brought up in the tradition of being *'paraya dhan'* (literally, property or wealth belonging to someone else, implying the in-laws). Generally married off in early childhood,[5] she never looks upon her natal home as her own, nor her father's property as anything but her brother's; her descent group is not that of her father, but her husband's. In north India, a woman marries into another descent group after avoiding several prohibited degrees of kinship.[6] She is considered, and considers herself, as belonging to another descent group, so automatically no rights in her natal family are accepted.

Her paraya (outsider) status is made clear in the marriage rituals. For example, the concept of *kanyadan* (gift or offering of a virgin), considered one of the *mahadans*, the highest form of *dan* in the Brahmanical tradition and in the *sastras*, as it earns the giver the greatest religious merit,[7] is also an intrinsic part of the wedding ceremony among the rural Hindus of Punjab and Haryana, who have never been under strong Brahmanical influence. The importance of kanyadan can be evaluated from the popular local saying, common to the whole of northern India, which I found in extensive use:

sona ko dan, chandi ko dan, aur kanya ko dan duhela ho Ram[8]
(The giving away of gold, silver and a virgin earns you religious merit.)

As kanyadan is considered an act of religious charity in which the *kanya* is gifted to her husband and the entire responsibility for her is transferred from the giver to the husband and his family, the giver has no further

---

[5] The customary age of marriage for girls in the early 1920s of this century was early childhood, although *muklawa* (the entry and establishment of the wife in her husband's home when the marriage is consummated) was much later, after her puberty. See 1911, *Rohtak District Gazetteer, 1910*, III-A, Lahore: Civil and Military Gazette, p. 87. The age at marriage for girls has certainly gone up now, but there is a difference of opinion about what it is in different villages: early and mid-teens seem to be the consensus, with muklawa following a little later.

[6] For details of the customary Got prohibhition and rules of territorial exogamy observed in marriages see Chapter 9 in this volume.

[7] P.V. Kane, 1941, *History of Dharmasastra, Vol. II*, Part I, Poona: Bhandarkar Oriental Research Institute, p. 869.

[8] Shankar Lal Yadav, 1960, *Haryana Pradesh Ka Lok Sahitya* (Hindi), Allahabad: Hindustan Academy, p. 191.

rights on her, only duties. Associated ideology reinforces the formal and almost total severance of the woman from her natal home.

The ritual songs associated with marriage or the kanyadan ceremony called *bidai geet* (farewell songs) are sung from the point of view of the kanya and vividly describe her public acceptance of her own *parayapan* (as one who does not belong to her natal kin). While leaving her parental home, the bride says:

yo ghar le mera jami, choddi teri dehli[9]
(Father, giver of my life, I leave your threshold forever.)

In another bidai geet, where the girl makes a request to be invited back after marriage as soon as possible, she is reprimanded by her *bhabhi* (brother's wife) who says:

bebe kaun yahan tera kaam[10]
(Sister, now you don't belong here.)

The song goes on to mention 'the lightening of the burden' of her parents who had her in 'their safe keeping' for a long time, after having gone to 'her rightful owners'.

The rituals performed at the bidai ceremony also underline changed status of the bride. After completion of the wedding ceremony when the bride leaves with her husband to go to '*apne ghar*' (her own home), she is required to wear clothes gifted to her by her husband. This symbolizes the change in her status from the daughter of her father's descent group to the wife of her husband's descent group. From then onwards, she is just a visitor in her father's house.

This cultural ideology which moulds the woman from birth has had its socio-economic fallout. Not considering herself a part of her natal family, the woman cannot conceive of having a share in that property. Therefore, not only do the family males not accept her right to property, which they reserve for themselves, but the women are not socialized to accept it. Culturally accustomed to being a part of her husband's family, she foresees having a share only in her husband's property.[11] A claim

---

[9] A very popular bidai geet sung at marriage of daughters; also, see ibid., p. 165.

[10] Another very well-known song; also, see ibid., p. 193.

[11] This is most forcefully expressed in the concept of *hamara khet* (our field/farm) used by rural women but only in relation to their conjugal property and not natal property. The latter is always referred to as *bapu ke* (father's) or *bhai ke* (brother's).

to her natal family property is seen by her as a second share, and she questions why she should have two shares.[12]

VALORIZING TRADITION: BROTHER–SISTER BOND

A daughter's claim in her natal family property is basically perceived as a sister's claim against her brother. This at once challenges the strong cultural tradition of great love and solidarity between brothers and sisters, specially marked in the rural areas. Any challenge to such a relationship, hinting at possible irregularities, reflected in the abuse 'bahen-chod' (sister-fucker), is enough to arouse violence.[13] Nevertheless, it is significant that it is a sister's *izzat* (honour) alone and not her material status which is valorized to such as extent. This morally sacrosanct relationship is celebrated in songs, festivals, folk, and other rituals. The bond established at the time of birth, continues ideally till death and even after.

The festivals and accompanying rituals associated with the sister–brother bond are among the most important in north Indian Hindu society; in these, sister honours her brother and prays for his bright future and long life. These include the widely observed annual festival of *raksha bandhan* and *bhai dooj*, the latter being observed primarily by the Banias and the Brahmins. The ritual of *ponchi bandhai* (tying of the sacred thread to the brother's wrist) in the raksha bandhan festival; putting a sacred *tikka* (red auspicious mark) on his forehead on the bhai dooj festival with *arti* (worship); the ritual of feeding him sweets while the brother gifts money or presents to his sister and bestows blessings on her, all symbolize the relationship which continues between them for life. The festivals highlight the life-long protection which a brother should extend to his sister.

In the post-colonial period, this social role of the sister has continued to be stressed, specially in northern India. This is amply illustrated in the depiction of the sister and brother theme in calendars which are very popular as wall decorations in rural and urban areas. Patricia Uberoi draws attention to a calendar depicting a sister and brother engaged in a *rakhi* tying ritual, emphasizing the Rajput/Kshatriya/non-Brahmin

---

[12] This attitude and viewpoint could be generally observed in all the villages that I visited.

[13] 'Bahen-chod' is considered to be the worst of abuses in the whole of northern India. Some even opine it to be worse than '*ma-chod*' (mother-fucker).

tradition in the backdrop of war and agricultural prosperity.[14] The martial traditions of Haryana and Punjab inspired a spate of calendars from 1960s onwards, depicting sisters tying rakhis to the *jawans* (soldiers) and applying tikka; enhancing the identity of women as sisters and actively advocating the bonds of love, symbolizing an exchange of metaphysical for material protection, these images do not appear, as suggested by Patricia Uberoi, as a site of resistance against dominant patriarchal ideologies of past and present. In fact, they further insidious patriarchal constraints, specially when placed in the new social context of the inheritance question. Any deviation or reversal of the relationship, according to a popular Punjabi saying, is a sure sign of the coming of *kaliyug* (the age of darkness):

na man put nun dekh ke raji
na put mainun dekh ke raji
bhra kiha na mainun bhain dise
bhain kiha na mainun bhra dise[15]
(When a mother is not pleased to see her son
Nor a son pleased to see his mother
When a brother disowns his sister
And a sister disowns her brother.)

The brothers, throughout their lives, are traditionally duty bound not only towards their sister or sisters but her children as well. As the children's *mama* (maternal uncle), they perform rituals and make presentations at various rites-de-passage.[16] This dual relationship is very well expressed in the popular saying:

ma ri mera mama aya
an de, bhai te mera sai[17]
(My uncle has come, oh mother
Let him come, he is my own brother.)

The mama to children in north India is the giver of gifts; he is greatly loved and his visits keenly awaited by his sister and her children. Indeed,

[14] Patricia Uberoi, 1990, 'Feminine Identity and National Ethos in Indian Calendar Art', *Economic and Political Weekly*, vol. XXV, no. 17, 28 April, pp. WS41–8.

[15] Paul Hershman, 1981, *Punjabi Kinship and Marriage*, Delhi: Hindustan Publishing Corporation, p. 65.

[16] For the details of various rites-de-passage and a mama's role in them, see ibid., pp. 66, 217–19.

[17] A very common and popular saying. Also, in Bhim Singh Malik, 1981, *Haryana Lok Sahitya: Sanskriti Sandarbh* (Hindi), Pilani: Chitra Prakashan, p. 86.

all kinds of help from the mama are expected as a matter of right and obligation. A local saying from Uttar Pradesh (UP), often repeated in somewhat the same form in Haryana and Punjab as well, epitomizing the relationship maintains: 'a mother's brother cannot stop his sister's son even from taking his only buffalo'.[18]

The goodwill of the brother is important to a woman because even though she is supposed to belong to the descent group she gets married into, it is a group which takes very long to accept her as their own. A large number of folk songs from northern India portray her real acceptance in the family only when she produces a son. As a *bahu* (daughter-in-law), after her marriage, she occupies the most inferior status in the family hierarchy and only slowly works her way up. As a young and inexperienced bride, she enters a strange and hostile household; the practice of village exogamy reinforces her isolation. The restricted life in her in-law's household, where she is burdened with work, contrasts very sharply with her natal family, where on visits she observes no *ghunghat* (veil), and is relieved of most of the work—even the care of children is taken over by other women like her bhabhi or her mother. Even the memories of these visits in her otherwise monotonous life make her nostalgic; she would never willingly cut off this source of escape.[19]

A woman who breaks away from her brothers and has strained relations with them is not 'respected in the *sasural* (conjugal home)'.[20] In fact, the woman bends backwards to praise her *meka* (natal home) and its 'generosity' by showing off the presents and money she receives from them. A very popular saying mentions this:

neem ke nimoli laga, sawan kad avega
aye ri meri ma ka jaya, ke ke chijji layavega[21]
(The neem tree has blossomed, the rainy season will come.
It will bring my brother along, laden with gifts and presents.)

[18] Cited in M.C. Pradhan, 1966, *The Political System of the Jats of Northern India*, London: Oxford University Press, p. 76.

[19] The nostalgia for the parental house was marked in all the younger women interviewed. One even vividly described how, while on her way to her parent's village, she 'by smell alone' could accurately guess the distance still to be covered; observation made by Meena, 24 years, in village Dighal, district Rohtak. She was on a visit to her parent's house, having come from village Firozpur Jhirka, district Gurgaon.

[20] A general opinion voiced by both males and females of different ages, classes, and castes.

[21] Nadan Hariyanavi, 1962, *Haryana Lokgeet Sangrah* (Hindi), Delhi: Dehati Pustak Bhandar, p. 57.

Not having a brother is indeed a cause for sorrow:

sooni hai bhai bin bahan[22]
(A woman without a brother is poor indeed.)

IMPORTANCE OF BROTHERS: CONTEMPORARY REINFORCEMENT

The attachment to the brother or brothers and the need to nurture these bonds has been heightened in the post-colonial period because, for a sister, the importance of maintaining good relations with her natal family, specially her brother, has increased. This is due to the growing popularity of *punar vivah*, that is, the remarriage of widows. The institution of widow remarriage in this region has no longer remained only in its *karewa* or levirate form, as it had primarily been in the colonial period, when both the widow's late husband's family as well as the state frowned upon any form other than the levirate and actively intervened to stop it.[23] Punar vivah, as pointed out by a *Haryana District Gazetteer* of 1982, has gained popularity among the traditional caste-conscious critics like the Rajputs, Banias, as well as the Brahmins.[24] However, even in those castes, the first choice in remarriage is karewa in its levirate form and only 'when none of the brothers accept their widowed sister-in-law as wife, *punar vivah* is performed anywhere in their caste'.[25]

Even though limited, punar vivah has certainly come to mean that remarriage is no longer the sole concern of the widow's late husband's family. It has necessarily brought her natal family back into the picture, as they alone can find a second match for her in case she or any of her husband's brothers refuse to accept karewa. Such breaches in levirate have occasionally occurred in recent years, as the young, issueless widows in many cases go back to their parents and get married again.

The increasing acceptability of punar vivah, highlighting the role of the brother, is also reflected in folk tales and local proverbs. A folk tale titled, *Rand Kaun* ('who's a widow'),[26] portrays a woman whose

---

[22] A common utterance. Also, see ibid., p. 80.

[23] See Prem Chowdhry, 1993, 'Conjugality, Law and State: Inheritance Rights as Pivot of Control in Northern India', *National Law School Journal*, vol. I, special issue on "Feminism and Law', pp. 95–116. Also, see Chapter 4.

[24] Government of Haryana, 1983, *Haryana District Gazetteer, Bhiwani District, 1982*, Chandigarh: Government of Haryana, p. 67.

[25] Ibid.

[26] Narrated by Chhotu Devi, 1986, village Dujjana, district Rohtak, 6 June. Born in 1921, her late husband was a big landowner in Dujjana. Also, in Malik, *Haryana Lok Sahitya*, p. 131.

husband, son, and brother are held responsible for having committed a major crime. The king inflicts the death sentence on two of them and asks the woman to choose the one she wants to save. The woman opts for her brother and observes: 'If my brother dies, I shall never get him back again, as the source from which he sprang has already dried up. If he lives I can always get married again and also beget a son'. A popular proverb also says:

rand te va jis ke mer jan bhai
khasam te aur bi ker le[27]
(A woman is truly widowed if her brother is dead,
for a husband can be got again.)

The theme of the story is in fact very old; it forms a part of the Jataka repertoire of stories where the emphasis had clearly been on the distinctly lesser importance of acquirable relationships and the impermanence of widowhood.[28] In accordance with present-day realities, the interpretation of the tale, as given by the narrator Chhotu Devi, extends the notion of protection to a new situation: the different social realities have manifestly thrown up allegiances which have material bases apart from emotional ones.

In fact, the lives of a woman's brother and his sons are also considered very important to her; a common blessing bestowed upon the young women by the older ones is:

bebe bahu, tu buddh suhagan ho
tere betta ho, tere bhai bhatije jiven[29]
(May you enjoy married life for long;
May you be blessed with a son; may your brothers and brother's son live long.)

In another song sung at the time of the arrival of the new bride into her sasural, the mother-in-law blesses her by blessing her brothers, their sons, and her sons:

jeo he tere bhai bhatije, banna rahe bhartar
mere bete ki bal badhai jamme he raj kanwar[30]

---

[27] This proverb is known among both men and women.

[28] The Uchhanga-Jataka tale is identical to the one mentioned. See E.B. Cowell (ed.), 1957, *The Jataka or Stories of the Buddha's Former Births, Vol. I*, London: Luzac and Company Ltd, pp. 164–5.

[29] A common blessing known to most. Also, see Yadav, *Haryana Pradesh Ka Lok Sahitya*, p. 454.

[30] Ibid., p. 166.

(May your brothers and nephews live long;
may your husband have a long life.
May you continue my son's line and bear him fine sons.)

In such a cultural milieu, the inheritance claim of a sister against her brother would be termed an 'unnatural act'.[31] Rural public opinion, as a study from Punjab shows, is so much against it that the girl after 'so shameful an act may never dare show her face in her father's house again'.[32]

The woman needs to remain on good terms with her brothers since marriage is a relationship in which troubles can be expected, if not from the husband, then certainly from his family. The constant tension between the incoming bride and her in-laws is a frequent theme of a large number of folk songs. One folk song about a girl complaining to her brother draws attention to this vividly:

sasu to beera chulhe ki ag
nanad bhadon ki bijli
susra to beera kala sa nag
devar sanp sanpolia
jetha tore beera bichchu ka dank
uple pathan dus jae ji
raja tore beera mehndi ka ped
kadi rache re kadi na rache[33]
(O brother, my mother-in-law is the flame of a stove
My sister-in-law is monsoon lightning
My father-in-law is a black snake
Younger brother-in-law is a viper
Older brother-in-law is the sting of a scorpion
ready to strike at all times
My husband is like the henna shrubs
sometimes congenial, sometimes not.)

---

[31] Observations made by Surinder Pal Singh, 44 years, and Dharam Pal Singh, 47 years, 1986, village Dujjana, district Rohtak, 6 June. The two brothers together own 25 *bighas* of land in this village. Their wives, Phool and Bimla, and their sister, Sheela, have all written off their inheritance claims in favour of their brothers. Such observations are widespread in rural areas.

[32] See case cited (year not specified) in Hershman, *Punjabi Kinship and Marriage*, p. 74. The sister in this case threatened to move the court to claim her share. She was, however, 'bought off' by being paid an amount supposedly equivalent to the value of the land.

[33] Yadav, *Haryana Pradesh Ka Lok Sahitya*, p. 126.

Here, both women and men are included among the potential trouble-makers for the young bride; even her own husband cannot be trusted to take her side.

Although both husband and brother are morally considered to be a woman's protectors, folk and oral tradition showing women's perception emphasize the husband as the lover and the brother as the protector.[34] In fact, it is only the brother who can protect a woman against her husband and therefore, he emerges as the 'real protector' in preserving 'her interests' against her husband's, as also in preserving 'her and her husband's interests' against others.[35]

The most pronounced role of the brother in his sister's house relates to her marital affairs. In fact, whenever a problem arises in her marriage, a woman, in most cases, turns to her brother for moral and economic support. This need has been reinforced as broken marriages are not infrequent today. The idea of divorce was legalized under the Hindu Marriage Act of 1955. Under this act, a Hindu male and female can sue for divorce and dissolve the marriage on certain grounds.[36] This act has also aroused intense resentment from the rural populace. The *bhajni* and *pracharak* (singers and preachers), as commentators on contemporary realities, expressed the wrath and contempt evoked by this measure in

[34] See Susan S. Wadley, 1986, 'Women and Hindu Tradition', in Doranne Jacobson and Susan S. Wadley (eds), *Women in India: Two Perspectives*, first edition, 1977; reprint, New Delhi: Manohar, pp. 113–40.

[35] See Nirmala's case, cited in Veena Das, 1976, 'Masks and Faces: An Essay in Punjabi Kinship', *Contributions to Indian Sociology* (NC), vol. 10, no. 1, pp. 1–30.

[36] The grounds provided by the act were as follows: if she or her spouse is living in adultery; has ceased to be a Hindu; has been of unsound mind for a period of three years preceding the presentation of the petition of divorce; or has, for the same period, been suffering from an incurable form of leprosy or venereal disease in a communicable form; has renounced the world by entering a religious order; has not been heard of as being alive for seven years; has not resumed cohabitation for two years or more after the passing of the judicial separation decree; has, during this period, failed to comply with a decree for restitution of conjugal rights. There are two more grounds on which a wife may seek divorce, that is, if she is one of two or more wives taken by her husband before this act came into force; or if her husband has been guilty of rape, sodomy, or bestiality after the marriage. See Government of India, 1956, *The India Code, Vol. II, Part IX*, New Delhi: Ministry of Law, pp. 149–56. The Marriage Law (Amendment) Act 1976, introducing categories of divorce by mutual consent, has further facilitated divorce by either party.

a highly dramatized conversational piece created and propagated in the aftermath of the act:[37]

An old woman to Nar Singh bhajni: *"beta Nar Singh, Hindu Code Bill ke sai"*? (Son, what is the Hindu Code Bill?).

Bhajni: *"tai, aaj, tu mere tau ke pas, kal use chhod tu mere ghar a ja, yo Hindu Code Bill sai"* (Aunt, today you are living with my uncle, tomorrow you leave him and start living with me. This is what the Hindu Code Bill means.)

Divorce was not unknown in the past, but cases were rare and nearly always originated from the man. He could expel his wife for unchastity through a practice called *tyag* (renunciation) which practically amounted to divorce; if he changed his religion, the marriage was automatically dissolved. Usually the man left his wife with her parents and never called her back.[38] There was no formal procedure for ending a marriage. Once the marriage or remarriage status was accepted, a Hindu woman could on no account claim release from it. The male's wrath is therefore directed at the right that the Act awards to women. For a woman ever to be given the right to initiate divorce violated the well-recognized cultural norms of male authority and respect for the husband.

Despite its legalization, statistically the number of those granted divorce in the district courts remains a mere 0.09 per cent of the total married males and females of rural Haryana.[39] The few who do go to court are mostly educated and aware of the provision against polygamy. In fact, formal divorce has come to be associated with the educated and as such, it is the educated females who are held responsible for breaking the societal norms.[40]

Legal divorce is considered a very serious step. The exposure arising out of the divorce proceedings, and the expense incurred has given it a bad name. However, the informal separation known as *chhordena*,

---

[37] Narrated by Khem Chand, 1988, village Govad, district Sonepat; a 65 year old *sangi* (singer of local folk songs), 15 October.

[38] E. Joseph, 1911, *Customary Law of the Rohtak District, 1910*, Lahore: Superintendent Government Printing, pp. 35, 40.

[39] 1986, *Census of Haryana, 1981*, series 6, part IV-A, Social and Cultural Tables, New Delhi, pp. 46–77.

[40] Government of Haryana, 1970, *Haryana District Gazetteer, Rohtak District, 1970*, Chandigarh: Government of Haryana, p. 48. The lawyers dealing with divorce cases in Haryana talk of 'increasing visiblity' of divorce cases initiated by women. The number of such cases, however, cannot be ascertained.

continues to be customarily accepted by both low and high caste and class groups.[41] This practice is sanctified by the caste *panchayat* or a panchayat of the village elders, or just an assembly of the elders of the *kunba* (joint family) of the two sides. This custom has the validity of a socially recognized divorce. A woman may also leave her husband on her own and return to her parents' house if she is unhappy in her marriage and may refuse to return. Many women, unable to bear the marriage situation, for whatever reason, are known to have taken this initiative, perceived to be unthinkable before the 1955 Act. This 'defiance' has, therefore, come to be associated with the after-effects of the Act. Such divorce cases in the rural areas are directly related to the changed society and its consumerist demands. Among these, dowry has emerged as the foremost cause for the practice of 'chhordena', or the woman is tortured so much that she leaves the husband voluntarily.[42]

Although most divorcees are known to have remarried, the resulting insecurity from divorce is very natural for women. In the remarriage situation, the woman must have the cooperation of her natal kin. Mostly uneducated, and totally untrained, with no job opportunities, a woman continues to be dependent on her husband or on her brother. This dependence reinforces her attachment to her brother and makes her extremely chary of closing her options in her natal family, controlled in effect by her brother or brothers. In fact, any inquiry as to why she does not claim her share brings out a kind of aggressiveness, as if one is teaching her to be immoral: '*bebe galat seekh mut de*' (Sister, do not give me wrong advice).[43]

---

[41] Several people placed special emphasis on the chhordena form of socially accepted divorce, considered essentially different from the divorce instituted by law by the rural populace. That is the reason why till the late 1960s, most people denied the existence of divorce in the rural areas which was considered to be an anomaly of the city urban life and education. Now the fact that even an informal arrangement actually means a divorce seems to have dawned upon the populace. Personal interview with Ram Meher Hooda, Rohtak, 17 June 1986. Hooda was born in 1933 in village Makrauli-Kalan, district Rohtak; practises law at the district level and specializes in divorce cases. He and his brother jointly own a landholding of 25 bighas in their ancestral village.

[42] This was the consensus of opinion among both men and women. Among other reasons are included beating of women. Although incidents of beating 'as a habit' are opined to have declined, the rising demands of dowry are said to be substatially contributing to its present existence.

[43] Voiced in village Bandh, district Karnal, and village Dujjana, district Rohtak.

The loss of the 'goodwill' of her brother is seen as enormous, both psychologically and morally, without the hope of gaining very much in return. As one woman confidentially pointed out: 'The inheritance if claimed would only deprive my brother and go to my husband'.[44] In effect, it would mean that both she and her brother would be deprived of it. Behind this reality lies the realization summed up effectively in an old proverb narrated in village Bandh of Karnal district:

bhai sa sahu na bhai sa bairi[45]
(No friend like a brother, no foe like a brother.)

However, when women were asked their opinion regarding the inheritance claims of male collateral, other than their own brothers, a clear ambivalence was noticeable. Many of them maintained: '*woh kya mahare bhai na hain?*' (are they not our brothers?). Most women held the same opinion about their classificatory brothers as about their blood brothers. Yet, in reality, the instances of women, given later, who claimed their inheritance because they had no brothers, belies this assertion.

A PATRIARCHAL CONSTRUCT: INHERITANCE RIGHTS VS DOWRY

As a justification for continuing to deprive a woman of her inheritance rights, rural male opinion is almost unanimous in contending that the girls receive their share of patrimony at the time of marriage in the form of dowry. Some anthropologists have gone so far as to equate this 'inheritance' of moveable property at marriage with immovable property which the brothers receive, as a kind of ante-mortem substitute for the land.[46] This view has been effectively refuted by a number of scholars.[47] The significant point about this contradiction lies in showing that the so-called property which a rural woman takes as dowry does not generate

[44] Opined by Meena in village Dighal, district Rohtak. Significantly, Meena voiced her opinion while on a visit to her parents and not in her sasural.

[45] Also, recorded by S.W. Fallon, 1886, *A Dictionary of Hindustani Proverbs*, Benaras: Lazarus and Co., p. 39.

[46] J. Goody and S. Tambiah, 1973, *Brideswealth and Dowry*, Cambridge: Cambridge University Press.

[47] For an effective contradiction of the anthropologists' claims, see Bina Agarwal, 1988, 'Who Sows? Who Reaps?: Women and Land Rights in India', *Journal of Peasant Studies*, vol. 15, no. 4, July, pp. 531–81; Hershman, *Punjabi Kinship and Marriage*, pp. 79–80; and Ursula Sharma, 1980, *Women, Work and Property in North-West India*, London: Tavistock Publications, pp. 489.

income in the same sense as land does. In rural Punjab, Haryana, and UP, it is quite inconceivable for a daughter to be given land as dowry.[48] The only way in which land might be used indirectly as dowry is if the guardian is forced to sell his land in order to offer the necessary money for dowry, and/or to pay the expenses of the marriage itself.

Indeed, in the general voiced opinion of both males and females, dowry is all that a woman is entitled to; customarily, it is pointed out, daughters have only been entitled to maintenance and to be 'suitably betrothed and married'.[49] Plea of custom reinforces more current argument about the rising cost of girls' marriages and the dowry demands which, men assert, frequently land them into debt, and is used to clinch the issue against female inheritance rights. The tendency has been for the amount of dowry to increase among all castes and classes.[50] It is a part of a general and widespread tendency to cultural convergence all over northern India. Firmly associated with prestige and status considerations, the custom of lavish and ostentatious weddings has tended to spread.[51] Even in colonial times, it had become a 'sign of social rank'.[52] However, social protest against this practice was not slow to emerge. A series of resolutions against dowry and excessive expenditure on weddings were passed by different village and caste panchayats.[53] After independence, several conferences of different castes

[48] *Ludhiana Customary Report* of 1911 mentions three cases in 1870s, when girls had been given about 5 bighas of land as dowry in marriage. See J.M. Dunnett, 1911, *The Customary Law of the Ludhiana District, Vol. V* (revised edition), Lahore: Punjab Government Press, p. 113.

[49] 1907, *Hissar District Gazetteer, 1907*, vol. II-A, Lahore: Superintendent Government Printing, p. 229.

[50] For a comprehensive overview, see M.N. Srinivas, 1996, *Village, Caste, Gender and Method: Essays in Indian Social Anthropology*, New Delhi: Oxford University Press, pp. 158–80. Also, see Sharma, *Women, Work and Property in North-West India*, pp. 137–43; Sylvia Vatuk, 1975, 'Gifts and Affines in North India', *Contributions to Indian Sociology* (NS), vol. 9, no. 2, July–December, pp. 155–95.

[51] 'It is an unwritten acknowledgement that jewellery, clothes, television, a vehicle, refrigerator, VCR—all indicate that a high level matrimonial alliance has been effected', says Phoolo Devi, 1968, village Singhpura, 6–7 August.

[52] T. Gordon Walker, 1985, *The Customary Law of the Ludhiana District, Vol. I*, Calcutta: Central Press Co., p. 26.

[53] See Vernacular Tract, no. 111, '*Sandhya Jatiya Sabha ka Dwitya Varshik Utsav*', Agra, India Office Records, London. For details of resolutions passed by different caste panchayats against marriage expenses, dowry, and the like, in

and *Gots* held in different villages have been making similar attempts to curb the practice, but these efforts have proved fruitless so far.[54]

On a broad estimate, a marriage in 1984 cost the subsistence level cultivators, 'who could ill afford it', a minimum of Rs 25,000 in expenses, with the dowry items including a radio, a transistor-cum-cassette player, gold and silver jewellery, furniture, and clothes.[55] 'A reasonably rich farmer' was known to spend (in 1987–8) anything between Rs 2 lakh and 5 lakh on a marriage, and offer a car among the dowry items. A class now exists of even richer farmers, who are said to offer as dowry all modern household gadgetry. Some rural marriages are boastfully declared 'to match marriages in any big town or city'.[56] The few who can emulate, even to some extent, try. One estimate suggests that in real terms, the cost of marrying a daughter in north India has increased tenfold in the past fifty years.[57] Expenses over the years have accelerated not only due to an increase in prices but also due to the tendency to add to the list of expected dowry items.

Dowry, earlier regarded with contempt and as a form of greed, has acquired a new legitimacy today. In this connection, it is also significant that in the villages the dowry brought by the bahu, although prohibited by law, continues to be displayed by most families.[58] Anyone not displaying the dowry is automatically assumed to have been married into '*kamino ke ghar*' (home of low castes / paupers), and to have received nothing worthy of display.

---

the 1930s of Punjab–Haryana, also see *Darling Papers*, Box No. II, Tour Diary, 1930–1, pp. 152, 227.

[54] *Rohtak District Gazetteer, 1970*, p. 47. For extensive reporting of the work by such *sabha*s and panchayats, see *Hindustan Times*, 1984, New Delhi, 20 May, p. 9; *Times of India*, 1983, New Delhi, 18 June, p. 5.

[55] See Bharat Dogra, 1984, 'How they Revalued Dowries', *Hindustan Times*, New Delhi, 20 May, p. 9; also, see *Times of India*, 1983, New Delhi, 18 June, p. 5; *Times of India*, 1989, 8 December, p. 7.

[56] Comment made by Chander Bhan Saini, whose three daughters were married: one in 1978 and the other two in 1986. Each received a car in dowry plus all the other household gadgetry. On an average, each marriage was estimated to have cost Rs 2.50 lakh. Interview with Chander Bhan Saini, 52 years, and Subhash Chander, 35 years, 1988, Hansi, district Hissar, 25 September. The Saini family of five brothers are leading agriculturists of Haryana. They reportedly own 700 bighas of land in village Dhani Peer Wali near Hansi, district Hissar.

[57] Sharma, *Women, Work and Property in North-West India*, p. 140.

[58] Personal observation in villages Alipur, Chhara, and Dujjana.

A large measure of legitimacy has been provided to this custom by women themselves, primarily because rural women have accepted dowry as a substitute for property for which their legal claim has been established. This acceptance is perhaps best explained by Leela Dube, who points out that the daughter is looked upon as a temporary member of the family and the son, a permanent one.[59] The women's main concern, therefore, is to establish themselves in the new family and acquire a status there; and dowry is looked upon as a necessary contribution towards this process. Moreover, realizing the increasing 'heavy expenditure' which marriage entails, women tend to view dowry, and not property, as their due. When directly questioned about their inheritance rights, annoyance is visible and also, counter questions: 'haven't our brothers got us married?' In their opinion they (that is, married women) have already taken a share of their parental property in the form of cash and kind at the time of marriage, 'so where is the question of more share'.

Significantly, the acceptance of dowry as a substitute for inheritance by women underlines their awareness and knowledge of their legal entitlement to property. It shows an ambivalence in their attitude indicating a distinct change. This ambivalence explains how and why a few women have started to demand 'what and how much they want in their dowries'.[60] There are yet others who believe that they were not given enough, as much as their other sisters had received, for example. The older women complain of younger women, 'the more shameless ones', who have started to ask for certain specific items; the plea being that they want to maintain 'the status of their *meka*' (natal family). Significantly, both men and women acknowledge that without dowry 'no good alliance can be made'.[61] Indeed, the dowry items have started to provide a ready index for gauging the level of a 'good alliance' procured.

The contradiction between inheritance as a matter of right and dowry as a matter of goodwill or faith of the father and/or brothers,

---

[59] Leela Dube, 1988, 'On the Construction of Gender: Hindu Girls in Patrilineal India', *Economic and Political Weekly*, vol. XXIII, no. 18, 30 April, pp. WS11–19.

[60] Phoolo Devi, 1988, 60 years, wife of Raghbir Singh, ex-*sarpanch*, village Singhpura, district Rohtak, 6–7 August, made this observation. The other women standing by nodded in assent. The comments of others are also reproduced above following this observation.

[61] Observations of Bimla and Phool, 1986, village Dujjana, district Rohtak, 6 June. Similar ones were made in village Gochchi and Chhara.

along with the dictates of the market and male considerations of their 'status' are far from being voiced.[62] Yet, the above cited demands and attitudes show an unvoiced but crucial link-up of dowry with questions of inheritance and the awareness of women regarding their entitlement rights located in material grounds rather than mere 'goodwill' of the brother. The brothers, on their side, have become more careful about fulfilling their 'obligations' regarding traditional gifts, be it for a particular festival or dowry.[63]

In fact, our analysis shows why the plea made by academics and activists for a retention of the custom of dowry till the inheritance rights are activated, based on the argument that dowry gives women, and is perceived by them to give, a share in their father's property, cannot be accepted.[64] On the contrary, unless this substitution of inheritance rights by dowry, which is a patriarchal construct, is done away with, the law of inheritance cannot be expected to succeed. The continuation of dowry acts as a justification imposed by patriarchy and accepted by women. On the other hand, it is also true that dowry as a custom among the landowning classes, apart from several other reasons, has been invigorated by the inheritance law and the resultant potential claims of women. Almost unwittingly, the law has reinforced this custom in rural society.

This background provides a valuable clue as to why the Dowry Prohibition Act of 1961,[65] the first major attempt by the state to do

---

[62] Several men spoke of the '*izzat*' involved in giving a dowry. The frequently mentioned, '*hum ne itna diya*' (we have given so much), went into establishing their 'status'.

[63] See Hershman, *Punjabi Kinship and Marriage*, p. 74.

[64] See Lucy Carroll, 'Daughter's Right of Inheritance'. Also, for the details of this highly controversial plea and the debate that followed, see Madhu Kishwar, 1988, 'Rethinking Dowry Boycott', *Manushi*, no. 48, September–October, pp. 10–13; 1989, 'Dowry and Inheritance Rights', *Economic and Political Weekly*, vol. XXIV, no. 11, 18 March, pp. 586–7; 1989, 'Continuing the Dowry Debate', *Economic and Political Weekly*, vol. XXIV, no. 49, 9 December, pp. 2738–9; C.H. Lakshmi, 1989, 'On Kidney and Dowry', *Economic and Political Weekly*, vol. XXIV, no. 4, 28 January, pp. 189–90; Rajni Palriwala, 1989, 'Reaffirming the Anti-Dowry Struggle', *Economic and Political Weekly*, vol. XXIV, no. 17, 29 April, pp. 942–4.

[65] *The Dowry Prohibition Act, 1961*, Act no. XXVIII of 1961, *Gazette of India, Extraordinary*, 1961, II, Section 3 (ii). Under this act, the definition of dowry is too loose to be legally binding. Further, both the giver and the taker are liable for penal consequences. This makes the giver reluctant to report the matter for fear of being prosecuted.

away with this social anomaly, and its amended versions in Punjab and Haryana in 1976 could hardly be successful.[66]

THE SON-IN-LAW PREJUDICE: *JAMAI* AS GHAR JAMAI

The increased giving and taking of dowries among the landowning classes which has come to be intimately connected with the inheritance rights of women, is closely connected with the physical and structural impossibility of a married woman 'taking charge' of her inheritance of land. This is specially so because of the custom of village exogamy and patrilocality still followed all over northern India.[67] Location of a married daughter within the natal village spells danger to patrilineal inheritance as it facilitates and could lead to assumption of land inherited by her.[68] Thus, enforcement of restrictions on marriage

[66] Government of India, 1982, *Report of the Joint Committee of the Houses to Examine the Question of the Working of the Dowry Prohibition Act, 1961*, New Delhi: Ministry of Law and Justice. This committee was appointed on 19 December 1980 and submitted its report to the Parliament on 6 August 1982. Consequently, an amendment was brought about which came into force on 2 October 1985. See *The Dowry Prohibition (Amendment) Act, 1984*, no. 63 of 1984, *Gazette of India, Extraordinary*, 1985, Section 3 (ii) Government of India, Ministry of Law and Justice, New Delhi, 1985. This amendment is hardly an improvement. It changed the words defining dowry from 'as consideration for the marriage' to 'in connection with marriage'. Yet, in effect, this substitution is not any better and as legal opinion shows, it ends up in protracted litigation on the meaning of the words. The basic problem of dowry still remains with its definition, the legal difficulties of proving it, and the varied forms under which it operates, extending from the pre-marriage, marriage, and its continuation into post-marriage years. Also, to be taken into account are its hidden facets, which defy the net of legal definitions termed, 'in connection with marriage'. Further, there is no amendment of the original deficiency of the 1961 Act, which had equated the 'giver' with the 'taker' of dowry and had made them share the onus of crime equally. This continues to deprive the pressurized giver of any initiative against the dowry taker. See Ranjana Kumari, 1989, *Brides are Not for Burning: Dowry Vicitims in India*, New Delhi: Radiant Publishers, pp. 74–6.

[67] North India has a clear preference towards distant marriage alliances. Caste groups such as Jats expressly forbid marriage with any village which shares even a border with the natal village or in which other clans of one's village are well represented. For details see chapter 11 in this volume.

[68] In the South, where marriage usually takes place within small areas or villages and often with relatives, ownership of land by women (usually received as dowry) is much more practicable than in the North, and is also widely found. See Carol B. Upadhaya, 1990, 'Dowry and Women's Property

practice, emphasizing village exogamy and caste endogamy among the landowning classes of north India (leading to violence in several cases), is crucially connected with questions of female inheritance.[69] This also provides a valuable clue to the near failure of the inheritance enablement effected by the state for women.

In other words, inheritance of land by women would, in effect, mean inheritance of land by her husband, for unless she moves into her natal home with her husband and family, she cannot take charge of her inheritance. In north Indian rural terms, it would mean a *ghar jamai* (resident son-in-law). In UP, Punjab, and Haryana, the cultural prejudice against ghar jamai among landowning caste groups is so strong that it has become the butt of many jokes and stories. A popularly quoted proverb runs:

sohre ke ghar jamai kutta
bahen ke ghar bhai kutta[70]
(A man living in his father-in-law's house,
a brother living in his sister's house,
are both akin to a dog.)

In fact, in Haryana, Punjab, and UP, a jamai is generally referred to as the *bateu* or a *mehman*, both words literally meaning a guest, and his honour lies in remaining one, that is, a jamai, and not a ghar jamai. The collaterals would not like to see an outsider taking a share of their property. So, if he were to go and live in his wife's village and become ghar jamai, he would be despised and would incur considerable shame. The word ghar jamai has become almost a term of abuse. It connotes the greed of a man who instead of taking away his wife from her natal home after kanyadan, comes back with her. He is guilty of reversing a time-honoured social norm. More importantly, this action severely compromises the rights of collaterals.

The ghar jamai is regarded as a *kamin*, which literally means a low caste. Indeed among the kamins or the lower castes, who also follow the village exogamy rule in marriage, the ghar jamais are known to 'move

---

in Coastal Andhra Pradesh', *Contributions to Indian Sociology* (NS), vol. 24, no. 1, January–June, pp. 29–59.

[69] For details, see Prem Chowdhry, 1998, 'Enforcing Cultural Codes: Gender and Violence in Northern India', in Mary John and Janaki Nair (eds), *A Question of Silence: The Sexual Economies of Modern India*, New Delhi: Kali for Women, pp. 332–67. Also see Chapter 11 in this volume

[70] Also, recorded in Rattigan, *A Digest of the Civil Law for the Punjab*, p. 198.

about and settle down freely' wherever they wish, that is, in their wives' village or even with the parents-in-law. They are not considered *bure* (bad) because of this or suffer the kind of status accorded to them by the landowning castes.[71] Among the lower castes of Haryana, the ghar jamais share the same status as enjoyed by them among the *chuhras* (sweepers) across the border in western UP, where their residence implies availing of the best opportunities, even if it is in their wives' natal village or home.[72]

The fact that the son-in-law could become the resident son-in-law among the lower castes also meant that the daughter could easily inherit land if she had no brother. Yet, following the example and custom of higher castes, the collaterals in such cases, also, have successfully challenged and deprived the daughter of her inheritance as the colonial judiciary recognized only the landowners' custom.[73] Clearly, this customarily sanctioned right of the son-in-law among lower castes to take possession of property on behalf of his wife has prompted the landowning castes to ascribe a kamin status to their own sons-in-law should they behave in a similar fashion.

Among landowning castes therefore, a ghar jamai is taken to be someone who has renounced his own parental house (like one of a low caste) for the greener pastures of his father-in-law and is looked upon as a *chutiya* (a coward) who eats off his wife instead of supporting her. Even in folklore, he is portrayed as belonging to an inferior and poor household if he comes to his wife's to better his prospects.[74] The word ghar jamai has become synonymous with a parasite, a greedy person, an exploiter, and usurper, who has no right to be where he is. A popular

[71] Information given by Phate, age 40 years, in village Chhara, district Rohtak, belonging to a scheduled caste, and confirmed both by the males and females among lower castes in other villages of my fieldwork.

[72] For the untouchables' practice, see Pauline Kolenda, 1982, 'Widowhood among Untouchable *Chuhras*', in Akos Ostor, Lina Fruzzetti, and Steve Barnett (eds), *Concepts of Persons: Kinship, Caste and Marriage in India*, Cambridge: Harvard University Press, pp. 170–230.

[73] Among the lower castes, the few cases that came up in the colonial period were decided according to the recorded customs of the agricultural castes and the judges ruled that daughters could not inherit their father' property. See the case of *Mussasmat Bajudi vs Maula Baksh*, 1896 in C.C. Garbett, 1910, *Riwaj-i-Am of Panipat Tehsil and Karnal Pargana in the Karnal District*, Lahore: Civil and Military Gazette, p. 23.

[74] *Vernacular Tract*, No. 1103, '*Mansukhi aur Sunder Singh ka Vartant*'.

proverb among the landowning caste groups contemptuously dismissing him maintains:

Jat, jamai, bhanja, rebari, sunar
kabhi na honge apne, saluk karo sau bar[75]
(A Jat, a son-in-law, a sister's son, a shepherd, and a goldsmith,
can never be your well wishers.)

For such a daughter, or sister who might bring her husband to her natal home, the most frequent advice tendered by women is to avoid such a degraded status for themselves. So naturally, even women would be against a ghar jamai status for their husbands:

ladki to apne susral mein hi aachi lagti hai[76]
(A girl's place is only in her in-law's house.)

Such 'truisms' are liberally scattered in the various *ragnis* (songs) of this region which seek to advise the people thus:

sayanni, nanad, bahan aur beti apne ghar aachi sai[77]
(Grown up sisters-in-law, sisters, and daughters should be in their own houses.)

Although inheritance through a daughter in the absence of a son and against distant male collaterals had been upheld in certain cases in the colonial period, this did nothing to mitigate the virulent feeling against a ghar jamai who might inherit his father-in-law's property through his wife.[78] In fact, whenever the ghar jamai had been accepted in the past, it

---

[75] Yadav, *Haryana Pradesh Ka Lok Sahitya*, p. 421.

[76] Interviews in village Bandh, district Karnal, 20–1 August 1988.

[77] Ibid. Also, see Fauji Meher Singh, 1983, *Mewati Ragniyon ka Guchcha: Fanne Khan Ragnian*, Delhi: Jain Pustakalaya, p. 83.

[78] In colonial Punjab, that trend of custom was given recognition by the compilers of customary rights and the later jurists in which, as a rule, daughters and their sons, as well as sisters and their sons were excluded by near male collaterals. Accepted as the general custom, the onus of proving a case to the contrary then lay on anyone challenging it. The colonial evidence, however, shows that women's rights, specially as daughters, were much wider than was accepted by the colonial authorities, leading to legislative confusion and conflicting judgments. For example, in 1890, in the case of Lado, a Jat woman of Jaurasi Kasba in Panipat district, who had taken over the land cultivation and management after the death of her father and in the absence of near collaterals removed to the seventeenth degree. The revenue officials decided in favour of the daughter 'not because she was entitled to the land' but because 'she was in actual possession of it'. Another case of Gujars of village

was for the benefit of the daughter's son. The daughter acted either as a stand-in for her husband or held the land as a custodian for her son; in both cases, acting as a mere 'conduit pipe'.[79] The benefits, if any, to her were merely incidental. In other words, this arrangement, if brought about at all, avoided the direct inheritance of property by the daughter; there was logic, however, in providing for an heir. Even in such cases, the infamy stuck to the son-in-law and even to his son. This was because the 'intruder', even though the daughter's son, still established a different Got line from that of his mother's father's collateral, and was, therefore, also unpopular.

Known as *bhanje-ki-aulad* in a derogatory manner, a daughter's son is still generally considered in rural areas, 'an outsider and an appropriator of ancestral property'.[80] In cases where there was no *bhanja* (sister's son), the land reverted to the donor's male agnates in case of the daughter's death.[81] Even if land was directly gifted to the resident son-in-law, it reverted to the male relatives of the last male holder on the wife's death in many cases. The practice, therefore, remained a rare one. Even now, in most cases, the woman either gives the land or sells it to her father's closest agnates for a nominal sum, or failing that, pressure is applied in making the bhanje-ki-aulad sell the land.[82]

COUNTERING CLAIMS: PATRIARCHAL FEARS

Cultural constraints and popular prejudices, however, did not entirely prevent the jamais from making claims on behalf of their wives. The colonial administration recorded a series of cases in which ghar jamais were turned out of the house after the father-in-law's death and

---

Chaprian in Panipat district in the same year can be cited when the revenue officials similarly effected a mutation of land in favour of Bir Dei, the daughter of the deceased landowner against the claims of far-removed collaterals. See Garbett, *Riwaj-i-Am of Panipat Tehsil and Karnal Pargana in the Karnal District*, p. 24.

[79] Sripati Roy, 1986, *Customs and Customary Law in British India*, first published in Calcutta, 1910; reprint, Delhi: Mittal Publications, p. 447. Also Rattigan, *A Digest of the Civil Law for the Punjab*, pp. 86, 298.

[80] Cited in Pradhan, *Political System of Jats of Northern India*, p. 80.

[81] A series of such cases between 1890–1928 are cited in Rattigan, *A Digest of the Civil Law for the Punjab*, pp. 327–39.

[82] Personal interview with Harpal Singh and Ratan Singh, 1988, village Bandh, district Karnal, 21–2 August. They along with another brother own 33 bighas (11 bighas each) of land in the village.

forcibly deprived of the land or given only half.[83] In some cases, the ghar jamais had been in possession for twenty years or more. This feeling has not changed. A son-in-law claiming inheritance is bound to meet a hostile reception.

After the 1956 Act, it soon became evident that a son-in-law could, and some of them did, lay claims through his wife. A number of factors contributed to this: the great increase in population after independence and the consequent pressure on land; the continued existence of population below poverty line, which some academics put at 45 per cent of the cultivating population of Haryana;[84] along with enormous affluence due to the impact of green revolution, increase in income and in land prices which shot up several hundred-fold in the last quarter of a century or so. In village Dujjana of district Rohtak, for example, 1 *kila* or 5 bighas of cultivable land is estimated to approximate of Rs 35,000 in 1988; the cost of this land was less than a thousand rupees about twenty years ago.[85] In Karnal district, the centre of the green revolution, the price of 1 kila is estimated to have risen from anything between Rs 2,000–4,000 per kila available before the green revolution to something like Rs 50,000 to one lakh rupees and above. The increase in the prices of agricultural land in those areas of Haryana which encircle Delhi as well as the major towns of Haryana itself, has been phenomenal. This land and income hunger are reinforced by the rising social expenditure, along with the greatly strengthened custom of dowry and the social demands of a new generation with a taste of urban life and consumerism. The rural male opinion holds these factors responsible for the subversion of customary norms by some jamais.[86]

Certain instances of a son-in-law shifting residence to take over land entitled to his 'brother-less' wife could be noted. In a series of cases after the 1956 Act, sisters successfully claimed their inheritance having contested the claims of the collateral. Significantly, all these were cases in which the sister did not challenge the brother, there being none, but effected land claims in opposition to distant collateral. I would like to

---

[83] Dunnett, *The Customary Law of the Ludhiana District*, pp. 107–8. This was also the general consensus of opinion in the villages.

[84] Usta Patnaik, 1987, *Peasant Class Differentiation: A Study in Method with Reference to Haryana*, New Delhi: Oxford University Press, pp. 152–8.

[85] Personal interview with Surinder Pal Singh and Dharm Pal Singh, 1986, village Dujjana, 6 June.

[86] Personal interview with Harpal Singh and Ratan Singh, 1988, village Bandh, 20–1 August.

cite one of the earliest cases from Punjab decided in the wake of the 1956 Act in which the sister successfully claimed her inheritance as illustrative of this.

The case decided in 1960 concerned the inheritance right to certain plots of land in village Sultanwind Tehsil in district Amritsar.[87] Sahib Singh, the last male owner of the lands under dispute had died in December 1918. The widow, Nihal Kaur, succeeded to the lands, but on her remarriage soon thereafter, she was divested of them and they passed to Sahib Singh's mother, Kishen Kaur, who died on 12 November 1942. On her death, a dispute arose between Sahib Singh's sister, Jeo, and Sahib Singh's agnatic relation, Ujjagar Singh, as to the ownership of the land. Jeo filed a suit asking for ownership. The court upheld her claim.

Similar decisions which were taken in the wake of the 1956 Act made it clear that inheritance of land cannot be denied to daughters or sisters. It should be emphasized that all these cases relate to situations where women had no brothers. Indeed, a member of the Haryana Vidhan Sabha testified to the 'greed' among people who, after the 1956 Act, wanted their sons to marry only those girls who had no brothers.[88] The act made the possibility of jamai becoming ghar jamai not only a legal possibility but in some cases, also a reality, specially as some of the son-less fathers showed preference for their daughter over their male relatives. Yet, the cultural ideology which has been safeguarding patrilineal interests for so long has been too powerful to be breached in any substantial way. Such attempts, therefore, have been confined only to those cases where some tradition exists. But the final outcome of these few rare cases does not entirely depend on the court decisions. Its implementation has always had to depend upon the agreement and goodwill of the reversioner, which despite the enabling law, has not often been forthcoming.

In a few cases, the staking of a claim by a son-in-law on behalf of his wife has led to ostracizing of the couple by the villagers, till they agreed to give up their demand.[89] In the face of such vehement opposi-

[87] *The Supreme Court Journal*, 1960, vol. XXIII, Civil Appellate Jurisdiction, *Ujjagar Singh vs Jeo*, pp. 16–26.

[88] 1979, *Haryana Vidhan Sabha Debates*, 25 September. See speech of Jagjit Singh Pohlu, a landowner of considerable stature from village Chattar.

[89] See Urvashi Butalia, 1979, 'Haryana's Women: Problems with Property', *Hindustan Times*, New Delhi, 16 December, Sunday Magazine.

tion, one rural woman in western UP actually signed away her share of land, which had been decreed to her after a prolonged court battle, to her brother without even the 'permission' of her husband;[90] an almost unprecedented step in rural areas. The following case from Haryana is illustrative of the fate of a female taking over her patrimony.[91]

A man from village Kasandi, married to the only daughter of a widow, came and settled in village Bandh of Karnal district in 1982 where his wife had inherited land from her widowed mother. His own landholding, being much smaller, was given out on *batai* (share cropping). This arrangement, with great difficulty, lasted only for two years. The male collaterals did not allow him to settle down. He was openly taunted; quarrels were picked up with him at the slightest pretext. Socially he was unwelcome everywhere; animals were let loose in his fields; crops were destroyed; water channels were cut and water diverted elsewhere; special irrigation arrangements made from the neighbouring tube wells for two hours would dry up only after half an hour; and so on. He finally sold the land at a much lower price than the market price to his tormentors, that is, his late father-in-law's male collaterals, and moved back to his own village.

The situation is, therefore, one of potential violence and bloodshed, in cases where the inheritance rights are sought to be claimed by the jamai. In September 1989, the Haryana Vidhan Sabha members openly acknowledged violence, and even murder, in such cases.[92] The situation is the same in rural areas of Punjab in Pakistan. In Pakistan, the officers of the law have often found it impossible to marshal witnesses, and collect evidence to take action against the offenders because such crimes are committed with the connivance of the *biradari* (community).[93]

[90] Case cited in Sylvia Vatuk, 1972, *Kinship and Urbanisation*, Berkeley: University of California Press, pp. 108–9.

[91] Narrated by Harpal Singh and Ratan Singh. It was interesting to note that the woman, the actual inheritor of land, was hardly mentioned in this narrative, the whole thing being the concern of her husband and her father's male collaterals.

[92] See debate relating to the Hindu Succession (Haryana Amendment) Bill 1979, 1979, *Haryana Vidhan Sabha Debates*, 25 September.

[93] Hamza A. Alavi, 1972, 'Kinship in West Punjab Village', *Contributions to Indian Sociology* (NS), vol. VI, no. 6, December, pp. 1–27.

Yet, some male observers in Haryana insist on seeing a 'trend' showing the sons-in-law shifting to their wives' villages to claim land.[94] This incidentally has also been the view projected by the Haryana Vidhan Sabha.[95] I have not been able to confirm any such 'trend'. Statistics regarding the number of cases which may actually have been effected are not available. But more than the actual numbers, it is the likelihood of such cases being effected which has aroused fear among the landowners, and thus is more significant.

ERASING ENABLEMENT: A DAUGHTER'S SHARE

Because of fear, landowners take steps to counter such an eventuality. Many lawyers testify to the stream of males with potential female inheritors in tow, to get women to write off their land claims in favour of their brothers in anticipation of the enforcement of the act.[96] In the court, one of the routine questions asked before *likhat-padhat* (formalization of rights) takes place, is *'tum khush ho kar bhaiyon ko de rahi ho'*[97] (are you giving the land to your brothers on your own sweet will?). Several gift and sale deeds were registered in favour of males at this time. This pattern has been generally followed since then.[98]

In some cases, the land is automatically registered in the girl's name but remains in de facto possession of the brother. However, she cannot always sign away her inheritance as her brothers would have her do, as rural consensus of opinion puts the marriage age well below the age of attaining majority. In cases where she does sign away her right, she is invariably taunted after marriage for having been 'so very generous to have gifted away the land'.[99] However, a way out of this has been found, which is not infrequently adopted. This is to seek the prior sanction of the husband-to-be and his family to not claiming the inheritance due

[94] Observations and comments of Chhattar Singh, 1988, village Kaloi, district Rohtak, 6 December; Khem Chand, 1988, village Govad, district Sonepat, 15 October.

[95] 1979, *Haryana Vidhan Sabha Debates*, 25 September.

[96] Personal interview with Jasbir Singh Malik, 1988, advocate, village Gohana, 17–18 June.

[97] Ibid. This was confirmed by both males and females in different villages.

[98] In some cases, certain other steps are taken to ensure that only sons inherit: the use of testamentary power to disinherit daughter or to make a pre-mortem legal transfer of land in favour of sons.

[99] Personal interview with Khazani Devi, 1988, village Sherjabad, 6–7 August.

to her.[100] In many cases this is forthcoming, perhaps because the wife takers, too, have daughters and are afraid of establishing a precedent which may recoil on them, or they are unwilling to withstand the social taunts regarding the obvious double standards. Significantly, in one case from Meerut district in UP, the parents of the boy opposed the inheritance suit instituted by him on behalf of his wife and tried to persuade him to abandon it.[101] But in those cases, where the assent is not forthcoming, the de facto control of the father and brother retains its upper hand.

These tactics to side-step female inheritance rights also prevail among the Muslims of Haryana, specially those concentrated in Gurgaon (and parts of Rajasthan), known as Meos. In questions of inheritance, they still follow the customary practices of their Hindu counterparts, as they had done in the colonial period.[102] Among them also, property is inherited strictly in the male line and Meo females have no claim to their father's property, even if he has no male heirs. The only way a female can inherit is through her father's will. But a woman who tries to press a claim to her father's property, even on the basis of his will, invites the hostility of her consanguine relatives. In the 1970s, there were a few cases of married women legally claiming their inheritance rights through the courts. This invoked such hostility from the villagers against the women that such moves have not been taken again. Significantly too, although in the post-1947 period there has been a greater Islamization, they have refused to adopt cross-cousin and parallel cousin marriages as followed by other Muslims.[103] Meos consider all such marriages incestuous and continue to practise village exogamy. The rejection of this marriage pattern by Meos implies that to keep the property in the male line, they still prefer to follow the established and familiar customary law, rather than adopt a different practice as it has the similar effect

[100] Personal interview with Ram Chander, 1088, village Bandh, district Karnal, 21–2 August. Born 1940, he is the brother of Harpal Singh and Ratan Singh mentioned earlier.

[101] Case cited in Sylvia Vatuk, *Kinship and Urbanisation*, pp. 108–9.

[102] Pratap A. Aggarwal, 1976, 'Kinship and Marriage among the Meos of Rajasthan', in Imitiaz Ahmed (ed.), *Family, Kinship and Marriage among Muslims of India*, New Delhi: Manohar, pp. 265–96.

[103] Pratap A. Aggarwal, 1996, 'A Muslim Sub-Caste of North India: Problems of Cultural Integration', *Economic and Political Weekly*, vol. 1, no. 4, 10 September, pp. 159–61.

of keeping the landed property with the *khandan* (family) and lineage, as shown by a case study of UP.[104]

Even in Pakistan Punjab, as reported by Zekiye Eglar and Hamza A. Alavi, similar tactics have been adopted by landowners to deprive females of their inheritance rights, even though the *shariat* entitles, and has always entitled, them to inherit (although it is a share not equal to that of their brother). Like their Hindu and Muslim counterparts in northern India, the Pakistani landowners, rather than permit any share of their land to pass after their death to women, are known to have transferred their land to their sons during their lifetime. Many others have reached agreements about claims to property with the families in which they have married their daughters even prior to their marriages. On occasions, the sisters themselves have transferred property to brothers by declaring that they had sold the land to them and had received money.[105]

In other cases, depending on the 'greed' or 'need' of the husbands, women are constrained to act whether they like it or not. Quite clearly, the Act of 1956, giving the women inheritance rights, has injected a potential source of violent conflict between the husband's interest and that of the wife's father and brothers. Consequently, the need to control women has become even more crucial. Given the strong hold of patriarchy in the rural areas, this male control over woman, minor or major, is never slackened throughout her life; it is a mere change of authority, from that of her father and brother to husband and son.

---

[104] Shibani Roy's study of certain Muslim groups of UP shows how the consanguineous marriages are most effective in keeping the landed property within the khandan. Since the women are not allowed to marry outside the khandan, there is no dispersal of the landed property. In effect, it means that the question of females claiming their inheritance rights granted under the Quranic law does not arise. Moreover, an exchange of women between two khandans also nullifies the fear of a daughter claiming her inheritance, as a counter-claim can always be initiated by the other family. See Shibani Roy, 1984, 'Concept of *Zar, Zan* and *Zamin*: A Cultural Analysis of Indian Islamic Tradition of Inheritance and Kinship', *Man in India*, vol. 64, no. 4, December, pp. 383–96.

[105] Zekiye Eglar, 1960, *A Punjab Village in Pakistan*, Columbia: Columbia University Press, pp. 187–8; and Hamza A. Alavi, 'Kinship in West Punjab Village'. The reasons given for doing this are similar to the ones given in Punjab and Haryana, that is, the risk apprehended by women of losing their parental home visits, gifts, goodwill, all of which enhance their 'prestige', and so on.

This ideology of control and dependence has actually operated for centuries, and its operation can be seen in the rural women still being known largely in terms of their familial relationships, denoting her dependence rather than her individuality. For example, a woman will be called 'Girdhari *ki Chhori*' (daughter), 'Nanku *ki lugai*' (wife), 'Ramchander *ki* bahu' (daughter-in-law), or 'Kishan *ki ma*' (mother). In all these familial relationships, her own name is all but forgotten or lost.[106]

Such an ideology of dependency and control hardly entitles her to any decision-making powers. As I show elsewhere, a woman does not have much space to make decisions, whether they be in her personal life, the disposal of her jewellery, the allocation of money in household matters, the economics of animal husbandry and agricultural production, or in the distribution of agricultural surplus.[107] Although there are always exceptions, it is not very likely that a woman would take entirely independent decision regarding the activating of her inheritance rights.

The force of the ideological reality of a woman's relations of dependence on both her brother and husband, prevents her from becoming an independent property holder, even when there are no institutional or legal obstacles to her doing so. In relation to the former, she signs away her right, and in relation to the latter, she claims her right; in both cases, she is just an instrument, the land remaining de facto a male possession.

Yet, even within this rigid framework, certain voices are discernable; negative voices and ones which are openly disgruntled. For example, there are a few women who have successfully withstood pressure from the husbands to claim their inheritance by maintaining, '*tu pahle apni behnon ko haq de mein phir apna haq lungi*'[108] (you first give your sister's share to them, then I shall claim my own), thus putting the husbands under pressure and successfully withstanding all attempts to institute legal claims to inheritance on their behalf. The women when questioned,

---

[106] This fact was highlighted when during the course of conversation, I wished to take down the identity of a particular woman; invariably, the woman was referred to as 'so and so's bahu or chhori', and the like. This was significantly different from the way a male was identified. His name took priority and then the familial relationship followed.

[107] See Chapter 8 in this volume.

[108] Personal interview with Mohran Devi, 1990, village Jhojho Chamani, district Bhiwani, 7 June; wife of Mange Ram, an ex-army man. They have 60 bighas of land in the dry belt of Haryana.

showed a distinct preference for their brothers. In this connection, a woman's realization cited earlier that it is her husband who will get the land and she will end up by losing both, that is, the goodwill of her brothers and her land claim, may be kept in mind.

Some of the women, however, who are openly disgruntled are reported to be asserting:

hamen bhat thora diya, chhuchhak thora diya,
hamare naam zamin hai, hum to lenge[109]
(We have been given so little in marriage and on other social occasions. Now that we can inherit property, we shall claim our share.)

Along with this is also asserted: '*koi leti nahin, per latkaye rakhti hain*' (no girl claims her land right but keeps the issue hanging). Yet, these disgruntled voices are no proof that married women are activating their inheritance rights. These certainly underline awareness of inheritance rights on the part of women and the use of it as a threat which has legal sustainability. In few cases where these threats concretize into reality and the lower courts are moved to claim inheritance, almost immediately an out-of-court settlement is reached, which may well have been the point of staking a claim. I was able to track down two such cases, in which married daughters moved the court to lay claim to their inheritance. Immediately, an out-of-court settlement was arrived at and they withdrew their claims.[110] There are, therefore, no recorded cases as such. Also, clearly it is money which is exchanging hands and not land.[111] In the considered opinion of lawyers dealing with the inheritance question, it is the unambiguity of the 1956 Act which has created all these 'problems'.[112] The act, being very clear on

[109] Personal interview with Daya Kaur, 1988, Sonepat, 12 October; born 1929, her three sons are employed in various government services; the land in the village is being looked after by her brother-in-law and his wife.

[110] In these two cases, one in village Gochchi of Rohtak district and another in district Karnal, a lot of money, running into couple of lakhs, was claimed to have exchanged hands to bring about a withdrawal of the case as the property was considerable. The names of the concerned parties are being withheld on request. This is significant, as it shows social stigma which sticks to such claims.

[111] It is certainly true that land can be bought out of this money, but the decision to utilize this money is in male hands. In the two cases just cited, the women concerned were silent on the way this money came to be spent or who decided to spend it.

[112] Jasbir Singh Malik, 1986, advocate, village Gohana, district Rohtak, 17–18 June.

legal inheritance right of females, has meant that such a claim, if made, cannot be denied them.

ATTEMPTING AMENDMENTS: A MATTER OF TWO SHARES

Despite the highly successful restrictions imposed on the widow, or daughter, or sister exercising her right of absolute inheritance, the enabling legislation continued to create anxiety and apprehension in the rural areas. And slowly, as tension mounted, voices to abolish or amend the 1956 Act gained momentum. The Haryana Assembly passed a resolution in 1967 and the Punjab Assembly in 1977, both requesting the central government to change the said act.[113]

The centre did not oblige. In 1979, the Haryana Assembly tried to force the issue by unanimously passing a Bill amending the Act of 1956, and sent it for the President's approval. This was not granted. The statement of objections of the Haryana Bill No. XXII of 1979, called the Hindu Succession (Haryana Amendment) Bill 1979, read:

The proposed amendments to the Hindu Succession Act, 1956 seek to take into account the general feeling in the state that a female Hindu should inherit the property of her husband and not that of her father. It is felt that the operation of the Act, whereby the daughters, married or unmarried, get a share in the property of their father, has had the effect of accelerating fragmentation of holdings in the state. The existing provisions have also led to serious disputes between brothers and sisters and have contributed to the disruption of harmonious life of the village community.

It is proposed to meet the situation by excluding married daughters from the heirs of Class-I and making other consequential changes. It is also proposed to restrict the right of a Hindu female to alienate the property inherited by her from any source so as to bring her at par with the Hindu male.[114]

[113] 1979, *Haryana Vidhan Sabha Debates*, 25 September. The Haryana Vidhan Sabha had four women members at that time: Shanti Devi, Shakuntala Bhagwaria, Sushma Swaraj, and Kamala Verma. Not a single one protested. For their social and educational background, see 1979, *Haryana Vidhan Sabha, Who's Who 1971*, Chandigarh: General Branch, Haryana Vidhan Sabha Secretariat.

[114] Government of Haryana, 1979, *Haryana Government Gazette Extraordinary*, Chandigarh: Government of Haryana, 21 September. Interestingly, whereas a Hindu female has been termed an absolute owner of her inheritance with full rights of disposal, the Hindu male, in the case of his coparcenary property, continues to be guided in accordance with the principles of the Hindu law, where the property devolves on the surviving members of the coparcenary, except in the case of his female heirs or her heirs, who under the 1956 Act, get preference in inheritance entitlement of coparcenary property as well. See *Hindu Law, Vol. II*,

It may be noted that the amendment sought to curb the right of only the married woman, not the unmarried one. This is significant as there are hardly any unmarried women in the rural Haryana. In 1981, females who remained unmarried after the age of thirty-five in rural Haryana were only 0.08 per cent.[115] In the rural areas, even the 'langri, looli aur andhi' (maimed and blind) women get married.[116] The exclusion of married women from the purview of the act, in effect meant exclusion of all women (as daughters) from inheritance. Besides, land claims of married women or widows, in effect, are generally viewed with much less antagonism than those of daughters, since with widows there is a greater chance of the land remaining with agnates, specially under levirate. Significantly, the 1981 Census of Haryana shows less than 1 per cent of widows among the rural women between the 'marriage-able age of 16 and 44 years'.[117]

The debate[118] which followed the introduction of the Bill also sought to defend this amendment on the basis of 'long established tradition of brother/sister love', which was projected to be 'in grave danger of being severely disrupted'. This defence of tradition has a wider signifi-cance, as this fraternal love can apparently only be sustained if the sister relinquishes her inheritance rights. The speakers also laid emphasis on the 'enormous increase in the fragmentation of land holdings' and creation of uneconomic holdings. Figures provided by the then Irri-gation and Power Minister, Chaudhary Rizak Ram, showed that the below 5 acres uneconomic holdings increased in 1956 by 73 per cent in 1975. Female inheritance introduced in 1956 was held responsible for this. But there are other possible causes. These extended from a natural process of inheritance in view of increase in population in those twenty years leading to sub-division of land among heirs on account of the break up of joint and extended families into separate households during the lifetime of the head, to the resumption of rented land for self-cultivation, and the impact of the green revolution, which in the opin-

---

p. 475 and Government of India, 1950, *The Hindu Code 1950*, New Delhi: Ministry of Law pp. 147–8.

[115] *Census of Haryana, 1981*, pp. 46–7.

[116] Personal interview with Shanti and Kalawati, 1988, village Bandh, district Karnal, 21–2 August.

[117] *Census of Haryana, 1981*, p. 46.

[118] For the entire debate, see 1979, *Haryana Vidhan Sabha Debates*, 25 September.

ion of some economists, activated a division of holdings.[119] Moreover, there is nothing to indicate that a sizeable number of females have been able to exercise their rights. In most cases, either their rights, if claimed, have been written off or bought out by the males. In others, the land may have remained with them only in name, the actual possessors being the male members. It appears that the amendment has been proposed more out of the fear of landowning males who remain apprehensive of the potential female claims than the actual claims made.

The Bill was defeated by the President's veto. Ten years later, in August 1989, Devi Lal, then a Member of Parliament from Haryana and Deputy Prime Minister, again proposed an amendment in the Succession Act, in an attempt to deprive married women of their share in the parents' property.[120] The spate of protests which followed this move could not be ignored. Devi Lal was forced to drop the proposal in view of, as he acknowledged himself, 'adverse comments in the media and elsewhere'.[121] In Punjab also, in the wake of agitation, the demand for the promulgation of the Sikh personal law that denies land rights to women and advocates remarriage of a widow with her brother-in-law had been put forward.[122] All these moves stand defeated, but not the spirit that had moved them. This continues unabated, cutting across differences of gender, class, caste, and even political parties.

* * *

The near failure of this gender progressive legislation is not exclusive to India. This fate is shared by other South Asian countries (Pakistan, Bangladesh, Sri Lanka, Nepal), where few women inherit landed property and even fewer control it.[123] There remains a vast gap between law and its implementation. The legal creation of women's inheritance rights in these regions sought to reverse the custom of keeping women excluded from inheritance, which the near century of British rule had

[119] Sheila Bhalla, 1977, 'Changes in Acreage and Tenure Structure Land-holdings in Haryana, 1962–72', *Economic and Political Weekly*, vol. XII, no. 12, 19 March, pp. A2–15.

[120] *Hindustan Times*, 1989, New Delhi, 9 August, p. 1; *Times of India*, 1989, New Delhi, 10 August, section 2, p. 4; *Tribune*, 1989, Chandigarh, 9 August, p. 1.

[121] *Times of India*, 1989, New Delhi, 19 August, p. 6. See letter to the editor.

[122] For details, see Amrita Chhachhi, 1989, 'The State, Religious Fundamentalism and Women: Trends in South Asia', *Economic and Political Weekly*, vol. XXIX, no. 11, 18 March, pp. 567–8.

[123] See Agarwal, *A Field of One's Own*.

legally established. Such a reversal of long-established custom, therefore, meant that the implementation of the act was not going to be easy. The sharp resistance of the men whose interests were drastically affected was to be expected. In fact, the post-colonial legislation which gave women, not only in India but in neighbouring countries too, the right to inherit land was not viewed with favour by men in patrilineal communities. Several ethnographic writings have commented on this.[124]

The female reaction, on the other hand, hinged on her knowledge and acceptance of the new legislation. Regarding this, the generally held opinion is that the rural women have a very low or no knowledge of their inheritance rights.[125] This factor is important as it is a crucial prerequisite of women exercising their rights. Contrary to this opinion, I found a very high level of knowledge and awareness of legal changes among rural women of Haryana. Yet, despite this knowledge, I also found ambiguities in their attitude towards this enablement, and contradictions in their voiced opinions and behaviour. These contradictions are crucially linked to the social stigma which such claims attract and the wholesale condemnation and resistance such claims face. The long-standing kinship system and its rules about patrilocal post-marital residence and village exogamy, in combination with the low position of ghar jamai, makes the implementation of the law of inheritance difficult and impractical to accomplish. Consequently, I found the 'idealized norms' of a patriarchal and patrilineal society not openly challenged but subverted by younger generation of women in certain cases, or used as bargaining counter to effect a better deal for themselves. The agency they assume in this respect is a complex one: emanating out of the material basis provided by the act, it ranges from their becoming a willing or unwilling tool in laying claims to property or in consciously asserting or rejecting their claims to property. Similarly, the male reaction to inheritance changes is also not of unqualified hostility. In some cases, their support or even initiative is available: from the husband of a

---

[124] For a comprehensive list of these works, see ibid., pp. 271–3.

[125] According to M.S. Luschinsky, one half of the women he interviewed knew nothing about the Act of 1956; see his 1963, 'The Impact of Some Recent Indian Government Legislation on Women of an Indian Village', *Asian Survey*, vol. 3, no. 12, December, pp. 573–83. Generally, Luschinsky's observations regarding women's access to information about inheritance laws, made in the early 1960s, tends to be accepted even now. See, for example, Agarwal, *A Field of One's Own*, p. 271.

brother-less wife or from the father of a son-less daughter, with varying degree of success.

Although the moral economy of the peasants, the cultural valuation of women, the ideological constraints, and customary practices are all inextricably working for the conservation of male rights, the right granted to women to inherit land and the potentiality of their claim has created a very genuine fear among the patrilineal/patriarchal forces in rural areas. So far, these forces have been apparently aided in their endeavours by woman as well, whose logic makes her reject the two shares which she has come to inherit, but for how long? As breaches become visible, the uncertainty inherent in the situation is heightened.

10

Private Lives, State Intervention

Cases of Runaway Marriage in Rural North India*

The introduction of modern concepts like adulthood and sanctity given to individual rights has legally turned the individual settlement of marriage between two consenting adults to be legitimate. Under the Hindu Marriage Act of 1955, except for certain incest taboos, the legal restrictions on marriage of two adult Hindus are almost non-existent.[1] Briefly speaking, this means that under the law, both *sagotra* (same *gotra*) and inter-caste marriages are permitted. Yet, the customary rules regulating marriages in most parts of north India are based upon caste endogamy, village and clan exogamy. While keeping within caste, they adopt the gotra or Got, as is known in rural north India, rule of exogamy (gotra are an exogamous patrilineal clan whose members are thought to share patrilineal descent from a common ancestor). For marriage, certain prohibited degrees of kinship have to be avoided. As a

---

* This chapter was originally published in 2004, *Modern Asian Studies*, 38(1): 55–84, Cambridge University Press.
    [1] The Hindu Marriage Act (no. XXXV) of 1955, in combination with an earlier Act called The Special Marriage Act, 1954, enabled two heterosexual adults to be legally married by a Registrar irrespective of their caste, creed, and kinship (with few exceptions). Sunderlal T. Desai, 1966, *Mulla Principles of Hindu Law*, Bombay: N.M. Tripathi Pvt Ltd., pp. 468–9, 616–751. For further details also see Chapter 11.

rule, three or four Got exogamy is followed by most caste groups, upper or lower.[2] Any break in this, though legally allowed, is not acceptable.

To overcome these caste and customary rules, some couples run away from the village to get married. Such cases are generally dealt within the close preserve of the family, and/or its kinship network. Yet, some of them spill over voluntarily or involuntarily into the public sphere and assume a different form, as issues concerning the sexuality of women, almost entirely confined to the family, are thrown open for judgement. This public sphere is dominated by two diametrically opposing authorities, one informal and the other formal. The informal is under the domination of the wider community (*biradari*), acting through the traditional panchayat with no legal standing; the formal is regulated by the state, based upon modern egalitarian laws. In this essay, I shall concentrate only on the latter.

In the case of a runaway marriage, the state apparatus gets galvanized on a complaint generally made by the woman's male guardian. The police registers a First Information Report (FIR) and accepts such cases as criminal cases involving abduction and kidnapping and very often, rape. In police and judicial vocabulary, these are termed as 'sex crimes' and are dealt with as such. The couple is hounded and caught. The man is taken into custody for questioning, leading to his imprisonment. His wife (if they have managed to get married, as very often is the case) is handed over to her male guardian, father, or brother. The family pressurizes her into indicting her husband as an abductor and a rapist, and deny the marriage. Any claims made or even proof of marriage supplied by the man is discounted on grounds of the woman's testimony, or on the minority age status of the girl, or on the allegation of the use of force to compel the girl to get married in order to have 'illicit intercourse' with her.

The criminal case that follows is instituted by the state against the alleged criminal/criminals. In such cases, I argue, the state colludes with the patriarchal family in controlling females, and in maintaining the caste and kinship ideology which governs the marriage alliances and cannot be sustained legally. It uses the ambiguities in the legal system to circumvent the rights of individuals. It selectively believes and disbelieves the testimony of the woman. In tackling the runaway

---

[2] For details of customary marriage prohibitions see Chapter 11 in this volume.

cases, the post-colonial state emerges resembling its predecessor state which operated norms clearly at odds with modern egalitarian principles. The colonial government worked under the ideology of guardianship, which turned runaway marriages illegal. The post-colonial state, despite different set of legal norms, continues to labour under the same ideological hold.

This essay analyses a series of court cases from Haryana–Punjab involving runaway couples, to argue that legal intervention not only delegitimizes such individual attempts at breaking out of the traditional system of marriage alliances, it also criminalizes all such attempts. It highlights the pronounced gender bias against women whose consent is taken cognizance of, without recognizing her right to consent or make individual choices. A mutual act is turned unilateral, condemning the woman and holding her responsible to the exclusion of the man, though contradictorily, it still punishes him. A man who seeks to divest a guardian of his possession / control of his daughter is termed a criminal. The punishment underlines an ideology of guardianship which also means a total control of woman and her sexuality, not withstanding her adult status.

The judgement delivered in such cases is premised upon moral and ethical grounds, overriding questions of legal and human rights of individuals. In such matters, the state acts, and is used by patriarchal forces, as a primary legitimating institution of popular cultural practices. Standing as an overarching patriarch and acting on behalf of the male guardians of a woman, the state criminalizes female sexuality, and constructs it as essentially transgressive, illegitimate, and morally reprehensible. It denies the woman autonomy over her body or assume agency to gain control of her life. Instead, it imposes an identity on her which is not her own. This collusion of the family, community, and state ends up in tragedy.

THE CRUCIAL AGE FACTOR: FLEXIBILITY
IN LEGAL POSITION

The runaway cases, officially reported as cases of kidnapping and abduction, are acknowledged to be 'nothing but cases of love affair with the abducted woman being the consenting party'.[3] Legally, kidnapping and

---

[3] Government of Haryana, 1988, *Mahendergarh District Gazetteer*, Chandigarh: Government of Haryana, p. 233.

abduction are two distinct offences.[4] Kidnapping is used only in the case of minors. It is an offence against the right of the parent from under whose guardianship the person is taken away. Consequently, in the case of a runaway woman, kidnapping case is most often registered to prevent her from exercising her choice in marriage against the wishes of her parents. In such kidnapping cases, the consent of the woman is immaterial or irrelevant. In order to prove kidnapping, the prosecution must establish that at the time of offence, the prosecutrix was a minor, that is, under 18 years of age. The entire case hinges on this. Kidnapping is punishable per se in terms of Section 363. In runaway cases, the registration of kidnapping charges is a must and many a times, even advised by the police.[5]

Abduction, on the other hand, as defined under Section 362 of Indian Penal Code (IPC), is an offence when a person is by force compelled or by deceitful means induced to go from any place. Such a person could be a minor or an adult. Abduction is punishable only when accompanied by a particular purpose as laid down in Sections 364, 365, 366, and 376 of IPC. This means that the intent of the abductor needs to be proved for conviction. The intent behind kidnapping or abduction under Section 364 relates to murder; under Section 365, to secretly and wrongfully confine a person; under Section 366, to induce a woman or compel marriage in order that she may be forced or seduced to illicit intercourse; and Section 376 relates to rape of a woman. Where the prosecutrix, if above 18 years, is herself responsible for taking the accused to another city on the pretext of getting married to him, Section 366 cannot be activated. Clearly, it is in the age factor that the legal ambiguity lies.

The legal age of majority, as also the minimum age for marriage, for girls, is eighteen. However, Section 375 of the IPC lays down the age of consent for sexual intercourse to be 16 years for all unmarried women and 15 years for all married women.[6] Sexual activity below these age groups is prohibited and considered illegal. Apart from this blatant discrepancy maintained in ages between married and unmarried women

[4] For a judicial understanding and application of these terms in criminal cases, see Criminal Law Journal, 1995, vol. 101, part 2, Biswanath Mallick vs State of Orissa, Orissa High Court, pp. 1416–19.

[5] Interview with a police officer, 2000, Rohtak, 24 January. Name withheld on request.

[6] Pratiksha Baxi, 2000, 'Rape, Retribution, State: On Whose Bodies?', Economic and Political Weekly, vol. XXXV, no. 14, 1–7 April, pp. 1196–200.

who do not observe patriarchal standard of morality, it also means that the illegal marriages of women below eighteen are accepted as legal under Section 375. This contradiction has led to an anomalous situation. In effect, it has meant that the charge of illegality is activated when the girl makes her own choice in marriage but not when her guardian makes it for her, even when she is well below the age of marriage. In runaway cases, marriage or indulging in sexual intercourse, if claimed and proved, is held invalid in view of the minor age status of the girl, who as a minor is legally not eligible for marriage. Consequently, the question of the age of the girl emerges crucial in all the runaway cases.

In most cases, it is difficult to establish the correct age of the girl. Given the general paucity of records regarding births and widespread apathy in recording births in rural India, a girl's age cannot be conclusively proved. It remains a matter of speculation. Interestingly, the school certificate, accepted universally as a proof of age, is not considered creditworthy in cases such as these. In such cases, it is contended that the birth date of a student is recorded as given by the guardian without substantiating it with any medical certificate or municipal record. According to the police, such records are easily manipulated. The high court judges have almost invariably refused to place any reliance upon it. Very often, there is a discrepancy between age given in the school register and the municipal birth register or the *chowkidara* register in the villages, or other records maintained in the office of the civil surgeon. The judges have observed that parents, while getting their children admitted into schools, do not provide the correct birth dates.[7] Most often, the birth date is held by the judges to be under-reported. Under- reporting of age is perceived to give an advantage to the child later in life: to a boy in his studies and in other competitions and career; and to a girl, in her marriage. In popular perception, the younger the bride, the more malleable she is considered to be to the wishes of her conjugal family.

Since the age factor of the girl is crucial, the court almost always gets the radiologist's opinion on the basis of bone X-ray examination, known as ossification test, to establish the age of the girl. However, this test is not considered infallible by the judges. Even after this test, the age given could well be an approximation to indicate the minimum and

---

[7] *Punjab Law Reporter*, 1969, vol. LXXI, *Jai Narain vs State of Haryana*, pp. 688–94; *Criminal Law Journal*, 1994, vol. 100, *Hira Lal vs State of Haryana*, Punjab and Haryana High Court, pp. 2471–3.

maximum age limit of the prosecutrix. This emerges clear from a 1969 case of *Jai Narain vs State of Haryana*. In this, the judge exercising his discretion regarding the fixation of the age of the prosecutrix, rejected the reading of the radiologist by maintaining:

It will be safer in the face of the unimpeachable character of the evidence pertaining to the birth entry of the girl supported by the oral testimony of the parents of the girl to take that on the date of occurrence the girl was 14 years of age. In her case, the maximum age limit of 17 given by the Radiologist is not conformable to the entry of the date of her birth. There is nothing to show that the entry is wrong or could pertain to a child other than Santosh Rani. Even if the lower age limit of 15 and a half years is adopted because of its being approximate to the age proved by her birth entry, she would be less than 16.[8]

In some instances, the margin of error regarding the age of the prosecutrix is taken to be the age claimed by the girl's guardian, plus three years.[9] In most cases, the individual judges decide whatever weightage they wish to give to evidence regarding the age of the girl coming from as different sources as medical test, oral testimony, school certificate, or birth certificate. The judicial flexibility about judging the age tells us a great deal about the flexibility or restrictions with which the given legal standards are evaluated and imposed. For the girl concerned, more often than not, this flexibility works against her rather than in her favour.

SEXUAL INTERCOURSE AND MARRIAGE:
LICIT AND ILLICIT

The existing court cases show how the court passively accepts, as also actively promotes, the regulation of a woman's sexuality through marriage rather than challenge it in accordance with her legal rights. Such a stand reiterates that the male guardian has the right to settle and give her in marriage to a partner of his choice. I shall take up some of the cases to illustrate the analysis. In *Harmel Singh vs State of Haryana* case of 1972,[10] all the evidence pointed to the girl's marriage. But the marriage was discounted by the court on the basis of her minor age status. Her intent to get married was also disregarded. Her active sexuality, well

---

[8] *Punjab Law Reporter*, 1969, vol. LXXI, pp. 688–94.

[9] *Criminal Law Journal*, 1994, vol. 100, *Balasaheb vs State of Maharashtra*, Bombay High Court, pp. 3044–50.

[10] *Criminal Law Journal*, 1972, vol. XII, *Harmel Singh vs State of Haryana*, pp. 1648–50.

within the fold of marriage, as per the requirement of the court, was condemned.

This case concerned Harmel Singh, a teacher by profession, who was convicted by the additional sessions judge, Hissar, on 23 August 1969, for abduction and rape of an allegedly minor girl, Asha Rani, daughter of Gela Ram of village Mandi Dabwali in Hissar. Harmel Singh was sentenced to one year rigorous imprisonment under Sections 363 and 366, and his associate, Harbhajan Singh, for aiding and abetting him, was sentenced to six months. Separate criminal appeals filed by the two convicts in the Punjab and Haryana High Court were decided in 1972. The case of the prosecution presented at the lower court was as follows.

Gela Ram's family used to live in village Mandi Dabwali, while Gela Ram, who worked as a *Patwari*, was posted at Gobindgarh. Both the appellants, Harmel Singh and Harbhajan Singh, were neighbours of Gela Ram in Mandi Dabwali and had friendly relations with him and his family. A month before the occurrence of the case, Gela Ram's wife and their only child, Asha Rani, the prosecutrix, shifted to Fatehabad to her grandparents. On 22 July 1968, Asha Rani left her home to go to the house of her maternal uncle. The two accused met her on the way and told her that her father had met with a serious accident and they had been sent to take her to Dabwali. Without verifying this fact, she accompanied them. She was taken by them to Sirsa. At Sirsa, Harmel Singh disclosed to her that she had been brought there because he wanted to get married to her. She was threatened that she would be killed in case she refused to get married or divulged this to anybody. The threat was given by Harmel Singh by flaunting a big knife. Asha Rani was then taken by train to Bhatinda to the house of one Jagdish Rai, an advocate. The two accused and Asha Rani stayed at the house of Jagdish Rai and during this period, the court noted that 'Harmel Singh the accused, committed sexual intercourse with Asha Rani and also took her to the Gurdawara on 24 July 1968 and performed the marriage ceremony.' The next day, the police, accompanied by Asha Rani's father, arrived in Bhatinda and arrested Harmel Singh while he was with Asha Rani. Gela Ram had lodged a report at police station, Fatehabad, on 24 July 1968. And it was based on this report that the police arrested the accused. After the completion of investigation, the accused were *challaned*, convicted, and sentenced by the lower court.

The High Court disputed the evidence provided by Asha Rani that she had been threatened and forced to accompany the accused or had been duped into accompanying them. Citing from the defendants' testimony, Justice Man Mohan Singh Gujral noted:

It was clearly admitted by Asha Rani that at no stage did she seek the help of any person though she had met a large number of persons. It is further in her statement that even at the house of Jagdish Rai she did not disclose it either to Jagdish Rai or to his family that she had been brought there by deception and force and was being kept there against her will. Asha Rani has further admitted that even at the Gurdawara while the marriage ceremony was being performed and a large number of persons were present the fact that she had been brought against her will was not brought to the notice of either the *granthi* who was performing the ceremony or other respectables who were present in the gurdwara. She has also admitted that photographs were taken at the time of the ceremony and she was forced to put up a happy face to show that everything with her was all right. All this leaves no manner of doubt that Asha Rani was a consenting party and that the story that she had been made to accompany the accused on the false representation that her father had met with an accident was false and that she had willingly accompanied the appellants first to Sirsa and then to Bhatinda...Coming to the facts of the present case, the circumstances show that Harmel Singh and Asha Rani lived in neighbourhood at Dabwali and that Harmel Singh used to visit the house of the prosecutrix. Gela Ram has stated that their families used to meet and were known to each other. It is further in evidence that Asha Rani and her mother shifted to Fatehabad and the suggestion made was that this was done to persuade Asha Rani to get married to some other person and not Harmel Singh. From this it can be safely inferred that there was some sort of liaison between Harmel Singh and Asha Rani before Asha Rani was brought to Fatehabad. The medical evidence also shows that Asha Rani was used to sexual intercourse before her elopement.

It is quite clear that the judge was aware of this case being one of elopement and marriage. He was also aware, as all judges sitting in judgement (I am told) over such cases are aware, of the fact that the girl was lying and the case had been fabricated under pressure from her family members.[11]

Legally the case hinged upon the age of Asha Rani. Regarding this, the High Court accepted an ambiguous position and maintained that the evidence showed her to be certainly above 16 years but below 18 years of age at the time of her elopement. This meant that she could certainly give her consent to having sexual intercourse but, not being

[11] A criminal lawyer from Rohtak candidly admitted that all parties concerned, including the judges, know about the nature of such cases and the pressures exercised by the concerned parties in this connection.

an adult, she could not give her consent to marriage. The judgement, however, did not stop short of this. It went on to deliver a highly moral judgement upon the woman's active sexuality to condemn and degrade her. Citing a judgement of the Supreme Court, often cited in cases such as these, delivered in *Brij Lal Sud vs State of Punjab*, 1970–2, the High Court elaborated:

The medical evidence showed that the girl was fully developed and used to sexual intercourse and her physical appearance showed that she had been perhaps indulging in it for quite some time. It was not, therefore, the only occasion when she was in the company of men. This reflects on the question of her consent, but consent is immaterial because she was below age. All the same in the case of a woman of this character the offence (of the man) is just little more than a technical offence. Because of this it is not necessary to insist on the full sentence.

The age factor made Harmel Singh liable under Sections 363 and 366 of the IPC. The High Court found him to be 'rightly convicted for these offences'.

But the court also maintained that as Asha Rani was clearly 'a consenting party', 'the accused could be regarded as facilitating the fulfilment of *the intention of the girl*' (emphasis added). The important question that arises is: what is the intention of the girl? Without specifying, the court makes it clear that her 'intention' was to have sexual intercourse with her lover.

This implicit intent was explicitly stated in a similar runaway case from Bombay. It formed part of the judgement delivered in 1994. The judge maintained that 'the conduct shows that there was complete consent on the part of the prosecutrix to be in the company of the *appellant in order to satisfy her sexual lust*'[12] (emphasis added). The obvious fact that her 'intention' was to get married or that she had indeed got married to the accused, as testified by the appellant, was ignored.

The question of marriage could not be entertained as she was a minor and her consent could only be for intercourse and not marriage. In other words, there was no way she could enjoy, what in the legal terminology is 'licit' sexual intercourse. Without marriage, her indulgence in sexual intercourse became illicit. The stand taken by the court reveals that it considers only marriage as a legitimate forum for sex, and the only marriage it recognizes is the one which has the guardian's sanction and blessings. This is a patriarchal norm of marriage and female sexuality.

[12] *Criminal Law Journal*, vol. 100, pp. 3044–50.

It may be reiterated that sexual intercourse by a man with his wife who may be above 15 years of age, but below the age of marriage, is considered legitimate in case the marriage of such a minor is performed with the sanction of the guardian concerned.

MARRIAGE: CONSENT OF THE GUARDIAN VS CONSENT OF THE WOMAN

As matters stand, the contemporary judicial attitude towards runaway marriages harks back to the Brahmanical strictures given recognition by the colonial judiciary. Proclaimed as an 'inferior form of marriage', it was looked down upon by the high caste people. In the eight forms of marriage traditionally recognized by the Dharmasastra of Manu, as given in chapter V, the lowest was the Gandharva form. The runaway marriage of a female fell in this category. Based upon self-regulation of sexual activity by a woman, with the basic purpose of indulging in sexual intercourse it was denounced vehemently. This understanding and attitude permeated all the judgments of the British Indian courts.[13]

A 1925 Allahabad High Court judgement described a runaway marriage as 'the *Gandharva* form', where the marriage takes place 'with the mutual desire of the parties'. It was declared to be 'one of the three most primitive forms of marriage', which in their opinion was 'really nothing more than the unregulated indulgence of lust'.[14] Such an assumption is rooted in the popular perception of the local people. A marriage without the consent of the parents, even if it was within the community, is not accepted as a marriage. Consequently, sexual relations in such a marriage are held to be illicit. I repeatedly encountered this attitude in rural Haryana. As the ex-*pradhan* of village Mitrao put it, 'where marriage rituals are not observed and parental consent is not forthcoming, such marriages are love marriages, based upon *badmashi* (lustful intercourse). We have nothing to do with them.'[15]

During the colonial days, a runaway match of an unmarried girl was not given the legal sanction of a valid marriage as the 'consent' of the guardian was considered necessary.[16] It was moulded on the

[13] Thomas R. Trautman, 1981, *Dravidian Kinship*, Cambridge: Cambridge University Press, pp. 288–91.

[14] *Indian Cases*, 1925, vol. 90, *Kishan Dev vs Sheo Paltan*, Allahabad, pp. 358–64.

[15] Daya Kishan, 2000, interview, village Mitrao, 14 September.

[16] C.A.H. Townsend, 1913, *Customary Law of the Hissar District* (except the Sirsa Tehsil), vol. XXV, Lahore: Punjab Government Press, pp. 12–21.

local custom under which minor and adult females were always under the guardianship of some male member. This turned the question of her legal age of majority in such cases, placed to be at fifteen, totally irrelevant.[17] Moreover, this consent was essentially a male guardian's consent. The colonial judiciary recognized the tradition of male guardian's right to arrange a daughter's marriage as a superior claim over and above any female claim. In a 1884 case, a marriage celebrated by the mother without the consent of the father was set aside. The father brought a suit and got a decree. The judges in this case held that under no circumstances other than that of abandonment by the father would a contract be binding without the father's consent.[18]

Consequently, a combination of the local preference and practice as well as the ideology that underlay Brahmanical texts came to be enshrined in the colonial judicial records. Such runaway cases in the colonial period were considered to be 'very frequent', next to that of 'rioting and hurt'.[19] I cite here as illustration a 1929 case.[20] Jamila from Meerut, alleged to have been 16 years of age, eloped with Sultan and got married to him. In her testimony to the court, she confirmed her marriage and declared her age to be between seventeen and eighteen. The judge held Sultan guilty by maintaining:

The consent of the girl does not exonerate the seducer. The underlying policy of the Section 366 is (1) to uphold the lawful authority of parents or guardian over their minor wards (2) to throw a ring of protection round the girls themselves and (3) to prevent sexual commerce on the part of persons who corrupt or attempt to corrupt the morals of the minor girls by taking improper advantage of their youth and inexperience.

---

[17] According to the Indian Majority Act, 1875, 18 years was deemed as an age of majority for both men and women, except in matters of marriage, dower, divorce, and adoption. This turned the minor and major categories extremely flexible. For instance, the Child Marriage Restraint Act, 1929, defined the word child for a male under 18 years of age and a girl under 15 years of age. See Desai, *Mulla Principles of Hindu Law*, p. 523.

[18] *Punjab Law Reporter*, 1917, vol. XVIII, *Kalumal vs Jai Karan*, pp. 323–5.

[19] See Baijnath *vs* Emperor, AIR, 1932, Allahabad, 402, cited in Usha Ramanathan, 1999, 'Images 1920–1950: Reasonable Man, Reasonable Woman and Reasonable Expectations', in Anita Dhanda and Archana Parashar (eds), *Engendering Law: Essays in Honour of Lotika Sarkar*, Lucknow: Eastern Book Co., pp. 1–32.

[20] *Criminal Law Journal*, 1930, vol. 31, Allahabad High Court, *Sultan vs the Emperor*, pp. 85–8.

The Allahabad High Court, however, reversed this judgement in view of the complicity of the woman. The judge maintained:

Upon a consideration of certain features of the case the learned judge was morally convinced of the guilt of the accused; and this moral conviction marred his judicial vision to such an extent that he failed to view the evidence in its true perspective.

Both the judgements adopted moral ground for proclaiming the verdict. The moral vision of justice in the lower court constructed the woman as a victim, a weaker sex in need of protection and not as an agent of her free will. The higher court's reversal of this was also on moral grounds and emanated from the same ideological base, except that the lower court placed the onus on the man and the higher court placed it on the woman. Both reflected the judicial premium not merely on the guardianship of women as mentioned earlier but also on moral concepts which were implied and stood breached. These concepts were of chastity, virginity, and premium on marriage.[21] The consent of the woman was used to absolve the implied 'sin' of the man. This consent designated her promiscuity. Such an approach continues to be the guiding ideology in deciding all cases dealing with runaway marriages.

For instance, in the earlier cited 1972 case, Asha Rani (as also all other girls who make runaway marriage) gets projected as a promiscuous and lustful woman who (desiring sexual intercourse) could not even wait to get married. Clearly, the court judgements underline the popular perception rather than deny it. Once such a woman is caught, as one of the judgements noted, she can only escape from 'the stigma attached to her character' or hide her promiscuity and lustfulness, by making allegations of kidnapping, abduction, and rape in order to 'saddle the appellant (man) in this crime'.[22] The fact of her marriage is not even entertained or speculated upon.

The appellant is seen by the judiciary as fulfilling the wishes of a promiscuous woman. In other words, the woman is held responsible for the man's behaviour. He is only seen as someone who succumbs to her wishes. For this, he too must be punished. Clearly, the judicial eye is

[21] The fact that in contemporary times, the judicial accent on these concepts is the same has been well argued by the feminist scholarship. See, for instance, Flavia Agnes, 1992, 'Protecting Women against Violence? Review of a Decade of Legislation, 1980–89', *Economic and Political Weekly*, vol. XXVII, no. 17, 25 April, pp. WS19–33.

[22] *Criminal Law Journal*, vol. 100, pp. 3044–50.

gendered. It sees a woman's sexuality in one way and a man's sexuality in another way. Sex for an unmarried woman is severely condemned but for an unmarried man, it is not a matter to comment upon. At best, he is seen as a 'victim' of woman's desire and lust. Such an attitude only naturalizes a man's sexuality and accepts it as a part of his masculinity. This is specially so as men do not suffer either a social stigma or a psychological scar as it is acceptable behaviour given the assumptions about the nature of male sexuality and women's consent for cohabitation. This gendered approach produces, at the judicial level, inequality rather than equality between men and women. It also severely negates consensual sex, for women, which is legally recognized for her if she is above 16 years of age.[23]

The ruling of the lower court in runaway cases, by and large, is for the conviction of the man. For this, they accept readily the minor age status of the girl. Such a reading is in tune with the popular feelings of anger, shame, and dishonour brought about by the runaway cases. The popular desire is to have the man convicted as a possible face-saver for the family in question and to reassert the male guardian's right of ownership of the woman. However, in view of treating these cases, which are essentially runaway, as those of abduction, kidnapping, and rape, the logic of deciding these cases as those of rape takes over. The cases of rape, for a variety of reasons, as a large number of studies indicate, have a notoriously low rate of conviction.[24] Consequently, even in a runaway-turned-'rape' case, the alleged culprit is given, what may be termed (in a rape case), a light sentence. In most cases, the sentence is further reduced on appeal, and sometimes, even reversed by the High Court.[25]

---

[23] See Nivedita Menon, 2000, 'Embodying the Self: Feminism, Sexual Violence and the Law', in Partha Chatterjee and Pradeep Jeganathan (eds), *Subaltern Studies XI, Community, Gender and Violence*, New Delhi: Permanent Black, pp. 66–105.

[24] See, for example, Agnes, 'Protecting Women against Violence?', pp. WS19–33; Baxi, 'Rape, Retribution, State', pp. 1196–200; Veena Das, 1996, 'Sexual Violence, Discursive Formations and the State', *Economic and Political Weekly*, vol. XXXI, nos 35, 36, and 37, pp. 2411–23; Vasudha Dhagamwar, 1992, *Law, Power and Justice: The Protection of Personal Rights in the Indian Penal Code*, New Delhi: Sage, pp. 237–87.

[25] The only way out in tackling rape cases to the satisfaction of the raped woman, as argued by the feminists, is to take cognizance of the body integrity of the woman, breached by the rapist. However, in the runaway cases treated

In essence, the judgements reflect a contradictory verdict. On the one hand, it puts the onus of the runaway cases entirely on women for consenting, even enticing the man, and on the other, it still punishes the man. This punishment inflicted upon the man despite a woman's consent reiterates the ideology of guardianship of women. Explaining this, Usha Ramanathan argues that, as a father or guardian, the man has the right to possess and control a woman.[26] Any man who challenges or neutralizes this right must be punished. The state takes upon itself to punish the offender on behalf of the guardian to reassert the criminality of anyone else taking over the control/possession of the woman. This turns a woman into a possession and the man into a criminal. At this juncture both are divested of their individual rights; human relationships are turned into material relations. Significantly, even mutuality is not recognized; for mutuality suggests consensual sex, for which, as indicated earlier, legal provision exists. Moreover, such a recognition may well suggest something more 'honourable'.

CLAIMS OF MARRIAGE: PRESUMPTION OF THE COURT
The legal cases stress the criminalization of a woman's sexuality outside of marriage. Her active sexuality, under open scrutiny to the public at the time of trial, is used by the judges to accept her as an adult, on one hand, who consents to sexual intercourse, and to morally and ethically condemn her for that consent, on the other. Disregarding her wishes, the modern judiciary sees a runaway woman as transgressing traditional norms and morally reprehensible. Their gender-biased cultural attitudes influence their judgements in passing comments upon the behaviour of a woman which is in resonance with the dominant opinion of the community and society at large. In *Kala Singh vs State of Punjab*, 1997,[27] the case put across by the prosecution was as follows.

Kala Singh had been engaged to Rajwant Kaur, the prosecutrix, one-and-a-half years before the occurrence of the case in March 1990.

---

as rape cases, in which consent is established and judicially accepted, the body integrity of the woman doesn't and should not matter. What she does with her body is her own concern. Whether she is habituated to sex or not should not be a matter of concern or comment by the judiciary. In such cases, mutuality or consensual sex should be accepted by the court as legally such a provision exists.

[26] Ramanathan, 'Images 1920–1950', p. 50.

[27] *Criminal Law Journal*, 1997, vol. 103, part 11, *Kala Singh vs State of Punjab*, pp. 1313–18.

For certain reasons, the engagement was called off and Rajwant Kaur was subsequently engaged to another man by her parents. Kala Singh retaliated by kidnapping the girl forcibly while she was with her brother and raping her. The police, acting on Rajwant Kaur's brother's report of this, arrested Kala Singh and started court proceedings on charges of abduction, kidnapping, and rape. The lower court held Kala Singh (and his associates) to be guilty under Sections 452 and 366 of IPC and inflicted rigorous imprisonment of five years plus a fine of Rs 3,000. Kala Singh was, however, acquitted of the charge of rape, as the prosecutrix, though underage, was held to be a consenting party.

The case of the defendant/appellant, Kala Singh, was that he had been framed by the prosecutrix's brother. According to him, although his engagement had been terminated by Rajwant Kaur's parents, the girl had wanted this association to continue and had indeed got married to him. Kala Singh produced records relating to the registration of his marriage with Rajwant Kaur. The appellants significantly focused on the anomalous fact relating to the court's behaviour. They maintained that since they had been 'acquitted of the charges under Section 376 of Indian Penal Code with a finding that the testimony of the prosecutrix was not credible or acceptable, her testimony regarding the alleged offence of criminal trespass and kidnapping ought not to have been accepted.'

In this regard, the High Court noted that since the state had not appealed against the acquittal of the accused of the offence of rape, the acquittal had become final. The only matter to be decided was that of criminal trespass and kidnapping of the accused. This decision had been taken by the lower court after accepting the minor age status of the girl. The High Court rejected this and set aside the conviction. The observations made by the High Court judge are revealing of their attitude and legal ambiguity existing in matters such as these. The judgement maintained:

It may be repeated that the trial court while acquitting the appellant for the offence under Section 376 of the Indian Penal Code had given sound reasons to disbelieve the prosecutrix of her allegations that the appellant had committed sexual intercourse with her against her consent. This fact is further clear from her medical examination report to the effect that her vagina admitted two fingers easily. In other words the prosecutrix who was admittedly unmarried on the day of the occurrence was habituated to sexual intercourse. It may be clarified that there was no fresh vaginal tear or external mark of injury on the private parts or around the same of the prosecutrix nor was there any bleeding from her vagina. These facts are important to ascertain as to the evidence of the prosecutrix who said at the time that she was not married to any person. Once she had been discredited and disbelieved on this major aspect of the case, it is difficult to believe her version regarding the allegations of criminal trespass and kidnapping by the appellant.

The judge also disbelieved the prosecutrix's testimony regarding her confinement in a *kotha* (roof) or in a deserted place, or the fact that she was kept in a moving van by the appellant. This was discounted on the bases of photographs supplied by the defendant/appellant which showed the prosecutrix, Rajwant Kaur, in a house inhabited by a family consisting of children and at least 'one prominent female'. These photographs, in the opinion of the judges, belied the use of force. Consequently, the High Court decided in favour of the appellant and set him free from custody.

It is clear from this account that the judges acknowledge the fabricated nature of such cases. In most cases, the fabrication is acknowledged by the judges by maintaining: 'The facts are clearly pre-designed and have been worked out only to saddle the appellant in this crime.'[28] They also accepted that lies were 'habitually fed to the court'. Yet, in all this, the proof of Rajwant Kaur's marriage is not commented upon. Her testimony regarding her kidnapping and rape was disbelieved, yet her denial of marriage was believed. The fact that Rajwant Kaur was married to Kala Singh and habituated to sexual intercourse was ignored. Instead her unmarried status, as claimed by her, or rather forced to be claimed by her, was believed. In this, her underage status came handy in determining her marriage status. She was not given the benefit of doubt regarding her age (as in other cases cited earlier), which may have legalized the marriage.

Ironically, if her parents had agreed to this marriage, even her underage status would not have mattered and her sexuality would have been accepted as natural and legitimate, well within the fold of marriage. The illegality of the marriage emanated out of the fact that Rajwant Kaur's parents did not accept this marriage and consequently, neither did the state. Her own autonomy over her body was never recognized. If the marriage status of a woman in keeping with her autonomy over her own body is recognized, then some uniformity can be achieved in relation to her age of consent which is put at sixteen, and the runaway cases would assume an entirely different angle.

[28] *Criminal Law Journal*, vol. 100, pp. 3044–50.

In yet another case, *Om Prakash vs State of Haryana*,[29] Sumitra ran away with her lover in May 1985, carrying Rs 4,000 and some ornaments of gold, weighing about 30 grams. Her father traced her after eleven days with the help of the police. The judge at the Hissar Session Court agreed with her father's contention that she was 14 years of age and inflicted ten years of imprisonment and a fine of Rs 200 on the accused. In 1988, this sentence was revoked by the High Court on an appeal on the basis that the girl was above 18 years of age and was a willing party to the whole affair. Apart from her 'character' and sexual behaviour in which she was medically acknowledged to be habituated to sexual intercourse, it was held that it was a case of runaway affair as she had even carried money and ornaments with her. The fact that the girl had runaway with money and ornaments with the intent to get married and/or had indeed got married was not subjected to any discussion.

In a 1991 case of *Hira Lal vs State of Haryana*,[30] Bhagwanti of village Chautala ran away with Hira Lal who lived as a tenant of her uncle. They were caught and brought back by the police and in the case that followed in Sirsa, Hira Lal was given four years of imprisonment and a fine of Rs 500. Hira Lal was acquitted in an appeal to the High Court in 1994. The High Court agreed with the lower court that the girl was complicit in the whole affair and was sexually active as well. As she was held to be above 18 years of age, the accused could not be held responsible for charges of abduction and rape. The question of marriage was not raised as the girl denied it.

It may be noted here that the runaway couples are not known to take recourse to the state-sponsored civil marriage. More often than not, the runaway couples opt for an Arya Samaj marriage ceremony. Although legal, this ceremony is not necessarily held at par with the civil registration of marriage. The former marriage is a quick affair, with hardly any questions asked of the couple. The latter, with its mandatory notice period of one month prior to the marriage, along with proof of age and residence, is taken to have checked the antecedents of the couple, before declaring them man and wife. These precautions act as buffers against the illegality of marriage. Yet, these also provide a valid reason

---

[29] *Criminal Law Journal*, 1988, vol. 94, *Om Prakash vs State of Haryana*, Punjab and Haryana High Court, pp. 1606–9.

[30] *Criminal Law Journal*, 1994, vol. 100, part 2, *Hira Lal vs State of Haryana*, pp. 2471–3.

to couples for not opting for the state-provided civil marriage. The in-built obstacles instituted by the state strength the man-made obstacles, emanating out of deep prejudices regarding such marriages, and makes the possible discovery of the runaway couple very real.[31] In such cases, the state and its functionaries emerge as obstructing the marriage rather than facilitating it.

Whatever the married status of the runaway couple, in almost all the court cases cited earlier, the question of their marriage is usually not raised, and if raised, it is hardly discussed. Evidence suggests that even when marriage is discussed, it is disposed of quickly and the woman's testimony disclaiming marriage is accepted readily, although she herself is dubbed as a liar who cannot be relied upon. The presumption of the court is against the marriage rather than in favour of it. In the three to four years that it takes a case to proceed from lower to the higher court level, the girl is either married off or physically eliminated. In case of her arranged marriage, this may well be her second mar-riage and, in fact, an illegal one. In other words, by the time the cases reach the High Court level, the girl is no longer available to be claimed as a bride.

In many cases, claims are not even made by defendant for a variety of reasons. One is the reservations of boy's family and his community regarding inter-caste marriages born out of their firm adherence to the concept of caste endogamy. To claim the runaway girl of another caste as the bride means not only an open violation of a traditionally honoured concept but it is also asking for trouble. As one of my infor-mants commented: 'It is like saying *aa bail mujhe maar* (come beat me up)'. Two, so concerned is the boy's family in getting him free that the question of claiming his bride is considered irrelevant and, at best, not broached. According to the criminal lawyers, such a claim is next to impossible to institute, specially in cases where the marriage is hypoga-mous, where the girl belongs to a higher caste group and the boy to a lower one. Indeed, not many lawyers are willing to accept the case of such a boy. Those who do, are well known to 'respect the sensibilities' of the dominant caste group. Many times, they are in regular touch with the opposing party belonging to the dominant caste group and very often, on their payrolls. This makes them less than enthusiastic in presenting their defence even to the point of neglecting the rights and

[31] For details, see Perveez Mody, 2002, 'Love and the Law', *Modern Asian Studies*, vol. 36, no. 1, February, pp. 223–56.

interests of the lower caste groups. In effect, it means that the accused languishes in jail, when he could be out on bail.

According to a criminal lawyer in Rohtak, many cases are indeed hypogamous and often the boy belongs to a Dalit community. The general impression gathered from my fieldwork was that the assertion of rights by groups suffering customary exclusion and disabilities meet with little encouragement, if not active hostility, at the hands of local officials, including lower level judiciary, who share the viewpoint of the higher caste groups. This factor helps explain partially the verdicts of the lower courts in runaway cases, which inflict heavy sentences upon the male—a sentence which is salutary and is inflicted to set an example. At the High Court level, where such bias is not so noticeable, and the appeal is contested on written testimony rather than oral, such sentence stands either diluted or done away with.

LEGAL AMBIGUITIES: CONFIRMATION AND DEPARTURE

It is true that in all these runaway cases, the girl is pressurized by her family members into denying marriage and condemning the concerned man of kidnapping, abduction, and rape. But not all of them succumb to it. There are a few rare cases in which the woman stands up for herself. If she does this, what is the outcome? In this connection, I shall take up two cases, one from Gohana and the other from Bhatinda, to give two different kinds of verdicts and the ambiguities inherent in legal system in dealing with such cases.

In the case of village Guddha of Gohana, a girl from Kashyap (Jhimmar) caste ran away to Goa in July 2000 with a Balmiki caste boy and got married.[32] They were caught by the girl's family and brought back. The Jhimmar panchayat met in this connection and instructed the father of the girl to get her married off elsewhere and not to take recourse to law. In the meanwhile, the girl's husband moved the court to take custody of his wife alleging that his wife had been forcibly taken by her father. In the case that followed in September 2000, the girl claimed that she was of age and had got married of her own volition, and wished to go back to her husband. The father put forward a counter-claim stating that his daughter was underage and the marriage was not legal. The case hinged on determining the girl's age. The girl was unable to produce any evidence as a proof of her age. The court chose to believe

[32] *Dainik Jagran*, 2000, 15 September, Gurgaon edition, pp. 1, 13; *Dainik Tribune*, 2000, 16 September, Delhi edition, p. 4.

the father. The girl was sent off to *nari niketan* (rehabilitation centre for women) as she refused to go back to her parents. The boy was sent to jail, awaiting trial for kidnapping, abduction, and rape.

It may be noted that even if the girl in question says that she is married of her own accord, the matter still cannot be settled because the court determines a woman's age out of a multiplicity of possible factors, indicated earlier. These factors remain flexible in most cases. In a situation where there are conflicting claims between a daughter and her father, regarding age, it is the latter's claim which is likely to be accepted, as this case shows.

In the Bhatinda case of October 2000,[33] Sukhjeet Kaur, who ran away and got married to Sunil Kumar of another caste, testified in the court that she had got married of her own accord and that she was an adult. Her father, Harvinder Singh, had moved the court that his minor daughter had been abducted by Sunil Kumar. He also moved the High Court to request for the cancellation of the bail granted to Sunil Kumar. In this case, Justice Nijjar gave what may be hailed as a historic judgement—possibly the first of its kind. He took the father to task and instructed him not to interfere with the married life of his daughter.

The case, I was informed, was solved due to two factors: one, Sukhjeet Kaur was able to furnish evidence regarding her adult age status. It is unclear as to the kind of 'proof' she was able to furnish. The important fact is that the court accepted her contention regarding her age. Second was her insistence and rendering the proof of her marriage, and its acceptance by the court. The legal acceptability of this runaway marriage made this case the first of its kind. The father was chastised by the court for taking his daughter as a 'commodity to be owned', rather than as a person and as an individual. The case made a major departure from the hitherto held ideology of guardianship of a woman and the right of bestowal of her sexuality in marriage.

It has not been possible to know the response to this historic judgement. Not many people are aware of it. It has not got the kind of publicity that it deserved and should have attracted. Those who know about it are reserved about their opinion. Apart from those who mouth politically correct sentiments, by and large, the impression gathered was that such a judgement has left the male guardians insecure. One such guardian opined that it will bring down the age of marriage. According to him, 'the decision offered unlimited freedom to an adult unmarried

---

[33] *Dainik Tribune*, 2000, 20 October, Delhi edition, p. 8.

woman, which is bound to go to her head. She'll be self-willed in matters she knows nothing about, make wrong choices, and inflict untold misery and dishonour upon her family.'

Interestingly, the law can be circumvented in a way to favour the runaway couples. This was brought home to me by an advocate in Rohtak who refused to be named, but gave me an account of the way he handles the runaway cases to help them. He deals with divorce cases as well as the so-called 'love cases', as he terms them himself, and likes to call himself, 'tudwane-judwane ka vakil' (an advocate who unites and separates couples). According to him, such cases come from all over Haryana, Punjab, Rajasthan, and Uttar Pradesh (UP). I give his modus operandi in his own words:

Young boys and girls come to me saying that they wish to get married and their parents will not allow them to do so. They are so wrapped up in each other that they cannot see beyond themselves. The girls often say, 'Uncle, if you pluck a flower from its stem and put it in honey, ghee or even in melted gold, would it survive? No! I can not survive with out him.' Yet others say, 'We are two bodies but one soul. We cannot be separated.' The boy says, 'I shall die without her'. Khub dramebaz hain (they are all very dramatic). It is the girl who is more vocal about her feelings. They are, however, both very innocent, and fearful of consequences. They are aware of the police investigations, and the boy being imprisoned, and its ending up as a criminal case. I take up the case after ascertaining certain facts: one, if they are above age and can furnish proof of it; two, they must not be related to each other in any way and have no got problem, which may customarily prohibit a marriage between them; three, they must not belong to the same village, in keeping with the principle of village exogamy; four, none of the parties should belong to the scheduled caste category. Such an alliance is not accepted at all. Khoon kharaba ho jata hai (ends up in violence). Ignoring any of these conditions is to invite trouble. Most of the runaway cases are inter-caste ones. Age wise, the girl is mostly a marginal case, close to adulthood but not fully adult. If any of these is not satisfactory I do not get into it. Main jhagde ke lapet me na aana chaahta (I do not want to get embroiled in any quarrel). I make short shrift of them as this would be inviting trouble to myself. In such a case I tell them, 'Bhai, yo to kanoon ke khilaf hai, main kuchch nahin ker sakta' (Folks, this is against the law, I can not do anything). I advise them to go back to their respective families. In case the matter is satisfactory from all counts I advise them to first get married in an Arya Samaj mandir or any other place of their liking. Then, I make the girl write a letter, enclosing an affidavit, to the local police officer, the district judge, the chief minister, the governor stating: Main balig hun aur maine apni marzi se shadi ki hai. Ye mujhe bhaga ke nahin laaya hai. Mujhe gharwalon se khatra hai, wo hamain katal ker denge (I am of age and have got married of my own accord, he has not compelled me to run away. I fear from my family, they may eliminate or punish me and my husband). After a couple of days I make her move the session court by declaring that she got married recently, but her husband refuses to stay with her or keep her with him. It is a plea for the restitution of conjugal rights. The police investigates and reaches out to the husband. The judge asks the girl: 'Tu apni marzi se aai hai?' (Have you come of your own accord?). The girl replies: 'haan. Ees ladke ne mujh se shadi ki thi eeb na le jaata, dus-pandrah din me mujhe chchod diya' (Yes, this boy had got married to me but now he refuses to take me back. He has left me after 10–15 days). A reconciliation takes place and the husband wife are together.

This move obviates a legal charge from the girl's family that the boy abducted the girl. In many such cases the girl, under pressure from her family, charges that the boy abducted her. This leads to the imprisonment of the boy and institution of criminal proceedings against him. It also establishes the fact of their marriage, willingness of the girl, and safeguards the boy against any charge of abduction and rape, as is usual in such cases. The parents can do nothing about it as they have no *local standi* to challenge it. The session judge notes that the girl herself had instituted a case for restitution of conjugal rights. The girl also cannot turn around or be compelled to say that she had been abducted. She cannot maintain that she had been pressurized by the boy. This means that the boy cannot be incarcerated. For instance, he can always say: 'All right, I abducted her from the village but there was no pressure on her when she faced the session judge and recorded her testimony.' The whole thing takes less than a month to be set right.

According to this advocate, he is the only one among vast numbers of legal luminaries who is able to successfully intervene in bringing about 'love marriages'.

What is the fate of such marriages? Do they survive or more correctly, do the couples survive? This advocate was not very certain as he had not maintained any links with such couples. In his opinion, the marriages do survive but mostly without the support of their families, who frequently disown them. He was not aware of anyone being killed in such cases. However, physical elimination cannot be ruled out. The other advocates have yet to find a way out of the legal tangle. They only advise registration of marriage, which is challenged by the parents. His fame, he says, is spreading 'fast' by way of word of mouth. According to him, he gets between twenty to fifty cases a year. Regarding the fees, he maintained that he charges according to 'the capacity' of the runaway couple. In this connection, he also observed that both the girl and the boy almost always run away from home with valuables and substantial amount of money. The boy also has friends and other network through which he is in a position to manage more resources. According to him, such 'love marriages' have increased manifold in the last 15–20 years, with 80 per cent of such cases coming from towns and only 20 per cent from the villages.

This observation highlights certain issues. One, the opposition to inter-caste marriages is not only in the villages but also, in a very large measure, in the urban areas. Two, there is also a higher awareness of law and legal matters in urban rather than in rural areas. In other words, the younger generation is not necessarily buying the older generation's claim that 'love marriages' or more explicitly inter-caste marriages are *gair kanooni* (illegal). This is often said to deter the potential cases. These reservations on inter-caste marriages are specially glaring in view of the fact that the state has instituted a scheme to encourage marriages in which one of the partners is a Dalit.[34] A cash reward of Rs 25,000 is reserved for such couples. In reality, the society does not accept such marriages and the couples who are determined to marry are forced to runaway. The state then steps in, not withstanding its own legal and constitutional position. It takes a lead in retrieving the girl and in setting aside her marriage.

RETRIEVED WOMAN: THE AFTERMATH

The fate of the runaway woman, who is either recovered by the family or by the state, is extremely uncertain. Once the judiciary places her in the custody of her guardian she is either married off quickly and quietly or disposed of equally quickly and quietly. In the former case, she is invariably married to someone who would not ordinarily have been entertained as her prospective husband, like a widower, an older man, a man with children, or a handicapped man. She may even have to accept becoming a co-wife. Her pregnancy, if any, is terminated.[35] In all this,

---

[34] The state claims to encourage such marriages by rewarding couples. The total amount of this reward money was increased from Rs 2,00,000 to Rs 3,00,000 in the financial year 2000. In an inter-caste marriage, each girl or boy from the scheduled caste receives Rs 25,000. This amount includes Rs 10,000 in cash and Rs 15,000 in fixed deposit for six years in the joint account of the couple. Two lakh rupees were stated to have been distributed under this scheme in the year 1999. See *Dainik Bhaskar*, 2000, 10 August, Gurgaon edition, p. 7.

[35] In the case of village Kheri in district Bhiwani, the runaway girl was caught, brought back, and remarried to an old man despite her four-month pregnancy, which was aborted. Significantly, the girl was an adult and all appeals to the police and district administration regarding this were ignored. The whereabouts of the boy, belonging to lower caste group, are not known or disclosed. The Jat biradari remains tight-lipped about him. He is rumoured to have been disposed of by them.

there exists a certain tacit consent among her kinsmen and affines, and even within the larger biradari, to observe silence (although not very effectively) about her transgression to enable her father/guardian to perform his duty of getting her married.

Clearly, the attempt at absorbing a runaway girl into traditional biradari network is not easy and often physical elimination of the girl is the only 'honourable' option. In village Barah Khurd, in Jind district, for example, Suman, a 15 year-old girl, ran away in August 2000, to get married to a man of her choice.[36] The father reported to the police, who caught the couple and brought them back. The girl was sent to her parents and the boy taken for questioning. Within ten days, the girl was dead and she was also hastily cremated. The family gave out the version that she died of some ailment. The police when contacted, maintained candidly, 'the girl brought shame and dishonour to her family by running away, so she was eliminated. What can we do about it.' The villagers openly stated, 'She was killed by her father and her two brothers, but no one will testify.'

There are several such cases. In a July 2002 case of village Talao in Jhajjar district, the elopement case of a Jat girl with a Chamar boy ended in tragedy. The younger sister of this girl, who had been helping her in this affair, had also accompanied the couple, as she apprehended violence from the family members. The parents of the girl had refused to even entertain such a hypogamous alliance. The Superintendent of Police, Jhajjar, maintained proudly that he worked 'very hard' on this case, spending a week in Talao and another week in following the trail of the girls. Within two days of being handed back to their parents by the police, both the girls were dead. They allegedly consumed poison. Earlier, the girls were reported to have made a request to the magistrate (a woman in this case) to be sent to nari niketan (remand home) instead to their parents. They clearly feared violence. This was not granted to them. The parents testified that it was a suicide and the police accepted it readily. The police claimed that the girls had threatened suicide even in the police station. The villagers maintained, in confidence, that the girls were killed. A Jat woman in village Talao opined that the girls were told to denounce the boy and testify that they had been 'lured and enticed' by the boy. The girls refused to oblige. 'It was because of this that they had to be killed,' maintained the Jat woman. Indeed, the older girl in her testimony to the magistrate had also stated that she

---

[36] *Dainik Tribune*, 2000, 3 August, Delhi edition, p. 3.

was married to the boy. The boy, charged with CRPc 363, 366, 376, and 120B, for abduction, kidnapping, rape, and criminal conspiracy, continues to remain in jail. Even the bail application was not moved by his advocate, showing his sympathy and complicity with the dominant caste groups, as mentioned earlier.

Not always is the woman or the couple eliminated or compelled to commit suicide. Although difficult to ascertain, in many instances, it may well be a voluntary act, specially when a woman's attempt to marry a man of her choice, or having married him to be accepted as his wife, fails.[37] At other times, the couple unitedly commit suicide even before they attempt to elope, because they already know that their desire for each other will never be allowed to culminate into marriage. The regional dailies are full of such reports. In other words, in many cases, violence erupts, inflicted or self-inflicted, even before the matter comes under the purview of the court. However, in a large number of cases, it is murder plain and simple. There are a few cases in which such a killing has been proudly claimed. In a case in Panipat, the runaway girl was hacked to death by her cousins, after she was restored to them by the police in March 2001.[38] The culprits killed her in front of the entire neighbourhood, but no one came to save her or be a witness to the crime. The culprits are still free.

There are some exceptional cases in which the guilty parties have confessed to committing such a crime, but no conviction has followed. In one of these rare cases where a man admitted to the police about strangling his retrieved daughter with her *duppatta* (long scarf), because she had brought 'dishonour' to the family by running away, could not be convicted.[39] The culprit retracted later on. The court held that a confession to the police was not admissible in the court and the police was unable to produce any independent witness to this crime. The man was set free.

---

[37] The regional dailies (and sometimes, national dailies) carry at least one news item regarding such suicides. For more prominent cases, see *Dainik Bhaskar*, 2001, 1 March, Gurgaon edition, p. 2; 5 November, p. 9; 28 November, p. 4; 22 December, p. 2; *Dainik Bhaskar*, 2001, 5 January, Gurgaon edition; *Dainik Jagran*, 2000, 9 September, Gurgaon edition, p. 4; 6 November, pp. 4, 13; 28 November, p. 4; *Dainik Jagran*, 2001, 31 January, Gurgaon edition, p. 4; 18 February, p. 3; *Times of India*, 2001, 31 January, p. 4.

[38] *Punjab Kesari*, 2001, 8 March, Chandigarh edition, p. 9.

[39] *Dainik Jagran*, 2001, 1 March, Gurgaon edition, p. 5.

The biradari is in the full knowledge of the violent end of the run-away woman, but observes silence. The silence signifies acceptance of violence as a just punishment for her transgression. In fact, the infliction of violence is considered the only 'honourable' course—more honour-able than her forced and severely compromised marriage or remarriage in an inevitably inferior household. It may be noted that there is great prestige attached to a status-oriented upward marital move and inferi-ority in a downward alliance which downgrades the standing and status of a family.

STATE INTERVENTION: LEGITIMIZING AND CRIMINALIZING

In this game of maintaining 'honour', where does the state fit in? After all, the public pronouncements of the state on the unmarried runaway woman's character, and her self-indulgence in sexual activity, turns her akin to a prostitute whose active illicit sexuality is in need of control. Such pronouncements, implicit and explicit, made by the judiciary, tarnish the honour of the family rather than redeem it. The family/biradari stands dishonoured. The question then arises as to why people take recourse to state apparatus and turn what is essentially private into public, and inflict public humiliation and dishonour upon themselves? An answer to this lies in the hierarchy of honour, which is essentially male honour, and what may be considered less honourable and what may be considered more honourable. The more honourable course, also, has implicit in it the concept of masculinity upheld by the male populace. For example, for men retrieving a female is more honourable than allowing a male belonging to a traditionally prohibited category of caste/community or just another community, higher or equal, to sexually appropriate her and claim her as his wife. Social taunts regarding this are a life-long affair; taunts of, '*Tu ke bolle sai, teri beti ne aisa kiya*' (what can you say, your daughter did this and this) and '*Woh to bhaj gaee, tu ke us ko laa paaya. Eeb to sharm ker*' (she ran away and you were not even able to bring her back. At least be ashamed of yourself now). The runaway woman, specially an untracked one, is considered to have disgraced the family or '*munh ko kalakh laga gaee*'.

In such cases, the allegations of the complicity of the guardian in making her run away are also made. It is maintained that so-and-so did not have the money or the *niyat* (inclination) to spend on his daughter's wedding. He, therefore, facilitated her running away. In the given dowry economy of Haryana, where giving and receiving of huge dowries and ostentatious weddings is considered important for status formation, this allegation has a tendency to stick. The crippling burden of dowry, leaving huge indebtedness for the families concerned, is compounded by the tight economic situation in Haryana with its huge unemployment problem and overburdening of agricultural sector, visible fragmentation of landholdings, and a downward price curve of agricultural produce in relation to other consumer items and declining profits in agrarian sector. Such a girl certainly increases the pecuniary burden of her family owing to the difficulty of getting her married.

Experiencing social pressure from all sides, people take recourse to state apparatus when they are unable to trace the woman themselves or know that they will not be able to trace her and the fact that her running away has already become a common knowledge. Here, the state is evoked to extend what may be termed as its familial functions of protection, support, and control. At a time when families cannot or are not in a position to exercise it, the state steps in to assume that role and restore the woman back to the family.[40] Clearly, it is not only in periods of collective violence such as war, insurgency, and widespread communal riots, as argued by Veena Das, that the state takes over the regulation of female sexuality and reproductive functions.[41] The state assumes this role even in ordinary times, as innumerable cases of runaway women show.

Taking recourse to court is, therefore, a kind of damage control to honour. The loss of face in the community is greater if the runaway woman is not traceable than when she is found and brought back and restored to her family. The family male members take recourse to lesser of the two evils, that is, recovering the girl through the state agency, or being called 'na mard' (emasculated). Once restored, her subsequent marriage or remarriage, however 'unworthy', still

---

[40] After the Partition, the state took upon itself to retrieve its abducted and kidnapped women from Pakistan. Even in their case, they were not allowed to exercise their right of choice. See Urvashi Butalia, 1998, *The Other Side of Silence: Voices from the Partition of India*, New Delhi: Penguin; Ritu Menon and Kamala Bhasin, 1998, *Borders and Boundaries: Women in India's Partition*, New Delhi: Kali for Women.

[41] Veena Das, 1995, 'National Honour and Practical Kinship: Of Unwanted Women and Children', in Veena Das (ed.), *Critical Events: An Anthropological Perspective on Contemporary India*, New Delhi: Oxford University Press, pp. 53–83.

underlines an important right—the right of the male guardian to give her in marriage and also, the principle of caste endogamy.

The court therefore emerges as regulating a woman's sexuality in accordance with the customary rules of alliance. This is best elaborated in Veena Das's work on sexual violence around rape cases. She argues:

a discourse on rape which places itself essentially on the intersection of the discourse of sexuality and the discourse on alliance, and which provides the essential function of protecting the system of alliance rather than protecting the body integrity of women, then the law can only function as long as normal classification of marriageable women; and of men who recognize themselves as partners in alliance versus those for whom such recognition is withheld since they are not likely partners in alliance, is in place.[42]

Applying this analysis to the runaway cases, it means that (just as in rape cases) the court moves beyond its concern with ideological and moral issues to regulate woman's sexuality in accordance with customary rules of alliance. A woman who has run away and is sexually experienced can hardly be integrated into the system of alliance based upon virgin girls by being gifted in marriage to 'respectable and acceptable families'. To follow this logic, it can be maintained that women who make runaway marriages violate the codes through which, to use Veena Das's phrase, 'the matrimonial dialogue of men is conducted'. This matrimonial dialogue is important for claims and formation of patriarchal status. A woman cannot be allowed to breach the rights of the patriarchal family. Such a woman deserves no sympathy and must be punished. Her self-made marriage has to be necessarily denied.

The state protection, therefore, means curtailing the right of such a woman with complete legitimacy, bring to close her illicit sexuality, and pave the way for legitimizing it within the cultural/caste codes of the family. The state, despite knowing the desire of the woman, acts blatantly against the wishes of the woman concerned. Rights of women are totally negated, which goes against the concept of equity and justice. In other words, the court passively accepts as also actively promotes the regulation of a woman's sexuality rather than challenge it in accordance with her legal rights, thereby reiterating that the male guardian has the right to settle and give her in marriage to a partner of his choice.

In such matters, the court acts and is used by patriarchal forces as a primary legitimating institution of popular cultural practices. Legal intervention, therefore, not only delegitimizes such individual attempts

---

[42] Das, 'Sexual violence, Discursive Formations and the State', pp. 2411–22.

at breaking out of the system of alliances, it also criminalizes all such attempts. Ideologically, both the state and the family are one in depriving a woman of her sexual agency. By exercising a control over her sexuality outside the dictates of the family, the state shows that such a woman is a threat and her sexuality illicit.

CONCLUSION: IDEOLOGICAL CONVERGENCE

In the coming together of the two opposing and mutually contradictory principles like tradition and modernity, signified by the family/caste/community on the one hand, and the state apparatus on the other, it is the former which is underlined. The patriarchal norms of society influence the state agencies: the police which is very dextrous in retrieving the girl, sabotaging her marriage, and later, in pleading helplessness in saving her life; and the judicial decisions which are a reiteration of caste/community and kinship codes rather than their negation on the basis of modern concepts such as individual rights and equity. The judges deliver a moral judgment rather than a legal one. These judgements reveal certain contradictions and tensions in which the female body emerges as a contested site. They also reveal a great deal about the flexibility or restrictions with which judicial standards of adulthood for a woman are evaluated and imposed. The contradictions between the official adult age and a woman's resultant rights could hardly make sense with the judicial insistence upon her underage status. Her adulthood emerges related more to her 'legally married' status rather than her age. The gendered judicial eye sees women's sexuality in one way and man's sexuality in another way. The former is condemned and the latter is naturalized, not even commented upon. Mutuality and consensual sex is denied outside of 'legal marriage'. This infringement of her rights over her body constructs an identity of a runaway girl for which she has to pay a heavy price—an identity of a woman habituated to sex, in effect, a prostitute. In marking the body of such a woman, the state agencies legitimize a new stereotype of a woman who has brought shame and dishonour upon her family, community, and society. The state officially confirms the popular prejudice against such women. The incorporation of such a woman in the society then becomes difficult, if not impossible. The elimination of such a body remains the only 'honourable' way out. This is a frequent recourse taken by the aggrieved 'dishonoured' family members and accepted by the community at large as well as the state agencies. Taking such a step evokes only relief all around.

In this ideological convergence of the state and the family, the woman alone stands as the discordant voice. Concepts such as 'purity' and 'honour' conflict with the life-world of women, their desires, and their priorities. In running away, a woman not only breaches and damages this 'male honour' but also underlines the value she herself places on such a concept. These concepts are given a subordinate position and value as compared to her fulfilment of marital and sexual desires and preferences. For this highly individualistic re-evaluation and the agency shown, she gets punished or silenced forever.

Yet, all is not lost. Although negated in practice, the law exists, over-riding all the traditions and customs; and evidence suggests that it can be handled in a way to give out a different verdict which is more in keeping with its letter and spirit. Also, the recent success of a case suggests the possibility of a change. It also suggests that the existence of such laws may indeed be acting as a deterrent in certain cases of runaway marriages in which the adulthood of the girl is unambiguous. However, the social acceptance of such marriages in rural areas remains uncertain. The urban areas do indicate the creeping in of a different sensibility, values, and concerns—a topic which needs a separate treatment. What is certain is that in cases where judiciary is true to the dictates of its law, the extra-judicial sphere gets activated.

11

Caste Panchayats and the Policing of Marriage in Haryana

*Enforcing Kinship and Territorial Exogamy**

In a caste group in the north Indian society, the principles of hierarchy and equality are articulated in complex ways. For example, all Jat *gotra* or *got*, as it is known in rural north India, are considered equal. Got is an exogamous patrilineal clan whose members are thought to share patrilineal descent from a common ancestor, and not from a single mythological sage as understood by the Brahmanical use of the term gotra. Yet, there is a social hierarchy within the caste, and especially among different Got within a village, which involves notions of dominant and subordinate Got. Often, there is considerable disagreement concerning the rank order. The changes occurring in ideas about rank and equality, along with the increasing differentiation of status, power, and wealth developing within each caste are contributing to a re-evaluation of the relative status of different clans and the collapse of the earlier relatively coherent, internally consistent ideology within the caste group. The attempt to translate the theoretical and ideological equality into social structural equality within a caste has evoked both a challenge—cultural, social, and political—as well as a fierce resistance.

* This chapter was originally published in 2004, *Contributions to Indian Sociology*, 38 (1 & 2): 1–42.

Difference and hierarchy are the two most widely acknowledged and characteristic features of the caste system.[1] To maintain these characteristics, the principle of strict caste endogamy has to be maintained. Inter-caste marriages lead to a blurring of the differences between different caste groups and disturb the recognized caste hierarchies. Anyone venturing to transgress this law is out-casted or expelled from the membership of the caste group. On the other hand, attempts at strict enforcement of ban on marriages between certain Got *within the same caste group* can be seen as attempts at enforcing a hierarchical and ranked order, effectively suggesting a reproduction of the caste system within a caste group, except that ritual hierarchy criterion like inter-dining are not entailed. In cases of such marriages, the hierarchical differences between Got get manifested as status rivalry, leading to social boycott and often expulsion of the transgressor, their families, and even an entire group from the caste. All this is done under the traditional ideology of *bhaichara* (brotherhood) that disparages competitiveness and contest within a caste group in order to maintain its *izzat* (honour) and *aika* (unity and solidarity). The collective strength of the caste panchayat (council) is used to socially control deviant caste members so that the cohesiveness of the caste group is maintained. Paradoxically, this blatant legitimization of inequality within a caste group leads to its further split and fragmentation, as well as its solidarity in different social contexts and relationships.

This essay looks at the phenomenon of the bitterly contested marriages in Haryana and analyses the issues thrown up by such marriages. Based on recent case studies, it examines the social factors operating behind the intervention of the caste panchayat and the success and limitation of this intervention. It reflects upon the working of the caste panchayat, which emerges as a collective body, wholly patriarchal, using its united power for repressive ends rather than egalitarian or democratic ones. It seeks to understand how and why, despite the post-colonial structural changes in law and polity, the caste panchayat continues to wield dictatorial power as an extra-judicial body, and how

---

[1] For a detailed exposition of caste and various opinions and arguments of eminent sociologists, see Dipanker Gupta (ed.), 1991, *Social Stratification*, New Delhi: Oxford University Press; and Dipanker Gupta, 2000, *Interrogating Caste: Understanding Hierarchy and Difference in Indian Society*, New Delhi: Penguin Books, pp. 1–85.

it is able to use social problems, specially those pertaining to questions of marriage, for legitimization of its authority, which has been severely eroded over the years. It tries to determine the role of the state agencies in abetting this traditional authority and in legitimizing the illegitimate, even while eroding the moral authority of the panchayat. The issue of contentious marriages reflects the degree of internal strife, conflict, and internal cleavage in contemporary rural society, highlighting the way in which a combination of forces are using traditional tools for traditional as well as modern political purposes.

CUSTOMARY RULES AND CASTE PANCHAYAT

The customary rules regulating marriages in Haryana stand diametrically opposed to the law of the land. Briefly speaking, under the Hindu Marriage Act (1955), except for certain prohibited degree of relationship, the legal restrictions on marriage are almost non-existent.[2] This implies that under the law, both *sagotra* (kin in the patrilineal line of descent whose members claim descent from the same gotra ancestor) and inter-caste marriages are permitted.[3] Yet, customarily, there are a variety of rules and practices and degrees of prohibited relationships observed in respect to marriage in different regions of India. This is specially marked in north/south divide.[4] Customary marriage rules in

---

[2] Certain persons, however, could not marry under this act: those related as *sapinda* (shared body relationship), unless the custom or usage governing them permitted marriage; those with a living spouse or those of unsound mind, suffering from mental disorder and incapable of giving consent; and those subject to recurrent attacks of insanity and epilepsy. See Section 5 of the Hindu Marriage Act, Sunderlal T. Desai, 1966, *Mulla Principles of Hindu Law*, Bombay: N.M. Tripathi Pvt. Ltd., pp. 599–751. The age limit of 15 years for the girl and 18 years for the boy sanctioned under this act was raised to 18 years and 21years, respectively, by the Child Restraint (Amendment) Act 2 of 1978.

[3] In 1946, The Hindu Marriages Disabilities Removal Act was passed, which permitted sagotra marriages between two Hindus not withstanding any text, rule, or interpretation of the Hindu law or any customary usage. This was followed by The Hindu Marriage Validity Act, 1949, which validated the inter-caste marriages and by The Hindu Marriage Act (no. XXXV of 1955), a far more comprehensive act, which incorporated both these acts and offered more freedom in marriage, separation, and divorce. For details of these acts, see S.V. Gupte, 1982, *Hindu Law*, Nagpur: All India Reporter, pp. 583–9, 635–69.

[4] For these regional diversities and their accommodation and articulation in the politico-legal regime of post-independent India, see Patricia Uberoi,

most parts of north India uphold caste endogamy and adopt the rule of gotra or Got exogamy. Most caste groups, upper or lower, follow three or four Got exogamy.[5] A person is not permitted to marry into his or her own Got, nor with the mother's, nor with the father's mother's, and nor usually with the mother's mother's. The last bar is, however, not universal and the restriction is apparently declining. In effect, the Got rules prohibit marriage with the first cousins of either the parallel or the cross variety. In certain instances (elaborated later), the principle of Got exogamy is enlarged by clustering several other Gots represented in the same village into an exogamous bloc. Marriage between these Gots is prohibited or restricted.

In extension of the principle of 'kinship exogamy', there is a rule of territorial exogamy. Most caste groups such as the Jats expressly forbid marriage within the same village, and every village which shares a border with the natal village, or in which other clans of one's village are well represented. The combined effect of these rules of exogamy is that, apart from the three or four Got exogamy mentioned earlier, a large number of Gots have to be kept outside the purview of marriage. The inhabitants of a particular village cannot inter-marry in a large number of villages, especially adjacent villages or those that fall in the *khap* area (the area held or controlled by a clan). In all these villages, the traditions and customs of the dominant Got are followed by all Gots. If the dominant Got observes the tradition of avoiding certain Gots for purposes of marriage, all other Gots in these villages will also follow this avoidance pattern. The inclusion of village exogamy (with its notions of locality being equivalent to consanguinity) observed by virtually all caste groups, high or low, and the existence of a large exogamous Got bloc, introduces considerable complexity to the marriage prohibitions. (However, parts of Haryana, namely, in Sirsa district which shares its boundaries with Rajasthan, as well as Fatehbad, which was a part of Sirsa district till 1997–8, there is no tradition of village exogamy as exists elsewhere in

2002, 'Kinship Varieties and Political Expediency: Legislating the Family in Post-independence India', International Symposium 19, International Research Centre for Japanese Studies, Koyoto, Japan, pp. 147–76.

[5] Gathered from field interviews. For the same norms in other parts of northern India, see Oscar Lewis, 1958, *Village Life in Northern India: Studies in a Delhi Village*, New York: Vintage Books, pp. 160–1; and M.S. Pradhan, 1966, *The Political System of the Jats of Northern India*, London: Oxford University Press, pp. 89–91.

Haryana. Fieldwork done in three villages of these districts—Bhodiya Khera, Khariya, and Chautala—shows this abundantly.[6])

Culturally translated, the principle of village exogamy means that all men and women of the same clan, the same localized clan, and the same village are bound by the morality of brother–sister and, therefore, that both sex and marriage[7] are prohibited between members of any of these units.[8] This extends to the khap area involving more than one village and more than one Got. Significantly, terms like *bhai* (brother) and

[6] This region has a different tradition, which dates back to the time of village settlements when a large number of people from neighbouring regions migrated to settle down in this part of Haryana. Sirsa, for instance, came to be termed in the colonial period as the 'meeting place where the Bangru Jats from the Bikaner region, the Sikh Jats from the Malwa and the Muslim Jats from the Satluj valley, meet the Jats of Hissar.' See Denzil Ibbetson, 1981 (original 1916), *Punjab Castes: Races, Castes and the Tribes of the People of Punjab*, New Delhi: Cosmo Publications, p. 126. The large-scale migration meant the existence of twenty-four to thirty Gots in a single village. This made it impossible to follow a tradition of village exogamy in marriage alliances. Moreover, these families had all migrated along with their *rishtedars* (families related through marriage). Since the villages included both the affines as well as consanguines, the tradition which allowed marriage alliances within the village or in the neighbourhood was consolidated. The second major migration to this area took place in the aftermath of the Partition (1947). The refugee population who settled down in this region also followed a tradition of making caste endogamous marriages within the village. The nature of the settlement patterns of these villages also meant the absence, in this region, of a khap panchayat, tracing its origins to a common ancestor. This provided another important reason for following a different tradition. This absence meant that neither a caste panchayat could be as powerful as in the rest of Haryana nor could there be an imposition of its dictates. I thank Dr D.R. Chaudhary for a discussion on this aspect.

[7] Athough clandestine sexual relations not infrequently occur between classificatory or village brothers and sisters, any social approval of them in the form of marriage is considered an approval of incest and therefore, violently resisted. The semi-secret liaisons tend to be overlooked, as they require no realignment of social relations; as marriage is forbidden, the relationship is also necessarily of limited duration. Marriage, on the other hand, affects the alignment of relationship between groups; it has to be publicly validated by overt transaction and it provides a precedent for similar arrangements in the future.

[8] Paul Hershman, 1981, *Punjabi Kinship and Marriage*, Delhi: Hindustan Publishing Corporation, pp. 133–4.

bahen (sister) in villages are even used for persons who are not related to each other. Transcending ties of biological kinship, they embrace all males or females of the village of one's own generation, not withstanding caste affiliations. One of the important connotations of the term bhai is that a bahen's care and protection are entrusted to him. He is to safeguard her honour and not sully it. These prohibitions create the bhaichara which establishes equality between all and denies all hierarchy. This is the idealized *biradari* (community)—both that of the village and the caste—which has full aika. Clearly, the most hallowed cultural concepts like aika, izzat, biradari, and bhaichara are contingent upon maintaining the traditional marriage prohibitions.

It is a breach in these prohibitions that provokes the biradari to use the traditional tools available to them in the form of caste or village panchayats to stem such attempts. The term biradari is variously defined according to usage. McKim Marriott, for instance, notes that 'the term *biradari* refers not to just one concrete structural unit at the village level but rather to patrilineal connection, real, putative or fictional, at any level of segmentation.'[9] Although usually it is the agnatic kin who form the biradari, in some instances, it may include cognates as well.[10] In the context of a caste group, a biradari is a social group made up of males who believe they are descended from a common male ancestor, which makes them equal and brothers. But used in the context of the village, biradari refers to the entire village, overriding differences of caste, class, and creed. Territorially, this may extend from a single village to a group of villages.

Customarily, the biradari uses the traditional panchayat[11] or rather, one of a series of traditional panchayats to settle a variety of disputes regarding caste and inter-caste matters, transgressions, questions of property rights, inheritance, and disputes which threaten the peace of

[9] McKim Marriott, 1962, 'Communication: Rejoinder to Rhoda Metraux', *Journal of Asian* Studies, vol. 21, no. 2, p. 265.

[10] Veena Das, 1976, 'Masks and Faces: An Essay in Punjabi kinship', *Contributions to Indian Sociology* (NC), vol. 10, no. 1, pp. 1–30.

[11] I am using the term 'traditional' panchayat to distinguish it from the statutory panchayat established in the post-independence India. This usage in no way means that this pre-colonial and colonial body was in any way a non-changing, static institution. Like the caste, traditional panchayat has also undergone changes over time. .

the village or the immediate region.[12] Questions of marriage and sexual affairs form a significant proportion of such disputes, and it is in this sphere that the panchayat frequently intervenes to impose 'justice' according to its own definition. Although very little is known about the working of traditional panchayats in contemporary times,[13] they remain an active force in rural north India.[14] In cases of contentious marriages, it is the caste panchayat of the biradari concerned that is called upon to settle matters.

Certain recent cases in Haryana show the frequent use of the caste panchayat, which has no legitimacy in law, attempting to change relationships and impose one of their own liking, subsuming the individual/family will to that of the village/collective, and prioritizing the village and biradari's izzat over that of individuals. To illustrate, I shall present an in-depth study of a case that occurred in village Jondhi of district Jhajjar. This study is based upon my fieldwork done during 1999–2002. In the course of discussion, I shall introduce other cases to emphasize some of the major points. The account that follows will throw light on the working of the caste panchayat and accentuate some of its more important features.

[12] Ralph H. Retzlaff, 1962, *Village Government in India: A Case Study*, Bombay: Asia Publishing House, p. 18, distinguishes four different kinds of traditional panchayats in northern India: one, caste panchayat; two, general meeting panchayat or the village multi-caste panchayat; three, the farmer–retainer panchayat; and four, the single purpose panchayat.

[13] For a succinct resume of the work done by different scholars on traditional panchayat, see Bernard S. Cohn, 1990, *An Anthropologist among the Historians and other Essays*, New Delhi: Oxford University Press, pp. 55–61; and D.G. Mandelbaum, 1990, *Society in India*, Vol. II, Bombay: Popular Prakashan, pp. 278–93. It may be noted that most such studies touch upon traditional panchayats as part of their research and fieldwork around village society. The one full length study of panchayats from Uttar Pradesh (UP) by Pradhan, The *Political System of the Jats of Northern India*, remains shrouded in controversy about its authenticity.

[14] According to Hershman, pp. 35–6, the clan and caste panchayats in Punjab have lost the authority that they had exercised in the past, when they acted as courts and arbitrators in disputes affecting their members. According to him, cases are seldom submitted, as they once were, to the elders of the biradari or caste panchayats to decide. The situation in Haryana and UP would appear to be different in this regard from that of Punjab.

DICTATING RELATIONSHIPS: THE CASE OF
VILLAGE JONDHI

A case which took place in early July 2000 in village Jondhi demonstrates the awesome power of the caste panchayat; the brutal extent to which the village culture and tradition can be extended, the continued hold of caste customs and traditions, and the challenges that these traditions and customs are facing. This case raises various questions regarding marriage and highlights the social ambivalence regarding issues of control, of prohibitive degrees, and of incest.

In February 1998, Ashish, a Jat boy of village Jondhi in Jhajjar district, 25 years of age, married Darshana, a 16-year-old girl from village Dabari. This village adjoins Haryana but falls within Delhi. When the case surfaced in July 2000, the couple had a one-and-a-half year old son. Ashish, a truck driver by profession, used to take export items from Delhi airport to Bangalore. He had been operating on this route since 1993. As is usual with the majority of people from rural Haryana who work outside their village and state, Ashish had his wife and child living with his other family members in village Jondhi. His immediate family included his father, Satbir Singh, and his grandfather, Daryav Singh, who lived with them. His extended family in this village, consisting of his five uncles and their families, comprised some forty members.

Trouble around Ashish and Darshana's marriage arose nearly three years after it had taken place when it became public knowledge that a Dagar Got boy had married a girl from the Gehlot Got. Under the rule of exogamy, these two Gots in village Jondhi fall in the category of prohibited Got and cannot inter-marry. According to a 'tradition', allegedly dating back 500 years, the founder of the village Jondhi, a Jat called Jondh, Gehlot by Got, had gifted 2,000 acres of land to Jats of the Dagar Got, a destitute family then living in the jungle, and settled them in the village. This was a time of great paucity of population when all hands were needed to till the land. Around 5,000 acres of land remained with the Gehlots. This gesture was claimed to have established a relation of brothers between the two Gots that prohibited inter-marriage between them. This tradition was claimed to have been duly respected by both the Got members till it was broken by this couple. It incensed the Gehlot Jats who summoned a caste panchayat of the village to thrash out the issue and avenge the alleged insult inflicted upon the *izzat* (honour) of the entire village by such a marriage. Although a caste panchayat, its attendance is open to all the villagers. However, as the concerned matter is internal to the caste, it is left to the villagers to attend it or not. This is important, as the decision taken at the caste panchayat is binding upon all the villagers. Indeed, the cooperation of the entire village is needed to implement the decision of the caste panchayat.

This panchayat appointed a committee of twenty-five members in July 2000 to go into the matter, and a series of meetings were held to allow the two parties to compromise their differences in some way. The Dagar family was repeatedly asked to appear before the panchayat dominated by the bigwigs of the Gehlot Got in the village. From Ashish's immediate family, only two of his *taus* (uncles) attended the meetings. Other members of the family, fearing the worst, stayed away. His father, unable to bear the social strictures, went into deep depression, increased his liquor intake, and was unable to talk to anyone. Only a few members of the Dagar family appeared before the panchayat. The importance given to this 'breach' in marriage prohibitions can be made out from the fact that, within a span of two weeks, eight meetings of the committee appointed by the panchayat and three meetings of the panchayat were held to come to grips with the problem. During these two weeks, almost every conversation in the village and surrounding villages revolved around this issue. All that the villagers could talk about was this 'disgraceful affair', as someone put it.

The couple's absence from these meetings incensed the villagers. The panchayat, noting this as a further defiance, issued an ultimatum to the Dagars at the end of two weeks. The entire Dagar family, including the couple, was ordered to appear before it on 17 August 2000. Failing this, the panchayat declared its intention to deliver their verdict and have it implemented. On the appointed day, a truncated Dagar family, minus the couple, attended the panchayat. The latter announced its verdict by inflicting heavy punishment on the Dagar family.

In a public pronouncement, the caste panchayat held the concerned Gehlot and Dagar families guilty of wilfully breaking a time-honoured village tradition. The Gehlot family of village Dabari came under severe strictures for marrying their daughter to a Dagar boy. The family was expelled from the biradari of Gehlots. In future, no Gehlot was to have any contact with them. The Dagar family was also vehemently denounced. It was alleged that the Dagars brought about this marriage knowingly, stealthily, and calculatedly. For this, it was pointed out, the number of *baratis* (marriage party) was kept deliberately low. It consisted of only 15–20 people, so as to keep the matter under cover.

It was even reported that at the time of wedding when someone raised the question of prohibited Got, he was misinformed that the girl's Got was Solanki—the Got of the dominant Jats of village Dabari. This village has only 10–12 households belonging to the Gehlot Got, the rest are Solanki. It was also given out that the father and grandfather of the bridegroom, who knew about the Got prohibition, had calculatedly stayed away from the marriage celebrations.

Unequivocally condemning the marriage, the caste panchayat ordered it to be nullified. This decision was in keeping with the popular concept of woman as the honour of the community. Such a concept turned Darshana into an object of honour for the Gehlots—an honour that could not be allowed to be abused at any cost. If this honour had been compromised or defiled by an act of marriage, such an act must be reversed and her status of an unmarried girl must be restored. Consequently, the couple was ordered to revert back to their brother–sister fictive relationship, in keeping with the Got status that had existed prior to their marriage. This was the only relationship between Gehlot and Dagar Got which the Jondhi caste panchayat was willing to recognize.

To affect this transformation, the panchayat prescribed a ritual to be observed. One, Darshana was to unveil herself in the full assembly of the village. This was a symbolic turning of the *bahu* of the village into a *beti* (daughter). (No daughter is required to veil herself in her natal village.) Furthermore, she was to tie a *rakhi* on Ashish, that is, publicly accepting him as her brother. Two, as a daughter, Darshana was to be married again. Her father-in-law, now transformed into her father, was to perform the *kanyadan* ceremony for Darshana and give her away as a bride. The Dagar family was to bear the entire cost of her marriage. This also meant that Darshana was demoted from her 'superior' Gehlot Got to 'inferior' Dagar Got. This made the Dagars responsible for remarrying her.

Three, the son of Ashish and Darshana was to remain with Ashish. Ashish's family was ordered to deposit Rs 5,000 in the account of his infant son as security. Four, all forty members of this family were to be expelled from the village. They were given a week to make their departure. Five, the members of Ashish's family were ordered to sell off their land and other property in the village within a period of two weeks. Failure to comply with these injunctions would result in confiscation of their land and property by the panchayat and forcible eviction from the village. Six, in case the Dagar family allowed a week to lapse without complying with the panchayat's orders, they alone were to be responsible for any untoward happening in the village. The panchayat refused to accept any responsibility for their lives or property after a week.

The latter stricture was certainly a tacit approval of violence. Such cases are far more pervasive than acknowledged. They play an important role in maintaining structural and assumed hierarchies and are considered normal and legitimate. Violence as an expression of power would certainly have been used by the male Gehlot biradari of the village against the couple, and against Darshana in particular, in order to reproduce and reaffirm the relative status and authority of the two Gots. The Dagars' defiance offered the Gehlots a pretext to punish them for wrongdoing and to assert the importance of maintaining or exercising their authority. With the belligerent tone of the panchayat and rising tempers, wide-scale violence was apprehended.

Yet, the police stood by silently. The Deputy Superintendent Police (DSP) of the Jhajjar police station, when contacted regarding this, admitted: 'No one bothers about the police in the village. Our decree does not work in the village.' The Station Police Officer (SPO) maintained that the police intervene if and when the law and order breaks down or a complaint is lodged by one of the parties. This 'official' policy of wait-and-watch adopted by the state agency in such cases helps establish the might of the caste panchayat. Even after the complaint was made to the police, the latter advised the complainants to pressurize the elected *sarpanch* to make her act. Such matters, according to the SPO, should be settled by the caste elders: 'What are they (the elders) for?' he asked. The precise nature of state intervention in such cases is context specific rather than principled, and does nothing to reinforce the objectives on which the state structure is based, that is, equality, egalitarianism, citizenship, adulthood, and the like. It merely acts to restore law and order and that too reluctantly, encouraging the illegitimate forces to take over. In other words, the police overlook social problems to seek a settlement through the panchayat. Similarly, the sarpanch of the officially instituted and elected gram panchayat not only supports the decisions of the caste panchayat but also actively promotes it, as we shall see presently.

The caste panchayat's belligerent stand put the Dagars on the defensive. They reportedly requisitioned a larger body, that is, a khap panchayat (a multi-clan council drawn from wider clan areas, also known as *maha*panchayat) to review the case. On 23 August 2000, a khap panchayat of both the Gots assembled from different villages took place in village Jondhi. An estimated 1,000 people gathered in the village for this purpose. The Dagar Got from *panchgama* (of five villages) was massively represented. Representatives of the Gehlot Got from eighty-three khap also assembled on special request from their Got kinsmen of Jondhi village. The proceedings of this panchayat took place under the chairmanship of Daya Kishan, the chief representative of Gehlot Got from village Mitrao in Gurgaon district. He was also the former *pradhan* (head) of Gehlot khap panchayat of forty villages and had also served as a sarpanch of the gram panchayat in the initial years of independence. Both sides were given a hearing for more than two hours. In this, the Gehlots were aggressive and the Dagars defensive and repentant. The senior Dagar, Daryav Singh, placed his *pagri* (head-gear) on the ground and apologized profusely with folded hands for the mistake unwittingly committed. The *phupha* (uncle) of Ashish, Ishwar Singh, the go-between in the marriage, acknowledged his mistake by holding his ears in repentance and promised never to repeat it. The Dagars pleaded for leniency maintaining that the earlier decision of the Jondhi caste panchayat was too harsh on the couple, especially in view of their child.

The khap panchayat appointed a committee of eleven—five representatives of each Got, headed by the president of the khap panchayat. A written declaration was taken from both the Got representatives and the concerned families that they would honour the decision of this committee. The decision taken after a great deal of consideration was communicated publicly. The khap panchayat did not dissolve the marriage but refused to condone it. It also refused to review the decision taken by the Jondhi caste panchayat against the Gehlot family of village Dabari. Darshana'a natal family was thrown out of their Got for giving their daughter to a Dagar boy in marriage. They could no longer call themselves Gehlot. Socially boycotted for life, no member of the Got was to associate with them in any way. All pleas for clemency were rejected by the khap panchayat. The khap panchayat further expelled the couple from Jondhi village for life. They were not even granted visiting rights. Their male child was exempt from this punishment, clearly on the grounds of patrilineage and sharing of blood. The other forty members of this family in Jondhi were allowed to stay in the village but were expelled from the biradari for two years. After two years, they could request the Jondhi caste panchayat for a review in order to seek re-admission to the biradari. Till then, there was to be complete social boycott of the family. Their *huqqa–pani* with other members of the village was banned. Neither could they participate in any of the village festivities nor could anyone else participate in theirs. Any infringement was to be severely punished.

These, briefly, were the major highlights of the case. Further investigations and interviews revealed certain nuances of the case, which bring into relief the contest around popular cultural and customary practices in rural areas.

A social profile of village Jondhi reveals it to be a Jat-dominated village. The Jats constitute 75 per cent of its population. In this, an overwhelming 50 per cent belong to the Gehlot Got and about 25 per cent to the Dagar Got. The Gehlots certainly own the bulk of the land in the village, but they are lagging behind in education and other professions compared to the Dagars, who are financially better off. Having taken to education, they have branched out, perhaps noticeably more so than the Gehlots, to jobs other than that of cultivators. A large number of them are in the army, the police, and other government services. Many have migrated to foreign lands and still others have come to own *sharab ke theke* (liquor shops) and *bhattas* (brick kiln), and are among the leading businessmen of this region.

The success of Dagars has been a source of tension between the two Gots for some time now. The ex-pradhan of village Mitrao spoke of *khundak* (tension/resentment) which some people in the village had against the Dagars which, according to him, was reflected in the Jondhi caste panchayat's decision. Although he refused to elaborate, it is clear that in a scenario of unemployment and growing population, there is severe competition over material resources. The Dagars, according to my Gehlot informants, were not sufficiently respectful towards them (Gehlots). They refuse to ascribe this self-confidence of the Dagars to the changed social milieu and the improvement in their economic standing. They put it down to their arrogance and the existence among them of anti-social elements. The Dagars' claims to equality clashed with those of Gehlots who looked upon the Dagars as subordinate partners, and of inferior status.

In the traditional Got hierarchy among the Jats, a Gehlot girl marrying a Dagar boy was bound to raise extreme resentment. It would be considered a *pratiloma* (hypogamous) marriage by the girl—a marriage beneath herself. Although the question of incest (based upon fictive sibling relationship between the two Gots which prohibits any sexual contact and marital exchange between the two) was easily the most important issue around which the local and regional opinion was mobilized, an important associated aspect was the question of status and hierarchy, based upon kinship and power. The rejection or non-inclusion of the subordinate Got in the structure of kinship alliances is a critical means by which senior lineage members manage the reproduction of power for themselves.

The marriage of Ashish and Darshana, therefore, was not merely a matter of transferring a kinship principle—the superiority of bride takers and inferiority of the bride givers—to the clan level, as suggested by Madsen in his study of a similar contentious marriage among the Jats of western UP,[15] for the inferiority of wife givers is limited to the immediate family only, due to certain factors, and does not automatically apply to the entire clan group.[16] The Dagars were not actually claiming a *superior* status, but merely an equal status with the Gehlots in village Jondhi, in keeping with their changed politico-economic standing and the egalitarian ideology of bhaichara existing among different Gots. In other words, what was essentially a hypogamous marriage in the eyes of the dominant Ghelot Got was seeking legitimacy not as a hypergamous match but as an isogamous one. Such an attempt brought to the surface the ongoing contest around status hierarchy that is continuously under

[15] Stig Toft Madsen, 1991, 'Clan, Kinship and Panchayat Justice among the Jats of Western Uttar Pradesh', *Anthropos*, vol. 86, pp. 351–65.

[16] In real terms, according to Hershman, p. 216, the scope of inequalities created by marriage alliances is circumscribed by the following factors: (i) this inferiority is largely limited to specific ritual contexts, for example, at weddings and at funerals; (ii), only the husband aquires any real honour for being a wife taker, and only the wife's immediate family shares the dishonour of being a wife giver. The other kinsman have their status affected in only the most nominal ways; (iii) the interaction of the affines is restricted to the relationship of a man to his wife's family, the marriage alliances of any one family tending to be widely dispersed across different villages and families; (iv) the inequalities created by wife giving are limited because they are not significantly related to control of the means of production, that is, land. Dipanker Gupta, 1997, *Rivalry and Brotherhood. Politics in the Life of Farmers in Northern India*, New Delhi: Oxford University Press, pp. 167–8, similarly argues that in western UP, the concept of wife takers as superior to wife givers is not strictly observed. As an example he takes up the case of Mohinder Singh Tikait, the Bhartiya Kisan Union supremo. Though Tikait is locked in an intense rivalry with the father-in-law of his daughter, no one considers Tikait's behaviour improper.

challenge, and offered an opportunity to the contesting parties to settle scores once and for all.

The Jondhi case is not an isolated case. It symbolizes a social phenomenon that is more widespread. Concerns of status hierarchy among different clans of Jats are crystallizing around questions relating to marriage, contributing substantially to the redefinition of traditional practices and status claims. A conflict (October 2000) between the Shyrano and Sangwan Got of Jats can be cited as an example. In the overwhelming Sangwan-dominated village of Damkaura in district Loharu, the attempt of one Bhagwan Singh of Jhajhodiya Got of Jats who wanted his son to marry one of the Sangwan Got girls was objected to by the Sangwans. The Sangwans considered Jhajhodiya Got an inferior/subordinate Got in the village, and this marriage, therefore, as a pratiloma marriage. The caste panchayat maintained: 'Sangwan got ki ladki Sangwano ke gaon me bahu ban ker nahin aa sakti' (a Sangwan girl cannot come as a bride in a Sangwan village) and gave a verdict against it. The two parties were told to break off the engagement or face dire consequences. Bhagwan Singh's plea to the panchayat rested on the claim of his Got being allied to the Shyrano Got of the Jats both as wife givers and wife takers. The Shyrano Got men had been instrumental in settling the Sangwans in village Damkaura. Traditionally, therefore, the Shyrano held a higher status than the Sangwans. As a higher status Got, it was claimed that they were traditionally entitled to take wives from the Sangwans and not vice versa. This tradition came in conflict with the ground reality of the Sangwans dominating numerically and materially in the village Damkaura. In seeking to upset this marriage, the Sangwans not only challenged the earlier tradition but also appropriated it for themselves. As dominant partners, they claimed the right to take and not give brides, from subordinate Got represented in the village.

The matter was resolved by evoking the ubiquitous concept of bhaichara. Based upon equality and brotherhood, any marriage between the two Gots would have been incestuous. Significantly, the objection in terms of incest was nothing but a proxy for objection to status reversal. The relative claim of the two regionally powerful sub-clans was subsumed and tradition was recovered/reconstructed to the satisfaction of all. The marriage did not take place but a rescheduling of the status claim did. Clearly, there cannot be a uniform application of status claims. Such claims have to take cognizance of village as well as wider regional equations.

STATUS COMPLEXITIES: RESOLVING CLAIMS

In the case of Ashish and Darshana's marriage, the social aspect of the disturbance of status hierarchies is somewhat more complicated and blurred. The ambiguity of approach towards the prescribed norms is likely to spillover in this case onto more and more cases of breach. For a variety of reasons (discussed later), individual concerns may take priority over the collective village and biradari concerns. In the case of village Jondhi, Darshana's natal family was clearly not so well off. Darshana's father, a former state bus driver in Delhi, had been disabled due to a stroke since 1988. He struggled to bring up his family of six children—four girls and two boys. Daughters meant having to provide dowries in a situation of steeply escalating marriage costs. Anxiety about their marriages was further compounded as the eldest girl was physically handicapped, and the next daughter engaged to be married. The family's scarce resources were already stretched. Their land in the village was under dispute and the family lived on the father's pension. This meagre income was augmented by letting out part of their dwelling (consisting of three to four small rooms). This fetched them only a little extra, as the rents are low in the villages. Darshana's two younger brothers, still in school, were nowhere near contributing financially to the family. In Ashish then, this family found a good match by any standards. Ashish was reportedly drawing 5,000–6,000 rupees per month in his job as a truck driver. His immediate family owned a *pacca* house, milch cattle, and one *kila* (five *bighas*) of land in Jondhi. With his wife and child living in the village and helping the other male members in looking after the land, it would mean a comfortable life with a large surplus income in the form of his salary.

In such a situation, Darshana was clearly entering into an advantageous match and marrying above herself in so far as economic status of her natal family was concerned. However, from the point of view of the large community of Gehlots of Jondhi, this view was not sustainable on two counts. First, in kinship terms, the Gehlots, as wife givers, hardly stood to gain in status by alliance to the Dagars as wife givers. Indeed, this marriage could well symbolize the ground reality, that is, the changed status and power equations between the Gehlot and Dagar Got of Jats. Second, the Gehlots evaluated the social and economic status of Ashish's family not in comparison with that of Darshana, but according to the traditional village ranking. In Jondhi, Ashish's family occupied a low status. Ashish was the only male member with a regular income. The family landholding was too small by itself to offer a worthwhile standard of living. The household consisted of three males and no females, as Ashish's mother was dead. In the eyes of the villagers, it hardly constituted a 'family'.

It is possible that if Ashish had belonged to one of the more prestigious and economically sound families of Dagars in village Jondhi, the strictures passed by the Gehlots could well have taken a different form. The caste panchayat is likely to be more lenient in passing judgement on a powerful man than on one who is inconsequential; the important man may resist or even nullify the panchayat's decision.[17] Daya Kishan, the ex-pradhan of Mitrao village, dismissed Ashish as someone to be pitied, someone otherwise unable to get married because of his family and financial status. What made things worse was Ashish's overriding concern and haste in getting married soon after his mother's death (a breach of one year mandatory mourning period). With no woman at home to look after the household and prepare food for his old father and grandfather, specially when he was away, Darshana, from a financially strained household, was quickly chosen to step in. That she was a Gehlot, if considered at all, may well have looked a minor hindrance.

For the Gehlots of Jondhi, this was a major breach of social and cultural norms, and indeed a political challenge. The Gehlot family of Darshana was held responsible for this, and the onus fell on Darshana's mother, since the father was an invalid; she had humiliated the family and brought on the united wrath of their Gehlot biradari. The suspicion of her active agency in bringing about the marriage was not without foundation. With a realistic assessment of her own financial position she had indeed actively promoted the marriage, and had even hastened it in order to get Darshana and her sister married at the same time. For this, she was roughed up by Darshana's two uncles (*tau* and *chacha*) and her life threatened. Darshana's mother complained that Gehlot women from Dabri village had also come over to her house to openly criticize the marriage alliance and to abuse her and take her to task.

The Jondhi Gehlots, on the other hand, opined that Darshana's family should have contacted their Got people in village Jondhi to help procure an equal, if not a superior, Got match for Darshana. The Gehlot biradari, they also pointed out, could even have been asked to share the cost of the marriage in case the *karta* (head) of the family was unable to meet his family's requirements. In a cultural milieu where masculinity and power are linked to the ability to protect and materially support a

[17] Mandelbaum, *Society in India*, pp. 302–3.

family, the males of Darshana's natal family stood emasculated, damned, and reduced to pariah status. As one Gehlot of Dabri village was to point out: *'inki na-mard harkat ne sub Gehloton ki naak katwadi'* (their unmanly deed has emasculated all the Gehlots). The Gehlot families of Dabri village severed all relations with Darshana's family.

The Gehlot community pressurized the families, Darshana's and Ashish's, to nullify the marriage. This forced the couple to go underground for a while in the month of August 2000. Darshana pointed out later that, had it not been for the child, the ending might well have been sordid and gruesome. Indeed, in several marriages that had transgressed the principle of territorial exogamy, the couples concerned had been physically eliminated. The whole of north India is replete with such cases.[18] A violent ending took place in village Narnaul of Rohtak district, Haryana, where in June 1999, a Jat girl and a Jat boy had run away to get married. The caste panchayat instructed the family members to kill the girl. The family members, however, sent the girl to her *mama* (maternal uncle). Incensed at this defiance, the panchayat decided to carry out the sentence themselves. They sent a party of ten Jat boys from the village to get her from her *mama*'s house. The girl was killed and cremated by them, significantly against the decision of the family. The elected sarpanch of the gram panchayat, who was a mute onlooker, feigned ignorance. It is alleged that the girl was also raped by her so-called brothers. The contradictions underlying the ideology of 'brotherhood' come violently and blatantly to the surface on such occasions.

The caste panchayat remained tight-lipped about the identity of the culprits, clearly protecting and shielding the rapists. In episodes such as these, which are not uncommon, the guardians and protectors of 'community' end up as violators. A First Information report (FIR) registered by a Rohtak women's organization to investigate the crime came to nothing. No one was willing to testify. The Jat boy, her runaway partner, has been in jail since then on charges of rape and kidnapping.[19]

---

[18] Prem Chowdhry, 1997, 'Enforcing Cultural Codes: Gender and Violence in Northern India', *Economic and Political Weekly*, vol. XXXII, no. 19, 10–16 May, pp. 1919–28.

[19] A similar case was handled by an individual family and not by the caste panchayat. In village Padanna, a Jat boy ran away with a Jat girl from the same village. They were not found despite an extensive search. The Jat family of the girl, belonging to the dominant and prosperous Got, took violent revenge on the lower class/status family of the Jat boy. They dragged the sister of the absconding boy by her hair in full view of the villagers in the daytime and took

It is openly acknowledged that a large number of cases, which are taken up by the traditional panchayats, are concerned with women. Yet, no woman is allowed in the panchayat premises, not even the one who is a party in the dispute. Although this may not be true of all regions and all caste groups,[20] in Haryana, a woman is represented by her male family members. The male head of her family is held responsible for her conduct. Similarly, in the almost all-male gathering of the traditional panchayats in Haryana, the female audience is missing. This again may well be region specific.[21] Curiously, Darshana was compelled to confront the caste panchayat twice. Once, when she was hauled up to the house of Pushpa Gehlot (the elected sarpanch of the gram panchayat), the woman sarpanch, complying with the caste panchayat's dictates, lifted her *ghunghat* (veil covering her head) in the presence of 30–5 people. On the second occasion, her ghunghat was lifted once again by Pushpa Gehlot, in front of the caste panchayat consisting of 500–50 people, all of them men. She was directed to comply with the panchayat's decision. Interestingly, what was considered humiliating by Darshana personally was projected by the panchayat members as bestowing *izzat* upon her, more as an attempt to retrieve her honour than to defame her. Darshana considered the lifting of her ghunghat as a great humiliation for herself. But for the *panches* or the villagers, reclaiming Darshana as a daughter was bestowing honour upon her. It was pointed out to me that to call your bahu (daughter-in-law) your beti (daughter) was indeed upgrading her status and honouring her, not demoting or dishonouring her.

---

her to their double-storey house. They openly announced: 'You have sullied our girl and dishonoured us. We shall also soil your girl in return.' Once on the roof, the girl was raped by three of the family members, while the mother stood guard at the entrance. The matter was taken up by the Mahila Jagran Committee who moved the court on behalf of the girl's family. However, convictions could not be made due to lack of evidence and witnesses. The girl's family subsequently left the village for some unknown or undisclosed place.

[20] In village Senapur in Jaunpur district of UP, when the case of a lower caste Kahar woman was decided by the dominant Thakurs of the village, the Kahar woman was present. Her preference for a sexual mate was given full recognition in deciding the case. For details, see Mario D. Zamora, 1990, *The Panchayat Tradition: A North Indian Village Council in Transition, 1947–1962*, New Delhi: Reliance Publishing House, p. 56.

[21] Ibid. In the above cited case, both the Kahar as well as the Thakur women formed part of the panchayat audience.

In Haryana, it is the beti's or bahen's honour that is given precedence and rated high. For illustrating this, the Ramayan story is held as an example. In the matter of honour and dishonour, it is maintained that it was Ram who gravely dishonoured Rawan, and not vice versa. Ram had refused to marry Shrupnakha, the sister of Rawan, and had been instrumental in cutting off her nose. Rawan, on the other hand, had only abducted Ram's wife. In the scale of dishonour, Ram's action far outweighed that of Rawan's. Out of the two insults to a man's honour, it was a sister's honour rather than a wife's honour that deserved drastic action. Summing up, the commentator remarked: 'You may say anything against my wife and I may, if I like, choose to ignore you. But if you say anything against my sister, it is a different matter altogether. You will have to bear the consequences.' Although clearly far-fetched and exaggerated, this contention needs to be understood rather than dismissed. It may be noted that the concept of bhaichara, whether that of the caste or of the village, covers sisters and daughters, but not wives.[22] In terms of abuses, those relating to sisters and mother, like *bahen-chodh* (sister-fucker) or *ma-chodh* (mother-fucker), though colloquially often used in rural areas even in ordinary conversation, are the ones most likely to arouse violence. Also, there is no equivalent abuse in relation to the wife.[23] Moreover, it is the brother who is considered the 'real protector' of a woman in Punjab and Haryana.[24] He safeguards her interests against others, including her husband.

For Darshana, the sudden appearance of her 'brothers', claiming to protect her 'honour', was totally unsolicited. She showed her mettle by fighting back throughout this crisis. Her strength and assertiveness

[22] Indeed, the most brutal retribution is reserved for an unmarried girl. In contrast to this, a married woman's liaison may or may not invoke a similar reaction. Violence as a response towards a runaway wife, for example, remains confined to individuals or families, and such cases are not known to get the support of the wider caste/community networks, or cited as a matter of 'honour' for the entire village. Consequently, what appears to exist is a noticeable difference of approach in the rural areas towards the handling of an unmarried and a married woman's amorous liaisons.

[23] A wife is generally humiliated by abusing her natal family, specially her brother and her father, by casting aspersions of incest upon them. For an interesting structural analysis of Hindi terms of abuse, see Amrit Srinivasan, 1976, 'Obscenity, Address and the Vocabulary of Kinship', *Journal of the School of Languages*, Winter, pp. 72–7.

[24] See Nirmala's case cited in Das, 'Masks and Faces', pp. 1–30.

can be gleaned from the interview of 21 August 2000 that she gave to *Dainik Jagaran*,[25] a local Hindi daily published from Haryana. In this interview, she condemned the illegality of the caste panchayat's dictates. Educated up to class ten and generally well aware, she maintained that there was no law of the land which could force her to acknowledge her husband as her brother. Showing tremendous agency and spirit, she also approached the police for help against the illegal ways of the panchayat. As usual with these cases, she was not encouraged to pursue this line. Critical of the caste panchayat, she voiced her strong resentment against its arbitrary decisions. It was she who defied its verdict by refusing to accept Ashish as her brother. She also greatly resented having been subjected to the humiliating ritual of unveiling in the full assembly of the village. She equated it with the behaviour of Kaurvas with Draupadi. A fully alert Darshana pointed out that 'no law can stop me from entering the village,' but maintained that she herself was willing to stay away from the village 'in order to maintain peace.' Darshana also showed herself willing to contact a women's organization in Delhi. In all this, her husband supported her fully but silently. He merely added, 'if they trouble us unnecessarily we will also not keep quiet.'

The lead taken by Darshana in the interview and the low profile kept by her husband reiterated that she was taking on the combined might of the Gehlots, as a Gehlot. Her Dagar husband, apparently inferiorized by the Gehlots (an inferiorization which was perhaps internalized by many of his Dagar kinsmen, who were not so well-to-do as other Dagars), implicitly accepted his lower ranking and powerlessness in the caste hierarchy by keeping in the background, allowing his wife to take the lead, an unheard thing in the villages. Ashish also never faced the caste panchayat, whereas Darshana was compelled to confront it, which she did with great composure, recall the eyewitnesses.

An interesting aspect of this case lies in the time factor. Why did it take three years for the news to become public, and why did it become public knowledge at all? The Gehlots give out the story that this news was accidentally discovered by some women from Darshana herself, who had gone to fetch water from the village well. When asked by the village women about her Got, Darshana disclosed that she belonged to the Gehlot Got. From there, the news caught on like whirlwind. Investigations suggest a different line, however. It is acknowledged

[25] 2000, *Dainik Jagaran*, 21 August, pp. 1, 13.

that the fact of the marriage was already known to quite a few people, though it was ignored till the younger generation of Gehlot men made an issue of it. This happened during the election to the post of sarpanch of the gram panchayat in July 2000. Reserved for women, this was won by a Gehlot woman candidate. Until then, for 52 years, the post had been won by the Dagars. Though numerically strong, the Gehlots have been faction ridden, and it was this fragmentation that had enabled the Dagars to get their sarpanch elected. The repeated triumph of the Dagars in the gram panchayat elections had confirmed the general perception among the Gehlots regarding the attrition of their sphere of influence in the village and the growing clout of the subordinate Dagar partners.

In the July 2000 elections of the gram panchayat, the Dagars did not offer their candidate for the post of the sarpanch.[26] Instead they supported one of the Gehlot factions. Because of the split in Dagar votes, the Gehlot faction that they had supported, lost. This was flaunted in the village as a Dagar defeat. The change in the political fortunes of the Gehlots was soon reflected in their behaviour with the Dagars. Having come to power democratically, it seemed important to assert themselves. The victorious Gehlot faction in the village took to ridiculing the Dagars whenever the occasion arose. The Dagars retaliated by calling them their *rishtedar*. Translated in English, rishtedar merely means a relative. Colloquially, however, it means infinitely more, depending upon the occasion and its usage. It is often used in rural areas in a pejorative way. In a conflict situation, it is used as an abuse, like the word *sala* (brother of the wife). It designates the other person as a wife giver who hands over his sister or daughter to another man for sexual use. According to Daya Kishan, the ex-pradhan of village Mitrao, the actual taunt thrown by the Dagar boys at the Gehlots was, 'We are your *jija* (sister's husband)'. Elaborating, he maintained that, in a situation

[26] Reportedly, in the previous election of the sarpanch of the gram panchayat, an understanding had been arrived at between the Dagars and one of the Gehlot factions. In that election, a non-Dagar man (son of a sister of a leading Dagar family who had settled in Jondhi) had become the sarpanch with the help of a faction of the Gehlots. The understanding was that if the Gehlots supported the 'Dagar *Bhanja*' (as he was known) in this election, the next sarpanch would be from among the Gehlots. The Dagars agreed not to put up their candidate, so that the Gehlot faction may have a chance to win. Ram Chander Yadav, State President, Democratic Youth Federation of India, 2001, interview, village Rampura, district Jhajjar, 28 February.

where brotherhood is accepted, this claim by any one party could only be an abuse directly suggesting 'I fuck your sister'. Claiming to indulge in incest with impunity can only lead to extreme violence and murder. As sexual abuses, the use of words such as rishtedar, jija, and sala in a conflict situation in the rural areas invites immediate retaliatory behaviour.

Aspects of the marriage that had remained under cover so far could now hardly remain so. Cut to the quick, the young Gehlot men used this pretext to settle scores politically. They exploited it to the full to trounce the politically powerful Dagar Got in the village and to make the rival faction of Gehlots fall in line with the others and to settle the contentious status claims of the rival Gots once and for all. Traditional tools were being used to bring the different factions of the Gehlots together, both for modern political purposes as well as in line with traditional status claims within the caste—in an attempt to dislodge the rival 'Other'. In this, a traditional panchayat, although ostensibly a non-political body, ended up making political gains.

In the aftermath of the election, loud announcements by some Gehlot men that this marriage was a 'grave insult' to their caste, Got, village tradition, and custom found immediate favour with the older generation of Gehlots in the village. Confident of the latter's support, as one of them put it, they 'decided to teach the Dagars a lesson they'll never forget'. The whole matter was portrayed in highly emotional tones by declaring the marriage designated as *vishwasghat* (traitorous), a '*kalank*' (slur) on the village, and *ochchi harkat* (low-level underhand activity) by the Dagars. Widely projected as inexcusable behaviour, young and old, men and women, were all united in condemning the marriage. Dissenting voices surfaced much later.

The issue of the wilful transgression of caste, family, and village norms succeeded in mobilizing the villagers across caste, class, Got, gender, and age divisions. For instance, the younger generation, students and other educated youngsters, echoing the older generation, openly stated that 'any one wishing to stay in the village must respect its traditions and customs and not go against it'. They also accused the predominantly urban job-holder Dagars of having succumbed to 'urban values' and practices at odds with the cultural norms and customary practices of the village community. Posed in such terms, even the Dagars could hardly voice another opinion. They supported it fully. A Dagar youngster, for instance, pointed out that 'such breach of village tradition must be punished.' With the girl's father openly accepting his mistake, the case against the Dagars was clinched. The caste panchayat was quick to cash in.

The Gehlots isolated the concerned Dagar family and stopped their interaction with anyone, within or outside the village. They stationed their strong men to shut out sympathizers. The Dagars, clearly on the defensive, accepted the 'fairness' of the panchayat's charges and criticized the marriage as well. Ashish's father and grandfather openly accepted their mistake and admitted their responsibility.

Dissenting voices were raised only when the extreme verdict was pronounced. This was especially in view of the fact that the infant son of the couple had been rendered not only illegitimate, but one born of an incestuous union. Darshana reported that a few people who protested against this extreme step were quietened down and threatened. These included not only the Dagars but also some of the Gehlots. However, with the harshness and unreasonableness of the verdict, this dissent of the Dagars turned more vocal. Pratap Singh, a former office holder in the gram panchayat, summed it up by declaring it *anhoni* (unnatural).

However, no voice was raised against the right of the caste panchayat to dictate marriage alliances. There was unanimity in the village about this matter being punishable. Opinion differed only on the nature of the punishment. When approached, villagers observed that: 'If the culprits are not punished for breaking the moral and cultural code of the village there will be no difference between sisters, daughters and *bahus* of the village.' The hold of the caste panchayat on ruralites was complete in this respect. The village surpanch, Pushpa Gehlot, summed up the popular sentiment by observing that: 'caste panchayats are empowered customarily to deliver judgements on various social issues. These must be honoured. In this alone lies the unity and prestige of the village generally and that of the *biradari* specially.'

Indeed, the role and attitude of the elected sarpanch is important to give legitimacy to matters such as these, which may not stand scrutiny under the law. The sarpanch, as the elected head of gram panchayat, instituted by the government, has a lot of power and political leverage to intervene in matters which go against the law of the land and constitutional rights of individuals. But the sarpanchs are not known to act against the dictates of the traditional panchayats. The traditional panchayats represent the *vox populi*, and to go against it would be electorally suicidal for them. It is a fact that *panchayati raj* is increasingly becoming a training ground for leadership at higher level and it is widely felt that the state leadership in Haryana may emerge from these institutions.[27] Therefore, instead of distancing themselves from the decisions of the traditional panchayats, the elected gram panchayat members and the sarpanch seek to emerge as supporters of the decisions of these panchayats. Indeed, in many cases, the sarpanch leads from the front. As noted earlier, this was done by Pushpa Gehlot and her husband, the de facto sarpanch of village Jondhi. Such unqualified support from important personages associated with the state and government stands to stem any criticism and weaken any resistance that may arise.

This is not to say, however, that the sarpanch or the other members of the gram panchayat do not share the opinions of the traditional panchayats on social matters. They do. When approached, one of the gram panchayat members, endorsing the stand taken by the caste panchayat, maintained: 'We cannot allow the whims of individuals to divide our society.' Culturally, rural north India prioritizes the collective interest over and above individual interests. The members of a family are expected, as a matter of course, to place the interests of the group above their personal desires.[28] According to this reasoning, the request of the Dagar couple for rehabilitation in the village was unjustified. It is also clear that in matters such as these, the caste panchayat enjoys even wider and higher political support than that of the gram panchayat. For example, the Chief Minister, O.P. Chautala, who visited Jondhi in the wake of this trouble, firmly maintained that 'whatever the panchayat (caste) decides is right'.[29]

REVISION OF DECISION: SHIFTING CONCEPTS

Why did the caste panchayat inflict such an extreme and unrealistic punishment on the couple? Having inflicted it, why did it retract, even though partially? This revision is not peculiar to the Jondhi case. While the traditional panchayats not infrequently revise their decisions, due

[27] Har Bhagwan Bathla, 1994, *Panchayati Raj and Political Parties*: An Empirical Study at Grass-root Level in Haryana, Kurukshetra: Nirmal Book Agency, p. 178.

[28] This sentiment has been borne out by a number of sociological studies, for instance, I.P. Desai, 1964, *Some Aspects of Family in Mahua: A Sociological Study of Jointness in a Small Town*, Bombay: Asia Publishing House; T.N. Madan, 1989 [1965], *Family and Kinship: Pandits of Kashmir*, New Delhi: Oxford University Press; and A.M. Shah, 1974, *The House-hold Dimension of the Family in India*, London: Tavistock Publications.

[29] Jagmati Sangwan, interview, Rohtak, 28 February 2001.

to social as well as political pressure,[30] in the case of village Jondhi, the answer to this revision lies in the concept of honour, and what the public holds as honourable and esteemed. Neither the concept of public honour nor the perception of this honour is static or fixed. It is fluid, and differs from time to time and from situation to situation. One concept of honour can indeed even cancel out or override another concept of honour. When the caste panchayat of Jondhi took the extreme step, there were large-scale undercurrents of hostility and competition between the two Gots of Jats. These feelings were exacerbated by the recalcitrance shown by the Dagar couple to attend the panchayat meetings even when specially instructed to do so. This happened repeatedly. A gesture of self-protection born out of fear of reprisals on the part of Dagars was perceived as yet another example of their arrogance and assumption of superiority, as wilful defiance, and as a challenge to the panchayat's honour and authority.

The Dagars' alleged defiance of the caste panchayat had shifted the onus from the village to the panchayat. Only the most severe and exemplary punishment could restore the honour of the panchayat. The extreme decision which followed certainly helped establish the awesome power of the caste panchayat and village elders. But it also, paradoxically, eroded its honour and public prestige. The absence of most of the Dagars turned the panchayat into an exclusive and one-sided body, detracting substantially from its popularly projected democratic, united, and representative face. The one-sidedness of the caste panchayat's decision was a serious charge on the honour and fair name of the panchayat and its tradition of honourable decision making.

The traditional panchayat, ideally perceived as *parmeshwar* (godly) and *panch* as the five gods,[31] is generally known to work on the principle of balancing antagonistic factions and effecting a compromise. The

---

[30] Madsen, for example, argues that in the case of western UP, the caste panchayat, after banning the Malik Got giving brides to the Balyan Got of Jats, lifted it subsequently. Jats belonging to these two Gots, who had already planned weddings of their wards, exercised the pressure. See Madsen, 'Clan, Kinship and Panchayat Justice among the Jats of Western Uttar Pradesh', pp. 351–65.

[31] Many ruralites, especially members of lower caste groups, the educated, and the politically oriented challenge this view of the panches. They believe them to be biased in favour of individuals, factions, and even political parties.

power of the panchayat lies in its fairness and its ability to carry the popular opinion of the village in its decision making and the social acceptance of its decisions.[32] This face of the Jondhi caste panchayat was severely undermined and its decision was neither considered fair nor accepted by the Dagars nor, reportedly, by some Gehlots who were friends of the Dagars. Consequently, a revision was very much on the cards. A non-compliance with the decision of the panchayat also meant a failure of the panchayat to implement its own decision. This challenged the very legitimacy of the caste panchayat.

Criticism began to mount. The caste panchayat was said to have gone berserk. It was suggested that it was attempting 'unnatural' things, as one school teacher of Jondhi put it. What perhaps remained unvoiced was the status of the child. The scathing attack on the panchayat's decision made by Darshana in her interviews with the press[33] and implying that there was greater authority in the law of the land, was devastating to the panchayat (as one member pointed out on condition of anonymity). The media, in reporting the case, had initially appeared awe-struck by the panchayat's might and its undisputed authority to dictate to its people but changed its tenor in two of its later editorials, pointing out the illegality of extra-judicial authority exercised by the panchayat.[34] For instance, *Dainik Jagran*, one of the most widely read papers in the whole of northern India, criticized the panchayat's decision, declaring it contrary to the law of the land and against human and moral rights. Assuming highly censorious tones, the two editorials condemned it as *kabilon ka kanoon* (literally, 'tribal law', but more appropriately, 'barbaric law'). There was, however, no questioning of the values involved. I was informed that the local correspondent of *Dainik Jagran* stationed in Jhajjar, who was responsible for filing reports on village Jondhi, was *gheraoed* by some of the caste panchayat

---

[32] Judgement in a panchayat is not reached unless there is unanimity or near unanimity among the presiding leaders. There is little point in a decision unless it can be enforced. Bailey has pointed out that councils in any society whose members have to implement their own decisions are impelled to search for such consensus. See F.G. Bailey, 1965, 'Decisions by Consensus in Councils and Committees', in F. Eggan and M. Gluckman (eds), *Political Systems and the Distribution of Power*, London: Tavistock, pp. 1–20.

[33] *Dainik Jagran*, 2000, 22 August, pp. 1, 13; 23 August, pp. 1, 5; 24 August, p. 13; 26 August, pp. 1, 9.

[34] *Dainik Jagran*, 2000, 19 August, p. 6; 24 August, pp. 1, 8; 26 August, pp. 1, 9.

members, who complained ab ut his adverse reports. This pressure resulted in his being shifted from Jhajjar, putting an abrupt end to the so-called adverse reporting. By then, other social institutions like the Meham *chaubisi*, a *sarv* khap panchayat (all clan council) of twenty-four villages also moved in on this matter. They were also highly critical of the extreme pronouncement of the Jondhi caste panchayat. The panchayat's move to uphold the honour of the village and prestige of the community had obviously backfired.

The public, which had hitherto shown a unanimous face, soon split—cutting across class, caste, gender, and age divides. A section of villagers refused to recognize the extreme verdict as an 'honourable' settlement flowing from the decision of a 'just and fair' panchayat. Summoning of a khap panchayat was on the cards. In this connection, the Gehlots allege that the Dagars requisitioned the khap panchayat. This was contested by Ashish and others, who insisted that the khap panchayat was called by the Gehlots who felt that the caste panchayat of Jondhi had gone too far, and not by the Dagars. Whatever the truth, many of the Gehlots were as much involved in the revision of the verdict as the Dagars. The reported initial reluctance of some of the Gehlots of Jondhi village to participate in the khap panchayat was soon overcome. In this, Gehlots from other villages played no small a part. Significantly, the verdict of the khap panchayat leading to a partial reversal and a partial reiteration of the earlier verdict, as elaborated earlier, nipped in the bud the dissent that was unmistakably raising its head and threatening to take wider social dimensions. It also restored, though belatedly, the prestige and honour of the caste panchayat. Paying heed to the internal critique which had emerged restored the panchayat's image of impartiality and balance as the upholder of traditional moral values and culture. The media applauded the *samjhadari* (wisdom) of the panch and congratulated them for revising their earlier decision.

Yet, all the criticism did not lead to the rehabilitation of the couple in the village. Darshana and Ashish's request to be allowed to come back to the village was a cultural claim in that they were challenging the splitting of their family. The caste panchayat was dictatorially threatening the existence of a family, by severing family bonds and compelling them to live apart. It is a well-known fact that in Haryana, many of the educated, or those who work in service occupations or in the army, prefer to settle in their respective villages and pursue parental occupations after retirement. The attachment of the landowning caste groups to land cannot be underestimated, so that the upholding of certain cultural norms (of kinship and territorial exogamy) by the panchayat was at the expense of other cultural norms (family unity).

Within a year of this decision, Ashish's father passed away, making this separation permanent. Ashish visited his village with a police escort. The cremation was boycotted by most of the villagers on the grounds that 'hamen koi matlab na sai' (it does not concern us). The caste panchayat members maintained: 'It is the administration which has allowed Ashish. His coming here is against the wishes of the village.' The gram panchayat sarpanch refused to attend the ceremony saying that she could not go against the wishes of the village. Abstaining from the cremation ceremony of a caste member being held in the village is unprecedented in rural north India, and a breach of this time-honoured cultural practice indicates the extent of prejudice against such marriages. The fear of penalization, decreed by the caste panchayat, may certainly have acted as a deterrent. Photographs were taken as evidence of attendance, in case the panchayat wished to take stern action against them in future

The Dagar community, despite offering initial support to Ashish, backed out after their own position in the village became secure. If Ashish's family had been economically sounder and socially more prestigious, his case probably would not have gone unrecognized and unsupported by his otherwise powerful Dagar community, for there are instances where socially and economically influential families have breached the Got restrictions successfully. The case of Jagmati Sangwan and Inderjeet Ahlawat whose marriage (1982) was opposed on the grounds of breaching the bhaichara norm of the village was a case in point. A few families of Sangwan Got lived in the otherwise Ahlawat-dominated village of Bhembheda, district Jhajjar, who objected to this marriage. Inderjeet's family was able to ignore them because of the economic strength and the social standing and influence he commanded in his own Got and the village. The two Gots, Ahlawat and Sangwan, are dominant and powerful Gots in different regions of Haryana. In Bhembheda, however, the Sangwans households are fewer and wield far less influence. The marriage reiterated the status hierarchy existing in the village and upset the concept of equality of the village bhaichara. Yet, the charge of 'incest' raised in the case of Jondhi was not raised in this village. The Sangwans' attempts to call the caste panchayat were not successful. Inderjeet's father openly challenged the move. Consequently, no move could be initiated against this breach. According to Jagmati, if the social and economic status of the family is not sound then the caste panchayat succeeds in its dictates. Influential families get away with breaking the 'traditionally sanctioned norms' which they uphold for others, or appropriate different norms, as it suits them.

To return to Ashish's case, I was told that except for his grandfather, Ashish's family was held in contempt due to his father's alcoholism and his gross misbehaviour after his drinking bouts. It was hinted to Ashish by his biradari-*walas* that, if he so liked, he could sell off his house and property to the other Dagars. Ashish chose to ignore these hints. Since then he has taken up a private job as a driver in Mahendergarh, while his wife and child are staying with his relatives in a different village. Until 2000, the caste panchayat had not changed its decision, maintaining that the gravity of the charge would not allow them to make any concession. The social boycott of Ashish's family also remained in force for a period of two years.

SELECTIVE APPLICATION: BHAICHARA AND THE CATEGORY OF INCEST

In arriving at its decision, the caste panchayat of village Jondhi had treated the concept of bhaichara and the breach of the incest taboo by the couple as the central issue. As pointed earlier, incest in rural areas is a very wide category. It embraces all inhabitants of a village, all Gots represented in the village who may be located anywhere, as well as the inhabitants of those villages which share a boundary with it, by creating fictive brother–sister relationship between them. Any breach in this is considered a serious transgression and dealt with summarily. Yet, experience shows that the charge of incest is not applied uniformly to all caste groups in the village. In case one of the parties is of a different caste, the issue is altogether different. It becomes a caste issue and not one of incest.[35] Moreover, it is a well-known fact that most love affairs are within the village itself, clearly indicating that fictive relationships are not really accepted. Most such alliances result in elopements. However, it is also true that, although highly idealized, cross caste ties in a village expressed through fictive kinship are valued by both men and women, but they become operative only after the marriage of a girl and especially

---

[35] This understanding is based upon my wider study dealing with inter-caste marriages in Haryana. See Prem Chowdhry, 2007, *Contentious Marriages, Eloping Couples: Gender, Caste and Patriarchy in Northern India*, New Delhi: Oxford University Press.

in her conjugal home. The fictive bond establishes for both of them the desired support structure and solidarity cutting across caste, class, and status ties.[36] Inside the village, with its emphasis upon segregation of the sexes, communication between fictive brothers and sisters hardly exists. It is frowned upon and looked at with suspicion—underlining the imposed nature of this relationship, which all concerned recognize. Yet, as an ideal it works and is upheld by all caste groups as the 'village norm', which must not be broken. Consequently, transgression of this norm is considered incest.

On the other hand, incest within the family is generally buried under the carpet. The concept of incest is not extended to family relationships involving unequal power relations between senior males and junior females or any other prohibited category of people. This counterposes fictitious incest *versus* real incest. Activists involved in the women's movement in Rohtak, based upon their experiences in the villages of Haryana, informed me that incest has assumed truly frightening proportions. The daughters and sisters are however afraid to voice it, as it would reflect on the 'honour' of their families, for which they feel responsible. Police officers, similarly, vouch for the widespread incest in families. According to them, these cases come to light only when they result in suicides or murders.[37] Some of these cases involve either the *dewar* (younger brother-in-law) or the *jeth* (older brother-in-law), and may not strictly fall in the category of 'incest', because the prevalent practice of levirate accepts them as sexual partners of a woman.[38] In other instances, the woman may approach the caste panchayat. The

[36] Helen Lambert, 1966, 'Caste, Gender and Locality in Rural Rajasthan', in C.J. Fuller (ed.), *Caste Today*, New Delhi: Oxford University Press, pp. 93–123, in her study of Rajasthan argues that the fictional relationships established by women with persons from their natal village offer them a support structure in their conjugal home. These cross-caste ties are of strategic political and economic importance even for men when visiting other villages where their married sisters reside. Other men establish fictional kinship ties of solidarity stretching across caste, class, and status through their women. For a similar reading see Leigh Minturn, 1993, *Sita's Daughters: Coming out of Purdah*, New York, Oxford University Press, pp. 59–63.

[37] In January 1998, for example, in village Ichhapuri, district Gurgaon, a woman killed her jeth for his incestuous designs on her. *Dainik Jagran*, 1998, 7 January, p. 4.

[38] In some instances, even the father-in-law was known to have taken his widowed daughter-in-law as his wife in the colonial period. For details, see Chapter 4 in this volume.

few cases that are brought to the notice of the panchayat, however, are not dealt with in any satisfactory way.

A recent example from village Hathanganna in Gurgaon district is a case in point. The caste panchayat, summoned twice in a case where a woman accused her father-in-law of attempting rape, did precious little. On the first occasion, the panchayat summoned the father-in-law, gave him a strict warning and advised the couple to ignore the instance and settle it among themselves. The second time, when the father-in-law repeated his offence, the panchayat expressed its inability to do anything and advised the woman to take recourse to the law, but when the woman tried to register an FIR at the police station, the police refused to do so. In matters such as these, the bonds of community or ideology shared by the police and the traditional panchayat, and not the law of the land, determine the action or inaction of the law-enforcing agencies. The woman then moved the court at Firozpur Jhirka. It was here that the judge instructed for a criminal case to be instituted against her father-in-law.

The caste panchayats are clearly uncomfortable and unwilling to deal with the question of incest within the family, especially when it concerns their own caste members. This may not necessarily be the case while dealing with other caste groups, specially the lower castes. When it comes to other so-called inferior caste members, the upper caste members take a high moral stand and impose very stringent sanctions.[39]

The iron fist shown in village Jondhi case is totally missing in certain cases and not in others, as just cited. What is it that creates different categories of incest? Why is it that the concept of honour is said to have been abused in one case but not in the other? The analysis suggests that caste, class, and status considerations articulate with patriarchal concerns to determine the action or inaction of the caste panchayat and other community members. Also involved is the concept of honour in its dual capacity—private and public. Questions of public honour can be embraced and turned into a cause celebre by the village, but not issues

[39] In a 1994 case from village Bhiwadi, the all-caste panchayat, dominated by the dominant Ahirs of the village, blackened the faces of a woman and her father-in-law and paraded them naked in the village, for allegedly indulging in incest. Reportedly, the lower caste members of the victims' community sided with the Ahirs in inflicting this punishment. A few villagers who protested were hounded out. The police did not even turn up. The matter was later hushed up under directions from the politicians. Case reported in *Dainik Jagran*, 1994, 19 April, pp. 1, 11.

of private honour. The latter are best tackled privately and under cover, even though they fall squarely in the category of incest as generally recognized.

The use of incest by the caste panchayat, in its wider meaning, was challenged by Ashish. Talking about it to the correspondent of *Dainik Jagaran*, Ashish reportedly suggested a quid pro quo situation in which a Gehlot man could marry a Dagar girl and call it quits.[40] Ashish also pointed out that there were twelve Jat Gots in Jondhi and if all of them were excluded for marriage purposes, it would be extremely difficult and cumbersome to select mates. This, incidentally, is an oft-cited, though off-the-record, and confidential opinion on the prevalent norm of Got exogamy, at least among some of the male youngsters of Haryana. Ashish's marriage, notwithstanding his Got status in relation to Darshana, and his proposal of a quid pro quo suggests that not only are the set social hierarchies being challenged, but new identities related to a man's work and occupation, and importantly, his status outside the village are being asserted.

Importantly, Ashish's proposal indicates that he did not consider the marriage as incestuous transgression and therefore immoral, but a matter of status between wife givers and wife takers. In other words, the status reversal brought by his marriage could be set right by a Gehlot marrying a Dagar girl. Paradoxically, in suggesting this, although he was not claiming a higher status to the Gehlots, he was certainly claiming one in which the bride's and groom's families are of equal status. Such a status was firmly denied to the Dagars by the Gehlots. Although Ashish was to deny having ever made such a proposal, the proposal itself had validity, both theoretically and ideally. Indeed, in Haryana, a Jat may marry his daughter into the same clan from which he has received a bride for his son.[41] Although this does not disprove clan hypergamy per se, it certainly shows a disregard for the immediate hierarchy of wife givers/takers.[42] Evidence suggests that local patterns of clan hypergamy

---

[40] Ashish denied this when I asked him about his reported statement in the newspaper. The reporting correspondent, however, stands by it.

[41] Satya P. Sharma, 1973, 'Marriage, Family and Kinship among the Jats and the Thakurs of North India: Some Comparisons', *Contributions to Indian Sociology* (NS), vol. 7, no. 1, pp. 81–103.

[42] See, for instance, the system of reciprocal marriage or exchange marriage adopted by the rural Kashmiri Pandits, as noted by T.N. Madan, 1989, *Family and Kinship: A Study of the Pandits of Rural Kashmir*, New Delhi: Oxford University Press, pp. 101–2.

do not necessarily exist at the regional level. In village Jondhi, such an exchange would have been contrary to the dominant and subordinate positions as traditionally perceived to be occupied by the two Gots of Jats, the Gehlots and the Dagars.

The Jondhi case offers somewhat complex reading. The opposition to the marriage emanated out of the concept of village exogamy, incest taboos, along with distinct shades of hypergamy, in which a girl in a lower clan can marry a man of a higher clan, but not the other way round. Yet, theoretically, all Jat clans or Gots are considered to be equal. But in reality, several factors intervene to determine their social ranking in particular areas, especially in view of the changed socio-economic and political position of different Got groups.[43] The above cited cases also show the status of different clans to be in flux, with different groups either claiming a higher or equal status or attempting to maintain their status against challenges and erosions effected by other clan groups within the caste fold. As marriage alliances are a significant means to establish one's status in society, they assume great importance and demand sharper vigilance. The contradictory reactions of certain groups to the demands of caste status show the contemporary multi-directional pulls within a caste which account for confrontation and violence in relation to contested marriage alliances.

CUSTOM VERSUS LAW: LIMITED APPLICATION

Although the collective decision taking by the caste panchayat is presented as a united and unanimous voice, there is dissent and challenge to this front. This may not arise or be allowed to arise immediately, but may force the panchayat's collective decision to be reviewed or revised, for the united voice and front of the panchayat cannot be allowed to crumble. Besides, there is always the potential danger that dissenters may move the court. Indeed, courts are being increasingly used to settle questions of material interests but the internal disputes, specially such as these, continue to be handled by caste men, and are thus, effectively delinked from the state and its law and order apparatus. Recourse to the court over 'personal' issues internal to the caste is not generally approved,[44] and remains a last resort. For the ruralites, the

---

[43] The notion of 'Rajputization' may be useful for understanding such status claims of upwardly mobile groups within a caste. See Jonathan P. Parry, 1979, *Caste and Kinship in Kangara*, New Delhi: Vikas, pp. 195–231.

[44] For details, see Chapter 10 in this volume.

financially draining courts, based upon different principles, are hardly equipped to resolve or bring about a compromise to the 'status claims', which are intrinsic to the confrontations and disputes occurring within the same caste group on questions of marriage.[45] In case recourse to law is taken, it is done only against grave social pressure, and incurs a great deal of community displeasure. Moreover, in cases regarding contentious marriages, the state agencies like the police and the local administration, as noted earlier, are well known to throw in their lot on the side of traditional authority. The court, on the other hand, can be moved only after the community has taken an unconstitutional or illegal decision or step. Not many people exercise the option of going to court, but some do.

One such case occurred in mid-2000 in village Daddhi Banna of district Bhiwani. It concerned the alleged breach of a marriage prohibition relating to an extended principle of territorial exogamy. In 1999, Satbir, belonging to Pilania Got, had his two sons, Sanjiv and Rajkumar, married into a Sangwan Got family of village Kubja Nagar. Village Daddhi Banna falls in the *chalisia* (a circle of forty villages) of the Sangwans, which means that all these villages follow the traditions and customs of the dominant Got of Sangwans, even though the latter are not represented in this village. Daddhi Banna is dominated by the Pilania and Bajado Got members. Yet, traditionally, all the Jat Gots in this circle of villages are committed to observing ties of bhaichara with the Sangwans. This made the marriages incestuous. A Sangwan Got panchayat declared the marriages invalid and socially boycotted all the Pilania Got families of village Daddhi Banna. This was later revised and only Satbir's family was expelled from the village. Satbir moved the court. The court gave a stay order and he could not be expelled from the village. Yet, the Got panchayat's diktat regarding Satbir's social boycott persisted and was observed in the village. The panchayat had also imposed a fine of Rs 100 in the first instance on anyone disobeying their order. Anyone defying the order a second time was to be socially boycotted. These penalties continued despite the court intervention.

In an earlier case of 1998, Surinder of village Dhatta, Jaglan by Got, had his daughter engaged to a Jat boy of Saharan Got in village Khaded. The Jaglans of his village raised objections to this alliance by pointing

[45] For the villagers' perspective of the legal pluralities, see Cohn, *An Anthropologist among the Historians and Other Essays*, pp. 575–631.

out that there were a few families of Jaglan Got in village Khaded and, traditionally, this Got could not be entertained for marriage. A Got panchayat of the Jaglans instructed him to terminate this engagement, failing which they ordered a social boycott of his family. Surinder moved the court and amidst tight police security had his daughter married off. When interviewed, Surinder accused his fellow Jaglans of being envious of him. He declared himself a 'victim' of factionalism within his Got. He also pointed out that several Jaglan girls, including his niece, had already been married in village Khaded and no one had raised any objection. His action reportedly earned him great ill will and the villagers showed this in their behaviour towards him. He and his family remain socially ostracized.

Both the cases show the aggrieved party taking recourse to the law in order to challenge the panchayat's decision. In the case of village Dhatta, the marriage did take place with police intervention. It was the same in village Daddhi Banna, where legal protection overruled the panchayat's orders to evict Satbir's family. But in neither case could the court intervene to set aside the social boycott of the families. This is a reality that is well known to the ruralites. Ashish of village Jondhi, for example, when advised to take recourse to the law to prevent his expulsion from the village, had very firmly declined to take such a step, asking how long the law could protect him against the 'joint might' of the village. How many times, he asked, could he take the help of police to visit his own village, when the caste panchayat of the village had decreed to the contrary?

Taking recourse to the law is no solution in cases such as these. Also, any attempt to reverse the panchayat's decision may well lead to permanent antagonism, revenge, and violent retribution.[46] I was told of a case in which the lawyer of the man who sought to challenge the caste panchayat's decision was severely beaten up. This was apparently to issue a warning to all lawyers who may venture to help people take recourse to law against the panchayat's verdict. Nonetheless, it may be noted that the villagers utilize the indigenous and official law, panchayat and the court, in accordance with their own calculations of propriety and advantage.

---

[46] In this connection, see an interesting case of 1927, analysed by Saurabh Dube, 1996, 'Village Disputes and Colonial India: Two Cases from Chhattisgarh, Central India', in N. Jayaram and Satish Saberwal (eds), *Social Conflict*, New Delhi: Oxford University Press, pp. 423–44.

On the one hand, an approach to the court of law or its enforcing agency, the police, as an alternative structure for conflict resolution, certainly leads to a dramatic loss of the caste panchayat's prestige as well as its delegitimation. It is a public demonstration of the refusal to obey its dictates. On the other hand, going to court means a further transgression of the norms of community, compounding the earlier transgression. It is construed as an even greater challenge to the panchayat's decision, leading to a further hardening of its posture. The traditional leadership considers the judiciary, run by people who have no knowledge of rural culture and customary practices, to be working against caste and community's norms. Anyone taking recourse to it is similarly condemned and stereotyped as 'westernized', 'urbanized', and 'modernized', and out of touch with rural realities. The state and its laws are blamed for all marriages which go against traditional norms and customary practices.[47] However, even while eroding the moral authority of the caste panchayat, the legal authority itself stands undermined, when the state agencies confirm and validate the actions of this collective body.

The one question which still needs to be answered is: why are the parents of young girls and boys breaching what are claimed to be the village and caste traditions? First, one should be clear that such breaches are not new; they have taken place even in the past. The post-colonial political economy suggests an increase, but it is difficult to confirm it with any degree of accuracy or certainty. The general impression at the local level also suggests an increase. In this connection, it is worth remembering that all the cases cited earlier are not so-called 'love matches', which may raise the ire of the caste and communities. These are arranged matches, brought about by the respective individual and extended families and attended by members of their community. It is because of this factor that, not only the individuals concerned come under grave pressure of the panchayat, but also their immediate as well as extended families.

The answer to this phenomenon of breaches lies in understanding Haryanavi society. Customary regulations governing marriages have had the effect of creating a very tight market for prospective brides and grooms. With the increase in population, the prohibited categories of people have tended to increase. For example, inter-village and

---

[47] This includes not only the Hindu Marriage Act, 1955, but also the Hindu Succession Act, 1956. See Chapter 4, n9 in this volume.

regional migrations have resulted in a severe drop in the number of very small villages and corresponding increase in that of large and very large villages.[48] This has had the effect of multiplying the number of Gots represented in different villages. An extension of the principle of village exogamy, indicated earlier, means that all the Gots represented in a village cannot be entertained for marriage. This leaves the marriage market much restricted. The extension of the concept of bhaichara also means that all the neighbouring villages have to be similarly excluded.

The growing popular sentiment against Got prohibitions can be evidenced in the readers' letters to the regional newspapers. For example, one of the letters pointed out the difficulties faced by the inhabitants of village Dhannana of district Bhiwani.[49] This village, he maintained, was surrounded by several villages like Badesara, Seesar, Talu, Mandanna, Jatai, Mitathal, Ghuskani, Pur, Siwada, and Munddaal. All these lie in and around 3–6 kilometres distance and some are indeed derived from the other. All these have to be excluded by the inhabitants of village Dhannana for purposes of marriage. Opinion is divided, though those who support the tradition are noticeably in the majority.

Wide-scale prohibitions traditionally imposed on marriages are great-ly compounded in a social situation labouring under multiple problems: the extremely unfavourable sex ratio, the presence of a large number of unmarried men, and the dowry economy of Haryana. All these are interconnected. The widespread foeticide practised in this region, in combination with suspected female infanticide through neglect and other causes,[50] has led to an adverse ratio of only 865 females to 1,000 males in 1991.[51] In a situation where status hypergamous marriages

[48] For details of changes in Haryana village size and its population, see Government of Haryana, 2001, *Statistical Abstract of Haryana, 1999–2000*, Chandigarh: Planning Department, Economic and Statistical Organization, pp. 48–9.

[49] *Dainik Tribune*, 2000, 3 September, pp. 1, 9.

[50] For details, see Prem Chowdhry, 1994, *The Veiled Women: Shifting Gender Equations in Rural Haryana, 1880–1990*, New Delhi: Oxford University Press, pp. 14–15, 54–7, 238.

[51] In 1991, this ratio was the second lowest in the whole of India. It stood next to that of Arunachal Pradesh which had a ratio of 859 females to 1,000 males. Reportedly, this ratio has gone down even more in the subsequent ten years. (Government of Haryana, *Statistical Abstract of Haryana, 1999–2000*, p. 74).

are the norm, there is a surplus of brides at the top but a pronounced deficit at the bottom. Consequently, unemployed lower class males find it difficult to get married, causing a great deal of anxiety. This situation is compounded by the very large number of unemployed men in Haryana. The unemployment figures have more than doubled in less than twenty years from 3,59,255 in 1980–1 to 8,11,359 in the year 1999—a staggering rise of 125 per cent,[52] whereas between 1981 and 1991, the population increase in Haryana was 27.40 per cent.[53] In the marriage market, it is the employed and not the unemployed that is a 'suitable boy'. The limited number of 'suitable boys' means a competition to net them in marriage. This competition creates a surplus of girls in this stratum, feeding into the dowry economy. This market-like situation with a 'suitable boy' out for highest bidder may well lead to the families of both the girl and the boy ignoring the traditional Got prohibitions imposed on marriages. At this juncture, the individual and family status concerns override the collective concerns of the community. Such concerns leave the unemployed to either settle for lesser matches or not get married at all. Although it is difficult to give figures of the overlap between unmarried and unemployed status of males, in the opinion of ruralites, there exists a very real connection. A substantial number of the unemployed are to be found among those who are unmarried. In the 1991 census, 36.24 per cent of men in the category of 15–44 years of age (the so-called reproductive or marriageable age) are shown to be unmarried.[54] In districts like Rohtak, the percentage of unmarried males between the ages of 15–44 years is as high as 44 per cent.[55]

Clearly, the marriage restrictions are extremely hard on both the sides—for the boys as well as for the girls. The defiance of the Got norms, both at the individual and the family levels, corroborates this. The attempt by the family members is to open out the marriage market. There is also evidence to suggest that some members of the older generation are also apprised of this social situation. That is the reason

[52] Ibid., pp. 530–1.

[53] Ibid., p. 40.

[54] A total of 14,38,997 males in the age group of 15–44 years out of a population of 39,70,390 males are unmarried. See 1994, *Census of India, Haryana, 1991*, socio-cultural tables, series 8, part IV-A, Chandigarh: Directorate of Census Operations Haryana, p. 22.

[55] In Rohtak, out of a total male population of 9,77,075 between the age group of 15–44 years, 5,47,922 were unmarried (ibid., pp. 22–3).

why, from time to time, caste panchayats have initiated certain alleviating measures to correct the situation by relaxing the prohibitions on marriage between certain Gots. For example, the Gulia and Kadyan Gots were deemed to have originated from two brothers and marriage relations between them were prohibited. This was relaxed even under British rule. Similarly, marriages between Kadyan and Jakhad Gots were also prohibited, and it was only in 1946–7, that four khaps—Gulias, Kadyans, Sangwans, and Jakhad—met and took a historic decision to allow marriage relations between them (Kadyan and Jakhad Gots).

More recently, in April 1995 at village Ismailpur, a sarv khap panchayat of the Chhahal and Mor Got declared that members of these two Gots could inter-marry. The occasion was provided by the contentious marriage of a Chhahal Got girl of village Narad to a Mor Got boy in village Ismailpur. The prohibition on inter-marriage between these two Gots had apparently been instituted so long back that no one even remembered its origin. A form of punishment imposed upon them is the common explanation of such prohibition. However, what is clear is that the ban on marriages is considered not merely a breach of bhaichara but also a 'punishment'. The conflation of punishment with bhaichara in popular perception is itself revealing.

In May 1995, such a prohibition was also lifted for the Mor and Singhmar Gots though marriages between them had been taking place. The decision of the sarv khap panchayat was a ratification and formalization of the already changing, and indeed changed, position. Such changes require the support of Gots other than the ones directly involved. For example, in the historic sarv panchayat of April and May 1995, Gots present, other than Mor, Chhahal, and Singhmar, were Goyat, Nain, and Sheyokand. The wider the participation of persons of different Got in the panchayat, the wider the acceptance of the changes affected in the traditional patterns of marriage relations.

PANCHAYAT'S INTERVENTION: SUCCESS AND CHALLENGE

Such emendations, however, are few and far between. By and large, the traditional panchayat asserts itself to the detriment of the 'erring' individuals and families. This intervention is also an assertion of the united power and domination of upper caste, senior male members over younger men and women. It represents a direct attempt at retention of power by the caste leadership which is fast being eroded and challenged by aspirants from different socio-economic strata as well as by the younger generation. In post-colonial India, the traditional power base stands considerably eroded with the introduction of different state structures such as the elected statutory panchayat (since 1950) and election mechanism based upon equal citizenship and adult franchise. The statutory panchayat, which has become the focus of political life of the village, has thrown up new socially mixed groups, in many cases drawing substantial representation from the lower social strata. In the changing scenario, the traditional leadership of village bigwigs derived from the ranks of those born to power and prestige is being pushed to the margins of power structure.[56]

This diminishing power is sought to be resurrected through the traditional panchayat who use social problems, specially cases relating to questions of marriage, for legitimation of its authority. In this, a large collection of people come together temporarily and rather promiscuously for a certain specific purpose. What follows is claimed to be an open, fair, and democratic decision in respect of a specific problem facing the community. A close observation of the proceedings suggests the contrary. On many occasions, one of the concerned parties is not even present or is too thinly represented. Women are not even allowed to enter the panchayat premises although, more often than not, the decision involves them in an important way. The traditional norm regarding their attendance was certainly broken in the case of village Jondhi. This breach has meant that the applicability of this norm lies in the hands of the panchayat, who may or may not apply it, or may apply it selectively if not whimsically. The leadership of such an assembly closely monitors the discussion. Dissent is either ignored, kept dormant, or not allowed to surface in any effective manner.

Youth, usually the affected party, is not allowed to voice its opinion, especially when any other older male member of the family is present. They are reprimanded, 'Why do you speak when your father/elders are present?' In rural north India, age and experience are still respected, though change, howsoever slow, now favours the youth. The decision of such a body, with the older generation monopolizing and directing its course, is projected and implemented as a unanimous decision democratically arrived at. It is asserted as *'sab ka mat yo hi sai'* (all have

---

[56] Many from this social group had indeed been elected to the newly constituted official panchayats in the aftermath of independence. However, over the years, they have had to make way; or as an ex-sarpanch of village Mitrao, district Gurgaon, insisted, they 'willingly made way' for the younger generation of men.

the same opinion), and dissenters, as pointed out, are dismissed as of 'no importance'.

For arriving at a decision, the traditional panchayat mobilizes a large number of people on the basis of family, kin, Got, caste, community, and village, including persons from outside the local area. By bringing in a wider biradari from outside the village, links are activated which make the panchayat look more powerful. Issues such as the breaking of social taboos, customs, rituals, and hierarchy are used as mobilizing strategies. Being highly emotive strategies, these succeed in uniting people and closing ranks and cleavages in rural society. In this, the concept of village honour based upon idealized norms and village aika produces a powerful plank.

Significantly, the utopian principle of village unity stands acknowledgedly fragmented in post-colonial India. The pressures exercised by the unprecedented expansion of participation through adult franchise, competitive elections, and state intervention have sharpened caste and status cleavages on the one hand, and polarized villages into fluid cross-caste factions on the other. The politicization of village India is a fact. Existing factionalism and litigation in the villages feed into unstable political conditions, fragmenting it more. Growing conflict over caste, community, and land has become an important aspect of rural politics in India. This fragmentation has meant that no particular group has been or can be in a position to speak for the whole village or for the entire membership of a particular caste community. Yet, the intervention of the traditional panchayat in preserving certain values of village life—its culture, customary practices, and the like—has the effect of closing ranks, imposing a temporary aika through a fragile cohesiveness on what has been and continues to be a highly fragmented village life. The political labels are obliterated to impart a non-partisan apolitical look to the panches.

In matters other than those related to village culture and tradition, the panchayat may or may not be effective, for example, in the frequent conflicts relating to land use or to other material resources. In such cases, the traditional panchayat's decisions are often challenged because there is a clear division or factionalism in the village. As the economic stakes are high, the aggrieved party, egged on by others, is quick to move the court. But in cases involving village honour, culture, and tradition and its breach by individuals, a united front is maintained. All dissidence is quietened by the show of unity achieved by threatening the isolation of the dissident/s, or through use of force, if necessary. The dominant caste groups, though severely divided into factions and interest groups, throw their might behind the traditional panchayat. In cases such as these, they cannot afford to split their own ranks or caste. A show of solidarity serves them in a two-fold way: (i) it helps them to present a united caste biradari front despite their political and party differences. Such a front comes in handy in demanding political and economic concessions from the state; (ii) it helps them in establishing their might in the village against other caste groups, specially the lower castes, reaffirming the existing hierarchy and caste/community domination. In cases where violence is resorted to, to implement the panchayat's decision, an even more effective weapon is placed in their hands. The desire to enforce their domination and prove their strength is an interest that is amply shared by other members of dominant caste groups.

Yet, despite tradition of acceptance, dissenting voices and challenges to collective decision making do exist. These may not arise or may not be allowed to rise immediately, but may become a source of embarrassment as in the case of village Jondhi. These may force the panchayat's collective decision to be revised and reviewed. Indeed, the cases cited earlier indicate that decisions may be reviewed, though with limited effect. Yet, the very existence of an alternative structure, power, and authority has created uncertainties among traditional wielders of power. The aggrieved and penalized party can approach the court, whose decision stands over and above that of the panchayat. Although the law works on principles contrary to that of the traditional panchayat, it may have only limited success in a society based upon various hierarchies. Despite challenges, the traditional panchayat's activities may remain a successful intervention to maintain a state of affairs that the state has attempted to change, at least legally. In other words, the extra-judicial power and activity of the traditional panchayat has severe implications for the state and the state stands devalued, unable to protect its citizens or implement its own laws. Ironically, the danger to Indian democracy stems from the grass roots level.

12

'First Our Jobs then Our Girls'

*The Dominant Caste Perceptions on the 'Rising' Dalits**

pehle mahari naukriyan le li eeb choriyon len sain
(First, they take our jobs and now our girls.)

This is an oft-quoted sentiment in Haryana that neatly sums up the dominant but highly exaggerated apprehensions that the upper castes have against the lower caste groups, especially the Dalits. Issues of employment and marriage are extremely sensitive and volatile in this state. They are interconnected and bring into focus the 'changed' position of Dalits, perceived popularly as the 'rise of the Dalits'.[1] What is the nature of this 'change' and what constitutes the 'rise' of the Dalits that is observed to be so threatening to the upper caste groups? How is this threat dealt with? What is the social reality behind such a perception? What purpose and whose interests does it serve? These are some of the questions raised in this essay, which seeks to understand the mounting tension between the upper caste groups and the Dalits. In

---

* This chapter was originally published in 2009, *Modern Asian Studies*, 43(2): 437–79, Cambridge University Press.

[1] It may be noted that the generally used term for the scheduled caste groups in this region is that of '*chuhre–chamar*' (scavenger and tanner/leather worker), instead of the word 'Dalit'. They are also refereed to as '*neechi jati*' or *kamins* (literally low castes). These terms emphasize the low caste identification of the Dalits and express subjective meanings.

the post-colonial shifting of material, legal, and ideological bases, some of the given patterns of relationship between individuals and caste groups have changed and weakened due to the introduction of new, parallel, and alternative structures of relationships. This change has left the upper caste groups feeling palpably insecure in relation to the Dalits. While delineating this relationship, this essay seeks to argue that the cases of Dalit and upper caste elopement and marriage represent a high point in the ongoing conflictual relationship between them, as these are viewed as forms of Dalit assertion. Although many caste groups and communities are involved in inter-caste marriages and associations that defy customary norms and caste practices and have no social acceptance, it is in relation to a Dalit and non-Dalit association or marriage that certain aspects, which impinge on wider issues, come to the surface more pronouncedly.

For the purpose of analysis, this article is divided into two sections. The first section deals with the political economy and the changes that specifically concern the Dalits and the dominant caste groups like the Jats. These changes are internal to different caste groups and are a matter of grave concern to them. Yet, they also impinge upon the relationship between different sections drawn from the dominant and the lower caste groups. This section attempts to explore the reasons behind this conflictual relationship and its possible escalation over time. The second section takes up the conflictual relationship to the concrete levels of tension and deals with case studies of elopement and marriage involving lower caste and dominant caste groups, drawn from my fieldwork in Haryana. Locally, these cases are dealt with either individually, at the family level, or collectively, by the community. I propose to concentrate on the role of the community in such cases to highlight how the all-inclusive notions of *bhaichara* (brotherhood), *biradari* (community), and *izzat* (honour) are, in reality, highly selective concepts which in conflictual situations work against the Dalits rather than in their favour. For an in-depth analysis, I propose to concentrate on a single village where two such cases took place in 2000–1, within a span of six months. I shall also very briefly bring in a few more cases to further refine some of the points raised through the two main cases. The case studies draw upon the political economy dealt in the first section to establish the interlinkages between caste, class, and gender, which are constantly in play in determining the outcome of such relationships.

CHANGING PROFILE: POLITICAL ECONOMY

The post-colonial capitalist development, especially in agriculture, and introduction of democracy, policy of reservations, education, and acquisition of different skills, as also urbanization, migration, and movement of Dalits into new vocations than the traditional ones, has introduced mobility and stratification among the Dalits. The earlier predominant internal feature of possessing similar skills and having somewhat similar income levels has been undermined. The Dalits have come to be far more internally differentiated than in the past. Although it is true that even in the colonial period there were differential categories among them,[2] but they were not so marked as now. The Dalit castes that were earlier at the receiving end of patronage from the upper castes have found that the position has been partially changed by these processes.

This social change and mobility has been building up slowly among the Dalits. Under the colonial impact, sections of Dalits became upwardly mobile in different parts of India.[3] In colonial Punjab, for example, successful entrepreneurs emerged in the leather industry from among the Chamars.[4] Since dealing with hides was considered an impure calling by the upper caste groups, many among the Chamars were able to achieve relative prosperity from the sudden increase in demand for raw skins in India and abroad during the first decade of twentieth century. By this time, the number of people engaged in the skin trade more than

[2] Chamars, for instance, formed a sizeable proportion of the tenants of the landowners in Haryana–Punjab. For details, see Prem Chowdhry, 1984, *Punjab Politics: The Role of Sir Chhotu Ram*, New Delhi, Vikas, pp. 61–99.

[3] The Jatavs of Agra, Uttar Pradesh (UP), were one such upwardly mobile group. It was the same for other untouchable caste groups like the Shanars, located in the south of Madras Province, or the Mahars of Maharashtra, and the Ezhavas of Kerala. See R.L. Hardgrave Jr, 1969, *The Nadars of Tamilnad: The Political Culture of the Community in Change*, Berkeley: University of California Press, pp. 95–7; R. Jeffrey, 1974, 'The Social Origins of a Caste Association 1875–1905: The Founding of the SNDP Yogam', *South Asia*, vol. IV, October, pp. 43–5; O.M. Lynch, 1969, *The Politics of Untouchability: Social Mobility in a City in India*, New York: Columbia University Press, pp. 32–5; E. Zelliot, 1970, 'Learning the Use of Political Means: The Mahars of Maharashtra', in R. Kothari (ed.), *Caste in Indian Politics*, New Delhi: Orient Longman Ltd., pp. 29–69.

[4] M. Juergensmeyer, 1982, *Religion as Social Vision: The Movement against Untouchability in Twentieth Century Punjab*, Berkeley: University of California Press, pp. 36–7.

quadrupled. The Chamars, who set up tanning enterprises or became active in the more lucrative trading business, employed their own caste fellows in the leather industry. Such changes were, however, few and far between. Vast majorities of Dalits remained aligned with agriculture in some capacity or the other.

This association with agriculture has remained even now. A huge majority, that is, 82.29 per cent of Dalits are rural based and involved in agriculture and agriculture-related activities in Haryana.[5] Many among them continue to be engaged in traditional activities like leatherwork, handicrafts, weaving, tanning, scavenging, and carrying the night soil. Yet, there are others who have migrated to the cities and have become salaried workers by profitably utilizing their traditional occupation of sweeping and cleaning, or by undertaking work that would have been polluting for the upper castes to handle. Among those in urban areas, several are employed in the organized and unorganized industrial sectors; some end up in slums doing menial jobs for survival or rickshaw pulling; and others are petty shopkeepers or small entrepreneurs. Yet others have come to be absorbed in government, semi-government, or private jobs. Some of them have raised their living standards and life-style. Indeed, the Indian government's policy of reservation, embodying positive discrimination in favour of Dalits, has led to severing the link between caste and occupation and undermining its material base most effectively.

Altogether, an entry into new professions, the availing of employment opportunities along with reservation of seats in the elected bodies like the gram panchayats, legislative assembly, and the parliament has thrown up a considerable number of Dalits as a distinct middle-class category, albeit a highly differentiated and layered one. Noticeable in public arena, this class, as we shall see presently, is primarily responsible for creating a sense of insecurity and resentment among the upper caste groups. Clearly, despite the emergence of a middle class among the Dalits, the caste ideology continues to play an important role in the reproduction of relationships and behavioural patterns.

Agrarian Field: Growing Marginalization
Among the categories of Dalits mentioned, those aligned to agriculture, as labourers, are the most vulnerable. In agriculture, due to the

---

[5] 2000, *Census of Haryana, 1999*, part VIII (1), Special Tables of Scheduled Castes, Directorate of Census Operations, Haryana, New Delhi, pp. 780–1.

integrated nature of the economic system and the virtual monopoly over land, and their hold over the traditional panchayat,[6] the dominant caste groups are still in a position to control the lower castes. Over the years, the dependence of the Dalits on agriculture, both in absolutist and relative terms, has increased. The failure of land reforms in Haryana is well acknowledged. In their implementation, the land and tenancy laws were easily manipulated, specially against the Dalits.[7] The Dalits were not only evicted as tenants, but they also failed to take possession of the surplus land allotted to them. According to the 1991 census, there were 5,12,913 agricultural labourers and only 75,095 cultivators among the Dalits, making for just 14.6 per cent of Dalits having minuscule land-holding, or sharecropping, or some other types of insecure tenantry.[8] In the two categories of cultivators and agricultural labourers, the percentage of cultivators over time has gone down and that of the agricultural labourers has gone up. Between 1981 and 1991, there has been 11 per cent decline in the numbers of Dalit cultivators, implying a process of proletarianization (that is, of losing ownership of land for even those who had diminutive bits of land, or access to land in lease market) and a phenomenal increase of 41 per cent in those of agricultural labourers.[9] In the latter category, the Dalits also have come to face competition from members of non-Dalit castes, for a variety of reasons, in the wake of green revolution and now, liberalization of economy. Sheila Bhalla observes that in certain areas of Haryana, the upper caste groups have displaced the landless labour who are drawn from among the Dalits, leading to a great deal of tension.[10] In other areas, migratory labour

[6] For the use of the term 'traditional panchayat' see Chapter 2, n11 in this volume.

[7] Paramjit Singh Judge, 2001, 'Land Reforms in Haryana', in Sucha Singh Gill (ed.), *Land Reforms in India: Intervention for Agrarian Capitalist Transformation in Punjab and Haryana*, New Delhi: Sage, pp. 118–36.

[8] Calculated from Government of Haryana, 2001, *Statistical Abstract of Haryana, 1999–2000*, Chandigarh: Planning Department, Economic and Statistical Organization, pp. 68–9.

[9] Calculated from ibid. and Government of Haryana, 1990, *Statistical Abstract of Haryana, 1988–89*, Chandigarh: Planning Department, Economic and Statistical Organization, pp. 60–1.

[10] For details, see Sheila Bhalla, 1999, 'Liberalisation, Rural Labour Markets and the Mobilisation of Farm Workers: The Haryana Story in an All India context', *The Journal of Peasant Studies*, vol. 26, nos 2 and 3, January–April, pp. 25–70.

from other states has replaced the Dalits, causing severe deprivation to the local Dalits. In a situation of expanding dependence on agriculture, and growing marginalization of Dalit cultivators, increasing landlessness, and differential labour demand, erosion of the economic base of Dalits has taken place. In the capital-intensive agriculture, this has had the effect of sharpening the class polarization between rich peasants and landless labourers, primarily drawn from among the Dalits, who also stand confronting the lower sections of the upper caste groups. All this has added to the volatility of a conflict situation.

Historically, the Dalit agricultural labourers (popularly known as the *kamins* in this region) and the landowning castes have been at loggerheads, breaking out in open confrontations on a variety of issues. These ranged from levy of certain fees and cesses (like the hearth fee), payment of wages, rendering of *begar* (work without pay), use of village *shamilat* (common land), and sexual exploitation of Dalit women.[11] Some of these issues have remained, or assumed different forms, and some fresh ones added. The payment of wages remains a contentious issue, as the statutory wages are substantially higher than what the landowners are willing to pay. Among factors that cause constant friction between the Dalits and the landowning classes, the use of village shamilat has endured and emerged as one of the major factor behind violent confrontations. Large portions of shamilat have been illegally occupied by members of dominant caste groups and are being utilized for purposes other than traditional one of grazing of animals.[12]

Moreover, there has been a steep increase in the numbers of livestock kept by all caste groups in Haryana.[13] For the Dalits, the rearing of cattle, sheep, goats, and poultry provides a major source of sustenance as well as some income. This has put them in direct conflict not only with the landowner but also a segment of the same class drawn from among the upper caste groups. The village shamilat is, however, not even adequate for the growing needs of landowners given to dairy farming

[11] For details, see Chowdhry, *Punjab Politics*, pp. 64–81.

[12] The regional daily newspapers are full of reports and complaints from the public regarding usurpation of common land.

[13] In less than ten years time (1988–97), the total number of livestock went up from 87,694 to 1,13,574. See Government of Haryana, *Statistical Abstract of Haryana, 1999–2000*, pp. 302–3.

in their pursuit of white revolution. The successive shrinkage of the shamilat, and its appropriation by the landowners for their exclusive use, or for their own caste men, not merely contravenes the traditional grazing rights of Dalits, but also causes a great deal of loss and hardship to them. The usage of shamilat constitutes, often, an important area of friction between the two groups. Furthermore, any attempt by the Dalits at acquiring ownership of government lands or surplus lands, as decreed under certain welfare schemes of the government, is violently resisted by the dominant castes, leading to open confrontations.

The landowners, on their side, maintain that the kamins no longer deserve the same privileges as given earlier. In their opinion, 'kamin eeb oot ho gayen sain, Kaam na karte, pehle ke tiryan' (the kamins have become impertinent; they no longer work as they used to). There is clearly 'everyday form of resistance' of the Dalits to overwork, that James Scott speaks of, though without questioning the power and authority relations as such.[14] Restricted and declining employment opportunity in the agricultural field means that many Dalit youth have to leave the village in order to seek employment outside; others opt out of working as agricultural labourers and migrate to cities. For many of the Dalit youth, it is a survival strategy and for others, it is a move to break away from the subordinate pattern of the past, which is closely tied to agricultural work and means labouring for the dominant caste groups.

Education and Reservations: Competing Classes

Availing of the educational opportunities facilitates this break. Dalits are anxious to have their children educated with a view to following a different profession. An oft-quoted remark among the landowners is: 'Now kamins want their boys to get educated and want them to become officers. They do not want their children to work in the fields.' In the opinion of the upper caste groups, the one factor that has ignited a wide-scale change among the Dalits is education. According to them it is education, facilitated through government scholarships, which has made the lower castes avail of reservations in the government jobs, thereby giving them an edge over the rest of them. In the perception of the upper caste groups, a combination of education and reservations has therefore turned the lower caste groups into, what one man described

[14] James C. Scott, 1990, *Weapons of the Weak: Everyday Forms of Peasant Resistance*, New Delhi: Oxford University Press.

them as, 'government *jamais* (sons-in-law)' who have to be pampered. The popular refrain is that the government has 'spoilt' the Dalits. This has led many among the upper caste groups to opine that since many Dalits had moved into more remunerative occupations, the 'privileges', which they had been enjoying earlier by virtue of belonging to the 'poor sections', could hardly be offered to them any more. Curiously, this demand has an echo among the lower sections of the Dalits against the 'elite Dalits', as I shall show presently.

The Dalits do not belittle the 'help' which government scholarships and reservations have afforded them, but find them inadequate. For example, the government scholarships, given to about 40,000 children, start from class IX onwards only.[15] Despite the lower level education being free for Dalit children, many Dalit students do not even reach this level. Moreover, these scholarships are offered to school and college-going children from families earning less than Rs 500 per month. This leaves out vast number of Dalits who find education with its tuition fees, books, and stationery and uniform an expensive proposition to be accommodated in their meagre income levels. The seat reservation in colleges and universities, especially medical and engineering, is hardly honoured and in fact, ignored at various levels.[16] The reality is that the poor economic base of the Dalits has led to uneven educational progress. There is high level of illiteracy, massive dropout rate at middle and high school levels, and limited access to higher education. An uncertain employment future for the educated and loosing a potential earner by sending him/her to school operates behind the withdrawal or the massive dropout rate of the Dalit students. An additional factor has been the oppression of the Dalit students by many teachers and fellow upper caste students who make classroom an inhospitable and derisive space for the Dalits.[17]

Despite these handicaps, the numbers of literate Dalits has doubled (from 4,96,409 to 10,01,028) within a span of ten years between 1981

[15] Government of Haryana, 1981, *Prosperity with Justice*, Chandigarh: Director, Public Relations, p. 74.

[16] Partap C. Aggarwal and Mohammad Siddiq Ashraf, 1976, *Equality through Privilege: A Study of Special Privileges of Scheduled Castes in Haryana*, New Delhi: Sri Ram Centre for Industrial Relations and Human Resources, pp. 54–5.

[17] For similar observation, see Vijay Prashad, 2000, *Untouchable Freedom: A Social History of a Dalit Community*, New Delhi: Oxford University Press, p. 126.

and 1991.[18] Even then, the rate of literacy among the Dalits is only 39.22 per cent as compared to 48.80 per cent among the non-Dalits in Haryana.[19] Among the so-called literate Dalits, there are only 9 per cent who are matriculate and above.[20] Yet, the popular opinion among the upper caste groups holds that had it not been for education, the lower caste people would not have come into their own 'despite all the quotas (government allotted reservations for Dalits in the services) in the world'. *'Education ne sab ka bhatta bittha diya'* (education is at the root of all ills), they opine.

These viewpoints are not without some substance, though they smack of casteism. Out of a total number of 3,16,472 government employees in Haryana till March 1999, there were 55,697 or 17.59 per cent who belonged to the scheduled caste groups.[21] Most of this representation remains in the lower paid, Class IV jobs, like that of the sweepers, office messengers, gardeners, night watchmen, and others, but the ranks of Dalit recruits from category III upwards, that is, postman, or office employee, or clerk and above, have been increasing steadily. According to the 28th Report of the Commission of Scheduled Castes and Scheduled Tribes, 1986–7, 20 per cent reservation quota filled in Haryana was as follows:[22] 5.6 per cent in Class I, 4.7 per cent in Class II, and 8.7 per cent in Class III. In these three categories, the reserved quota was nowhere near the prescribed 20 per cent. In Class IV alone it was 26.20 per cent, which was far above the prescribed percentage. It is clear that in Class IV, the Dalits are more than proportionately represented mainly because sweepers are included in that category. Castes other than Balmikis and Dhanaks are not willing to take up this polluting work. In the case of sweepers, the caste and its occupational association has not broken down. In a way it stands strengthened as

[18] See Government of Haryana, 1983, *Statistical Abstract of Haryana, 1981–82*, Chandigarh: Govt of Haryana, Economic and Statistical Organization, Planning Department, p. 65 and Government of Haryana, 1993, *Statistical Abstract of Haryana, 1991–92*, Chandigarh: Govt of Haryana, Economic and Statistical Organization, Planning Department, p. 73.

[19] See Government of Haryana, *Statistical Abstract of Haryana, 1999–2000*, pp. 72, 73.

[20] Calculated from *Census of Haryana, 1991*, pp. 780–1.

[21] Government of Haryana, *Statistical Abstract of Haryana, 1999–2000*, pp. 690–1, 708.

[22] Cited in Ghanshyam Shah (ed.), 2002, *Dalit and the State*, New Delhi: Concept Publishing Co. See introduction, p. 35.

several young men from among the Balmikis, after working as semi-skilled labour, have taken up sweeping, a highly stigmatized job, for its attractive remuneration and the security of tenure.[23]

The real resentment of the upper castes is coming for reservations in Class III, which is the largest category of employees in the government service and does not require high academic qualification. And it is coming from the lower sections of the upper caste groups who greatly resent the intrusion of the Dalits into what could have been positions that they wish to avail, for example, that of peons or clerks, as distinct from sweeping, and so on. The same goes for low 'technical' or skilled jobs like that of motor mechanic available in government-owned workshop attached to public transport corporations such as Haryana Roadways and Delhi Transport Corporation. The Dalit job holders in these may be diploma holders or risen from apprentices in private workshops. Yet, they have succeeded in providing competition to the lower sections of the upper caste groups. It may be noted that it is not merely the 'reserved quota' but also the competition provided by the Dalits in the 'general category' that is causing a lot of heartburn among other caste groups.[24] Another coveted post, which attracts competition and hence resentment, is school teaching. It demands a higher academic qualification than the other jobs just cited. The resentment of the upper caste groups against the Dalits taking over teaching jobs is heightened because they do not want their children to be taught by Dalit teachers. There are instances when the dominant caste groups beat up the Dalit teachers, on discovering their Dalit identity.[25]

Although a large number of the reserved posts, especially in the higher category, remain vacant and not filled, yet, on the whole, job reservations have helped in redefining the identity of Dalit youth. Moreover, it is because of reservations that certain Dalits have even come to occupy posts from where some of them are in a position to disperse favours to the members belonging to the upper caste groups. Many upper caste people spoke of the humiliation they face when they have to make petty requests to the Dalit officers for gaining certain favours. The Dalits, on the other hand, feel resentful that even when

[23] Aggarwal and Ashraf, *Equality through Privilege*, p. 131.
[24] I found that a number of Dalit candidates were selected on merit, competing in the general category rather than in the reserved one.
[25] Aggarwal and Ashraf, *Equality through Privilege*, p. 128.

they are better educated than the upper castes, the latter expect a certain behaviour from them which is not at one with their status or rank.

It may be noted that the Dalits are not challenging the near monopoly of the landownership of the upper caste groups, but are providing competition in the services by accessing seats through reservations. In fact, it is noticeable that the young boys among the dominant caste groups are not willing to settle down to an agricultural life in the village. The income generation in the green revolution areas has driven away rather than attracted the younger generation to agriculture.[26] There is, therefore, a great scramble for any employment, high or low, whatever the social status. In a situation where there are more than eight lakh unemployed in Haryana, the competition for government jobs, with its secure income, is intense. The figures of the unemployed (including non-literate, semi-literate, graduates, and above, including those technically qualified), registered with the unemployment exchanges in Haryana, had more than doubled in less than twenty years from 3,59,255 in 1980–1 to 8,11,359 in the year 1999—a staggering rise of 125 per cent.[27] Out of these, more than half are matriculates, undergraduates, graduates, and above.[28] The enormous increase in the number of educated unemployed in Haryana, despite the limited growth in education, has meant a great deal of competition for the existing jobs, making even the petty jobs attractive. The intense competition provided by limited jobs offered (especially in the lower class categories) by the local district and state administration, tends to isolate and target the reserved posts, which are blamed for limiting the jobs for others.

[26] The village women opine that even those boys who have only studied up to matric (class ten) and had, in fact, qualified by '*nakkal*' (copying or cheating) wanted jobs in the white-collared professions. This observation is confirmed by another study which similarly comments that a large chunk of the educated and semi-educated rural population under the age of twenty-five in Haryana, ranging from the most difficult category of 'tenth class failed' to 'BA-third class', want non-farm jobs and cannot get them. Sheila Bhalla, 1981, 'Islands of Growth: A Note on Haryana Experience and Some Possible Implications', *Economic and Political Weekly*, vol. XVI, no. 23, 6 June, pp. 1022–30.

[27] Government of Haryana, *Statistical Abstract of Haryana, 1999–2000*, pp. 530–1. The caste wise break-up of the unemployed is not available.

[28] Government of Haryana, 1990, *Economic Survey of Haryana, 1989–1990*, Chandigarh: Planning Department, Economic and Statistical Organization, pp. 15–17.

Resisting Reservations and Accumulation of Social Capital

The reservation category, enlarged under the implementation of the Mandal Commission Report in 1990 on caste-based reservation of the Other Backward Classes (OBCs), has turned matters much worse for the upper caste groups. The OBCs are middle ranging caste groups which are just above the scheduled castes and though not 'untouchable', they have faced discrimination and are socially 'backward'. In Haryana, there are seventy-six castes listed as the OBCs, adding to the thirty-seven scheduled caste groups that already exist under the reservation category.[29] The OBCs, whose quota for jobs was put at 27 per cent by the central government, have been allotted 5 per cent reservation in government jobs and 2 per cent seat reservation in professional colleges in Haryana. The Mandal report evoked extreme reactions, especially among the upper caste groups comprising the dominant landowning caste groups like the Jats, Rajputs, and others, as also the trading and business castes, like the Banias and Brahmins. In August 1990, the students of Kurukshetra, Rohtak, and Hissar actively agitated against it. The lumpen element of the so-called Green Brigade, an outfit of the then ruling party (Bhartiya Lok Dal) and dominated by the Jats, which had entered the student's rank, was violent and undisciplined.[30] Public property worth several crores of rupees was destroyed. Significantly, the movement against the Mandal Commission Report was not so much against the backward classes as it was against reservations in favour of the scheduled castes. The agitation was used to demand abolition of reservations altogether. The dominant Jats of Haryana, while condemning reservations for the Dalits, have demanded to be included among the OBCs, like in Rajasthan and Delhi.[31] Indeed, Devi Lal, the former Chief Minister of Haryana and the then Deputy Prime Minister in 1990, had strong reservations regarding the implementation

---

[29] K.C. Yadav, 1994, *India's Unequal Citizens: A Study of Other Backward Classes*, New Delhi: Manohar, p. 70.

[30] Ibid., pp. 177–9.

[31] *Dainik Tribune*, 2000, 29 August, Delhi edition, p. 4; 6 September, p. 4; 17 September, p. 4; 19 September, p. 7. In Haryana, the demand to do away with reservations, although an unvoiced demand due to political exigencies, exists along with the demand of the Jats to be included among the category of OBC. However, being a dominant caste group, the Jats perhaps know that such a demand is impossible to concede. Doing away with reservations, according to them, alone will stop the 'rise of Chuhras and Chamars'.

of Mandal scheme.[32] He tried but failed to persuade the government to alter their view.

The current leading politicians of Haryana, including former Chief Minister, O.P. Chautala, are openly sceptical of reservations not only for the OBCs but also for the Dalits.[33] Under him, certain government measures have gone distinctly against the Dalits, especially in relation to facilitating the accumulation of social capital in the form of education and its use in gaining jobs through reservations. For example, in September 2003, the exemption of examination fee uniformly for all Dalit children was set aside.[34] Instead a selective criterion was initiated. The Haryana School Examination Board introduced examination fee for those Dalit children who came from families having income above Rs 350 per month. This measure has worsened the support structure for Dalit education, which is quite inadequate and, in any case, poorly financed. Earlier in June 2002, recruitment of Dalits to the post of police constables was made more difficult by raising the required height of a candidate from 5 feet 6 inches to 5 feet 8 inches.[35] The change, according to the chief minister, was brought about because it was important that the law enforcers must be 'seen to be dominant'. As many Dalits held that 'their boys are not so tall', this move could only be perceived as 'anti-Dalit and anti-reservations'—a kind of reversal through the back door. According to the Dalits, this change has had an effect on their recruitment in the police. Although statistics are not available, there are said to be very few Dalits, especially at the officers' level, in the Haryana police. Clearly, as the police are a source of enormous power, both punitive and coercive (as well as illegal gratification), the ruling classes feel the need to guard these posts far more closely from 'encroachments'.

Another corresponding field of authority and power given equally close scrutiny is that of the armed forces. The opening out of the Indian Army, after independence, to all regardless of region, class, and caste,

---

[32] Christopher Jaffrelot, 2003, *India's Silent Revolution: The Rise of the Low Castes in North Indian Politics*, Delhi: Permanent Black, p. 339. Mohinder Singh Tikait, leader of Jats of western UP, also demanded abolition of reservations, which forms a part of his charter of demands.

[33] See a press report on the chief minister in *Dainik Jagran*, 2001, 9 Feburary, Gurgaon edition, pp. 1, 15.

[34] *Dainik Jagran*, 2003, 6 September, Gurgaon edition, p. 19.

[35] *Dainik Jagran*, 2003, 5 October, Gurgaon edition, p. 7. For general category, this height was raised from 5 feet 7 inches to 5 feet 9 inches. See the chief minister's answers to queries from the janata (public).

and allotment of 'recruitment quotas' to different states (according to a certain undisclosed percentage of male figures of recruiting ages),[36] added to heightening of the perception of 'the rise of the Dalit'. This opening out has led to a great deal of resentment among members of the traditional recruiting bases. In reality, this ideal could hardly be achieved all at once. As the earlier recruitment patterns based on the 'martial race' concept[37] (which excluded the Dalits) and 'regional preferences' stood to be gravely disturbed by this 'opening out', the new scheme has had to be introduced very gradually. Consequently, despite this 'opening up' of the army, by and large, the same 'classes' and 'castes' of people are still recruited in the army as in the colonial period.[38] The 'others', for example, the Dalits are known to be largely, though not exclusively, recruited in the non-combat forces. Consequently, the attention and pressure exercised by the two chief ministers of Haryana, Bansi Lal and Devi Lal (both Jat by caste), to increase the army recruitment quota,[39] turned out to benefit the traditional recruiting base drawn primarily from among 'martial' caste groups like the Jats, rather than the Dalits.

In a situation of severe unemployment, such open stand of the Haryana government in favour of dominant castes can only be received as anti-Dalit. The implementation of the new economic policies adopted since 1991, leading to successive withdrawal of the state from the economic management of the resources of the country, has meant not only a severe reduction of employment for all, including the Dalits, but also a dilution of the reservation policy.[40] Privatization, with its

[36] Personal communication by Lt General B.T. Pandit, Adjutant-General, 1991, Army Headquarters, New Delhi, 1 April.

[37] For details, see Prem Chowdhry, 1994, *The Veiled Women: Shifting Gender Equations in Rural Haryana, 1880–1990*, New Delhi: Oxford University Press, pp. 32–6.

[38] Thus, the contribution of states like Punjab and Haryana which had been sending an overwhelming number of recruits had to be whittled down in favour of other states, resulting in their total contribution to be less than what it was under the British. However, it still remains far above their population levels. Personal communication by Lt General B.T. Pandit, Adjutant-General, 1991, Army Head-quarters, New Delhi, 1 April.

[39] Ibid.

[40] For details, see B.L. Mungekar, 1999, 'State, Market and the Dalits: Analytics of the New Economic Policy', in S.M. Michael (ed.), *Dalits in Modern India: Vision and Values*, New Delhi: Vistaar Publications, pp. 287–302.

accent on 'merit', has shown itself against any sort of reservation for the Dalits or any other backward castes. Entry of multinationals and other firms (for example, catering to 'out sourcing' from the USA) has also shown its preference for urban, public school, English medium upper caste candidates, much to the disadvantage of local, Hindi-speaking ruralites from Haryana,[41] fragmenting the Haryanavi society even more. The existing socio-economic disparities and the rising cost of education do not allow the majority in Haryana, as elsewhere in India, the opportunity of gaining competition worthiness as the quality of education generally imparted remains 'sub-standard'. Those who are availing the advantages of recent changes are primarily either the urban or affluent ruralites and/or the non-Haryanavis. This has had the effect of deepening caste and class polarization of Haryanavi society even more sharply. The recent mushrooming of the English medium public schools in Haryana, considered to be the 'fastest growing private enterprise', is related to the demand in the private sector. Significantly, it is not only the majority of the Dalits who cannot avail of this expensive education but also the lower sections of the upper caste groups.[42] Unable and perhaps unwilling to raise the objections against their own caste men, the upper caste groups tend to locate competition elsewhere, deflecting it on to the shoulders of the Dalits.

The Stratified Layer: Middle Class and Politics

The universal chorus among the dominant caste groups that 'the lower castes are rising' is projected to be at the expense of the upper castes as a whole and not necessarily against sections of them. As a proof of how well the Dalits are doing, members of the dominant caste groups point out that most of them (Dalits) wear better clothes than what they can afford to! Many have cell phones, two-in-one with radio and cassette players, see films, and sing filmi songs! Dalits continue to be 'them' and the 'other'. It may be noted that like the landowning caste groups many Dalits also fall in the overlapping urban–rural category.[43] Although, among the Dalits, the migration of women to the urban centres is

---

[41] Such social stands have created a demand for the knowledge of English language in the whole of northern India.

[42] Even those who can avail of expensive English education, priority is given to the boys. In the same family, the boy goes to the English medium school and the girl to the Hindi medium.

[43] Chowdhry, *The Veiled Women*, pp. 388–9.

more noticeable,[44] it is also true that their attachment to the village or the small piece of land that they may have is no less than that of the landowning groups. Like the dominant caste groups, many among them live in the rural areas and commute daily to their work places. Some others have their families in the rural areas, while they may reside in urban centres. With their incomes, as the case studies in the next section show, they have been able to build *pacca* houses in the village and also own cattle. In some instances, their standard of living not only equals that of the lower class among the dominant caste groups but also sometimes has a distinct edge. This is all the more noticeable as the social geography of certain villages stands greatly changed. Because of the unplanned expansion and growth of population, the earlier open spaces between different *pannas* (sub-division of a village) and *thola* (sub-division of a panna) have been built upon and occupied, leading to mixed pannas of dominant caste and lower caste groups. This ostensible blurring of caste distinctions observed in segregated dwelling spaces, in combination with urbanization and homogenization regarding appearance, consumption, and life style has had an unsettling effect. The dominant caste groups know that sections of Dalits cannot be singled out from among them, as perhaps they could be earlier.

The forever simmering discontent and resentment of the dominant caste groups relates to the Dalits assuming city norms and causing confusion of identities and crumbling of boundaries between 'them' and 'us', and translates into an 'imagined threat'. This change is more immediately visible in the realm of family, living style, and marriage celebrations. Since occasions like marriage verge on public domain, it has even attracted violence from the dominant caste groups. The violence inflicted on a Dalit bridegroom riding a horse—a symbol of power and authority—and the accompanying wedding procession in village Lohari Jat of district Bhiwani in November 2002, is a case in point. More recently, in February 2003, in village Harsaula of Kaithal district, the Jats did not allow the Dalits to celebrate the Ravidas Jayanti festival. The Dalits were told to remain within 'their own boundaries', and were beaten up brutally for not heeding this advice. About 200 Dalits had to leave the village and take shelter in the district headquarters. It was only after a month that they were rehabilitated in the village by the intervention of the district administration. Many such sporadic

[44] Ibid., pp. 194–5.

cases can be cited as examples. Consequently, any breakdown in the correspondence existing between life style and caste, and caste and occupation, is construed as an attempt to change caste itself and hence, resisted by the other caste groups.

This disjunction in caste and occupation, and in caste and lifestyle, is most noticeable among the newly emergent 'middle class' of educated, in-service Dalits—a class that was not visible in the colonial period. If social status is evaluated with the help of an objective criterion such as level of education, income, or occupation, those Dalits who have advanced upward to higher government jobs have undoubtedly reached middle-class positions. The emergence of this nebulous middle-class category among the Dalits has proved disconcerting for the upper caste groups as there is a shift of emphasis from birth to one's acquired status through self-achievement, enterprise, and agency—all qualities associated with upper caste groups, masculinity, and their monopoly of power. The Dalits stereotyped as inherently inferior, endowed with a low intellect, supine, and docile are repeatedly breaking this image by their educational achievements, occasional assertive behaviour, and demands, and exhibition of consciousness of their power and rights in a democratic polity. The educated class among the Dalits has a new social perception as they have access to social mobility and portal of power, however limited. This advantageous approach was earlier the preserve of the high born. In other words, a different 'social rank' reflecting the occurrence of a 'class system', demanding a distinct degree of 'social honour' in which birth is in the background, has undermined the hereditary occupation/specialization and the hierarchically arranged society/groups.

Moreover, as Dalits, they may lack organization and coherence in the local context, but as a class category, they are vocal and 'leaders' of a different society. This class has the capacity to evolve towards greater socio-economic complexity leading to a transformation of stratification. In other states, this class has provided the fulcrum of rising criticism against the discrimination and atrocities committed against the Dalits. For instance, in the neighbouring state of UP, the Backward and Minority Communities' Employees' Federation (BAMCEF), established in 1978 by Kanshi Ram (a Ramdasia Chamar Sikh from a Punjab village and a government employee), was a successful attempt. The BAMCEF could organize the educated government employees, who had benefited from the reservations, and the subordinate sections of the middle class among the Dalits, as a core body to contribute to the welfare of their communities.[45] They later came to have a political thrust and proved to be the parent body of the present, highly successful Bhujan Samaj Party (BSP) established in 1984.[46] A middle class among the Dalits has been in the process of formation and consolidation in different parts of India. The educated among the Dalits act as leaders to unify their caste group to compete for jobs and political power in democratic/ electoral contestations.

In Haryana, too, the upper castes are aware that the contest—material, social, and political—is likely to come from this class segment of the Dalits. Politically, the Dalits have supported the Congress, by and large, since the colonial period.[47] In the post-colonial period, a greater diversification of their support for different groups and parties has taken place. Yet, the possibility of change, which may mean an identification of the problems of the community rather than individual mobility through a political party, has always existed. The likelihood of such happening has been very unsettling for the political leadership drawn from among the dominant castes, greatly troubled by the underlying tension between them. So far, they have succeeded in 'capping their rise', both socially and politically.[48] Yet, there are apprehensions that a Dalit middle class that has long been in the process of formation and

[45] Abhay Kumar Dubey, 2001, 'Anatomy of a Dalit Power Player: A Study of Kanshi Ram', in Ghanshyam Shah (ed.), *Dalit Identity and Politics: Cultural Subordination and the Dalit Challenge*, New Delhi: Sage, pp. 288–310.

[46] The BSP emerged in the 1980s and 1990s as a force to be reckoned with, in the four north Indian states of UP, Punjab, Madhya Pradesh, and Haryana. In the 1998 Lok Sabha elections, the party polled more than 20 per cent votes in two constituencies of Haryana. The total Dalit strength in Haryana is 19.75 per cent. See Pushpendr, 2001, 'Dalit Assertion through Electoral Politics', in Shah (ed.), *Dalit Identity and Politics*, pp. 311–54.

[47] Prem Chowdhry, 1991, 'Social Support Base and Electoral Politics: The Congress in Colonial Southeast Punjab', *Modern Asian Studies*, vol. 25, no. 4, pp. 811–31.

[48] For example, in the April–May 2004 Lok Sabha elections, the entire state unit of the BSP, including the state president, Ashok Sherwal, joined the Indian National Lok Dal (INLD) of Chautala. It may be noted that it was under the INLD government that the state witnessed a spate of crimes against Dalits. This action exposed the BSP concern for the cause of Dalits. On 29 April 2004, the lone BSP legislator in Haryana, Bishanlal Saini, declared his support for the INLD candidate from the reserved seat of Ambala. Saini even hailed Chief Minister Chautala as 'a well-wisher' of Dalits and backward castes. See T.K. Rajalakhmi, 2004, 'Oppressed and Marginalised', *Frontline*, 21 May, p. 25.

consolidation in Haryana is likely to throw up social and political leaders to unify their caste groups to compete for political power, as in the case of UP. It is clear that the Dalits are perceived as political opponents.

However, the position and role of this class, given to contradictory pulls, remains ambiguous and even opposing. Here, it may be noted that the concerns of the middle-class Dalits are different from the concerns of the majority of Dalits who are connected with agriculture. Moreover, in certain ways, the emergence of this class has had adverse implications not only for inter-community relations but also for the internal cohesion of the Dalits themselves.[49] The opinion surveys indicate that quite often the caste allegiance of successful Dalits recedes into the background, making it difficult for them to give effective leadership.[50] Similarly, the cross-caste connections of middle-class Dalits are also effective in negating their caste ties. The resultant social fragmentation prevents the forging of a sense of political community. Without such a sense, no political action can be effective.[51] There is, however, no appreciable group mobility among this class of Dalits vis-à-vis other social groups, although the individual upward mobility has taken place in many instances. A lack of social integration with the middle class of other upper caste groups does have the effect of pushing the Dalits towards their own caste men. It is also undeniable that the educated among them have a group identity that can be used to galvanize unity and wider support.[52] It may also be noted that it is not the lowest

[49] For the social fragmentation of Dalits and their inability to come together as a cohesive community which may form the basis of political action, see Ramashray Roy and Vijay Bahadur Singh, 1990, 'The Harijan Elite at the Crossroads: Results from a Survey', in Subrata Kumar Mitra (ed.), *Politics of Positive Discrimination*, Bombay: Popular Prakashan, pp. 321–39.

[50] E. Kulke, 1983, 'The Problems of the Educated Middle Class Harijans', in John P. Neelson (ed.), *Social Inequality and Political Structures*, New Delhi: Manohar, pp. 135–75.

[51] Confronted with this situation, the Dalit elite prefers the path of personal salvation through upward social mobility, better jobs, and access to power through different political parties. This prevents them from effectively identifying themselves with the problems of their community and making serious attempts to solve them. It puts distance between them and their community and arouses suspicion about their intent. It further fragments the community. See Yadav, *India's Unequal Citizens*, pp. 177–9.

[52] In Bihar, for instance, they have formed an informal association which is convened at irregular intervals to discuss topics of common concern.

sections among the Dalits who raise the issue of caste identities and social dignity, but the educated/employed and articulate.

There are also certain other factors that impede the coming together of the Dalits as a community. The benefits accruing through positive discrimination are neither enough nor shared by all. The overwhelming majority of successful candidates come from a few Dalit castes, sections of who had enjoyed a somewhat better position in the colonial period. Among these groups, the Chamars are leading in Haryana.[53] Also, the field experience shows that family members of those who have been earlier recipients of its benefits best avail of the gains of reservations. In effect, an elite has grown up within the Dalits that tends to reproduce itself and, thus, monopolize the advantages provided by the government leading to a kind of 'Brahmanization' of the upper crust of the Dalits. This is a point of great heartburn and division among the Dalits who, in their scramble for limited seats, demand a one-time use of reservation category for a Dalit family.[54] Not withstanding these internal fissures, it is clear that for the upper caste groups, middle-class sections of Dalits are posing a threat. Clearly, although the Dalits are spoken of and projected as a monolith—undifferentiated category—the reality is entirely different.

INTER-CASTE ASSOCIATIONS: ELOPEMENTS AND MARRIAGES

This more complex and stratified layer among the Dalits spells 'danger', especially in relation to miscegenation. The increasing liaisons between youth drawn from among the Dalits and upper caste groups signify and symbolize, in the opinion of the latter, 'the high point' in the social aspirations and social mobility of the lower caste groups. They find it threatening and greatly upsetting of the status quo. It may be noted that it is mostly, though not entirely, the second and third generation of such Dalits, with an entirely different experience of their caste disability than the first generation, who are perceived to be most involved in such associations.

The fear of such associations has assumed urgency because of the extremely tight marriage market, which has had deep repercussions for both intra-caste and inter-caste relationships. There are a variety

---

[53] Aggarwal and Ashraf, *Equality through Privilege*, pp. 125–6, 146–7.

[54] Voiced by the Dalit candidates belonging to the Indian Forest Service, Gurgaon, in January 2004.

of reasons for this constricted market that, as I have argued elsewhere, has heightened the internal crisis faced by the dominant caste groups like the Jats.[55] The status of different Jat clans are in flux with different groups either claiming a higher/equal status or attempting to maintain their status against challenges and erosions effected by other clan groups within the caste fold. The question of marriage is proving highly contentious and inviting the wrath of the caste council if it has not observed certain customary rules of kinship and territorial exogamy, equated with status and hierarchy. This extremely tight marriage market, apart from other reasons, has resulted in a large number of men remaining unmarried in Haryana. The figures available for unmarried men between ages of 15 and 44 years, as already pointed out in the previous chapter, show 36. 24 per cent in the whole of Haryana and 44 per cent in a district like Rohtak.[56] These frequently overlap the unemployed men, as the unemployed find it difficult to get married, causing a great deal of anxiety. A combination of the unemployed and unmarried men is especially noticeable among the lower sections of the upper caste groups who are pitted in competition against the upwardly mobile class from among the Dalits. In such a situation, the fear and threat from a Dalit assumes exaggerated proportions. The situation turns complicated, as the dominant caste men, convinced of the 'inherent lustful nature' of all women, perceive their women to sexually 'desire' men from the lower castes. From women's side, such sentiments are freely expressed in exclusive women's songs.[57] Several attempts to curb or replace these songs have failed. Since the higher castes can hardly blame their own women openly, the onus of such associations is put down to the Dalits' 'arrogance' in coveting 'our girls'. This sentiment turns the outcome of such associations more violent.

For condemning such 'social aspirations', an allegedly 'true incident', which took place recently, is popularly recounted and held as an example. It is narrated that a Dalit officer was heard boasting that he was getting marriage offers for his son from Jat families. He was soundly beaten up and publicly made to apologize to the Jat biradari by holding

[55] For details, see Chapter 11 in this volume.

[56] See *Census of Haryana, 1991*, pp. 22–3.

[57] Prem Chowdhry, 2001, 'Lustful Women, Elusive Lovers: Identifying Males as Objects of Female Desire', *Indian Journal of Gender Studies*, vol. 8, no. 1, pp. 23–50.

his ears. Recent research has pointed out that the majority of employed Dalits consider themselves equal to any other caste group.[58] Another study similarly states that Dalits, with a relatively high level of education, want to marry 'educated' girls from upper castes, since it is very difficult for them to find an appropriately educated girl from the Dalit castes.[59] Indeed, among the total number of Dalits in Haryana who are matriculate and above, only one-fourth are women.[60] Notwithstanding this 'desire' of the educated Dalits, it is difficult to entertain or accept this allegedly true incident or the viewpoint of some scholars in view of the strict rules of caste endogamy for marriage and pressure exercised by the village and caste community in making people observe it.[61]

Importantly, the given story underlines the changed class status of the Dalit that has put him in a different category than the popularly accepted undifferentiated mass going under the name of Dalit. This class status in the eyes of the Dalit is portrayed as having overridden his caste status, though not in the eyes of the Jats. It belies the suggestion that once a Dalit attains a certain status, his caste consideration falls away or is ignored. The narrative begins by hinting at the weakening or broadening of the all too familiar stereotypes of the Dalits held by the high caste, only to confirm it more vigorously. It expresses the underlying hope and insecurity of both the Dalits and the Jats vis-a-vis the possibility of the former commanding a different class status and the effects of such a posturing on the Jats. The likelihood of such an eventuality coming to a pass is a matter of anxiety for the non-Dalits. This is specially sharpened as in certain high profile cases, the Dalit and upper caste marriages have even been celebrated with

---

[58] This self-confidence extends from education, work, behaviour, lifestyle, and consequent high self-esteem. Only a minority of the employed, mostly in lower categories, did not feel themselves socially to be equal to other caste groups. See Richard Pais, 1990, 'Scheduled Castes, Employment and Social Mobility', in Mitra (ed.), *Politics of Positive Discrimination*, pp. 321–39.

[59] Kulke, 'The Problems of the Educated Middle Class Harijans', pp. 135–47.

[60] Calculated from *Census of Haryana, 1991*, pp. 780–1.

[61] In this connection, Partap C. Aggarwal maintains, on the basis of his interviews with certain members of Dalits, that in Haryana and Punjab, marriage alliances are being offered to educated youth by Jat and Brahmin families. I think further investigations and a more detailed study need to be undertaken to ascertain the validity of this contention. See his, 1983, *Half Way to Equality*, New Delhi: Manohar, pp. 8, 22, 44, 107.

much fanfare and gained social approval and media blessings.[62] The given narrative also underlines a reversal of roles and the jealousy/ resentment evoked by the 'progress' of the Dalits. Indeed, the charge of jealousy and resentment is openly thrown by the Dalits against the landowning castes.

Customary Rules and Traditional Concepts

Inter-caste alliances, especially among upper caste and lower caste groups, were not entirely uncommon in the colonial period. However, as I argue elsewhere, this was more often than not confined to a secondary alliance rather than the primary one.[63] More importantly, this practice did not go unchallenged. From the late nineteenth century onwards, attempts were made to move the court in those cases where caste endogamy had not been observed.[64] A large number of such cases involved lower caste women. Yet, taking wives from low caste never became a norm as such, nor was it practised on a wide scale. In the changed socio-economy of the post-colonial period, such secondary associations are no longer socially acceptable. Both men and women are under pressure to remain within the caste, though this pressure on men is not as great or equal to that exercised on women. There is certainly a constriction of opportunity not only for men but, more importantly, for lower caste women who earlier had the facility to marry in castes above them.

In this essay, however, the focus of study is essentially on primary association, which continues to be very strictly governed by certain

[62] A recent high class, publicly celebrated marriage of a Bania girl and a Chamar boy, both medical doctors by profession in Rohtak, and scions of noted families, is held as a case in point. This is a rare example of *pratiloma* marriage where an upper caste woman married a low caste man. A high profile inter-caste marriage, it even basked in societal approbation. For example, high government officials, political dignitaries, and business people made it a point to attend this wedding. In this case, caste as a marker of identification is subsumed under class, education, and personality of the two families and their status in society. It is undeniable that those from the younger generation with increased sense of self-identity, self-worth, and education are likely to have a different attitude towards inter-caste marriages.

[63] Prem Chowdhry, 1997, 'Enforcing Cultural Codes: Gender and Violence in Northern India', *Economic and Political Weekly*, vol. XXXII, no. 19, 10–16 May, pp. 1019–28.

[64] See Chapter 5 in this volume.

rules. The customary rules regulating the *biah* or *shadi* (marriage) for all caste groups, upper or lower, uphold caste endogamy and village exogamy. (Caste endogamy places all the caste groups, and not necessarily the Dalits, outside the system of alliance, although it has to be acknowledged that the reaction to an alliance with a Dalit evokes far pronounced and violent a reaction than the other caste groups.) This means, as stated in the previous chapter, that all men and women of ones own generation in a village not withstanding their caste affiliations are considered to be siblings and bound by incest prohibition which forbids sex as well as marriage between them.[65] Such restrictions are helpful in maintaining the highly idealized concept of biradari and bhaichara in a village, negating all hierarchy among different caste groups. The reality however is contrary to this. Not infrequently secret sexual liaisons are formed between these classificatory brothers and sisters. But there is no social approval of them in the form of marriage. They are violently resisted as they are considered incestuous. Legally however, such customary marriage restrictions have no validity.[66] Yet, in questions of marriage, as I argue elsewhere, the role of the state remains highly ambiguous.[67] It emerges as providing a space for social change as well as space for intervention to stem the process of social change. The customary law, on the other hand, unlike the law of the land, does not permit inter-caste marriages.

To overcome caste and customary prohibitions some couples run away from the village to get married, evoking great tension and violence in the rural areas. It may be stated here that these breaches are not new; they have taken place even in the past. The post-colonial political economy suggests an increase, but it is difficult to confirm it statistically with any degree of accuracy or certainty. The local dominant opinion, by linking these breaches to the 'rise of the Dalits', certainly propounds an increase. Such breaches provoke the biradari to use the traditional tools available to them in the form of caste or village panchayats to stem such attempts. For illustrating the outcome of such runaway cases, I shall take up a few case studies, involving the Dalits. Two of the more recent and intertwined cases belong to village Loharhedi in district Jhajjar. The resolution of these cases by the caste panchayat reiterated

[65] For details see Chapter 11 in this volume.
[66] The Hindu Marriage Act, 1955, however, did impose certain restrictions. For details see Chapter 11 in this volume, n2 and n3.
[67] See Chapter 10 in this volume.

the might of customary practices and cultural norms in the face of law. The study highlights how in the exercise of these norms, differential treatment is meted out to the concerned parties based upon their caste and class affiliations as well as gender considerations.

Unmatched Matches

In September 2000 in village Loharhedi, a Jat-dominated village, Ravinder, a Jat boy, and Sushila, a Balmiki girl, were hauled up before an all-caste panchayat of the village. Their 'love affair' was severely condemned. The panchayat decreed that blackening their faces, cutting off their hair, and taking them around the village on donkeys should publicly shame them. Ravinder's face was blackened and so was the forehead of a bitterly crying Sushila. A part of Ravinder's head was shaved off and Sushila's long hair was cut from the middle. Ravinder was also made to wear a garland of shoes. When they were being taken around the village on donkeys, Ravinder jumped onto his friend's scooter and escaped. The traumatized girl was taken home and later, dispatched to her relatives in Mumbai. The villagers were quiet about the whereabouts of the boy. He was known to have started to visit the village again within six months of this case. There was, however, no guarantee for the girl's safety if she were to return to the village. Her family feared for her life.

The Balmiki family was extremely bitter and resentful of the treatment meted out to Sushila. They pointed out that it was unprecedented and against all cultural norms and tradition for a girl to be publicly summoned and punished by the caste panchayat. They also pointed out that in another case, which took place about six months ago, involving Sarla, a Jat girl, and Ashok, a Nai boy, no one had dared behave towards the girl in such a manner. The couple had run away and got married. They were caught in Mandi, in Himachal Pradesh, and taken into police custody. Sarla refused to leave her husband to go with her father and brother. It was only after the Jats threatened Ashok's family of dire consequences and expulsion from the village that Ashok's family undertook to persuade Sarla to come back to the village on the promise that she would be publicly married to Ashok. Once home, she was handed over to her natal family, where she was brutally beaten and pressurized into disowning and condemning Ashok. This led to slapping of cases of abduction, kidnapping, and rape on him. According to Ashok's brother, apart from these cases, another equally fictitious and criminal case of an attempt to murder (the driver of the vehicle the couple had used to make a getaway) was slapped on Ashok. Because of the seriousness of the charges, Ashok was not granted bail by the court. In fact, Ashok's brother was not keen to pursue bail for him, as he feared that the dominant Jat community of the village might kill Ashok. He maintained that he would rather wait for this matter to die out, as he did not want to endanger Ashok's life. Till date (2003), Ashok remains involved in a protracted criminal litigation. These cases will take a long time to fold up.

Although both Ashok and Sarla are alive, in several cases, the couple is killed. In May 2002 case of village Shimli, district Rohtak, a runaway girl belonging to a Jat family and a lower caste boy were hounded and caught in Gurgaon.[68] The villagers confidentially admitted that they were brought back and administered poison and burnt while still alive. The police was informed only after a day of their cremation. The police rounded up several people for an inquiry. All of them were set free as no witnesses were coming forward. The police pleaded its helplessness.

Similarly, in 1998, in village Ratdhana, a Brahmin girl and a Lohar boy were tied to an electric pole and hacked to death, right in the middle of the village compound. No one came forward as a witness. Later, a Lohar relative of the boy was accused and booked of murder by the police. The general opinion of people in this region, cutting across caste and class, is that if a lower caste man is involved with an upper caste woman, he is invariably killed. And the girl, whether belonging to the upper caste or the lower, is almost certainly eliminated. This is observed to be the general pattern in Haryana, adopted by the dominant caste groups and decreed by the caste panchayat.

Sarla, by such standards, should certainly have been killed by her family members. Although not killed, Sarla was quickly married off, as an alternative action. Sarla belonged to a well-to-do family. Her family owned about a 100 *bighas* of land—the largest single holding in the village. Her grandfather had been a *sarpanch* and one of her uncles was in the police. She was married quietly, in a greatly compromised match, in village Nooran Kheda of district Sonepat. It may be noted that in cases such as these, where the girl's 'notoriety' becomes public knowledge, the much desired status hypergamy for the girl, or for the family, cannot be maintained. Sarla's husband and his three other brothers were all illiterate and unemployed. With inconsequential

---

[68] For a report of this case, see *Dainik Jagran*, 2002, 5 May, Gurgaon edition, pp. 1, 13.

landholding, they severely lacked income or other means of support. This factor had kept them unmarried. Sarla's husband was reputed to be an alcoholic who was given to beating her frequently. The villagers of Nooran Kheda held his family in great contempt. Having had to spend a great deal of money in marrying her off, Sarla's natal family showed no further interest in her. Informants say that for all purposes she might well be dead for them. Sarla was said to be extremely unhappy in her marriage and people opined that she might commit suicide as many of the girls are known to do in such cases.

Indeed, it is a well known and openly stated fact that a large number of girls who are forcibly 'retrieved' in cases of elopement or marriage are either murdered or pressurized to commit suicide. The girls are either administered poison (a popular pesticide) or pushed into the well—the two most well-known ways to eliminate them. These are then claimed as suicides. The police readily accept this contention and close the case. According to the police, this is because they know that no one will come to testify to the contrary. A girl's death is seen as the only way in which the 'honour' of the family can be salvaged. To this may be added the financial burden of marrying a girl who was said to have eloped. In the given dowry economy of Haryana, such a girl is more of a burden than in a normal case.

In keeping with the 'conspiracy of silence' maintained by the village and caste community, the caste panchayat that met immediately after the arrest of the couple (Sarla and Ashok) was absolutely quiet on the role of the girl. About this silence they pointed out that a *beti* of the village was shared by all and could not be dishonoured. The panchayat gave its verdict to socially boycott Ashok's family. Interestingly, this boycott could not be observed for too long and collapsed within six months. The only Nai family in the village, Ashok's family belonged to the middle caste group (OBC) and not to the scheduled caste category. Moreover, this family was not inconsequential in the village. Two out of six of Ashok's brothers were in government service. The rest were in family business as the leading suppliers of milk to the city. They also had moneylending as a side business.

Cases such as this, located in sound financial base, give substance to the general opinion voiced by many of the lower caste groups, mentioned earlier, who hold themselves in high esteem and find themselves to be equal to other caste groups. Indeed, Ashok's brother, when interviewed, repeatedly asserted that the Jat girl was 'after Ashok' and was determined to marry him and that it was she who took the lead. A similar opinion was voiced in another runaway case of village Narela, involving a Jat girl and a Dalit boy.[69] In this case, the family members of the Dalit boy had blamed the Jat girl by maintaining: 'koi mard nahin bhagaa sakta, aurat hi bhagaati hai' (It is always a woman who initiates an elopement. No man can do it). It may be noted here that the emphasis is not merely on gender here but also on caste. It implicitly accepts that no Dalit man can dare ask a Jat girl to elope.

The sound economic standing of Ashok's family turned the implementation of social boycott decreed by the Jat panchayat extremely difficult. The panchayat's decree was repeatedly infringed by their creditors, which included even some of the Jats. Imposition of fines on the violators by the panchayat became difficult to implement. Many a times infringements had to be overlooked, because the Jats were the culprits. As Ashok's brother maintained, 'addha gaon hamare paise se khata hai' (half the village is our creditor), made the panchayat's verdict infructuous. Consequently, when the second case, that of Ravinder and Sushila, erupted soon afterwards, the frustration regarding this case had built up considerably among the Jats.

The Power Equations: Dalits and Jats

The socio-economic profile of Loharhedi and a few details of the case establish direct linkages with the inter-community relationship between different sections of the dominant and lower caste groups analysed in the first section of this essay. It also brings to the fore certain dimensions regarding the selective use of cultural practices to settle scores in rural society which need to be highlighted. Loharhedi is an overwhelmingly Jat village with 80 per cent of Jat population. The Jats are severely divided. They occupy both the strata, that of the landowners as well as agricultural labourers. Many among the landowners also have additional income from sources other than agriculture, like the services. This gives them additional prosperity, prestige, and power. Ravinder's family, for example, not only had land but one of his uncles was in the police and his father, an ex-army man, had his pension, as well as his salary from his employment in a factory.

Apart from such families, there are a large number of Jats who own insignificant amount of land and some are even landless. They work as

---

[69] For details, see Peoples Union for Democratic Rights, 2003, *Courting Disaster: A Report on Inter-Caste Marriages, Society and State*, Delhi: PUDR, August.

agricultural labourers in the fields of their caste men, just as the lower caste groups. As the 'more hardy' Jats are preferred for agriculture labour by their caste men, there is perceptible tension between the lower class Jats and other lower caste groups. Yet, caste wise, the Jats have an upper hand and are keen to drive it home whenever the occasion arises. The former tend to gang up with their caste brothers against the latter. The lower castes, mainly consisting of Chamars and Balmikis, on the other hand, are numerically far fewer in village Loharhedi when compared to Jats. Most of them work as agricultural labourers. Yet, some of them who have been able to take advantage of educational opportunities have aspired, and some even gained, access to positions such as that of peons, clerks, drivers, or have been taken in the military service. Yet others, as mentioned earlier, have become salaried workers in the city centres by utilizing their traditional occupation of sweeping and cleaning to get into stable and gainful employment. Loharhedi Balmikis can be found as cleaners in hospitals in urban areas of Haryana like Chandigarh and even in places like Mumbai. Sushila's father, for example, was employed in a government hospital in Rohtak as a janitor and commuted daily to Rohtak. He earned a fair amount of money. Out of the money earned, he had also built a pacca house in the village. His children, Sushila and two sons, instead of providing their labour in the fields of the Jat landowners were being educated.

The antipathy of the dominant caste groups towards the education of lower castes, as observed earlier, is not merely directed towards their men but also their women. Here, it may be noted that, by and large, the landowning caste groups' attitude towards the education of their own women is ambivalent.[70] They are not really sympathetic. There is considerable anxiety about education as they hold it responsible for women going astray, even in the context of their own women. Parents are reluctant to get their daughters educated beyond a point, especially if it involves sending them out of the village. A large number of cases of runaway couples belong to the educated class. Educational institutions provide significant social context and spaces through which such

[70] The aversion of the dominant caste groups towards women's education is well acknowledged by the officials and remains a matter of grave concern to Haryana government. Yet, these caste groups also want an educated bride who is able to teach the family children. Many among them even want an earning wife or a daughter-in-law. On the whole, the societal opinion on educating women remains divided and uncertain.

liaisons surface. The enhanced mobility and the social space provided by the educational institutions are known to erase social divisions and hierarchy maintained in the village. The changed social geography of the villages, leading to mixed pannas, mentioned in the earlier section, has similarly encouraged an outward integration of population between different caste groups on the one hand, and generated tension between them on the other. More significantly, these changes are perceived as encouraging interaction between the youth of different communities and leading to elopements. Clearly, the younger generation, with increased sense of self-identity, self-worth, and education, has a different attitude towards inter-caste marriages. They may not be voicing it though. It is because of this 'threat' that, from time to time, there have been moves against such spaces that accommodate both girls and boys. A *sarv khap* (all-clan) panchayat held at village Sisana in district Sonepat on 21 March 1993, unanimously passed a resolution against setting up of the co-educational schools.[71] The 'danger' of a mixing of the sexes is commonly acknowledged by all caste groups and considered morally reprehensible. Sarla's case is touted as an example of this. According to them, it was education which gave her 'such ideas'.

The lower caste groups share this negative opinion regarding education of women. In Loharhedi also, they felt that 'too much of education' imparted to Sushila had led to this situation. Even the girl's parents blamed themselves for having 'educated' the girl. Sushila, a bright and disciplined student, stood out among other girls (majority being Jat) due to her diligent attitude towards studies. Her teachers in the village vouched this for Sushila. According to them, she was getting educated with a view to employment. In a way, it is not only Dalit men but also Dalit women who may be said to provide competition; this time to the upper caste women. The resentment is emanating from 'reserved' positions in institutions that offer vocational and professional courses like that of nursing and training for school teachers. As these courses

---

[71] Although not because of the panchayat's decision but because of the demands of political economy such a segregation of sexes at the school level is inadvertently coming to the surface in Haryana. An interesting development is taking place. The girls are being sent to government schools to save money and the boys to expensive English medium private schools. So stark is the discrimination that the local government schools can now be mistaken for being 'girls only schools'. See a news report in *Indian Express*, 2003, New Delhi, 7 December, p. 1.

offer a better opportunity for employment for women, the limited seats in such institutions attract bitter competition. Yet, it is also true that the percentage of female education among the lower caste groups is only 18.87 per cent as compared to the 40.54 per cent among the upper caste groups.[72] For example, Sushila was the only girl in her community to go in for high school education in the village. The rest of the lower caste girls were class IV or class VI dropouts. When this case erupted, Sushila was in tenth class and staying in the hostel in Sampla. Ravinder was doing his BA. As a child, Sushila had often sought his help in studies. Her teachers also hold Sushila's higher studies and her mobility, that is, travelling outside the village, responsible for her 'kharab hona' (going astray). The Jats, by and large, called her badmash (bad character) who coveted a Jat boy and aspired to marry him.

There are several such cases of 'unequal' inter-caste alliances, involving higher landowning caste groups and the Dalits, which can be cited.[73] Not all of them are dealt with by the caste panchayat. They are also tackled by the family male members of the dominant caste groups. In a notorious case of April 1998, violence was inflicted upon a Dalit family on suspicion alone. In village Juaan, district Sonepat, a landowning Jat family suspected one of their girls to be involved with a lower caste boy, whose family worked as agricultural labourers in their fields. The boy, like many others of his caste, had opted out of agricultural work and was studying towards a different vocation. The landowning males took the matter in their hands by beating up the male members of the Dalit family when they were working in their fields. The Dalits had to be hospitalized. They also raped the wife of one of them and mutilated her private parts. The police station officer at Gaunaur refused to register their complaint for three days. Only after the lower caste groups surrounded the police station was the First Information Report (FIR) lodged. The case got registered, but was opined to be extremely weak for any conviction of the culprits in a court of law. This left great bitterness all around. The accused are still free.

[72] Out of a total of 15,03,112 females from the scheduled caste groups, only 2,83,490 are literate. See Government of Haryana, Statistical Abstract of Haryana, 1999–2000, p. 67.

[73] In rural areas, such cases are on the increase, but very few convictions are made as the police act in consonance with the dominant caste groups, who also have political connections. For reports of this case, also see Dainik Jagran, 1998, 20 April, Gurgaon edition, pp. 1, 13; 12 May, p. 4.

Another hypogamous alliance of a high caste girl and a low caste boy which ended in tragedy took place in July 2002. In village Talao of Jhajjar district a Jat girl helped by her younger sister eloped with a Chamar boy. The police acted swiftly. The three were apprehended and brought back. The Superintendent of Police, Jhajjar, a Jat himself, openly boasted of the two weeks of special efforts which he put in personally in order to retrieve the girls. During this investigation, the Dalits were repeatedly humiliated by the Jat community in the presence of the police leading to the suicide of a young Dalit woman and an elderly Dalit man, both accused of helping the absconding youngsters. After two weeks, the girls surfaced, were taken into police custody, and handed over to their family. Within a couple of days, both the girls were found dead allegedly having consumed poison. The police readily accepted the suicide version handed down by the family members. The villagers, speaking in confidence, maintained that the girls had been killed. They also spoke of pressure exercised on the girls to testify that the Dalit boy had 'lured and enticed' them. The girls refused to give in and consequently had to be killed. In fact, the older girl had testified to the magistrate that she was already married to the dalit boy. The advocate defending the Dalit boy showed his sympathy and complicity with the dominant caste groups, as well as perhaps fear, by not even moving the application for his bail. The boy, charged with abduction, kidnapping, rape, and criminal conspiracy, remained in jail for one and a half years, even after the so-called 'victims' were dead.

'Honour' among the Lower Castes

An aspiration of alliance by the Dalits with the upper castes is construed as a move towards status formation and upward mobility by the latter. The Balmikis of Loharhedi denounced any such aspirations and maintained that they are as zealous followers of caste endogamy and village exogamy as the upper castes. Indeed, the marriage of their girl with a Jat boy was not considered hypergamous or raising of their status. As one of them put it, 'us ka to sawal he na ootthata' (the question [of such a marriage] does not arise). According to them, such a marriage did not and could not improve their status, as may be the case with other upper caste groups. Clearly, status hypergamy lies strictly within the caste and not outside it. On the other hand, in the opinion of the Dalits, the insistence of upper caste groups on this issue was a disturbing pointer to the fact that *neech log* (low castes) think about caste matters differently from them. It is perhaps because of the awareness of this perception that the lower caste groups displayed some anxiety about stressing 'no difference' in thinking from the high castes in relation to observing caste endogamy in marriage. In reality, opinion among different sections of Dalits remains divided. The defiance to the norm of caste endogamy is after all coming from the young Dalits. Also, as mentioned earlier, the younger educated Dalits are desirous of marrying educated girls (not readily available in their own caste) from upper caste groups. On the other hand, the older generation, both men and women, as also the overwhelming numbers connected with agriculture, is firmly against such marriages.

It may be noted that the lower caste groups are as much hierarchy ridden and caste status conscious as the upper caste groups. The following cases involve lower caste groups caught in the contradiction of village exogamy as well as caste endogamy, highlighting how most caste groups follow the dominant caste norms in this region. In October 1997, for example, a Khati girl of village Bigdanna, district Bhiwani, ran away with a Jogi boy from the same village. They could not be traced. Within the lower caste groups, Khati caste in Haryana is rated higher than Jogi. The multi-caste panchayat that met expelled the Jogi family from the village. The boy's parents and his five brothers were beaten up, their household things were either damaged or looted, and their meagre crops were destroyed.

The presence of upper caste groups in the multi-caste panchayat seems to suggest that their norms of caste endogamous marriage were being imposed on the lower caste groups. But this may not be strictly true. Each caste group has its own biradari to enforce its rules. Yet, the dominant caste of the region often could, if needed, arrogate to itself the power to enforce the internal behaviour of an endogamous group. Therefore, even the lower castes could not be allowed to breach the caste endogamous rules, as breaches are considered dangerous. If condoned, they may well spread to other caste groups. Although this sceptre exists, an occasion for such an intervention may not arise. The lower caste groups are as much 'honour bound' and status conscious as the dominant caste groups. They also observe the norms of caste endogamous marriage and deal with such cases individually or through panchayats in similar fashion as the dominant castes do. Yet, given their weak socio-economic position, they are unable to claim any such honour, especially in relation to the dominant castes.[74] They may vaguely share in the honour of the village as a whole. This identification may mean going willingly or unwillingly along with the dictates of the dominant caste leadership. The Dalits find it extremely difficult, if not impossible, to withstand the dictates of the caste or village panchayat in which they occupy the same peripheral and demeaning position as in the village society. Their consent is taken for granted, and even if the decision goes against them, they are considered a part of and a supporter of such a decision. This was clearly evidenced in the Loharhedi cases. In fact, the only 'honour' which the lower caste groups may 'honourably' claim is in relation to their caste members and lies in their ability to enforce it within their own caste group. Denied any claims of honour in relation to upper castes, the lower castes therefore become hypersensitive in defending it within their own castes. Such a concept of honour can not only be claimed but also defended and implemented.

In this connection, a recent case of October 2001 can be cited where a caste panchayat of the Chamars in village Dujjana in Beri district expelled from the village the family of the girl who belonged to the Balmiki caste for breaking the norm of caste endogamy. The boy she was involved with belonged to the Chamar caste. The whereabouts of the girl's family are not known and she is rumoured to have been killed. The boy is occasionally seen in the village. In another case from village Ahulana in district Gohana, a Chamar boy and a Balmiki girl committed suicide in April 2001 fearing opposition to their marriage.[75] The cases of youngsters committing suicide, to pre-empt opposition and violent retribution, are widespread among all caste groups. They are aware that their desire for each other will never be allowed to culminate into marriage. These cases are frequently and sensationally reported in the regional dailies. Such suicides or murders are acknowledged to be because of the well-known antipathy of all caste groups to inter-caste marriages.

[74] A few instances of the Dalit aggression have come to light. In July 2003, in village Jooan of Sonepat district, one Jat boy was killed by the Dalits. He was known to sexually harass the Dalit girls. The Dalits maintained that they had a right to 'protect the honour' of their women. In retaliation, the Jats burnt down the Dalit houses.

[75] *Dainik Bhaskar*, 2001, 25 April, Gurgaon edition, p. 1.

Dalits and the State Agencies

In Sushila's case, the humiliation inflicted upon her had the effect of bringing the two factions of the Balmikis together. A vocal lot, they said that they would not be bullied by anyone. They cited an earlier case in the village in which they had been in direct clash with the Jats over grazing rights. This case corroborates the analysis of the conflict between the Dalits and landowning castes given in the earlier section. For example, in village Loharhedi, the Dalits had a long-standing disagreement with the Jats over grazing rights. In the clash that ensued over the use of the shamilat, reportedly a Balmiki accidentally killed a *Jhota* (bull) of the Jat landowners. Such a killing, even though accidental, is considered a heinous crime—a crime that must be punished. It is entirely different matter that the landowners are themselves known to kill a bull for destroying their field and crop.[76]

This killing was made a pretext by the Jat panchayat of the village to fine all the Balmikis. Although unjust, according to the Balmikis, they had still paid the fine. They clearly were not in a position to resist the imposition. This had the effect of feeding into the existing resentment and tension between the two. The independent income of some of the Balmikis, through outside jobs and their small forays in education to fulfil aspirations toward jobs, had already laid grounds of this friction. So when the Balmiki girl was discovered to have developed intimacy with a Jat boy, the Jats pounced on her, 'to teach the lower castes a lesson'. In this, the targeted Balmiki girl was used as a prop for the otherwise divided and heavily factionalized Jats to come together to attack the lower caste groups in order to assert their dominance.

Rumours of Sushila's marriage with Ravinder were floated and stories were spun as to how Sushila would visit Ravinder attired in boy's clothes to spend her nights with him. The Balmiki family, unable to take this vilification, approached the police to register an FIR that they were being harassed by the Jats. In such inter-caste cases, the lower caste group may take recourse to the state agencies, specially the law, because they lack power in the village. The other alternative is to seek help from the National Human Rights Commission, which

---

[76] I was informed of this by the landowners in confidence. The intent however is not to kill the errant bull. The severe beating results in killing. Historically, this is a documented fact. See Government of India, 1935, F. no. Home Poll, 37/2/35, pp. 53–4.

is also resorted to, showing a high level of awareness among the Dalits. But the dominant caste groups may still block the legal writ, as the police protection is available sporadically, whereas the lurking danger or threat from the dominant caste group is constant. Consequently, the lower caste groups shy away from taking recourse to the law of the land.

Indeed, there is complicity between the perpetrators of violence and the police about the 'justice' done for the sake of 'honour'. Many times, it is known to take a lead in preserving this 'honour'.[77] Police in northern India, heavily drawn from upper caste dominating groups, is acknowledgedly casteist. Moreover, its criminalization and commercialization are well known facts: monetary considerations overrule merit in recruitment, promotion, and transfer. Because of its association with 'power' and dominance, the dominant caste groups' anxiety to retain their hold over it is greater. That is why, as noted in earlier, the appointment of Dalits in the reserved seats in the police department was sought to be scuttled by the then reigning Chief Minister, O.P. Chautala. In law keeping, the socio-political role of such a force has proved to be highly dubious. In matters such as these, they are known to watch from sidelines. In their opinion, the caste leaders or the caste panchayat and not the law of the land, which applies a different criterion of justice, must resolve social issues.

The police action or inaction has created nervousness among different communities, especially the lower castes, who fear open partiality and hidden biases in reporting the case or in not obeying the decision of powerful high caste panchayat. In worst cases, the community leaders openly assert: 'The police can do whatever they want, but we have to punish the culprit in our own way.' Even in Loharhedi case, as in most such cases, the police 'persuaded' or 'bullied' the Balmikis to take up the matter with an all-caste panchayat of the village, fully knowing the power equations working in such a body. As mentioned earlier, the panchayat that was overwhelmingly Jat not only broke its own tradition but also attempted to create new one. The verdict was delivered on the premise of 'maintaining time-honoured village customs and cultural practices'.

---

[77] In village Dharuheda, the police cut off the penis of a Dalit boy, accused of having an affair with a Jat girl.

Caste, Class, and Gender: The Deciding Factors

The caste panchayat that had hauled up the woman also hauled up the man. Yet, there was a perceptible difference in their attitude towards them. The eyewitness accounts were unanimous in pointing out that Ravinder was not only unrepentant, he was also openly defiant of the caste panchayat's proceedings. He certainly submitted to the decreed punishment quietly, but he also defied them. Eyewitnesses recounted how he dared to wipe out Sushila's tears in full assembly of the panchayat. Despite being slapped by his elder brother for this and threatened by his mother who, standing with a *gandasa* (cleaver), vowed to kill him, he ran away on his friend's scooter. The popular opinion maintained that the whole thing was stage-managed by the panchayat and the Jat biradari was complicit in making him run away.

It is true that Ravinder, too, was publicly punished, but it is equally true that he was also allowed to run away. Ravinder's mother (who in an unprecedented move attended this panchayat) provided a clue to this apparent contradiction. When interviewed, she abused Ravinder for giving a handle to the other faction of Jats to establish their *chaudharat* (ascendancy) in the village. As this matter concerned the dominant status of the Jats vis-a-vis other caste groups, it succeeded in uniting them across class and factional lines. There was no voice of dissident. Yet, it is also true that the faction of Jats to which Ravinder belonged stood particularly disgraced. This in return strengthened the opposing faction. As one Jat boy crudely put it, 'who wants to marry a *Chuhri*, we only have intercourse with them.' Sexual liaison of a dominant caste man with a lower caste woman certainly establishes his masculinity and virility. The same cannot be said of his serious intent to marry her. This intent introduces a kind of weakness contingent upon question of morality and ethics not necessarily associated with masculinity or virility. The much 'coveted macho qualities' stand above considerations of morality and ethics, especially in relation to women of lower caste groups.

Ravinder's serious involvement with a Balmiki girl to the extent of wanting to marry her not only stood severely condemned by the caste panchayat's treatment of him, but it was also meant to act as a future deterrent. The public spectacle made out of the two lovers was a move towards this. One of the *panch* opined that it was important to create *bhaye* (fear) in people's mind regarding recurrence of such incidence.He also said that another similar case was brewing which, because of this case, will be effectively nipped in the bud. Equally important is that this treatment brought the two factions of Jats together against the lower castes groups and had a more lasting effect on interrelationship between the two, rather than on Jat factional politics.

Clearly, the caste and class factors intervene to determine the decisions of the traditional panchayats. The treatment of the two girls in the same village, a Jat and a Balmiki, stands in sharp contrast, same as that of the Jat and the Nai boy. The Jat girl was not hauled up by the caste panchayat or even her name mentioned, for that would have slurred the honour of her caste and the village. Here, the word caste and village are held synonymous with the Jats. In all this, any punishment to be inflicted upon her was accepted as the concern of her family. It was considered a private matter best left to them to decide. The Balmiki girl, on the other hand, was hauled up by the panchayat. A private concern in her case became a public matter. There was also some talk among the Jats, supported by some Balmikis, of eliminating her for bringing 'dishonour' to the village. A Balmiki youth even agreed to do the hatchet job, but later withdrew. Though not killed, she was publicly punished and humiliated. It was thought fit not to leave her to her family but to make an example of her. Her 'honour' was not treated as the 'honour' of the village. Instead her public humiliation was treated as having saved it.

The punishment inflicted upon the Balmiki girl brings to the fore the differential treatment meted out to the two girls, Jat and Balmiki, by the caste panchayat members. When asked about this difference of approach, the panchayati members pointed out that they had been greatly criticized in the earlier case of Sarla and Ashok, involving a Jat girl and a Nai boy, for differentiating between the boy and the girl when both were equally involved in the affair. The former had been set free where as the latter had been punished. This anomaly was sought to be set right in the second case by inflicting punishment on both of them: the Jat boy and Balmiki girl. 'We cannot allow the fair name of the panchayat to be sullied,' they maintained. Regarding the hauling of a woman in the panchayat, they pointed out that traditionally the caste panchayat had the right to summon anyone, man or woman, they wished to interrogate. It is a different matter, they said, if they do not often exercise such a right in relation to women. This right could be activated whenever they found good enough reason for it and no one could challenge it.[78]

Indeed, the applicability of traditional concepts by the caste or village panchayats is conditional. For instance, the principle of bhaichara also translates into that of village exogamy. The involvement of the two couples belonging to the same village, though of different caste groups, strictly fell within the purview village exogamy as it breached the time-honoured tradition of siblinghood.[79] Yet, in Loharhedi, the concept of village exogamy was not raised in any of the two cases. In matters concerning dominant higher and subordinate lower caste groups, these concepts clearly have no relevance. In fact, this concept, as applied in village Loharhedi, made a difference between a Jat beti and a Balmiki beti. The former was the village beti but the latter was not.

Caste and class intervened again to determine the caste panchayat's attitude towards the two boys and the punishment meted out to them. It was the Nai boy who was the recipient of the Jat community's wrath, whereas the Jat boy was allowed to run away. With the help of the law and police, the former was imprisoned, and tied up in innumerable cases that may well take several years to untangle. Whereas the latter was free to lead his life without any fear whatsoever. The fate of the girls, however, was not so different. Both could have been physically eliminated, as 'tradition' seems to dictate. Yet both are alive. The Jat girl's legal marriage was turned illegal. She was forced to marry a second time; and she was forced into a ruinous match. The Balmiki girl's career aspirations were ruined forever. It is likely that she, too, was heading for a ruinous match like the Jat girl. The lives of both were tainted and lay in shambles. Again, in both the cases, the dominant caste group used women to settle wider issues at stake, notwithstanding their caste affiliations. The 'honour' at stake was not personal to the women but to the dominant community. The 'Jat honour', held synonymous with the village honour, was considered to have been redeemed.

Notwithstanding the caste–class matrix of power just described, the attitude towards the two women remained identical. Both were

[78] Even when women are called, which a few instances show, they are either not allowed to speak or are too terrified to speak in a wholly male body. They are also aware of the humiliation of being called by a panchayat.

[79] This is the stand taken by the caste panchayats when two roughly equivalent caste groups are concerned.

considered 'lustful' women, who had initiated and invited the men. However, such an insistence had a different fallout in relation to the two men. In the case of the dominant caste woman and the lower caste man, such a stand had the effect of denying the 'sexual conquest' of a woman by a man, a conventional sign of masculine identity. The agency of the man in this was denied or subverted. As argued by Anandhi *et al.*, this denial of 'sexual conquest' of upper caste woman by lower caste man negated the 'virile' image of the Dalit.[80] The lustful agency given to the dominant caste woman took away from the lower caste man his virility, sexuality, and masculinity. In the case of the dominant caste man and the Dalit woman, such a reading was at one with the stereotypical perception of the 'lustful nature' of Dalit women. The comments made by many dominant caste women in this respect were revealing. Many opined: 'What can our boys do when these women are so easily available to them.' Such sexual encounters are taken in stride, by most, as a part of the growing up process of the boys. However, the intent of marriage in a case like this clearly stood to weaken this image (of lustful low caste woman and virile upper caste man) rather than substantiate it.

Curiously, regarding inter-caste marriages, the general opinion in the villages is that they are outside the purview of the caste panchayat. They do not form a part of the traditional concerns of this body. Some of the caste panchayats are reported to have even passed resolutions to encourage inter-caste marriages. However, I was unable to trace out even a single one. When approached, it was always some other panchayat that had passed such a resolution. Officially, even the state is given to promoting the dalit-non-dalit marriage by rewarding the couples, but it can hardly boast of any substantial numbers of such marriages.[81] Ironically reward and killing exists side by side in the state. Essentially, it is pointed out that such marriages are considered to be a private matter. If the family concerned accepts an inter-caste marriage, then the panchayat has no say. The panchayat gets activated only when the family does not agree and requests it to intervene. Otherwise, primarily, the family members deal with such matters.

[80] S. Anandhi, J. Jeyaranjan, and Ranjan Krishnan, 2002, 'Work, Caste and Competing Masculinities: Notes from a Tamil Village', *Economic and Political Weekly*, vol. XXXVII, no. 43, 26 October, pp. 4397–406.

[81] The state gives Rs 25,000 to each dalit boy or girl. According to figures available, in 1999 there were only eight couples who received this reward. See *Dainik Bhaskar*, 2000, 10 August, Gurgaon edition, p. 7.

Yet, it is clear that the caste panchayat reflects the dominant popular opinion of the society at large. The basic concept of caste endogamy observed by all caste groups does not allow cross-caste associations. In many such marriages, it is indeed the family that takes the lead in dealing with such associations, but it still does not rule out the intervention of the caste panchayat. In cases where Dalits are involved, the panchayat sits on judgement not only on the erring couple and on the allegedly acquiescent Dalit family, but significantly, also on the entire Dalit community located in the village. This is where the exaggerated charge of 'rising Dalits' acts as ideological and political stratagem of the dominant caste group, which Dipanker Gupta has spoken about in relation to western UP.[82] That is the reason why only the Dalits and no other caste group are known to have faced such a violent retribution. Only the individual members or their immediate family or families, and not an entire caste group, have been at the receiving end of the traditional panchayat's decision. This differential treatment corroborates the weapon-like use of such cases in relation to the Dalits to settle wider issues at stake.

Any move against the Dalits sees the dominant caste, although severely divided into factions and interest groups, throw their might behind the traditional panchayat. In cases such as these, they cannot afford to split. It suits them to close their own ranks. Indeed, the two issues around which mobilization of the dominant castes, regardless of all factions, class, and age divides, gets easily affected in rural Haryana is that of 'women' and 'cow slaughter', as seen in the recent Dulina case of October 2002.[83] This closing of ranks against the dalits by the dominant caste groups helps them both politically and socio-economically. Politically this united front is used by them to pose as a vote bank and extract from the state certain concessions which otherwise may not be forthcoming. Socio-economically, it helps them to maintain their caste dominance greatly under pressure from the newly thrown up social groups in society . The use of violence to enforce their decision or that

[82] Dipanker Gupta, 2001, 'Everyday Resistance or Routine Repression? Exaggeration as Stratagem in Agrarian Conflict', *The Journal of Peasant Studies*, vol. 29, no. 1, October, pp. 89–108.

[83] In October 2002, five Dalits were lynched to death in front of a police post in village Dulina of Jhajjar district, allegedly by a mob acting on the rumour that the Dalits had killed a cow and were skinning it. For an insightful analysis of this crime, see Peoples Union for Democratic Rights, 2003, *Jhajjar Dalit Lynching: The Politics of Cow Protection in Haryana*, Delhi: PUDR, February.

of the panchayat only strengthens their hands further. The need to assert their strength and dominance is an interest that is fully shared by other members of dominant caste groups. Such an 'exploitation' makes the inter-caste marriages, where lower caste groups are involved, far more complicated and conflict ridden.

* * *

The post-colonial demands and compulsions of political economy have brought the 'Dalit' question—the challenge it poses and the conflict it arouses—to the forefront in a most pronounced way. And although the category of 'Dalit' continues to be used as a homogenized, undifferentiated, monolith category, it is the newly emergent, the still nebulous middle-class category which is primarily responsible for creating a sense of insecurity and resentment among the upper caste groups. It is in this class category that a major portion of the exaggerated threat perception regarding the 'rise of Dalits' is rooted. It is the upwardly mobile sections of the Dalits whose life-style and economic standing, in sharp contradiction to their socially and ritually lower status, stands as a challenge to the dominant caste groups, especially the lower sections among them. These sections among the upper castes have not been able to stem their declining status and hierarchical ranking within the caste and outside, and are pitted in competition against the better-off Dalits on a variety of occasions. Also, it is the youth, primarily drawn from these sections, who are defying and revolting against the social and caste/cultural norms by getting involved in inter-caste associations leading to elopement and marriage. On the one hand, such associations can be seen as highly individualized resistance against cultural practices located in an iniquitous system based upon assumed hierarchies and status claims. On the other hand, in a curious way, they also confirm and consolidate those very norms they seek to challenge. The state intervention in such cases is contrary to its own stated laws. The state agencies, drawn heavily from among the upper caste groups, are extra-enthusiastic in intervening and 'solving' such cases, in overlooking violence and crime inflicted on Dalits individually or collectively. For the dominant caste groups, such associations remain the most viable and potent issues to garner a wider collective support, cutting across class/caste/community and age divides. Such cases, which may be overlooked in relation to other caste groups, are selectively made a public spectacle by the dominant caste groups to settle wider issues at stake verging on contemporary political and economic interests. As such, the refrain of 'the rise of the

Dalits' is not confined to any one section of the upper caste groups. It emerges as a ubiquitous refrain of the non-Dalits. For the dominant caste groups, this refrain has the effect of deflecting inflammable intra-caste rivalry and competition concerned with matters of status and hierarchy, on to the 'other' and the threat emanating from them. Such conflicts become a front where local and factional inter-caste politics is played out. In doing this, traditions are invented/claimed/manipulated to serve several interests other than the immediate, private, or familial. Once the community gets involved, the applicability of traditional concepts like bhaichara (brotherhood and equality) and izzat (honour) either changes or collapses dramatically when confronted with Dalit social reality.

Index